The New Senate

The
New Senate

Liberal Influence on a
Conservative Institution 1959–1972

Michael Foley

New Haven and London
Yale University Press

Designed by James J. Johnson
and set in Linotype Caledonia type.
Printed in the United States of America by
Vail-Ballou Press, Binghamton, N.Y.

*Library of Congress Cataloging in
Publication Data*

Foley, Michael, 1948–
    The new Senate.

    Bibliography: p.
    Includes index.
    1. United States. Congress. Senate.
2. United States—Politics and govern-
ment—1945– 3. Liberalism—United
States. I. Title.
JK1161.F64   328.73′071   79-27751
ISBN 0-300-02440-1

For Frances

Contents

Acknowledgments   ix

1 The Old Senate   1

2 The Political Environment—From the 1950s to the 1970s   17
The Eisenhower Years: Liberalism amid Confident Caution.
The Kennedy Years: Liberalism's False Start. The Johnson
Years: The Fruits of Productive Consensus; Consensus of
Complaint. The Nixon Years: Liberal Disasters and Liberal
Opportunities.

3 American Liberalism and Senate Liberals   79
Liberalism: A Way through the Quagmire. Liberals: The
Dimension of Time. Liberals: The Dimension of Issue. Lib-
erals: The Dimensions of Time and Issue. Who Are the
Liberals?

4 The Liberals and the Folkways   118
Apprenticeship. Courtesy. Reciprocity. Specialization. Legislative Work and Institutional Loyalty.

5 The Liberals as a Legislative Force   170
Group Identity. Internal Communications. Group Mobiliza-
tion. Case Study: Liberal Mobilization and the Carswell
Nomination. Group Organization.

6 The New Senate: Change and Tradition   231
Structure. Culture. Style and Function.

Appendixes

  I List of Persons Interviewed   261

 II Notes on the Methods Used in the Construction of Guttman
Scales in the Senatorial Voting Study   264

III Issues Scaled through the Guttman Technique, by Congress   268
Distribution of Liberal Scores among the Scaled Issues, by
Congress   269

IV Distribution of Senators' Scale Rankings, 1959–1972   287
Classification of Senators into Individual Attitude Types   293

Notes   301

Index   334

Acknowledgments

It would not be exaggeration to say that this book is simply a testament to the generous support and helpful assistance that I have received from a profusion of individuals and organizations on both sides of the Atlantic. Limited space necessitates the injustice of mentioning only a very few of those who contributed toward the completion of this book. First, I must acknowledge my debt to those who actually taught me about American politics and who initially aroused my interest in this particular aspect of the American system. Their names are: Dom. John Main, O.S.B., of Ealing Abbey, London, Dr. John Lees of Keele University, and Dr. Larry Johnston of Essex University. Second, I am indebted to Mr. John M. Lewis, now at the University of Indiana, and to Dr. Alec Barbrook of the University of Kent, who both guided me very skillfully and patiently through the early stages of the project. Subsequently, I received much valuable support and critical analysis from a whole group of friends and tutors at Essex University. The individual of central importance to me in this group was Professor Anthony King. His unflagging application to the arduous business of sorting out my ideas and of impressing upon me the requirements of order, organization, clarity, and direction was of inestimable value. I wish to register a very sincere debt of gratitude to him. Professor King, along with his colleagues Dr. David McKay, Dr. Graham Wilson, Dr. Jim Alt, and Dr. Norman Schofield, succeeded in changing my diversified investigations into an altogether more rigorously analytical form of research.

Further thanks are due for all the assistance I received from so many sources in Washington. In particular, I would like to express my gratitude to the community at St. Anselm's Abbey for their generous hospitality, to Mr. John Hardy of the Senate Commerce Committee, who began many of the trails that led onward and outward, and to Senator Lee Metcalf, whose kindness and encouragement in the first interview I undertook gave me an appetite for more. Grateful acknowledgment must also be made to the Social Science Research Council, the Political Studies Association, and the Faculty of Economic and Social Studies at the University College of Wales, Aberystwyth, who provided me with the financial means to undertake research in Washington.

In assisting me in the difficult process of transforming the research into book form, I am grateful first to Dr. John Lees, to Professor Anthony King, and to Professor James L. Sundquist of the Brookings Institution for their many valuable and penetrating suggestions; second, to Mrs. Marian N. Ash and Mrs. Laurie B. Smith at Yale University Press for their excellent editorial and technical assistance; third, to Professor Ivor Gowan, Mr. Peter Madgwick, and the rest of the staff of the political science department at Aberystwyth for their support and forbearance; fourth, to Mr. John Smith of the Social Science Research Council, a good friend and fellow student of Congress, for his part in many long, productive, and entertaining discussions on Washington politics; and fifth, to Mrs. Doris Heywood and Mrs. Marian Rivers for their secretarial skills.

Finally, I must give my deepest thanks to my family for their patience and understanding. My mother, who set me an early example of professional dedication and diligence, gave me every possible encouragement during the early stages of this study. My greatest debt of gratitude, however, must go to my wife, Frances, for her tolerant support, her constructive suggestions, and for her help in drawing up the index. Problems and troubles were shared. Any errors and misjudgments in the book are not. They are mine alone.

Aberystwyth, Wales

1 The Old Senate

The Senate has traditionally been the center of political caution, restraint, and sobriety within the national government of the United States. It was originally conceived as a small chamber in which mature and experienced representatives, appointed by their states, would create a stable and responsible counterweight to the popularly elected and more impulsive House of Representatives. In James Madison's words, the Senate would act as "a defense to the people against their own temporary errors and delusions" by suspending proposed actions "until reason, justice and truth [could] regain their authority over the public mind."[1] Although senators became directly elected representatives in 1913, the Senate has not only maintained its distance from the House of Representatives, but managed to retain its status as the upper chamber.

The spirit of aristocratic detachment is quite evident for example in the privileges and perquisites afforded its members. To any casual observer there can be no doubt which end of the Capitol building accommodates the Senate and its members. While congressmen can be seen braving the elements in the journey from their offices to the chamber, senators travel by private underground railway and personal lifts to the Senate floor. Once there, they move amid chandelier-encrusted corridors with the self-assurance provided by their security of tenure (six years), their celebrity status, and the realization that they embody the major political entities of the United States. In contrast to the dignified atmosphere of the Senate is the turbulent arena of the House, in which groups of anonymous members meet and argue in conditions sufficiently austere both to withstand the bustle of their legislative business and to reflect their distaste for the arrogant pomposity of the Senate.

The Senate's style of operation, combined with its formidable capacity to obstruct the legislative process, has normally conveyed the impression of a chamber dedicated to critical review and reassessment. During the 1950s, however, this traditional image of the

Senate as an institutional lag in the federal government became radically transformed as the chamber was increasingly viewed as "the most secure bastion of entrenched, institutionalized conservatism."[2] Its role was no longer seen as one of reflective deliberation but rather one of intrinsic and self-contained conservatism, independent of external forces and ideas. Instead of a lag, the Senate appeared to be an insensitive block to legislation. As the 1950s progressed and frustrations mounted, the Senate's aristocratic demeanor no longer seemed so nostalgically antiquarian. On the contrary, it appeared to reflect the substantive fact that the whole ethos of the Senate was one of insular and unrepentent conservatism.

At first sight this conservatism appeared to be based simply upon a largely fortuitous concentration of conservatives in the leading positions of both the party and committee hierarchies. The vagaries of the seniority system had certainly produced a very strong conservative presence in the formal framework of internal power. Southern Democrats like Richard Russell (Armed Services), Harry Byrd (Finance), James Eastland (Judiciary), and A. Willis Robertson (Banking and Currency) dominated the powerful committee chairmanships. The conservative tenor of the committee system was further buttressed by such conservative Republicans as Styles Bridges, Wallace Bennett, John Williams, John Butler, Andrew Schoeppel, Carl Curtis, Frank Carlson, and Barry Goldwater. Their long tenures allowed them to occupy many of the leading minority positions in the system. It was not surprising, therefore, that the senior committee members often appeared to have more in common with each other than with other members of their own parties further down the committee pecking order. On many important committees, the chief political division lay not so much between the parties as between those who were seated in close proximity to the chairman and those who were out of earshot.

The southern Democrats and the conservative Republicans not only dominated the committees, but through their influence in the party organizations could control the flow of committee assignments and transfers within the committee system. All too often it appeared as if committee places were used as rewards and punishments for behavior in the Senate. The liberal senator Joseph Clark, for example, was convinced that assignments were deliberately manipulated by the conservative hierarchy in order to maximize the ideological consistency of the major committees. When a number of liberal senators were given poor committee assignments directly after a vote on cloture reform in 1963, Clark took the floor and clearly implied that the "conservative establishment" had discriminated against liberal freshmen in its distribution of assignments: "When the Democratic steering committee met, it became obvious that in filling committee membership vacancies, the establishment would ignore seniority when to ignore it would strengthen the establishment's control, but would follow it when to do so would have the same result."[3] He also claimed that the bipartisan elite had refused to alter the party ratios on the committees to their correct levels after the 1962 elections. It was suspected that the conservative elders had opposed these adjustments because they would automatically have benefited the crop of northern liberals that had arrived since 1958.[4] Assumptions concerning the motivations of the conservative group could not be proved absolutely. Nevertheless, such apparent discrimination cultivated the widespread suspicion that Democratic and Republican conservatives were engaged in a concerted effort to thwart liberal programs and to impair liberal careers.

The whole conservative ethos of the Senate did not rely merely upon the formal system of internal power. A less obvious, but just as significant root was considered to be the Senate's own indigenous code of ethics and procedures. This was the dimension of conservative power that particularly irritated the liberal members, for it appeared not only to create a perfect environment for conservative policies, but to provide the underlying political base for the conservatives' position of formal power. To liberals, the Senate's culture and its framework of status and informal influence were more insidious than the official system of committees and party agencies precisely because the latter was thought to be based on the former. This interpretation was not just confined to liberal senators. In the 1950s many journalists and political analysts endorsed the view that the Senate's form of private influence was not just an epiphenomenon of the formal distribution of internal power but was structurally related to the more visible superstructure of chairmanships and party positions.

Much of the evidence for this interpretation, and the chief cause of its extraordinary durability, was provided by two seminal works on the Senate written in the 1950s. Donald R. Matthews in *U.S. Senators and Their World* and William S. White in *Citadel*[5] both examined the nature of the Senate's social arrangements and their impact on the chamber's mode of operation. The two studies approached their subject from different angles. Whereas *Citadel* was a highly prescriptive work that revered and romanticized the Senate's legislative style and system of values, Matthews's study was a more factual analysis of the causes and effects of senatorial behavior. In spite of their different methods, there was a marked similarity in their observations of the Senate during the 1950s.

Both discovered that a senator was expected to comply with a series of internal norms or "folkways" in order to gain a measure of legislative effectiveness and to be accepted as a true "Senate type" (White) or "Senate man" (Matthews). They found that the Senate demanded a certain style and character from its members that could be acquired only through respectful observation of established Senate types. The conditioning of freshmen senators to "the moods and the habits and the mind of the place"[6] involved a period of apprenticeship in which they were expected to exercise restraint in debate, assume a large part of the unattractive work of the Senate, and place a high value on the experience of their elders. New senators had to seek advice continually, ask questions, and make acquaintances in order to absorb the subtleties of the traditional role of the Senate parliamentarian. They were expected to accept the frustrating task of presiding over the Senate, to restrain themselves from speaking excessively, and never to attempt to lead the Senate on an issue without gaining prior approval from the senior members. This initiation process of apprenticeship was not just another aspect of the seniority system; it was a reflection of the belief that the Senate was characterized by a special atmosphere that could be sensed only gradually, so that even "the most brilliant of arriving members [would] find that it require[d] years of learning to be able to be truly Senatorial."[7]

The folkways prescribed that a senator should be a legislator above all else. It was customary for his major efforts to be directed toward legislative tasks and for second priority to be given to personal advancement and publicity. The respect within the Senate for those who devoted themselves to the often dull and politically unrewarding work of legislation produced "a puzzling disparity between the prestige of senators inside and outside the Senate."[8] This is not to say that senators had to remain anonymous; personal publicity was acceptable when it flowed from a senator's legislative performance or when it helped to further a proposal or a member's chances for reelection. Persistent "grandstanders" and "headliners," however, were distrusted and disliked.

Because of the size and complexity of the Senate's workload, White and Matthews sensed a strong tradition of specialization. A member who dedicated himself to the subject areas of his committee gained respect from his colleagues as an expert and as a guide to certain aspects of policy. A generalist, on the other hand, was unable to develop the internal leverage that a specialist commanded and was consequently a disruptive influence in the framework of mutual trust and expertise that contributed so much to the accomplishment of Senate business.

To promote cooperation and compromise, senators were expected to conduct themselves in a courteous manner when dealing with their fellow members. By being forbidden to question the motives of other members or to criticize other states, it was hoped that popular rhetoric would be excluded from the chamber and that personal hostilities would be ameliorated.

The folkway of reciprocity or compromise was rooted in the Senate's traditional attachment toward John Calhoun's notion of "concurrent majority." Calhoun's deep distrust of a government that could operate on the basis of simple majority rule to the detriment of diverse minority interests led him to prescribe a crucial qualification to popular government.[9] As the representative of a region that was becoming progressively less influential in the union, he declared that government decisions ought to embody the diverse preferences of the nation's constituent communities. In order to secure such organic decisions, he recommended that each interest should not only have extensive opportunities to participate in policymaking, but ultimately a veto that "invest[ed] each with the power of protecting itself."[10] It can be claimed that Calhoun's concurrent majority doctrine was consistent with, if not a reaffirmation of, the Founding Fathers' objective of a complex constitutional system that would deter the formation of simple and durable majorities. Nevertheless, this additional emphasis on minority prerogatives had special relevance to the Senate as the institution's nonnumerical form of representation, and its function in offsetting the predicting excesses of the House appeared to provide it with the framework that necessitated a concurrent majority in its decisions. The Senate's ethos of conglomerate decision was further confirmed by the subsequent addition of restrictive rules and precedents that served to extend the protection afforded to minorities and to force majorities to accommodate themselves to minority objections.

With this heritage of concurrent majority and with the Senate's formal rules affording such a wide range of obstruction, it was essential that members be prepared to bargain, negotiate, and compromise. Where the immediate concern of constituents was not involved, senators were expected to participate in logrolling agreements, by which favors given one day were required to be repaid in the future. Although the "Senate man" had an understanding of national problems and of the pressures under which other senators labored, he was impatient with those members who refused to accommodate to the bargaining process. White described political compromise as the greatest raison d'être of the Senate and saw no place for politicians who persistently stood on their principles.[11] The "Senate type" would not expect members representing a minority to agree to policies or laws that were completely repugnant to them, as this would be contrary to the Senate's tradition of concurrent majority. Nevertheless, he would accept the fact that a senator could not "forever refuse . . . to make any compromise at all and remain a good, or effective, member."[12]

Finally, members were expected to take pride in the belief that the Senate was the "greatest . . . deliberative body in the world."[13] Suspicious of the nationalism of the presidency and slightly disdainful toward the simple majoritarianism of the House of Representatives, the Senate valued its tradition of "qualitative representation" and sought to preserve those aspects of it that were embodied in its customs. The election of a third of the Senate at a time gave the chamber a sense of historical continuity that encouraged reverence toward its established practices. Precedents were therefore changed only occasionally, and only after the most careful consideration of possible effects. The Senate type would be highly conscious of the chamber's dignity and would immerse himself in its past and present importance. For such a man, the Senate was an end in itself through which he fulfilled all his personal hopes and political aspirations. To the extent that a member had higher ambitions and used the Senate as a means to those ends, he was not a Senate type.

While legislative norms such as the folkways could be said to foster such functional attributes as role education, expertise, division of labor, cooperation, and collegiate identity, their main achievement in the view of White and Matthews was the maintenance of a conservative style and thereby the perpetuation of conservative decisions. According to White, any member could become a true Senate type. Lack of wealth, party loyalty, social status, and affability were irrelevant; the chief criterion was what White euphemistically described as character—"character in the sense that the special integrity of the person [had to] be in harmony with . . . the special integrity of the Institution."[14] A key to White's meaning of character and integrity was given by the relationship postulated between the institution and its southern members. To White the southern senator was the personification of the upper chamber. "He is preeminently *the* 'Senate man' and this is his great home. It is not so much that he is so like the Institution as that the Institution is, in fundamentals, so like him."[15] His aristocratic heritage, organizational skills, and traditional deference toward his elders gave the chamber much of its special atmosphere. He reflected the Senate's continuity through his own long tenure in office, which provided the basis of his institutional power and nurtured his respect for precedents and tradition. Since so much of the Senate's culture was constituted from southern traits, the southerner could expect to operate in an environment consistent with his legislative style and generally conservative disposition.

In addition to southerners like Richard Russell, Lyndon Johnson, James Eastland, and Harry Flood Byrd, the indefinable "inner tone of the place"[16] could also be sensed and appreciated by such conservative Republicans as William Knowland, Eugene Millikin, and Robert Taft. Together these disciples of the Senate, whose attitudes and behavior appeared to dovetail so neatly with the institution's norms, formed a bipartisan group of senatorial zealots dedicated to preserving and protecting the Senate's traditions. White called this group the "inner club." While it may have been a purely spontaneous union of like-minded representatives and its members may have employed innocuous methods as gentlemen's agreements and private understandings, the group represented a very real power bloc. It was generally agreed that this indistinct yet clearly discernible group of senior senators lay at the center of the institution's status and power

structure in the 1950s. "The Inner Club makes the decisions as to
what *in general* is proper in the Institution and what *in general* its
conclusions should be on high issues."[17] To White and many others,[18]
the phenomenon of a powerful inner group of conservatives appeared
to substantiate the notion that senatorial conservatism was not merely
a feature based upon contemporary political conditions, but a built-in
permanent ideological orientation founded upon institutional customs
and internal power.

The dynamic relation between senatorial culture and formal institutional power was perceived to operate in the following way. To
become truly senatorial, a member had to conform to tradition and
comply with the folkways. Folkways involved, first, a socialization
process in which new members were obliged not only to defer to
the Senate elders, but to strive to imitate their seniors in as many
ways as possible. Second, they buttressed the operating style of the
Senate by fostering a deep regard for the institution's ancient rules
and precedents. Third, they supported the Senate's formal hierarchy
by fostering conformity to those practices and conventions that had
in themselves determined the composition of the hierarchy. It was
apparent that, through the folkways, members were acclimatized to
the conservative atmosphere of the Senate and educated in the sanc-
tity and political relevance of its ethics.

The conservative leadership demonstrated its interpretation of the
Senate's rationale by asserting that there was a natural relationship·
between conservative ideology and the authentic values and practices
of the Senate. Lending weight to their view were the institution's
continuity, derived from overlapping terms of membership; its formidable capacity to obstruct the legislative process; its tradition of
concurrent majority; and its customary distrust of the nationalist and
reformist tendencies of the presidency. White, for example, called
the Senate a "basically unreconstructed"[19] body which not only continued to display its Madisonian distaste for majority rule and central government, but maintained an "essentially backward looking"
style that always placed a "heavy burden upon every changer."[20]

Although the theoretical validity of a natural link between conservatism and the Senate's culture remains open to question, the
conservative members had the power to fulfill their own assertion
in practical terms. The conservatives' access to informal sanctions
(e.g., misplaced bills, ignored requests, social ostracism, postponed

decisions) and formal inducements (e.g., party positions, committee assignments, memberships to select committees, foreign trips) completed a network by which the major facets of Senate life appeared to lead back to an impregnable conservative center.

The crucial theorem laid down by White and Matthews, therefore, was that of a self-perpetuating form of conservatism within the Senate generated by a symbiosis between the institution's culture and its official system of internal power. Traditional procedures and established customs produced and sustained a conservative leadership which in turn controlled leadership recruitment by maintaining the same procedures and customs. The leverage the conservatives had to impose their philosophy of the Senate on the Senate was completed by such rewards for past conformity as committee chairmanships and party positions. In this way the circle was closed. According to White and Matthews, traditions and customs were not just the superfluous vestiges of a lost aristocratic past, but the means by which the conservatives could claim the informal system of status as their own, come to dominate the closely related structure of power,[21] and finally secure passage of their policy positions. In Matthews's words: "The folkways of the Senate . . . buttress the *status quo* in the chamber, and the distribution of power within the chamber results in moderate to conservative policies."[22] In this way the conservatism of the Senate in the 1950s was transformed by White and Matthews from a purely contemporary phenomenon to a fundamental law of the institution. Given such inherently conservative traditions and the powerful socializing force of the senior conservative leaders, the Senate's conservative posture appeared to be an immutable characteristic. To White and Matthews, the dynamic interrelationship between internal culture and power had frozen the Senate's legislative style and policy orientation into a permanently conservative direction.

Within the logic of this scheme there was no room for liberal senators. Liberals were activists and reformists who stressed national standards and federal intervention over cultural diversity and states' rights. As such, they naturally gravitated toward the presidency, which to any true senator represented the chief source of emerging national sovereignty and administrative centrism. The liberals, therefore, were seen as members of the president's party within the very institution pledged to act as a counterweight to the incautious and

precipitous actions of the executive branch. As befits the liberal impulse toward swift and decisive movement, the liberals' legislative
style was inconsistent with the traditionally sedate and insular tenor
of the Senate. According to Matthews, liberal senators were both
unwilling and unable to display the customary diffidence within the
Senate, to wait for internal influence through the seniority system,
to limit their floor speaking and their appeals to audiences outside
the Senate, to specialize in a restricted number of subject areas, and
to compromise their principles to the pragmatist spirit of the Senate.
Consequently, the "liberals [were] more likely to challenge Senate
norms than the conservatives"[23] and so were more likely to remain
unsuccessful and "ineffective" legislators.

The liberals' policy positions, combined with their disturbing lack
of decorum, generated an atmosphere in which the conservatives and
the liberals consciously withdrew from each other. Since the conservatives were in a superior political position, the net effect of such
a dissociation was the creation of a small group of isolated liberal
outsiders. In this way another long-lasting rule of thumb for the
Senate was established. Just as the culture and power structure was
inherently conservative, so in Ralph Huitt's words "the Outsider [was]
more likely to be liberal, as his opposite number [was] apt to be
conservative."[24]

This classic view of the Senate, as portrayed by White and Matthews, has been disputed on a number of grounds. Matthews's methods
of assessing folkway compliance and legislative effectiveness[25] and
White's criteria for inner club membership can both be questioned.
There is concern that the concept of the inner club was erroneously
inferred from the liberals' neurosis over a pernicious conservative
clique that was, in fact, a purely spontaneous union of like-minded
men. Nelson Polsby, for example, asserts that the power of the inner
club was imaginary given the exceptionally diffuse distribution of
power within the Senate, which afforded some form of leverage to
even the most detached outsider.[26] Interesting as these points may
be, they do not affect the validity of the arguments put forth by
White and Matthews. Critics overlook the fact that whether the conservatives' cohesion was spontaneous or not, the net result to those
who were *not* conservative was the same. Even if the conservative
coalition was the result of pure circumstance, this did not prevent
liberals from acting on the belief that the conservative members used

their power to reduce the level of liberal participation and the scope of liberal influence. Critics also forget that while the Senate's power structure may be more diffuse than that of other legislative chambers, it was relatively centralized for the Senate during the 1950s and early 1960s. Technical disputes over the criteria adopted to determine the exact boundaries of inner club membership, or debates over the differences between Joseph Clark's "establishment" and White's "inner club," tend to conceal the overall framework of a formal conservative elite—whose members had much in common and who operated in an environment in which this commonality could be given political effect. It is true that not all the senior senators were conservative and not all conservatives elder members. But the degree of overlap was such, especially in the major committees, that the conservatives came to embody a structural and cultural hierarchy that was averse to liberals in general and to junior northern Democratic liberals in particular. It is in this light that the assertions of White and Matthews should be seen. Despite the methodological ambiguities in their studies, it was in precisely this light that the Senate was viewed by a wide circle of contemporary observers and analysts.

Tom Wicker; Randall Ripley; Ralph Huitt; Joseph Harris; Rowland Evans and Robert Novak; Roger Davidson, David Kovenock, and Michael O'Leary; and John Bibby[27] all perceived the existence of a group of conservatives which dominated both the informal and official Senate power structures in the 1950s and early 1960s. The full weight of the conservatives' leverage impressed itself most forcibly, however, upon just those individuals one would expect to feel it—the liberal members. To Gaylord Nelson, "The conservative committee chairmen all supported each other and created a bloc that was very difficult to break."[28] To Frank Moss, "During the 1950s and 1960s the inner club was fully dominant. . . . It could keep everything tied on top of the table."[29] To Edmund Muskie, "It was not a formal consultative group, but a body of men who were philosophically attuned to each other. They held the positions of power and leadership. . . . The establishment was hard to define but it existed. I do not think that anyone was not aware of its existence."[30] Finally, Joseph Clark summarized his views of *realpolitik* in the Senate in his famous speech on the Senate establishment. "The Senate establishment as I see it . . . is a self-perpetuating oligarchy with mild, but

only mild, overtones of plutocracy. . . . The two-thirds majority of
the Democratic Senators who are Kennedy men, and therefore liberals, and therefore want to get the country moving again . . . are
represented sparsely, if at all, in the Senate establishment."[31]

These observations reflect the irritation and anxiety experienced
by many liberals at that time. Their views appeared to be justified,
for they repeatedly experienced concerted efforts by the conservatives to obstruct the passage of liberal legislation. In this context
conservative cooperation was in no way a figment of liberal imagi-
nation, for the high level of conservative cohesion was evident in
the voting figures. Studies confirm that every time a coalition of
Democratic and Republican conservatives appeared in the 1950s it
won between 80 and 90 percent of the relevant votes.[32] With this
impressive voting power it is evident that the conservatives were not
a phantom moving amid the shadows of the Senate, but a real political force that could not only control the Senate when and if it
wanted to, but could impose its view of the Senate's appropriate culture and life-style.

Since their policy positions and legislative methods were anti-
thetical to the Senate's conservative ethos, the impression created
by liberal senators was that of a group of dissident and disruptive
mavericks. This remaining part of the White and Matthews equation
of institutional conservatism with liberal detachment certainly appeared to be well founded in fact. According to Bibby and Davidson,
for example, "most of the liberals elected before 1958 found themselves relegated to the role of outsiders."[33] It was widely known that
such members as Paul Douglas, Wayne Morse, Patrick McNamara,
William Proxmire, Joseph Clark, and Herbert Lehman reacted against
the internal organization of the Senate, their lack of access to the
leadership, the disproportionate representation of conservatives on
party and important standing committees, and the ritualistic subservience to the Senate elders and their folkways. Some even took the
drastic step of breaking ranks and making their complaints in public
on the Senate floor. While Joseph Clark and Paul Douglas denounced
the partnership of Democratic and Republican conservatives, William
Proxmire made a personal attack on the Johnson leadership. These
outbursts resulted in liberals being identified as even more nonconformist than they were before.

The impression of the average liberal senator conveyed by the

behavior of such members as Proxmire, Clark, Morse, and Douglas
was that of intransigence, isolation, and ineffectiveness. They were
not only unwilling to compromise their philosophy to the prevailing
ideology of the conservative establishment, but refused to be bound
by a set of rules that apparently served to maintain their opponents'
internal power and to foster policies contrary to their own. Consequently, the liberal of the 1950s was apt to divorce himself from
the safety of a group identity and to use his personal independence
in order to criticize the Senate, publicize problems, propose reforms,
and generally encourage the Senate to become a more responsive,
active, and national institution. The conspicuous position of the liberal outsider was, therefore, due not only to the isolation inflicted
upon him by the Senate's traditionalist forces, but also to the realization that such a course of behavior was the only valid role for a
liberal in the Senate at that time.

We have seen that the consensus of contemporary observers and
the general impression received by the public lent credence to the
basic thesis of White and Matthews. Although different writers
stressed different aspects of the Senate's conservatism and did not
emphasize the permanency of the culture and the power structure as
explicitly as did White and Matthews, they provided a background
of impressions and observations that was consistent with the two
seminal works. All in all, it seemed that White and Matthews had
successfully captured the mood of the Senate in the 1950s. Given
the additional material provided by other writers, White and Matthews's equating of the Senate with an intrinsic and self-perpetuating
form of conservatism did not appear to be an unreasonable conclusion.

White and Matthews succeeded in establishing a model of the
Senate's cultural and power relationships during the 1950s that was
generally endorsed by their contemporaries. The very success of the
model, however, has created problems, for it has endured in many
political and academic circles throughout a period when the Senate
is reputed to have undergone certain changes. This has led to confusion over the Senate's development during the 1960s. Some of the
literature on the Senate that appeared in the 1960s and early 1970s
reported that great changes had taken place. According to John Donovan, for example, the Senate in 1970 appeared "to be changing more
than any of the other political branches of the national government."[34]
Other observers, including Randall Ripley, Gary Orfield, Tom Wicker,

John Manley, John Bibby, Roger Davidson, David Kovenock, and
Michael O'Leary,[35] joined Donovan in declaring that the Senate of
the mid-1960s bore little relation to the Senate of the 1950s. Furthermore, this "revisionist school" of Senate analysts had no doubts
that the principal architects and chief beneficiaries of the changes
had been the Senate's liberal members, who had increased their
presence in the chamber so dramatically since 1958. Other writers,
however, appeared not to have noticed any major changes in the
Senate and continued to subscribe to the classic model laid down
by White and Matthews.[36] This perplexing situation becomes further confused by the continual references made to the two pioneer
works and to successive reprints of parts or all of their books.[37] A
virtually unamended edition of U.S. Senators and Their World, for
example, was published in 1973.[38] The speculative style of the new
literature exists uncomfortably with the established authenticity of
the old literature, which continues to freeze the Senate in a 1950s
mold. As a result, there is a good deal of doubt as to whether the
Senate actually changed with the infusion of large numbers of liberal
members.

The central purpose of this study is to examine the question of
change and to assess how much, if any, of White and Matthews's
classic model remains intact after the developments of the 1960s. If
the 1960s did witness the introduction of a new Senate, one would
expect this to be reflected in, if not characterized by, a change in
the position and behavior of the liberal members in relation to the
Senate's power structure. Since the dissaffection, nonconformity, and
ineffectiveness of the liberal senators might justifiably be regarded as
the touchstone of the traditionalist view of the Senate, this analysis
concentrates on the liberals in order to assess the nature and scope
of any institutional changes that may have taken place. More significantly, it seeks to analyze the liberals' own contributions in producing such changes. In particular, it attempts to discover the degree
to which the liberals either deliberately or unconsciously disrupted
the symbiosis between the conservative culture and the power structure, thereby invalidating White and Matthews's central tenet of a
self-sustaining institutional conservatism.

The framework of the study is broken down into four main parts.
Chapter 3 discusses some of the theoretical problems in the use of
the term liberal, suggests an operational solution, and uses this solu-

tion as a basis for a voting study which differentiates the liberals from their colleagues. Chapter 4 examines the liberals in relation to the Senate's behavioral norms. It studies the liberals' attitudes toward the folkways and investigates the notion that the liberal senator was an inveterate nonconformist whenever established customs were involved. Chapter 5 looks at the liberals in terms of actual institutional power. It questions whether all liberals were necessarily maverick outsiders who valued independent detachment above all else, and whether liberals had the capacity and the motivation to suppress their intrinsic indiscipline and to form themselves into an informal, yet structured and cohesive force. Through an examination of their problems it is hoped that it will be possible to assess how well liberals converted their increased membership into real political leverage. On the basis of the earlier analyses of liberal behavior both within and toward the Senate, the final chapter attempts to assess not only the degree to which the liberals changed the Senate, but the extent to which the Senate changed them. In this way, it is hoped that a balanced perspective of the contemporary Senate is achieved, relating the structural immobilism of the traditionalist school to the revisionists' assertions that the Senate has undergone a liberal revolution.

Research for this study was derived from three major sources. First was the written record, comprising both primary (e.g., *Congressional Record*, committee reports and hearings, government documents, party and interest-group literature) and secondary materials (e.g., magazines, journals, contemporary interpretations, legislative histories, biographies). A second source was provided by data on individual voting behavior in the Senate. It was through the information obtained from published roll calls and by the related *Congressional Quarterly* polls on the preferences of absent members that senatorial policy attitudes and commitments from 1959 to 1972 were studied. The third major source of material comprised interviews with a large number of senators, staff assistants, party officials, journalists, Senate officials, interest-group representatives, and other observers of Capitol Hill who all had firsthand experience of the Senate during the period under review (see appendix I for a full list of interviewees). The interviews, which were undertaken in February and March 1974 and August and September 1975, were usually conducted in the interviewees' offices and normally lasted for approximately 30

minutes. Although the impressionistic information and personal re-
flections gained in these interviews were valuable in themselves, it
should be pointed out that such material was only used as "hard"
evidence where there existed an alternative body of corroborative information, or where the same point was repeatedly made in a number
of interviews.

The product of the research based on these three sources of information is presented and applied to the central question of the
Senate's development during the "liberal era" of the 1960s in subsequent chapters. But before the Senate itself comes under close
scrutiny, it is necessary for the institution to be placed in an overall
political and historical context. Clearly, the main part of the study
is necessarily focused on the social and political relationships within
the Senate during the 1958–72 period. In an institution like the
Senate, internal considerations such as personal behavior and individual attitudes can be of crucial importance in terms of power distribution and policy decisions. Nevertheless, in concentrating upon
Capitol Hill, there is a danger of presenting the Senate as an institution disembodied from outside political life. No matter how much
W. S. White would like to think of the Senate as literally a citadel,
the reality of American politics demands that any individual political
institution should be interpreted against the kaleidoscopic background
of competing interest groups, multiple policy demands, changing
public opinion, and varied governmental organizations. In order to
comprehend and to assess the nature of the Senate's development,
therefore, it is necessary to review the major contemporary events
and trends in American politics during this period. It is the purpose
of chapter 2 to provide this political and historical framework.

2 The Political Environment—From the 1950s to the 1970s

THE EISENHOWER YEARS: LIBERALISM AMID CONFIDENT CAUTION

The 1958 congressional elections and their long-term effect on national and senatorial politics cannot be gauged without an understanding of the Eisenhower era that preceded it. If any period in the postwar years could be characterized as American "normalcy," it was the period from 1953 to approximately 1958. During this time, President Eisenhower consciously inspired the American people to improve their society without recourse to presidential guidance and to increased central direction. Eisenhower may have been a political general but he was not regarded as a politician. Yet it was this very deficiency that constituted much of his initial popular appeal. His avowed nonpartisanship and his dedication to American national purpose attracted millions of his countrymen who were seeking an escape from the frustrations, anxieties, and doubts generated by the immediate postwar period.[1]

Eisenhower's appeal was partly Republican and partly personal. Voters who were concerned over inflation, government corruption, union power, internal subversion, social dislocation, the international balance of power, or simply one-party dominance were drawn to the Republican leader. These deep anxieties were supplemented by a positive attachment to Eisenhower himself. His Horatio Alger rise to prominence from the wrong side of the tracks in Abilene, Kansas, and his personal principles of honesty, individualism, self-restraint, and thrift seemed to prove that the reassuring image of old America was not necessarily a chimera.

In 1952, Eisenhower ended the 20-year period of Democratic administration when he inflicted a decisive 55.1 percent majority defeat on Adlai Stevenson. Despite this victory, he failed to translate his personal popularity into a general electoral advance for the Republican party. Whereas Truman's victory in 1948 coincided with

17

new Democratic majorities of 91 in the House of Representatives and of 12 in the Senate, Eisenhower's weak coattails in 1952 barely secured a Republican Congress. By 1954, the Democrats had regained control of Congress, which they maintained throughout the remainder of the Republican administration despite Eisenhower's enormous electoral victory in 1956. Because of the volatility in voting behavior, which gave Eisenhower large majorities but control of Congress to the Democrats, the President's victories could not be interpreted as mandates for change. Given the tight party balance in Congress, the cleavages within each party, Eisenhower's desire for the Republicans to establish themselves as a center party, and the popular disenchantment with partisanship per se, the watchword of Eisenhower's approach to administration was consolidation. Neither the political capability nor the personal inclination existed to engage in bold New Deal advances or Taftite retreats in the sensitive area of domestic affairs.

The combination of Eisenhower's personal philosophy and a tight party balance produced a program of minimal conservative proposals mixed incoherently with a set of minimal liberal proposals.[2] On the conservative side, for example, Eisenhower was resolved to prevent any further federal intervention in the fields of electrical power and natural resources, which he regarded as two areas of "creeping socialism." With this in mind, he successfully pressed for state sovereignty over offshore oil deposits and attempted to obstruct the expansion of federal power projects in the Tennessee Valley area.[3] On the liberal side, he angered the right wing of the Republican party by refusing to dismantle the framework of Democratic social welfare programs. Eisenhower's pragmatism and his plans for the future development of the Republican party ensured that he would not try to counteract the achievements of Roosevelt and Truman. Under the confusing and inconsistent banner of "progressive-conservatism," the Eisenhower administration attempted to maintain the momentum of existing social programs while reducing expenditures and balancing the budget. The Republicans' fiscal orthodoxy of tight credit, lower taxes, and spending cuts tended to contradict their declared aim to preserve the New Deal. By 1955 and after two failures to balance the budget, the administration indeed became less doctrinaire in its economic management and in its approach to deficit spending.[4] The progressive component of Eisenhower's progressive-conservatism, however, was not just limited to abandoning balanced budgets and defending a static New Deal structure against the Republican right wing. His administration proposed cautious extensions to established social policies and gently prompted the public and Congress to reflect upon the *possible* need for change in such areas as civil rights and health insurance. Eisenhower's reticence in the field of domestic policy was not just derived from a fear of what the right-wing reaction to further progression would do to his party or from a fear that the congressional Democrats would convert his promptings into a clarion call for radical action. His caution was born out of a personal philosophy that concerned the government's social role in general and the president's political responsibilities in particular.

Eisenhower subscribed to the basic Republican premise that the free operation of private enterprise provided a self-regulating mechanism that both created wealth and resolved the problems generated by it. According to this doctrine, government was not a benign force that assisted the performance of the economy, but a form of political coercion that would probably destabilize the economy, prevent necessary adjustments, and thereby reduce competitiveness, profits, and production.[5] This did not mean that the Republicans thought that the government had no role in the economy and society. The lesson of the Great Depression, the growth of monopolies, and the realization that poverty and unemployment were neither necessarily indications of personal worth nor incentives to individual effort had made government intervention imperative. Eisenhower and most of his party had been led to accept the principle of a mixed economy. Despite this concession, the party considered itself responsible for subjecting the standards and objectives of government regulation to continuous reassessment. The onus was placed on government to justify even the validity of its established responsibilities. The fact that a program was in existence was not sufficient to warrant its continuation. Eisenhower revealed this sentiment when his skepticism toward high farm price supports led him to press for a policy of more flexible subsidies.[6]

In the field of social reform, Eisenhower revealed a similar skepticism toward the capacity and legitimacy of government involvement. He had a traditional conservative respect for those New Deal reforms that had become entrenched in society and absorbed into people's expectations. Nevertheless, he did not regard established

New Deal programs as an initial stage in an evolutionary process that would inevitably lead to increased government intervention. On the contrary, Eisenhower believed there were definite limits to what government could and should do. If it breached those limits, it would only exacerbate problems and undermine governmental authority. In the area of civil rights, for example, Eisenhower reluctantly requested new legislation to provide southern blacks with voting rights but designed the legislation only to enable the blacks to resolve their own difficulties.[7] Although the Eisenhower administration was credited with the first civil rights legislation in a century, the President's half-hearted commitment to the bill did little to assist its passage. Arguably, Eisenhower's attitude may even have contributed toward the subsequent challenge to black voting rights and school desegregation—thereby confirming the president's own suspicions of the efficacy of governmental intervention in such sensitive areas.[8]

Eisenhower's philosophy of government was reflected in his attitude toward his own role within it. Presidents Roosevelt and Truman had embodied and popularized the notion of activist leadership by which the president not only assumed a disproportionate share of power within the federal government but expanded the scope of federal authority through a process of publicizing social problems and advocating executive-inspired solutions. Eisenhower did not care much for social criticism—least of all from those who sought to elevate themselves by exaggerating the deficiencies of American society and declaring personal solutions to problems that would probably resolve themselves if left alone. To counteract the trend set by the preceding Democratic administrations, Eisenhower deliberately devolved power from the White House by giving greater discretion to his departmental secretaries, by reviving the cabinet as a decision-making body, by relying more on state and local governments to attend to social problems, and by attempting to restore Congress to a joint partner in the formulation of public policy.[9] Eisenhower believed that pressure for government action and social reform should come from below through a careful process of consultation and deliberation, not through unilateral and precipitative action from the White House. He did not think that people wanted, or needed, a "Roosevelt, sounding as if he were one of the Apostles, or the partisan yipping of a Truman."[10] While those dedicated to an activist presidency denigrated the Eisenhower style as an abdication of presidential responsibility, Eisenhower himself saw no reason to depart from his self-effacing paternalism and political gradualism.

It is precisely the fact that no real pressure was exerted on Eisenhower to change his presidential style that gave the Eisenhower era its special character. If a public mood can ever be said to exist, the mood of the 1950s was most certainly embodied in the figure of Eisenhower. He personified a political consensus that was a product not merely of cold war absolutism and national self-assertion, but of a complex social chemistry based on the insecurities, aspirations, and expectations of a suburban middle class increasing in scope and affluence.[11] As a result of these developments, American society took on the appearance of comfortable social conformity. According to Seymour Martin Lipset, for example, the problems of industrial society had been resolved by the 1950s and thus ended domestic politics for the many intellectuals who needed ideologies to motivate them to political action.[12] In the 1950s, Lipset's assertion seemed neither outrageously inaccurate nor dangerously complacent. Indeed, the notion that political dissent and ideological speculation had no relevance in American society was echoed by a variety of contemporary writers.[13] The prevailing philosophy of the Eisenhower era, therefore, was not concerned with a set of principles to be striven for but with the maintenance of an indigenous ideology that not only rationalized and celebrated naturally occurring social values and arrangements, but discouraged all forms of political skepticism. In this context, political problems were not seen as deep-seated malfunctions but merely as superficial disorders demanding only the slightest social readjustment.

Given this type of political optimism and social certitude, the position of the Democratic Senate and the role of Eisenhower becomes easier to comprehend. Moderation and nonpartisanship characterized not only the Eisenhower presidency but also the Democratic leadership in Congress. This reflected the prevailing spirit of consensus and accommodation. In addition, it was the product of the relative strengths within and between the two major parties. From 1954 to 1958, Congress was almost equally divided between Democrats and Republicans. In addition, both parties experienced potential or actual splits on a number of major issues. When these two disaggregative forces were combined with a presidency formally controlled by one party and a Congress formally controlled by the other, any attempt at full partisan mobilization by either Democrats or Republicans would have ended in damaging failure. Eisenhower, in particular, realized that an effort to rally Republicans around an unequivocal party program would have precipitated an immediate closure of Democratic ranks, a split between the Republican liberals and their Taftite critics, the disappearance of Eisenhower's chief political asset of nonpartisanship, the end of Eisenhower's hopes for a Republican majority-center party, and a public reaction against the party responsible for any breakdown in executive–legislative relations. Much to the chagrin of Democratic party zealots, their leaders in Congress (Lyndon Johnson and Sam Rayburn) also acknowledged the political utility of bipartisanship.

Lyndon Johnson believed that what was true for Eisenhower and his party was also true for himself and the Democrats. As a result, he saw his role as maintaining as much party unity as possible without irritating the more uncompromising members of his party and without causing a breach with an exceptionally popular president.[14] With this dual aim in mind, he sought to avoid those issues that would split the party (e.g., civil rights, congressional reform), and to exploit those issues that could unite the party against the Republicans, without directly embarrassing Eisenhower (e.g., minimum wage, publicly owned power projects, social security changes). In general terms, however, Johnson assumed a consensus approach. He preferred to engineer impressively large bipartisan majorities through a sustained virtuoso performance in personal persuasion, procedural manipulation, and coalition building.[15] Johnson believed that "in an era of national conciliation," the Democrats' road to power and his own route to the White House were "paved with modest bills actually passed [and not with] proposals that could not be enacted."[16]

Johnson's Democratic critics believed that he was in effect acting as Eisenhower's legislative manager and that instead of embarrassing the Republican incumbent, Johnson chose to save Eisenhower from the president's own ineptitude in legislative liaison and from his apparent indifference toward his own legislative proposals. According to Johnson's detractors, the power that he had developed as majority leader was employed to benefit Johnson's own political future and not to create a set of distinctive Democratic positions. Although Johnson proclaimed that great strides had been made in civil rights legislation and that social welfare reforms had been given congressional approval for the first time since 1941, the skeptics in his party were by no means impressed. Notwithstanding Johnson's declarations of legislative achievement and the clamor of senatorial self-congratulation, the skeptics believed that Johnson's Senate had done little more than launch a flotilla of empty ships. Such vessels contained neither legislative substance nor the promise of future reform. On the contrary, Johnson's marginal reforms were seen as techniques by which the conservative coalition sought to preempt any movement for more major reform.

In Johnson's defense, it can be said that as majority leader he was always in the position of having to satisfy both wings of the party at the risk of possibly alienating one wing or even both in the process. His inconsistency was the inevitable result of having to mollify the liberals and the conservatives in different issue areas. On some issues he seemed to support the party's progressive–national group (e.g., housing, education, social security), whereas in others he deserted it in favor of his southern power base in the Senate (e.g., oil, gas, labor, civil rights).[17] Perhaps what made Johnson so controversial was his capacity to integrate the Senate's diffuse power structure to a sufficient degree for it actually to produce legislation. Once the Senate began to pass bills, criticism came from purists on both sides, who would have preferred principled immobilism rather than consensus legislation. It was Johnson's belief, however, that the period demanded his consensus approach to politics.

The 1956 election was a disaster for the national Democratic party but for Johnson it represented a vindication of his legislative strategy, for, despite Eisenhower's landslide victory, the congressional Democrats actually gained seats. While Johnson settled back into his role as the "second most powerful man in Washington," an influential faction inside the Democratic party had already decided that Johnson and Rayburn had given the voters no reason to reject Eisenhower and elect a Democratic administration. From then on, party politics and presidential ambitions in combination with social demands and economic conditions began to disrupt Johnson's spell over the Senate and to weaken his strength among the cadres of the national Democratic party.[18]

After the 1956 elections, one of Johnson's most vociferous critics inside the party was Paul Butler, the ambitious and aggressive chairman of the Democratic National Committee.[19] Butler became associated with the Democrats' progressive wing when he sought to shift the party away from the flaccid bipartisanship of the congressional leadership. In order to achieve a set of distinct Democratic policies and priorities, Butler knew that, in some way, he would probably have to emasculate the power that the congressional leadership had in molding the public's impression of the party. By doing for the chairmanship what Johnson had done for the Senate majority leadership, Butler exploited all the possible power sources of his position to siphon influence over party policy away from Congress. Butler was undeterred by those who claimed that the party chairman's responsibilities did not extend to interference with the congressional element of the party, especially after the 1956 congressional elections had confirmed the leadership's effectiveness in maintaining seats at a time when the national party had been humiliated. In Butler's view, the party's national organization and the party's congressional representation could not be separated. With the Democrats formally responsible for congressional decisions, "the record of the Congress itself became the party record"[20] that would be of enormous significance to the next presidential election.

Butler finally precipitated an open breach with the congressional leadership by his plan to form a permanent central policymaking body within the party's structure. Butler hoped to draw together the party's elite figures (e.g., congressional leaders, key governors, Democratic National Committee members, Adlai Stevenson, Estes Kefauver, and Harry S. Truman) and to form them into a nationally prominent party organization capable of establishing authoritative party positions. Initially, Johnson showed a good deal of interest in the project. He appeared to welcome the invitation to become a member of what would later become known as the Democratic Advisory Council (DAC). However, after Rayburn unilaterally denounced Butler's plan as an unwarranted and intolerable encroachment on the congressional leadership's prerogatives in policymaking, Johnson saw fit to dissociate himself from the council. The decision of Johnson and Rayburn left the DAC with a decidedly northern and western flavor. When Butler found he could not attract a single southern governor to its ranks, the council quickly acquired the reputation of being a northern Democratic action group intent on pressing unpalatable policies onto Johnson and Rayburn. The council, which Johnson had originally seen as a possible national platform for himself, thereby became the source of a damaging gulf between his leadership and the party chairman. Johnson came to regard Butler's DAC as a challenge not only to his control of the Senate, but to his potential as a future presidential candidate. In Johnson's eyes, the council threatened to detract credit from his legislative achievements, to restrict his freedom of operation in the Senate, to disrupt the finely tuned machinery of his coalition building process, and to give disproportionate influence to the small group of troublesome liberals in the chamber. Johnson realized that if the DAC eventually became an effective policy unit, his controversial opposition to its strategy of partisan confrontation would almost certainly disqualify him from being considered as a presidential figure of party unity in 1960.

Given this tension between Johnson and Butler, the 1958 midterm elections assumed particular significance for the Democratic party. The question was not one of a possible increase in congressional seats for the Democrats, but rather what kinds of Democrats they would be—the areas they came from, the campaigns they ran, and the expectations they had. The election would be a test of the party's strength in the country, an indication of the vulnerability of Republicans, and possibly a guide to the effectiveness of Johnson's or Butler's strategy. For these reasons, it was expected to be an important election. But very few could have predicted the far-reaching effects that the election would have on party fortunes in general, and on senatorial and presidential politics in particular.

Although Johnson and Butler both claimed credit for the Democrats' success in 1958, the elections were decided largely on the basis of contemporary events and conditions rather than on the relative differences between the congressional leadership and the Democratic Advisory Council.[21] Because the Republicans had provided them with a number of issues that could easily be exploited for electoral advantage, the Democratic party found itself in a position to score an outstanding victory. First, the country was experiencing an economic recession more severe than previous depressions during the Eisenhower period had been, and thereby all the more disturbing for those who had become accustomed to ever-increasing expectations of economic expansion. Second, the launching of the Soviet Union's Sputnik satellite had created widespread anxiety over the status of the United States in space technology and nuclear deterrence. Third, a scandal had led to the resignation of Sherman Adams, Eisenhower's chief assistant at the White House. Fourth, the Republican administration's less than wholehearted commitment to the Supreme Court's desegregation decision was believed by many to have adversely affected race relations and even to have precipitated the crisis at Little Rock. Fifth, the Republicans had refused to weaken the Taft–Hartley Act, despite their promise in the Republican platform of 1956. Sixth, the Democrats' proposed policies in such areas as civil rights, education, unemployment, and medical care were evoking an increasingly favorable response from the public. Seventh, the administration was beginning the inevitable decline from power as the Twenty-second Amendment rendered Eisenhower a lame-duck president. And finally, under the strain of an approaching presidential election that would demand a new party leader, the Republican party was threatening to relapse into the type of liberal–conservative dispute that had plagued the party in 1952. These Republican misfortunes and mistakes, combined with an increasingly unpopular administration and the electoral phenomenon of an antiadministration swing in midterm elections, contributed to create conditions highly favorable to the Democratic party.

With regard to the Senate, the election provided an opportunity for the Democrats to break the party deadlock that had characterized senatorial politics throughout the 1950s. In this respect, Senate Democrats benefited from a quite fortuitous, yet very significant advantage. As only one-third of the Senate faces electoral contests in any election year, the potential of such politically promising conditions to the Democrats was dependent upon the number of Republican Senators campaigning for reelection in 1958. A highly significant factor, therefore, was the large number of Republican seats up for election. Only 12 of the 49 Democrats faced their electorates in 1958, but 22 of the 47 Republicans had to confront Democratic challenges in conditions highly unfavorable to the Republicans.

The potential of these conditions was more than realized, for the election produced a dramatic swing against the Republicans. In the Senate it resulted in the largest gain for a party (+16) and the largest loss for a party (−12) to be experienced in this century. (The difference in gains and losses was due to the addition of 4 members from two new states—2 Senators from Alaska and 2 Senators from Hawaii. These new members entered the Senate in 1959 shortly after those Senators from the older states who had been elected in November of the previous year.) The Democratic majority, which had never been more than 4 throughout the 1950s, suddenly increased from 2 in 1957 to 30 in 1959. The importance of the 1958 Senate class was not limited to its size; there had been large classes before—in both 1946 (25) and in 1948 (19), for example. But the class of 1958 was different because it contained such a large number of northern Democrats. Prior to 1958, there had been on average only 4.3 northern Democrats in each of the six classes that had entered the Senate since the war. In 1958, the northern Democratic ranks swelled by 16, to reach a level of 41 seats.

This influx of northerners changed the whole composition of the Democratic party in the Senate, for the northern wing suddenly achieved a large numerical superiority over the southerners. Throughout the 1950s the number of northern Democrats had been roughly equal to the number of southern Democrats, but after 1958 northerners outnumbered southerners by 41 seats to 24 seats. The election also changed the composition of the northern Democratic group itself, for it increased the element of progressivism within its ranks. Although the northern Democratic group contained some of the most progressively inclined senators of the 1950s (e.g., Morse, Douglas, McNamara, Lehman, Clark, Carroll, Murray, Humphrey), it was also noted for its more moderate members (e.g., Bible, Frear, Hayden, Chavez, Anderson) and for its conservative member (Lausche). In 1958, the northern Democrats gained many new liberals, who were to reduce the isolation of the existing liberal group and provide the initial momentum for additional liberal seats in subsequent elections.

According to the voting study that appears in chapter 3, nine new liberals were swept to the Senate on the wave of the Democratic resurgence in 1958. They were Clair Engle, Vance Hartke, Ed Muskie, Philip Hart, Eugene McCarthy, Harrison Williams, Stephen Young, Frank Moss, and Oren Long. In combination with the existing liberal group, this part of the 1958 class immediately posed a potential threat to the system of senatorial leadership. The exceptional effectiveness of Lyndon Johnson as majority leader was based very firmly upon his general conformity with the Senate's traditional code of legislative behavior. To William S. White, Johnson was the ultimate personification of the Senate, for he recognized the futility of doctrinaire intransigence, acknowledged the necessity for compromise, and appreciated the utility of such aids as returned favors,

logrolling, rewards, penalties, records of credit and debit, and tactical
timetabling. Given this form of leadership and his past record of
conciliation with President Eisenhower, it was not unreasonable for
Johnson to have expected a reaction from the new progressives.

Liberal protests against Johnson's Senate operations had not been
unknown in the past. He had suffered criticism from progressive
members such as Paul Douglas, John Carroll, Estes Kefauver, Wayne
Morse, Patrick McNamara, William Proxmire, and Joseph Clark during his rise to prominence.[22] Such dissent had rarely deflected his
sense of purpose or his approach to the party leadership. And yet
just prior to the 1958 elections, Johnson began to feel the first sen-
sations of irritation over the attitudes and activities of the progressive
group. It was difficult enough at the best of times to mold consensus
policies while preserving an appearance of party unity. With increased numbers of traditionally more intransigent and critical members, the task became even more difficult. Johnson's delicate formulas
of conciliation became increasingly vulnerable to disruption when a
distinct group of dissenters refused to shift their ground for the
sake of an impressive majority.

Of course, if the liberal members refused to join Johnson's network, he could effectively isolate them in the Senate. But Johnson
did not want to adopt that course because such an action would lead
to an open split in the Senate Democratic party. This would not only
damage the party electoral strength but would damage Johnson's
presidential prospects. If Johnson was going to preserve his potential as a national candidate, he would have to maintain the effectiveness of his majority leadership while appeasing both wings of
his party in the Senate. From Johnson's point of view, it was more
likely to be the liberals than the conservatives who would determine
the viability of such a strategy.

Johnson attempted to allay the fears of both the old and new
liberals in the Eighty-sixth Congress (1959–60) by launching a bold
program of New Deal–style reforms.[23] He hoped that this action
would unite his inflated Senate party against the Republicans and
provide legislation passed by "veto-proof" majorities. This party program was partly an offensive posture in preparation for the 1960
election, partly a response to the more aggressive Republican leadership in Congress (i.e., Charles Halleck and Everett Dirksen), and
partly a defense against the newly developed partisanship of the

lame-duck Eisenhower administration. While Johnson's policy declaration worried some Democrats and whetted the appetites of others, Johnson found it difficult to change from a style of public caution and private accommodation to one of partisan confrontation with President Eisenhower. He was sensitive to Eisenhower's attacks on the Democrats as a party of spendthrifts, and he was anxious that Eisenhower might veto any new legislation that Johnson could inspire the Senate to pass. Johnson was not accustomed to, and did not like, presidential vetoes. If he was going to lead the Democrats in an active way and dispense with his strategy of bipartisanship, he knew he would have to expect presidential vetoes. Given this approach, vetoes were tolerable to Johnson only if they could be overridden by Congress and legislation actually placed on the books. Johnson could not abide the notion of legislative effort without the prospect that there would be legislation enacted by the end of the day. However, with a lame-duck administration and such a severe loss of congressional seats, the Republican minority in Congress was closing ranks and refusing to give Johnson and Rayburn the extra votes needed to ensure that vetoes could be overridden. Faced with the prospect of legislative defeats and smarting from Eisenhower's unashamedly political attacks on the Democrats as the party of budget deficits and inflation, Johnson began backing down on his commitment to major social reform. Legislation in such areas as housing and unemployment compensation were scaled down to meet Eisenhower's objections. Predictably, Johnson encountered the full effects of liberal disillusionment.

Many liberal Democrats in Congress believed that the failure of progressive legislation was due not so much to the membership's political attitudes or to contemporary public opinion as to the internal organization of the institution. As a result, the cause of Congressional reform was renewed. While liberal congressmen were busy organizing themselves into the Democratic Study Group under Lee Metcalf,[24] the Senate progressives were suggesting changes in the rules and modifications to the party structure. The crucial significance of Rule XXII, requiring two-thirds of the Senate to enforce cloture on debate, was recognized by all parties as the southern Democrats' ultimate deterrent to unacceptable civil rights legislation. The rule had been a symbol of southern domination to small groups of northern progressives over the previous 15 years and there had been nu-

merous liberal attempts to reduce the degree of support necessary
to limit debate. In January 1957, Senators Anderson, Douglas, and
Humphrey launched another amendment proposal to Rule XXII. Even
with the vigorous support of Paul Butler and the Democratic Advisory
Council, the proposal was swamped by the Johnson machine. As
with so many other reform proposals, the pre-1958 group of Senate
progressives believed that the large class of northern and western
Democrats would dramatically transform the prospects for a change
in Rule XXII. Johnson, however, moved quickly to preempt any
chance of a major reform by suggesting a minor adjustment. Through
a series of unilateral approaches to individual members, he succeeded
in splitting the liberal group and securing his amendment by the
massive margin of 72 to 22 votes.[25] Many liberals were despondent;
Paul Butler was furious. Yet the determination of Johnson to scotch
maneuvers of this sort was quite predictable, for nothing threatened
his position as Senate leader and potential presidential candidate so
much as an attempt to expose, in embarrassingly explicit terms, the
fact that the foundation of Johnson's power lay in the South.

Before 1958, northern Democrats believed they were underrepre-
sented as a regional group not only within the Senate as a whole but
also in the Senate Democratic party organization. Since Johnson had
become majority leader, it had been possible for him to proceed on
the assumption that the Senate Democratic party was a moderately
conservative organization. Johnson could usually manufacture Democratic majorities by mobilizing the southern bloc and by drawing in
a large supplement of senators from the Rocky Mountain and Border
State regions. After 1958, it was no longer so easy to detect and exploit a center of gravity in the Senate party. Johnson could not even
be sure that one existed. Just as the Rule XXII issue could have
exploded all the appearances of a controlled party organization, so
could the liberals' other proposals for changes in the party structure.

Once again, these liberal proposals had roots that stretched back
over the long period of Johnson's leadership. After 1958, however,
they assumed a special urgency in the light of the progressives' electoral success and their interest in the Butler strategy of a clear party
record in preparation for the 1960 presidential election. During the
Eighty-sixth Congress, Johnson had to suffer the irritation of receiving complaints over the atrophy of the party caucus as a decision-
making body, the absence of any center of information and consul-

tation for the Senate Democrats as a whole, the unfulfilled potential of the Democratic Policy Committee, the underrepresentation of northern Democrats on both the Democratic Policy Committee and the Steering Committee, and the apparent power held by the majority leader.[26]

In response to the progressives' demands, Johnson agreed to hold a caucus whenever any member demanded one. Johnson assumed, correctly as it turned out, that it would be the liberal group which would require additional caucuses and that ultimately the liberals would be the only members present at such caucuses. In respect to the other complaints, Johnson decided to ride out the storm, for any changes in such areas would have struck at the heart of his control network. As Johnson clung tenaciously to the institutional sources of his power, the liberals became convinced that the failure of so many of their social reform proposals was due to a sustained corruption of the majority rule principle in the Senate.[27]

By the time the Eighty-sixth Congress was at an end, the liberals' early optimism had proved ill-founded. Major reforms were probably too much to hope for given the entrenched partisanship of an approaching presidential election between two nonincumbents. Nevertheless, the Senate's liberal group and the Democratic Advisory Council anticipated that the class of 1958 would have a profound effect on the Senate in terms of institutional change and policy output. As it turned out, advances in congressional reform were minimal, while the liberals' central planks of effective civil rights, medicare, aid to education, housing, and area redevelopment remained only proposals. The chief legislative enactments of the Congress were a watered-down civil rights act and a new piece of restrictive union regulation (Landrum-Griffin Act), which through a comedy of errors had become law just as the labor movement was demanding a reduction in the scope of the Taft–Hartley Act. The liberals were both despondent over, and outraged at, these legislative accomplishments. Their attempts to facilitate the passage of progressive legislation by changing the internal framework of the Congress had not been successful. To the liberals, the Senate exemplified congressional inaction and structural conservatism. As a result, the Senate and its leader were dragged onto the national political stage by the liberals, who secured "majority rule in the Senate" as a plank in the Democratic party platform of 1960.

Although the liberals believed that Johnson's mastery of the Senate had not been weakened to any significant extent during the Eighty-sixth Congress, it is possible to perceive the two-year period as one of impending crisis for the Johnson leadership. The civil rights fight provides the best example of a reduction in Johnson's influence. In contrast to 1957, Johnson was unable to dissuade the southerners from filibustering even a weakened version of the bill.[28] Johnson knew that civil rights was the one issue that split the Democratic party more than any other. The southernness of southerners, including Johnson, came starkly into view when civil rights was raised in public debate. If the liberals insisted on raising the issue, Johnson saw his role as formulating a minimal bill and foreclosing argument on the subject as quickly as possible. According to Johnson, the liberals should have been satisfied with almost any legislative advance in this controversial area, while the southerners ought not to have exacerbated the division by filibustering such a bill—thereby precipitating a large-scale northern movement against Rule XXII in particular and northern political and economic retribution against the South in general. In 1960, however, the southerners were not prepared to face their constituents without having used the procedure of last resort.[29] Meanwhile the liberals repudiated the adequacy of Johnson's civil rights compromises and believed that the southern filibuster was an extravagant piece of Johnsonian engineering. The actuality of the situation can probably best be conveyed by an observation of Evans and Novak. "Johnson was overcome with frustration, his Senate humiliatingly out of his control. He begged his Southern friends for relief, and when they turned him down, he was at the point of nervous exhaustion. For once, Lyndon Johnson simply didn't know what to do next."[30]

The civil rights fight reflected a general change in conditions that were no longer favorable to Johnson's form of control. Increased public attention toward the civil rights issue; the growing salience of Rule XXII; the resurgence of confrontation politics between Democrats and Republicans and between northern and southern Democrats; the impending departure of President Eisenhower, whose passive form of leadership had permitted Johnson to benefit from the subsequent prominence given to Congress; the possibility of a new Democratic president who would be an activist party leader and thereby restrict the operational discretion of the Senate's lead-

ership; and the appearance of the Senate's conservatism and of Johnson's mistrusted pragmatism as political issues in themselves must
all have led Johnson to consider very carefully his future effectiveness in the Senate.

Just as the disillusioned liberals regarded the turbulent and divisive Eighty-sixth Congress as an indication of what they could
expect in the 1960s, so Johnson must also have realized that the
political and institutional preconditions for his leadership style were
disappearing. It should have come as no surprise, therefore, when
the majority leader accepted the vice-presidential nomination from
one of the junior members of the Senate. Johnson knew that after
1960 the Senate would never be the same as it had been during the
Eisenhower administration. In fact, "Johnson's anticipation of the
difference made him ready, perhaps eager, to leave, thereby sparing
himself the agony of watching his prestige diminish day by day."[31]

THE KENNEDY YEARS:
LIBERALISM'S FALSE START

The initial complexity of the historical and political context within
which the Kennedy presidency was set has been compounded rather
than clarified by the ever-increasing number of interpretations given
it.[32] As a result, Kennedy has been portrayed as a liberal intellectual
with conservative policies; a liberal president who was cruelly frustrated by an alarmingly reactionary Congress; a rhetorician who
was not interested in substantive legislation; a president who inspired the civil rights movement and precipitated a break with the
South; a president who worked with the South to the detriment of
the civil rights movement; a president who exaggerated social deficiencies in order to intervene in the role of crisis manager; a foreign
policy pragmatist who would never have involved American troops
in Asia; and a cold war zealot who condemned the United States
to the Vietnam war and inaugurated what later came to be known
as the "imperial presidency." Since the Kennedy name has remained
both a potent political force in the Democratic party and an emotive
element in American contemporary history, the Kennedy era continues to be afflicted by a welter of skeptical revisionism and nos-
talgic counterrevisionism. It is not the purpose of this study to speculate on the validity of the numerous interpretations presented on

this theme, but neither does it seek to convey an oversimplified view of the political environment during the Kennedy period. Acknowledging the multiplicity of perspectives in this field, the study seeks to explain and clarify certain contemporary congressional developments by analyzing two major elements of the Kennedy era: first, the continuation in the early 1960s of many of the public attitudes and political forces that had characterized the 1950s, and second, the result and ramifications of the 1960 election.

Senator Kennedy would not have been the liberals' first choice for president, yet they derived great satisfaction from his electoral victory. Now they believed that there would be a dynamic relationship between themselves and the White House that would at last link the disparate elements of the party's national–urban–progressive wing. During his election campaign, Kennedy inspired the progressives not only by his policies but by the methods he intended to use to secure their passage. Kennedy excoriated the Eisenhower administration and challenged the American people to release themselves from the stultifying complacency of the past.[33] In the strident tones of national self-assertion and social confidence, Kennedy publicized the imperative need for just those policies that congressional liberals had been pressing for unsuccessfully during the previous few years (e.g., federal aid to education, medicare, housing reforms, revision of labor laws, civil rights). To the progressives in Congress, the unambiguously liberal form of the Democratic platform in 1960 and the mobilizing force of Kennedy's flamboyant leadership would not only redeem the wasted years of the Eisenhower period but end their own isolated ineffectiveness within Congress. Kennedy was speaking their language. He was making the right sort of promises. What was more, he was going to make things happen.

By associating himself with "getting the country moving again," Kennedy was inferring that it had stopped and that it was Eisenhower who had stopped it. In this way he related the failures of the 1950s to the general failure in national leadership. Kennedy did not equivocate as to how this could be improved. "In the challenging, revolutionary Sixties, the American Presidency will demand more than ringing manifestos issued from the rear of the battle. It will demand that the President place himself in the very thick of the fight, that he care passionately about the fate of the people he leads."[34]

Kennedy was determined to restore the virtues of Roosevelt and

Truman to the presidency. After eight years of Eisenhower's benign paternalism, it seemed quite plausible that a vigorous president could provide the necessary impulse to sustained social improvement and to economic expansion. Certainly, the liberals allowed themselves to become convinced of both the capacity and the legitimacy of presidentially inspired reform. To them, the policies were already there. The only element missing was a president that would shift the mountain of anachronistic conservatism in the Congress.

If the liberals had become disillusioned during 1959–60 as a result of their unrealistically high expectations after the 1958 elections, they showed no signs of guarding themselves against the same sort of disappointment in 1960. Kennedy's victory appeared to hail a radical change in American politics. A new president from a new generation had formed a new administration to usher in the New Frontier.[35] The elections had been fought in terms of the public's receptivity to change, and therefore Kennedy's win was seen by liberals as a vindication of their proposals and a license for the President to pursue immediate social reforms. Nevertheless, the Kennedy vote represented an acceptance of only a very generalized and diffuse form of change. Although Kennedy had secured enough support for domestic reform to offset what he had lost due to his religion and to the Republican's professed experience in international policy, he had by no means gained a mandate for radical reform. His supporters were inspired by Kennedy's reiteration of traditional American ideals, they were concerned about contemporary social and economic problems, and they were impressed by the administration's sense of urgency and optimism. Yet, there was no catalyst, such as a depression or a war, that served to disturb the prevalent atmosphere of continued prosperity and social certainty. In Tom Wicker's words: "There was no real public evidence that the country believed it was standing still [and] no overwhelming demand for new movement."[36] Too many people had been nurtured on the suburban affluence of the Eisenhower period and too many political attitudes had become entrenched during the relative tranquility of the 1950s. Kennedy himself had risen to public prominence during the 1950s and had grown to appreciate the resilience of the Eisenhower consensus. As president, he knew that he would have to work within the existing range of public tolerance.[37]

If the torch had been passed to a new generation, there was

every indication that the torch would continue to burn in much the same way as it had before and that the new generation was not very much different from the previous one. Reform in principle was acceptable, even attractive. The substance, however, would have to be negotiated with other power centers. In addition, expenditures on social reforms would have to be compatible with the declared objectives of maximum economic growth with close control of budget deficits, expanded government spending without tax increases, low interest rates without high inflation, and the protection of the dollar's value at home and abroad.

Kennedy regarded change as necessary but realized that it would probably have to be incremental in nature. To achieve even the latter, he knew he would have to utilize fully the presidency's capacity to publicize issues and to mobilize support—even if this raised the expectations of his liberal colleagues in Congress. While many liberals were seduced into believing that Kennedy's campaign rhetoric would be converted into reality, Kennedy himself realized that extravagant hopes would probably have to be satisfied by mild reform. Given the absence of crisis and the maintenance of much of the 1950s political infrastructure, even modest reform would necessitate full exploitation of the very limited potential for reform. Anything more radical was too much to be expected, especially when the election results were taken into account.

The second major influence on Kennedy's attitude to policies and on his relationships with the Democratic party and the Congress was his weak electoral performance in 1960.[38] Although he gained a majority of 84 in electoral college votes, he secured just 49.7 percent of the popular vote. In the twentieth century, only Presidents Wilson and Truman had gained lower percentages of the vote. In some ways, Kennedy had done quite well. He won most of the northeastern region and, despite his religion, succeeded in securing six southern states. Nevertheless, in other respects, Kennedy was a weak candidate. He did not do well in either the Midwest (winning only Missouri, Michigan, Illinois, and Minnesota) or in the West (winning only New Mexico and Nevada). The erosion of traditional party loyalties was particularly noticeable in the South, where Nixon succeeded in retaining four states (Virginia, Tennessee, Oklahoma, and Florida) that Eisenhower had won in 1956. While Nixon picked up 40 southern electoral college votes, the independent ticket of Senator

Harry Byrd took 15 electoral college votes away from the Democratic candidate. This hemorrhage of electoral support from the once solid South served as a salutary reminder to Kennedy that the South would probably provide the pivotal votes in any future presidential election. It is ironic that while Kennedy has generally been depicted as the president who won the office on the basis of his appeal to the industrial–urban constituency of America, his winning margin of electoral votes came from the South. If Kennedy in 1960 had lost as many votes in the Deep South as Lyndon Johnson lost in 1964, he would not have won a plurality of the national vote. The South's position as the soft underbelly to Kennedy's electoral constituency helps explain why Kennedy felt obliged to pay careful attention to the region during his presidency.

Kennedy's vulnerability was not, however, limited to the South. Instead of entering the White House on a wave of increased Democratic representation in Congress, Kennedy had to suffer the embarrassment of actually losing 20 seats in the House of Representatives. Although the number of Senate Democrats increased by 2, Kennedy's impact on the electoral fortunes of his party had clearly been minimal. The mediocre performance of the party was due to some extent to its inflated success in the 1958 elections. But even if most of the electoral potential had been fulfilled in 1958, that did not in any way reduce the need for an attractive presidential candidate to defend and maintain the high level of seats. In this respect, Kennedy was a liability rather than an asset to many congressmen. Although some candidates dissociated themselves from Kennedy, in particular from his religion, others regarded their own electoral performances as tantamount to coattails for the party leader. From the voting figures it is not hard to see why so many congressmen claimed responsibility for Kennedy's election. At the outset, Kennedy's 49.7 percent of the vote compares unfavorably with the 54.5 percent of the vote captured by the congressional Democratic ticket. However, this figure represents only the gross congressional party vote, which includes both decisive winners and individual Democrats buried in local Republican landslides. Kennedy's electoral weakness becomes apparent only when his vote is compared with those Democrats who won congressional seats. Taking the Senate as our example, Kennedy's 49.7 percent was in arrears not only in the popular vote but also in the number of states won. The average vote of the Democratic senators elected in 1960 (except those who were unopposed) was 61.5 percent. And of the 22 states to elect Democratic senators in that year, only 14 voted for Kennedy in the presidential election.

The tensions between northern and southern Democrats, between campaign promises and political compromises, and between Kennedy rhetoric and the prevailing consensus were reflected in the president's relations with Congress. Although he was the first president in a century to have served in both Houses of Congress, Kennedy was not, and never felt himself to be, a Capitol Hill professional. On the contrary, Kennedy knew "that he had always been too junior, too liberal, too outspoken and too much in a hurry to be accepted in [the] inner ruling circles [of Congress]."[39] Kennedy was aware that his efforts to secure the Democratic party nomination had been opposed by the congressional party leadership and that his reform proposals were not likely to be received favorably by important segments of his party on Capitol Hill. It appeared to Kennedy that the battle lines between the administration and the Democratic Congress had been drawn up before he had even won the election, when, in a special postconvention session of Congress, he failed to secure legislative passage of four major planks in the Democratic platform (i.e., minimum wage, housing, medicare, aid to education).[40] If Kennedy had been laboring under any illusions after his electoral victory, they were quickly dispelled by the celebrated campaign to increase the size of the House Rules Committee.[41]

Speaker Rayburn had always acknowledged the power of the Rules Committee in structuring and scheduling the legislative process but was loath to engage in attempts to restrict its discretion. His belief in the efficacy of gentle private pressure led him to dismiss liberal demands for the committee to be made more representative of the institution's overall membership. Rayburn was not convinced that the committee was unrepresentative of the chamber—but if it was, the House could force the committee to relinquish its grip on legislation through such procedural devices as the discharge petition, "Calendar Wednesday," and a suspension of the rules. To the liberals, these mechanisms were far too unwieldy to operate and were almost always bound to fail given the general inclination of members to support one another's privileges and powers.

It was precisely this network of interdependence that had deterred Rayburn from moving against the committee, even though its existence represented a continual threat to his position as the central planner of the legislative process inside the House. By 1960, however, even Rayburn was beginning to feel that the committee's threat was more actual than potential. At the beginning of the Eighty-sixth Congress he had promised the newly enlarged liberal contingent that he could deliver much of the legislation they wanted in time for the 1960 presidential election. His confidence in the power of discreet persuasion and the effectiveness of appeals to party loyalty was rudely shaken when Judge Smith's committee adopted an intransigent position on a whole series of important measures. The shift of the two most senior Democrats (Smith and Colmer) into the camp of the four Republicans activated a solid conservative coalition that split the 12-member committee in half. The consequent immobility jeopardized bills in such fields as civil rights, federal aid to education, medicare, minimum wage, federal pay scales, housing, and depressed areas.[42] Just at a time when the Democratic party needed to establish a clear legislative program for the benefit of its presidential candidate, the Rules Committee had publicly embarrassed both the party and its leader in the House. Rayburn sensed a threat to his power base, a contravention of institutional norms, and perhaps most significantly, a denial of basic loyalty. In Tom Wicker's words: "Rayburn was a Democrat, first and last; the Judge's affronts to him might be accepted, but could the Speaker put up with what he was bound to regard as a betrayal of his party and its candidates? He could not; his tolerance of Howard Smith turned to outrage."[43] Rayburn felt that if the Rules Committee was permitted to operate in the Eighty-seventh Congress as it had done in 1960, it would jeopardize not only Kennedy's Democratic program but also the Speaker's status within his own party and within the institution.

After threatening to purge Colmer from the committee, Rayburn settled upon a strategy of enlarging the committee by two Democrats and one Republican. Since the two Democrats would be sympathetic to Rayburn, the Speaker would then be able to depend on a majority of eight Democratic regulars outvoting a minority of two southern Democrats and five Republicans. Rayburn's campaign was strongly supported by Kennedy, who as president-elect realized that little of the Democratic platform would be enacted as long as the form of the Rules Committee remained the same. The obvious political importance of the proposed reform activated an intense lobbying campaign both by groups in support and by groups in opposition. The administration and the Democratic party organization raised the political temperature even further through their attempts to influence congressmen directly by electoral assistance and constituency benefits and indirectly by mobilizing pressure at the local party and constituency level. Rayburn's proposal had graduated not only into a test of the Speaker's political strength but into a vote of confidence in the Kennedy administration and its programs.

Despite the considerable pressure exerted on its behalf, the Rayburn reform of the Rules Committee was passed by only 217 votes to 212. It was a vote that haunted Kennedy throughout his presidency and probably conditioned his strategy on many subsequent political proposals. In Kennedy's pessimistic reaction to the vote, one sensed the sights of his administration being lowered: "With all that going for us, with Rayburn's own reputation at stake, with all the pressures and appeals a new President could make, we won by five votes. That shows what we're up against."[44] From a nominal figure of 263 Democrats and 174 Republicans, Kennedy found that he could not rely on nearly two-thirds of his party's southern wing in this most important vote. Kennedy was left depending on 22 Republicans for his marginal victory. As a result of this salutory lesson, Kennedy now knew what he had probably, if reluctantly, anticipated all along—that his election had not changed attitudes in Congress; that his platform, his lack of coattails, and the loss of Democratic seats may even have intensified opposition to him and his programs; and that if he wanted reforms he would have to negotiate them through Congress on the basis of coalitional support and reciprocal accommodation.

As the cartoon images of a reluctant president facing an impulsive Congress changed to that of an activist president confronting an obdurate legislature, Kennedy tried, whenever possible, to invoke policy changes without recourse to congressional approval. Impressed by the scope and effectiveness of his executive status in the foreign policy field, Kennedy exploited what independent executive discretion he possessed in the area of domestic policy. For example, when Kennedy wanted to stimulate production in the construction industry in 1961, he simply reduced the interest rate on loans provided by the Federal Housing Administration. He attempted to compensate for the absence of further civil rights legislation by tightening antidiscrimination provisos in federal contracts and in federally subsidized programs. Where executive action was insufficient or impossible and where congressional action was necessary, Kennedy tried to change the ground on which he fought for his policies. In addition to the Rules Committee fight, Kennedy launched himself into the midterm election campaign of 1962. At best, he hoped to produce a more sympathetic Congress, but at the very least he planned to prevent his congressional position from deteriorating further as a result of midterm Republican gains. As the Cuban crisis occurred in the middle of Kennedy's election campaign, it is difficult to determine whether the Democrats' success in maintaining their level of congressional representation was due in any way to Kennedy's partisan intrusions.

Finally, Kennedy attempted to use the presidency to publicize issues and mobilize support for his administration's policies. Kennedy realized that it was not presidential leadership "directly of the lawmakers so much as the public reaction to that leadership that [won] congressional votes."[45] Working on that basis, Kennedy took his proposed reforms to the people and alerted them to the need for immediate action in such areas as education, health, and the minimum wage. It is true that Kennedy always acknowledged the Neustadt principle—that a president has to preserve his public prestige and professional reputation from the debilitating effects of unattainable objectives and open failures. Nevertheless, Kennedy was prepared to identify himself closely with his administration's proposals and to exploit his political prominence in order to generate popular support for those proposals which he regarded as realistic and attainable.

Despite Kennedy's use of executive action and his challenge to the people to prepare themselves for the New Frontier, he was ultimately dependent upon Congress for many of his policies. In effect, this meant that Kennedy had to season his inspirational public rhetoric with plain political negotiation inside Congress.[46] It has already been acknowledged that Kennedy was electorally dependent upon the South. It was in Congress that the South would do most to remind Kennedy of the insufficiency of his northeastern constituency. If such a power base was not large enough to ensure a majority in a national election, it would most certainly be inadequate in a rurally biased Congress characterized by malapportioned con-

stituencies and a disproportionate number of committee chairmen
from the South. Kennedy lacked congressional support, therefore,
in both numerical and cultural terms.

Kennedy set out to win important friends and to strengthen his
congressional base by making every effort to accommodate the South.
Much to the surprise and irritation of many of his urban supporters,
Kennedy courted southern chairmen; channeled federal contracts, public works, and redevelopment subsidies into the South; raised price
supports on major southern crops such as tobacco, peanuts, rice, and
cotton; and devoted most of his congressional liaison efforts toward
bringing southern congressmen and senators into the administration's
policy clearance and legislative strategy apparatus.[47] In accordance
with this southern strategy, Kennedy felt unable, and probably unwilling, to press for legislation in the area of civil rights.[48] As his
efforts were directed toward maximizing party unity, he was loath
to approach the one issue that always split the Democrats. Kennedy
believed that black Americans would benefit far more from his executive actions and from reforms in such areas as education, welfare,
and minimum wage than from an embittered and probably sterile
civil rights campaign that would place in jeopardy all his other reform bills. While a civil rights fight may well have raised the morale
of his core supporters, many of whom had become disillusioned by
Kennedy's ineffectual congressional performance, Kennedy continued
to test the loyalty of those he counted on most by "reneg[ing] on
his own and his party's program"[49] in civil rights. Ultimately, Kennedy suffered from his reluctance on this issue by being seen to be
forced into a civil rights stance through the deterioration in race
relations that to some extent may have been due to Kennedy's own
apparent ambivalence toward black Americans. Nevertheless, up to
February 1963, Kennedy's position on civil rights typified his overall
strategy of compensating for his poor electoral position by working
with the established congressional leadership to secure a number
of long-established reform proposals.

Contrary to popular notions, Kennedy's strategy did achieve a
number of notable victories. He gained legislation in such areas as
housing, area redevelopment, minimum wage, Rules Committee reform, trade, unemployment compensation, manpower development
and training, public works, and aid to dependent children. In addition, the bipartisan tradition in foreign policy held firm to provide

Kennedy with congressional acceptance of the Development Loan Fund, the Alliance for Progress, the Peace Corps, the Arms Control and Disarmament Agency, and the ban on atmospheric testing of nuclear weapons. Although this could be viewed as a successful congressional record in terms of output, Kennedy was criticized not only for compromising bills to secure congressional passage (e.g., minimum wage) but also for failing to achieve acceptance of measures that were regarded as top priority by both the president and the Democratic party.[50] Conspicuous by their absence were the civil rights bill, the tax cut, medicare, and federal aid to education. By 1963, congressional liberals were joined by academic observers in being convinced that the perverse obstinacy of Congress in the face of such apparent demands for action could only be due to structural conservatism that necessitated large-scale congressional reform. According to this liberal view, Congress was not representative of the people and, to add insult to injury, the congressional leadership was not even representative of the membership. Liberal irritation was greatest in respect to the Senate, where liberals perceived the existence of an inner conservative clique that had the power to translate into reality its conservative philosophy of the Senate's institutional role and its conservative policy outlook.[51] Liberals, whose appetites had been whetted by the 1960 Democratic platform, were somewhat disenchanted with the failure of *their* president to effect change, particularly within the Senate. To the liberals, his conciliatory attitude toward the southern leadership was final proof of the disequilibrium in the American system that forced a nationally elected and progressive president to accommodate himself to a congenitally unrepresentative and conservative institution.

The liberals' criticism, however, was not confined to Congress. The "crisis in government" also extended to the presidency. If, as Wicker claims, Kennedy was "too astute to believe his own 'image,'"[52] the same could not be said of his liberal supporters. Kennedy had generated such high expectations among them that their disappointment seemed almost inevitable. In the Senate, the liberals had increased their numbers from 18 in 1958 to 26 in 1963, but even with this substantial increment, they had failed to secure many of their favored reforms. Some of them had pressed progressive proposals in the 1950s and had worked to publicize reforms and establish them on the agenda for future legislative actions (e.g., McNamara with medicare; Morse with educational aid). It appeared that the climax of their efforts would come with the crucial endorsement of and subsequent pressure from a Democratic administration. Just at the moment of impending fulfillment, however, the Senate liberals were held in suspense as Kennedy battled against his own political weakness and against the established forces in Congress. Their irritation led some of them to be privately skeptical of Kennedy's standard of congressional leadership and the depth of the president's commitment to the Democratic platform. Other observers—Henry Fairlie, for example—criticized Kennedy's leadership style for its excessively strident presentation of crises.[53] But to the liberals, Kennedy failed to take his case against Congress to the people. While the liberals had come to expect a jihad against congressional conservatism, Kennedy was seen to be inaugurating an ecumenical movement between the presidency and the established congressional leadership.

It is very much this liberal image of congressional regressivism absorbing presidential progressivism that characterized the Kennedy era. As this section has attempted to convey, Kennedy was confronted by debilitating economic problems, an apparent absence of social crisis, the continuity of the 1950s consensus in political attitudes, his electoral and congressional weakness, and intense and contradictory political pressures generated by the exaggerated hopes and fears associated with a new Democratic administration. From the perspective of all these problems and restraints, it is possible to assess the Kennedy period as one of unfulfilled potential. Nevertheless, it should be noted that by the time of Kennedy's assassination, at least some of the Democrats' seminal reforms (e.g., college aid, tax cut, civil rights) were showing signs of moving out of the chrysalis stage of congressional discussion.[54] Whether this development was due to Kennedy's increased prestige after the Cuban crisis, to improved legislative liaison work, to the onset of the presidential campaign season, to a decline in public anxiety over Kennedy and his policies, or just to sheer presidential attrition, the fact remains that Kennedy appeared to be succeeding in at least two major policies at the time of his death. The changes in the political environment led James Sundquist to conclude that "most of what happened would have happened—more slowly, perhaps, but ultimately—if Kennedy had lived."[55] The conditions necessitating a reassessment of the reactionary nature of the Congress were already evident before Kennedy's death. The assassination merely exaggerated preexisting political trends and precipitated the obsolescence that had been unwittingly built into the model of congressional conservatism by the disappointed liberal observers of the Kennedy presidency.

THE JOHNSON YEARS

The Fruits of Productive Consensus

There was no better politician than Lyndon Johnson for exploiting fully any opportunity for political achievement. With the Kennedy assassination, he inherited not only the presidency but all the political momentum of the Kennedy program and all the aspirations of the bitterly disappointed Democratic party. This rich bequest provided Johnson with power, and with frustration. As a new president after a nationally traumatic event, he entered the White House on a tidal wave of popular support that was generated more by sympathy for Kennedy and by deep public attachment to the presidency as an institution than by any spontaneous attraction to Johnson.[56]

On the contrary, Johnson was initially confronted by the prospect of becoming an embarrassed receptacle for the presidential seal and a lightning rod for all the bitterness of the bereaved Kennedy loyalists, who struggled to reconcile themselves to Kennedy's absence. While Kennedy became politically canonized, Johnson appeared as the Southern manipulator who had merely balanced the ticket in 1960 and gambled successfully on the vice-presidency. To many, the death of the sophisticated and urbane young president was made even more poignant by the figure of his successor, who appeared to be everything the late leader was not—uncultured, inarticulate, gauche, unattractive, provincial, and a southerner nursed on the raw intrigue of Texas politics.[57]

Despite the considerable disadvantage of not being the "recognized successor to the leadership of John F. Kennedy,"[58] Johnson succeeded in acquiring a position of central power after only a few months as president. Cultural sentimentality toward the presidency in general and to Kennedy's memory in particular were progressively displaced by respect for Johnson's burgeoning personal authority. Contemporary political conditions interacted with the personal philosophy and capabilities of the president to produce an individual aura that pervaded the style and direction of the entire government. In the words of Doris Kearns: "Lyndon Johnson dominated public life as almost no one before him. . . . His formidable presence seemed to infuse all the decisions of government, and he exacted a compliance from Congress unprecedented since the beginning of the New Deal."[59] The mid-1960s became literally the Johnson years—significant not only for Johnson's prominence but for his role in a pivotal period of American history that saw the culmination of so many political campaigns and the beginning of so many new political developments.

Johnson's profound influence on American politics and society was the result of his almost unique capacity to exploit the particular historical opportunity that presented itself in the mid-1960s. His capacity consisted not only of a set of formidable political skills but also of a set of absolute beliefs concerning American society and the role of leadership within it. Johnson's experience, background, and motivation appeared to be peculiarly appropriate to the milieu in which he had to operate as president. Johnson's prominent position as chief executive served in turn to fashion public attitudes toward his perspective of social development and political decision making. This interaction between Johnson's philosophy and the political circumstances favorable to his notions of government became known as consensus politics. The advantages and deficiencies, strengths and failures of consensus politics characterized the Johnson era.

Johnson had always been predisposed toward working within the established landscape of American politics for the purpose of maximizing the system's potential for change.[60] The continuous interplay of competing groups among different governmental levels and institutions characterized the American political system. While Johnson recognized that such a kaleidoscopic form of politics could generate excessive conflict and ultimately immobility, he also believed that it had the potential for inducing widespread agreement and cooperation—given the right conditions and the appropriate leadership. He supported this view on the basis of two premises: first, that the unique social history of the United States had blessed Americans with fundamental unanimity on social values and objectives. According to this view, more things united Americans than separated them. In Johnson's own words: "What the man in the street wants . . . is *not* a big debate on fundamental issues; he wants a little medical care, a rug on the floor, a picture on the wall, a little music in the house, and a place to take Molly and the grandchildren when he retires."[61] It was the function of leadership to remind people that they were already living within an achieved ideal and that different individuals' demands and objectives were basically simple in nature and compatible with one another.

The second premise was related to the first. Johnson acknowledged the existence and legitimacy of different groups with differing interests and political resources. Such groups were necessary to an effective democracy. Nevertheless, in Johnson's view, intergroup differences too often activated the debilitating and counterproductive checks endemic in the political system. The resultant political stasis led only to greater divisions between Americans and to intransigent political positions that needlessly jeopardized America's valuable social unity. To Johnson, this form of politics was not only myopic because it ignored what linked Americans but also completely unnecessary, because all legitimate American interests were by their nature consistent with each other. Johnson's experience in Texas politics had demonstrated to him that the interests of labor and big business, blacks and whites, farmers and bankers could be served by a single party sufficiently pragmatic to give concessions to each group. In such an environment, trade-offs between groups were regarded as an acceptable and necessary prerequisite to political action that would be generally beneficial to all groups involved. Johnson's term as Senate majority leader had taught him the same lesson. That institution was well known for its capacity to lapse into unproductive disorder. The role of the Leader, in Johnson's eyes, was to prevent differences from degenerating into principled intransigence and to rely instead upon a process of multiple accommodation between individual members that transcended simple group allegiances and appealed to an aggregate common interest. With this background in Texas–congressional politics, Johnson arrived at the White House convinced that presidential leadership should be concerned with a vivid appeal to the public in terms of its individual but mutually inclusive group components.[62]

Johnson was in politics to produce output and, as president, he was determined to generate tangible changes on the ground that would rank with the New Deal. However, Johnson was proposing to use different methods to secure such changes than those used by

Roosevelt. His pluralist recipe for effective political leadership depended upon the resolution of conflict by an essentially discreet process by which interest-group deals would be formulated and packaged by a president acting as a central intermediary. In contrast to Roosevelt and Kennedy, Johnson deplored partisanship as an irrational and negative phenomenon that reduced the system's potential for achievement through general agreement.[63] Johnson's working slogan, "come now and let us reason together," could not operate successfully if a president insisted upon explicit party appeal. Such partisanship tended to bind some groups together under the party flag while permanently excluding other groups that would undoubtedly become more inflexible in their positions. These two corollaries to partisanship reduced a president's discretion in drawing groups together and in activating bargaining relationships between them that would lead to compromised policy, but policy that would at least be enacted. Partisanship, therefore, "like race prejudice or class warfare, [was] the enemy of consensus."[64] Consequently, Johnson renounced the role of party leader in favor of that of a catalytic negotiator who would produce results by exploiting the existing configuration of political relationships.

Although Johnson was personally disposed toward consensus politics, he would not have been able to exercise his leadership techniques in conditions that were not conducive to this idiosyncratic form of political juggling. Fortunately for Johnson, the political environment during the early part of his presidency appeared in many ways to endorse Johnson's assumptions of American society and his belief in the productive potential of the political system. To begin with, the economy was recovering from its poor performance in the late 1950s and early 1960s. Kennedy's expansionist policies, in conjunction with the tax cut in 1964, had succeeded in stimulating industrial production in 1965.[65] The industrial production index had increased by only 7 points from 1955 to 1960, but between 1960 and 1965 it grew by 23 points.[66] As a result, unemployment dropped from 5.5 percent in 1960 to 4.5 percent in 1965, its lowest level in 10 years.[67] The boom renewed American confidence in its economy and in its capacity to generate unlimited goods and capital. Insofar as social problems demanded the application of financial resources, no challenge could fail to be met. The easy optimism of the mid-1960s was similar to the "end of ideology" era of the 1950s, during which Americans were convinced that all the problems of Western industrial society had been effectively resolved. This was the bedrock of the Eisenhower consensus. The economic certainties that reappeared in the mid-1960s were joined by a burgeoning awareness of social deficiencies such as poverty and racism. Disturbing as these blights on the American success story may have been, they were in no sense seen as indicative of deep cultural or political malaise. On the contrary, it was through wealth that such problems could be resolved, by a series of readjustments and technical modifications to a basically sound economic system. Such changes did not even appear to involve the need for setting priorities, for, given the abundance of resources, all problems could be resolved at the same time without excessive cost to anyone. Indeed, so strong was the economy that during the mid-1960s Americans had even begun to lapse into the luxury of speculating on the moral and human costs of assured economic expansion.

The development of Johnson's consensus was further assisted by the public reaction to the Kennedy assassination. The shock generated a powerful impulse toward Kennedy's reform program, not only out of a desire to reaffirm the integrity of the political system, but because the assassination itself had created serious anxieties over the state of American society. The killing of a president who had been calling attention to various social deficiencies in an apparently successful and tranquil society was deeply disturbing to many Americans. As a result, his successor was given the dual role of personifying the continuity of the presidency and responding to a general demand for government action that would resurrect America's diminished social confidence. Johnson reasserted American faith in its system by appealing for unity upon "a program which [was] wise, just, enlightened and constructive."[68] That initial program was composed of Kennedy's unenacted legislative proposals on aid to education, taxation, medicare, and most significantly, on civil rights. It was the issue of civil rights, which was being literally forced onto the government by widespread agitation, that allowed Johnson to allay many northern suspicions of his southern background and to win his liberal spurs from Kennedy's progressive–urban constituency. He gave Kennedy's civil rights bill the strongest possible endorsement by making it his top legislative priority and by indirectly supervising its passage through the Senate.[69] The successful campaign to impose cloture on the southern filibuster secured the most far-reaching civil rights act since Reconstruction. For the blacks, the act included a guarantee of equal access to public accommodations and further strengthening of federal policy in the areas of school desegregation and equal employment opportunities. For Johnson, the civil rights act gave him the opportunity to escape from the debilitating embrace of his sectional heritage and to present himself as a responsible centrist whose consensus methods produced results even on the most difficult of issues. It could be regarded as somewhat ironic that what Kennedy had failed to achieve in civil rights was accomplished by a southern Democrat. Yet it was precisely Johnson's electoral and political strength in the South that enabled him to press for civil rights legislation without the appearance of southern victimization. Far from being a disadvantage, therefore, Johnson's southern background appeared to make him the only available leader who could have mobilized widespread agreement on a strong civil rights bill.

To Johnson, what was true for the controversial issue of race was just as valid for any other issue. In Johnson's view, Americans were basically unified on values and objectives in the hands of the right leader. His only problem was to persuade the American people that he was that leader. To the extent that the people were unified, the president could claim to personify that unanimity and in turn provide an additional source of social integration. Conditions were conducive to this aim in terms of the economy, the Kennedy assassination, the public's renewed sense of social awareness, and the passage of civil rights legislation. It was the 1964 election, however, that provided Johnson with a decisive demonstration of public allegiance to his presidency and what he took to be a popular acceptance of his style of politics.[70] Goldwater's provocative statements on voluntary social security, "victory abroad," and states' rights poured votes into the center accommodated by Johnson.[71] The president's symbolic appeal as Kennedy's successor had always sustained his public approval level at around the 70 percent mark, but with Goldwater's candidacy, Johnson was able to translate this diffuse indication of acceptability into a personal victory of dramatic proportions. Johnson won by the largest margin of votes recorded in a presidential election up to that time. Whereas Kennedy had lagged behind congressional Democrats with only 49.7 percent of the vote in 1960, Johnson surpassed the performance of his party in congressional elections (57.4 percent) with a staggering 61.1 percent of the presidential vote. Johnson's popularity helped to bring in 38 additional Democratic congressmen. Although the number of Democratic seats in the Senate increased by only one, this represented a notable victory, for the Democrats succeeded in retaining the exceptionally large gains they had made in 1958. Despite the consistency in the party ratio, the changes in the Democratic seats, together with the Democratic gains over Republicans, produced a further increment of 3 liberal members (Tydings, Harris, Robert Kennedy). Since 1959, when the class of 1958 boosted the liberal ranks to 18, the number of liberal Senators had grown repeatedly in each election until in 1965 the citadel of conservatism had accumulated 28 liberal members. Johnson, therefore, had not only become President in his own right but had secured a Democratic Congress of Rooseveltian proportions. To Johnson, the election was both a vindication of what he had achieved up to that point and a mandate to expand the scope of consensus politics even further. At last, Johnson could present himself as the personification of a consensus which, with his leadership, could provide beneficial results for all Americans.

After his election, Johnson developed and exploited his position as national leader. Johnson became the central negotiator in terms of policy and physical position. He saw himself as the gravitational force that drew superficially opposed groups into a disjointed harmony of interests in which liberals and conservatives became indistinguishable from one another. To Johnson, this was an indication of presidential success: "You ask a voter who classifies himself as a liberal what he thinks I am, and he says 'a liberal.' You ask a voter who calls himself a conservative what I am, and he says 'a conservative.' You ask a voter who calls himself a middle-roader, and that's what he calls me. They all think I'm on their side."[72] Johnson had indeed incorporated, if not ingested, into his coalition those groups, such as the blacks, the intellectuals, the unions, the Democratic left, and Kennedy loyalists, that were initially hostile to him. Another major component of Johnson's consensus was the South. The region was not at all convinced by Johnson's view that civil rights was to its ultimate advantage. Nevertheless, through Johnson the South had finally secured the presidency and, as such, could be relied upon to offer slightly less opposition to certain policies than it might have done with a northern Democrat in the White House.[73] But perhaps

Johnson's "most striking achievement" lay in his successful appeal
to the business community to support a "liberal Democratic President, who meant to spend taxpayers' money for social purposes."[74]
This appeal was based upon Johnson's early image as a gas and oil
politician, his budgetary caution as Senate majority leader, his belief
in the necessity of a strong economy to facilitate social change, and
his known consensus style of individual rewards and sectional incentives. Just as Johnson was open to persuasion, so business interests
were prepared to bargain with him. It was in this spirit of mutual
accommodation that Johnson was able to combine his liberal coalition with the tacit, yet crucial, support of precisely that political
group which Kennedy was never able to claim. In sum, Johnson's
broad and heterogeneous coalition appeared to give some justification to his assertion that all groups and interests could be accommodated within the great tent of the Democratic party.

Johnson knew that to keep all these groups in his tent, he would
have to provide them with a positive stimulus. Thus began Johnson's
vast balancing act, in which a prodigious number of privately negotiated agreements was finalized and coordinated by the White
House. Johnson's central position in this network was maintained
only by the president's own formidable skill in political persuasion
and negotiation, by his attention to the conscious interdependency
of policy proposals, and by his intuitive knowledge of the capacity
and potential of the political system. The net result of Johnson's
multifaceted and multilayered maneuvers led to retraining for the
unemployed, poverty programs for the poor, tax rebates for industry,
medicare for the old, aid to education for the young, highways for
business, civil rights for minorities, rent supplements for needy ten-
ants, increased minimum wage for labor, automobile safety for drivers,
legal protection for consumers, clean air and water legislation for
environmentalists, and so on. In Sam Lubell's words, "no previous
budget had ever been so contrived to 'do something' for every major
economic interest in the nation."[75] Congress was inundated with legislative proposals. From 1965 to 1966 it was presented with 200 proposals for domestic legislation by Johnson. It was seen as a reflection
of Johnson's immense political leverage that the Congress passed
181 of the president's requests.[76] It appeared that the inveterate conservatism of Congress had given way overnight to an enlightened
progressivism inspired by the managerial skills of its most celebrated

former member.[77] To Johnson, congressional support was not only an essential prerequisite to consensus leadership but provided in itself the final element in Johnson's whole concept of consensus politics. Johnson's aim was to process the debilitating effects of divisions (e.g., regional, class, racial) out of politics. The apparent movement of Congress into the presidential orbit, therefore, represented the fusion of the last cultural duality and the final closing of the circle around the central figure of Johnson.

It can be argued that the seeds of Johnson's legislative successes had not just been sewn in the Kennedy era, but had been actively nourished by certain progressive elements in the Congress. The poverty program, for example, owed much to the early commitment by many congressional liberals to the notion of community action in the field of juvenile delinquency.[78] In addition, Kennedy had endorsed a program of direct relief to the poor in 1963 before Johnson flamboyantly declared his "war on poverty."[79] Thus, while the Economic Opportunity Act remains "a classic case in executive legislation"[80] by the Johnson White House, it should be acknowledged that, as with all policies, the roots of legislation were lengthy and manyfold. In fact, many Great Society programs consisted basically of old proposals applied to known problems by a Congress generally amenable to change. What was exceptional was Johnson's capacity to exploit the favorable conditions within Congress and to expedite the passage of the maximum amount of legislation. Johnson had always believed that the president should be his party's congressional leader, and with this in mind he exercised the same type of legislative artistry from the White House that he used to employ from the majority leader's office. The tactics were essentially the same—selecting only politically viable proposals for presidential leadership, negotiating with congressional elites for support, maintaining discreet but close contact through the liaison staff, carefully timing legislative initiatives, and privately engineering a winning coalition of votes.[81] Johnson believed that his "mandate" extended to inundating a breathless Congress with a large number of proposals and to involving himself actively in congressional politics to ensure the enactment of policies. In Doris Kearns's words: "He blended and obscured the usual relationship between the President and the Congress, mingling previously distinct functions together until he involved each branch in both proposing and disposing of legislation. He was seeking to fashion an American version of the British parliamentary system."[82]

Johnson's strategy, combined with his intuitive knowledge of Capitol Hill, led to significant legislative measures in such areas as poverty, housing, education, health, pollution, urban renewal, and civil rights. While it is true that Johnson was generally able to define the terms in which his success would be measured, he did provide the large Democratic majorities in Congress with the necessary ingredient of mobilization and direction. In conclusion, it can be said that the form and style of the administration's legislative victories from 1963 to 1966 appeared to give the final proof that Johnson's role as an activist-consensus president was not only a viable one but a political actuality.

Consensus of Complaint

It is ironic that just as Johnson's consensus began to look well-founded and politically resilient, it exploded in a ferment of disaffection and protest. Johnson was fully aware that the vivid colors of the Democratic Congress in 1965–66 would fade in succeeding Congresses, but he never thought that smaller and less intense Democratic majorities would reflect a disruption in what he took to be America's mainstream orthodoxy. Life as President would be harder. Consensus politics would be trickier. Yet the basic agreement on social principles, the political system, and the necessity of presidential leadership would remain. Johnson was incredulous, therefore, at the black riots during the long hot summers of 1965, 1966, and 1967. He had labored for, and had identified himself with, the Civil Rights Acts of 1964 and 1965 in the sure knowledge that such legislation would effectively resolve the race problem. But just as the southerner had succeeded in demonstrating the system's capacity to produce civil rights legislation, the supposed beneficiaries had reacted with more dissent than ever before.[83] And what was true for the blacks was true for many other groups and interests.

The reasons presented to explain the breakdown of Johnson's consensus are legion. They extend from social psychological causes such as "frustrated expectations" and "alienation in an affluent mass society" to simple economic reasons such as inflation. On a strictly political level, however, the demise of Johnson's consensus can be explained to a large extent by the very nature of the consensus itself. The consensus was a basically pluralistic framework of groups whose individual interests were satisfied by complex series of trade-offs.

Despite the illusion of unanimity based on the essential compatibility of American interests in partnership, the complex structure of interdependent groups was highly susceptible to internal disequilibrium. Once the imbalance had been perceived, it would have been almost impossible to reverse the trend, to restore confidence, and to retain the groups' working relationships with each other. The process of decay would be the same as that described by R. Downs and J. E. Mueller[84] in reference to simple majority rule. Mueller claims that even if an administration secures majority support for all its policies, it could still be defeated by the accumulation of minority dissent. "This could occur when the minority on each issue feels so intensely about its loss that it is unable to be placated by administration support on other policies it favors."[85]

The debilitating effect of minority dissatisfaction in a consensus would be even greater, for in a consensus, disaffected minorities are not even presumed to exist. In Johnson's consensus, groups that had apparently been ingested into it suddenly reemerged as identifiable and independent units. Johnson had to take criticism from labor complaining about the continuation of section 14b of the Taft–Hartley Act, whites objecting to black advances, blacks denying the effectiveness of civil rights legislation, the South opposing school desegregation orders, the poor appealing for further assistance, industrialists deploring the "fiscal drag" of government revenues, consumers outraged at inflation, farmers demanding increased price supports, and so on. The tide of disenchantment could not be stemmed by an appeal to party loyalty, for Johnson had always renounced partisanship as the enemy of consensus and reconciliation. Johnson's appeal had always been based on the mutual support and self-interest of individual groups. Johnson had always encouraged groups to follow their interests. Therefore, when these groups ultimately perceived that their interests could not be satisfactorily served inside the consensus, they simply excluded themselves from it. As a result, Johnson's consensus of a thousand groups died of a thousand cuts.

Just as Johnson's group consensus withered away, so did the partnership among major political institutions. The "creative federalism" of the Great Society had seriously disturbed the relations among federal, state, and local governments. The penetration of the White House into areas of local administration, the bypassing of state and even local governments by federal program administrators, and the provision of public funds to local nongovernmental bodies led to protests from state and local officials.[86] The federal bureaucracy was also straining to adjust itself to the programs it had been inundated with during the Great Society. Johnson had always emphasized the passage of legislation rather than its implementation. He thought that administration problems were merely technical in nature and could be sorted out after the hastily conceived programs had been rushed through Congress.[87] By 1967, however, it was becoming apparent that the disjointed form of many Great Society policies was being made worse rather than better by "the organizationally incoherent way in which many of [the] five hundred domestic programs [were] scattered throughout a crazy quilt of bureaus and divisions in the more than one hundred executive departments and agencies."[88] Johnson attempted to make the bureaucracy more responsive to the White House by a series of disruptive personal interventions and by efforts at reorganizing the executive apparatus. Without a period of consolidation, the bureaucracy began to lose morale and to react against the incessant criticism of its performance and against the progenitor of the Great Society legislation.

The Democratic party also became disenchanted with Johnson.[89] Unlike Kennedy, Johnson condemned the Democrats' national party apparatus because it restricted presidential discretion and generated destructive forms of crude partisanship. As a result, the organization that Paul Butler and John Kennedy had done so much to develop was purged of much of its personnel and resources by a president intent on depending on a more personalized machine for reelection.

Johnson's spell over Congress began to evaporate after 1966.[90] The midterm elections had reduced Democratic seats in the Senate from 67 to 64. But it was in the House that Johnson suffered his most serious losses. The level of Democratic strength there fell from the heady heights of 295 seats to 248, a figure lower than Kennedy had had to depend on in the early 1960s. Although the Republican resurgence in 1966 had a sobering effect on the remaining Great Society Democrats, they had already begun to react against the political exhortations of the president and the private harassment of his liaison staff. A growing realization among congressional Democrats that the enhanced scope of Johnson's power was a reflection of the legislature's own emasculation produced a growing renaissance in institutional consciousness and independence. Even among Johnson's most fervent congressional supporters, there developed a marked antipathy toward many of the president's secretive and manipulative tactics. For example, Johnson refused to release to Congress the five-year financial projections of numerous urban programs after the estimated five-year costs of the model cities policy almost led to the program being rejected by Congress in 1966. Johnson privately explained his strategy in graphic terms: "A Congressman is like a whiskey drinker. . . . You can put an awful lot of whiskey into a man if you just let him sip it. But if you try to force the whole bottle down his throat at one time, he will throw it up."[91] Congressmen complained that they needed the financial projections in order to come to informed decisions, but Johnson's political judgment decreed that such figures would only jeopardize policies by providing political ammunition to liberals and conservatives alike. As usual, the attainment of Johnson's objectives was more important than the means. By 1966, growing numbers of congressmen were objecting not merely to Johnson's methods but even to the goals that he was pursuing.

In the Ninetieth Congress (1967–68), Johnson progressively lost touch with Congress as he became more distracted by foreign policy issues that he felt were not directly the concern of the legislature. Congress not only objected vigorously to Johnson's definition of its foreign policy role but was increasingly left to review and assess the Great Society's domestic programs at a time when they were being subjected to the most intense political and financial criticism.[92] Johnson won some victories in this Congress (e.g., open housing, tax surcharge, increased poverty program funds). But he also had to suffer painful defeats and criticism. His poverty, rent supplemental, and model cities programs were cut back; a financial spending ceiling, $6 billion under budgetary expectations, was imposed on the administration in 1968; and in an atmosphere of increasing personal and political criticism, Johnson had to withdraw his nominee to the Supreme Court chief justiceship after an unfavorable reaction to him by an increasingly sensitive Senate.

The disaggregation of political groups and institutions was serious enough to undermine the working operations of Johnson's consensus politics. In itself, however, it would not have been fatal to Johnson's presidency. He could probably have survived in weakened form had it not been for the enduring crisis of Vietnam. Ironically for the master of consensus, the final coup de grace to the Johnson period was inflicted in precisely that area of policy that all postwar presidents had regarded as the assumed minimal core of American unity (i.e., presidentially controlled foreign policy).

It is impossible to overstate the significance of Vietnam as an issue in American politics after 1966. A war that had had no real beginning gradually lost its earlier anonymity and developed into a full-blown military and political crisis in every sense of the term. Although the causes of the war are constantly disputed by historians, its effect on the political life of the nation was apparent. The United States found itself in 1966 with 500,000 troops committed to an Asian land war that many Americans did not fully comprehend but whose demands they complied with because of the strictures of established foreign policy guidelines, the authority of presidential judgment, and the fundamental threat of expansionary communism in Southeast Asia.[93] Ultimately, the lack of military success, the rising casualties, the ambiguous relationship of the war to U.S. interests, the apparently ineluctable process of ever-greater commitment at ever-increasing costs, adverse world opinion, and misleading information on the conduct and expense of the war generated every variety of disaffection against the war, the political system, and the commander-in-chief.[94] Criticism of the government in wartime produced, in turn, a backlash of equal diversity and complexity. The subsequent encounter between the critics and apologists developed into a moralistic dispute concerning the ethics of guerilla warfare, military retreat, political speculation, patriotic commitment, nuclear restraint, and presidential authority.

The division between "hawks" and "doves" was highly confused and was not based consistently on other established social and political divisions. Nevertheless, from 1966 onward, the war personally affected increasing numbers of Americans and continually forced people into the unaccustomed and uncomfortable position of reassessing social principles, political objectives, and America's international role. As a result, the war assumed a divisive prominence that tended to implicate other issues within it, thereby making consensus politics almost impossible.[95] The Great Society programs, for example, came under immediate pressure from conservatives, who sought to offset increasing military costs by reducing domestic expenditures. Johnson had always claimed that the Vietnam war would be financially painless and therefore would not affect the Great Society. But as the costs of the Vietnam engagement rose from an estimated $0.1 billion in 1965 to an estimated $25 billion in 1968, and as consumer price increases rose from 1.7 percent in 1965 to 4.2 percent in 1968, Johnson was faced not only with the need for increased taxes but, more significantly, with the need to select national priorities in the federal budget.[96] Contrary to Johnson's principle of consensus, the war forced him to concede that the United States could not afford benefits for everyone. Just as the Great Society programs were coming under attack from a less sympathetic Congress and Johnson's negotiating ability was needed to maintain the program's political momentum, Johnson was forced to divert federal resources and presidential attention from domestic concerns to the Vietnam crisis.

While the war hastened the decline of Johnson's domestic consensus, it finally began to eat into the president's foreign policy consensus. If the constitution had originally invited Congress and the presidency to compete with one another for the control of foreign policy, that contest, in contemporary historical terms, had effectively been won by the president. The sheer functional attributes of an executive agency in foreign policy (e.g., discretion, secrecy, initiative, immediacy, decisiveness) had always given the presidency an advantage over a legislature beset by cumbersome internal machinery and dependent upon legalistic prescription or critical retrospection. The president's exceptional position in international affairs was endorsed by the Supreme Court in *United States* v. *Curtiss-Wright* (1936).[97] In that case, Justice Sutherland went as far as any defender of the Constitution could go toward accepting the principle that presidential authority in foreign policy was extraconstitutional. According to Sutherland, the president possesses a "very delicate, plenary and exclusive power . . . as the sole organ of the federal government in the field of international relations" and therefore he should be given a "degree of discretion and freedom from statutory restriction which would not be admissible were domestic affairs alone involved."[98]

This double standard was developed even further after World War II. Public confidence in the presidency's wartime performance, combined with public anxiety over the motives and military capacity of the communist bloc, fostered a spirit of bipartisan unity in international affairs and an acceptance of presidentially directed foreign policy. Just as the cold war demanded the highest skill in international diplomacy, so the technical advances of nuclear warfare necessitated the most sensitive and responsive forms of decision making. In this atmosphere of ideological intransigence and sustained nuclear tension, America's strident anticommunist consensus elevated the presidency to a symbol of national purpose and afforded it constitutional license to defend American society and interests.[99] As part of this process, the Senate's position in the foreign policy field suffered a largely self-inflicted decline. Presidents increasingly circumvented the Senate's prerogative in treaty ratification by extensive use of executive agreements "involving the United States in far reaching commitments abroad."[100] Between 1964 and 1968, for example, 1,083 executive agreements were finalized compared to 67 treaties submitted to the Senate.[101] Even with formal treaties, presidents could retain a wide degree of discretion by employing the chief executive's prerogative of interpretation in response to changing conditions. The exact nature of treaties could also be defined by a number of supplementary, and possibly secret, executive agreements.

It was the role of the commander-in-chief of the armed services, however, that really enabled the modern presidency to assume such a pivotal position in foreign policy formulation. The power to deploy troops without a congressional declaration of war has been endorsed by historical precedent, but after World War II it became regarded as a natural concomitant to presidentially controlled foreign policy in an era in which any foreign crisis had the potential to shift the delicate balance of power, or at worst deteriorate into nuclear war.[102] The apparent vindication of presidential centrism in foreign policy came in the Cuban missile affair of 1962, when President Kennedy assumed close personal control of a crisis that demanded the most careful deployment of military force and the most sensitive direction of international negotiations. The successful outcome of Kennedy's crisis management led to the Cuban incident being established as the precedent that above all others validated the capacity, the legitimacy, and the necessity of presidentially directed national security policy. In Arthur Schlesinger's words: "Kennedy's action, which should have been celebrated as an exception, was instead enshrined as a rule. . . . The very brilliance of Kennedy's performance appeared to vindicate the idea that the President must take unto himself the final judgements of war and peace."[103] Apart from some grumbling about lack of consultation, Congress joined the public in celebrating the system's adequacy in meeting the challenge. Furthermore, many members of Congress insisted that presidential privacy in this field was essential to ensure that American foreign policy could in no way be compromised by the parochial myopia and impulsiveness of the Congress.

As late as 1966, Aaron Wildavsky could still claim that presidents retained an exceptional authority in the area of international affairs because "potential opponents [were] weak, divided, or believed that they should not control foreign policy."[104] However, as the Vietnam war became a more prolonged and frustrating encounter, Johnson began to suffer increasingly from public criticism and, at times, open hostility. Johnson's consensus techniques in such a situation proved ineffective, for not only was the Vietnam issue not susceptible to Texas-style pragmatism, but Johnson himself was a central participant in the war and not the negotiating broker that he was accustomed to being in political confrontations. Johnson's embarrassment and irritation at both the war and its public critics led him to withdraw even further from public debate and to depend upon an increasingly insulated unit of national security advisors and managers. The prevailing impression of presidential secrecy and deception surrounding an apparently intractable military engagement regenerated senatorial interest in the field of foreign policy decision making. On a wider scale, "Johnson's war" led to public disquiet over the whole notion of presidential power in the political system. To an increasing number of skeptics, the presidency was not an institution to be promoted and rationalized within the governmental framework so much as a disturbingly potent political force that appeared to have a momentum of its own.[105]

Johnson's problems with the war were further compounded by the growing dislocation in domestic politics and social behavior. Just as Vietnam had become "Johnson's war," so drugs, crime, urban riots, and sexual license were collectively characterized as "Johnson's society." Those who had always had doubts over the Great Society programs were now joined by those who, in various ways and for various reasons, perceived social evils to be directly related to both liberal experimentation in social reform and an unpopular war that only exacerbated existing social tensions. This sense of confusion and disenchantment among Americans in 1968 is captured well by Richard

Scammon and Ben Wattenberg: "The general disquietude . . . attached itself to certain lightning rods of dissatisfaction: crime, race,
morals, disruption. . . . This disruption worked against LBJ, even
though LBJ was the target of this disruption. The President, like it
or not, is blamed when the nation is in turmoil."[106] Thus Johnson,
who had always attempted to place himself and his presidency as a
cushion to conflict, had by 1968 become instead a political punching
bag.

Johnson's consensus, which had been substantiated by a landslide
election in 1964 and public approval levels of 80 percent in the heady
year of 1965, had dramatically collapsed under the strain of fighting
one war in Vietnam and another in "the streets of Newark and Detroit
and in the halls of Congress."[107] As the rate of public approval of
Johnson's presidency slumped below 40 percent in the summer of
1968, Johnson experienced the full force of the fissiparous energies
always present within American politics. His consensus of groups
evaporated in an atmosphere of mutual suspicion and complaint.
The consensus within the Democratic party ended with the challenge of Eugene McCarthy and Robert Kennedy to Johnson's policies and with the formation of George Wallace's independent party.
The consensus between the parties subsided once the Republicans
had regained their respect and their identity in the 1966 elections.
The consensus between president and Congress gave way through the
excessive demands that each made on the other. The consensus on
the strategy and objectives of contemporary foreign policy suffered
from increased skepticism and uncertainty over America's international role. The consensus on presidential direction of foreign policy
cracked under the strain of public misgivings over the president's
judgment in running the war and over the president's frankness in
informing the American people about the war. Even the well-estab-
lished consensus on the presidency had to experience the corrosive
forces of suspicion and public distrust. As a result of these multiple
injuries, the consensus centered on the figure of Johnson himself
dissolved amid recriminations, disappointments, and lost causes. For
a time, it appeared that the "mammoth Texan might be able to impose his personal configuration of the world on an entire society,"[108]
but in the end he was overcome by political conditions and social
forces that not even Johnson could master.

THE NIXON YEARS: LIBERAL DISASTERS
AND LIBERAL OPPORTUNITIES

In some ways the Nixon administration appeared to mark a departure from the past. After the turmoil of street politics and torrid infighting that had characterized the demise of the Johnson administration, Richard Nixon's masterful, if colorless, exploitation of the political center looked like the beginning of a new era. The Republican party, which had regained its reputation as the party of peace, promised initially to extend that image to the area of domestic tranquility. As Nixon appealed to Americans to "stop shouting at one another,"[109] he sought to put as much distance as possible between himself and the turbulence of the preceding administration. Nixon wanted his administration to be as distinct as possible from that of Johnson. In terms of personality, party, policies, and operation, the Nixon presidency did indeed appear to diverge sharply from Johnson's political style and social objectives. And yet, despite the appearance of change, the Nixon administration's significance and political effect lay precisely in its continuity with the past. Just as Nixon himself could never escape from his personal reputation established 20 years before, so his presidency could not disengage itself from the circumstances from which it had arisen. The past not only generated the problems that confronted Nixon, it affected his capacity to deal with them. The burden of established trends and entrenched political forces produced the sort of frustration in the Nixon administration that led to as much, if not more, acrimony and divisiveness than that of the Johnson administration.

While the problems that faced Nixon were deeply rooted in contemporary history, it was the 1968 presidential election that illustrated and clarified the nature of the difficulties that he had inherited. It was in that traumatic year that America's fundamental consensus on basic social and economic principles appeared to be under threat. Since this consensus was based on "the inarticulate premise of conformity"[110] to norms regarded as self-evident, any general skepticism toward it was by definition an indication of a profound dislocation in society. Hartz described the American consensus as one of the "most powerful absolutisms in the world"[111] because it was based on the ubiquity of implictly accepted social and political values. While the view of consensus theorists such as Hartz may, or may not, be valid for America's entire social development, the notion of consensus was significant in the cold war orthodoxy of the 1950s and early 1960s. It appeared to explain America's social and economic stability, its lack of class politics, and its avoidance of ideological conflict. In this context, "Johnson's consensus" was a successful piece of social engineering that was dependent upon, not a precondition of, America's underlying bedrock of basic social and political norms.

In 1968, however, "there was a sense everywhere . . . that things were giving; that man had not merely lost control of his history, but might never regain it."[112] The anxieties produced by urban riots, crime, pornography, campus dissidence, drugs, and so on, were deepened not only by the open contempt for authority shown by some groups but by the emergence of several radical movements that were critical of American society and its political system.[113] In varying degrees, these groups overlapped with one another in terms of ideas and members. The new left's intellectual critique of centralized bureaucracy, materialist technocracy, and individual alienation, and its advocacy of participatory democracy and human self-fulfillment, were clearly related to the aspirations of black power, peace, and community action groups. It was the fringe groups, however, that attracted most publicity and, as a result, an already shaken public tended to associate any form of political speculation with draft-card burning, violent demonstrations, direct action, and social revolution. "In the broad American public, then, there was a widespread sense of breakdown in authority and discipline that fed as readily on militant political dissent as on race riots and more conventional crime."[114] It appeared that not only had Johnson's consensus split apart but that the American consensus itself was crumbling away under the corrosive forces of political disruption and social polarization.[115]

The Democratic convention at Chicago, in which the Yippie movement attempted to use "guerilla theatre" to "freak out the Democrats so much that they disrupt[ed] their own convention,"[116] became a symbol of what was portrayed as the general struggle between the new values and the old. The result was a violent confrontation between the Chicago police and the demonstrators which fulfilled both sides' prophecies of each other. The significance of the televised conflict was that, despite widespread condemnation of the police by the media and by foreign opinion, the American public rallied behind the forces of law and order. For a nation supposedly wracked by deep internal divisions, only 20 percent disagreed with Mayor Daley's use of the police during the Chicago convention.[117] The figure is significant because what was widely described as a police riot embodying the political system's basic insensitivity to legitimate demands in no way became a *cause célèbre* that divided the nation. Instead, Mayor Daley's police appeared to unearth the hard-core consensus that had been overlain with vociferous dissent and protest rhetoric.

What was true for the Chicago police was true also for many other aspects of American society. Extensive majorities were registered against greater advances in civil rights, and were in favor of stricter laws on obscenity, tougher controls on students, and tighter restrictions on the use of marijuana.[118] Even a majority of opponents to the Vietnam war resented the civil strife generated by antiwar demonstrators and joined hawks in condemning them. The war itself, which had proved in so many ways to be a catalyst to contemporary anxieties and problems, was regarded in 1968 as the top issue in American politics. A majority of Americans thought it had been a mistake. Yet 75 percent of those polled were against pulling out of Vietnam, and only 3 percent were sympathetic to the antiwar demonstrators.[119] The electorate was clearly frustrated by the war, but Vietnam did not split the nation. Whether it was through sincere patriotism, simple inertia, grudging acquiescence, or actual conviction, Johnson was still "supported" in his Vietnam policy.

The Vietnam issue at home, however, was different. It became wrapped up in the overall malaise of urban disorder, crime, race, and inflation. These problems drained Johnson's support. As the personification of the administration responsible for economic management and law and order, Johnson suffered for society's problems and the economy's deficiencies. His ailing presidency was replaced by a candidate who had aligned himself as closely as possible with the configuration of contemporary attitudes. Nixon carefully cultivated the center. In a campaign that always threatened to subside into generalities and platitudes, Nixon managed to acknowledge the problems that divided the Democrats, to promise an honorable peace in Vietnam, and to "consolidate" social programs. At the same time, he absorbed much of George Wallace's message on law and order without recourse to incautious language. It was an uninspiring, yet effective performance.[120]

In what was termed "the greatest come-back since Lazarus,"[121]

Nixon secured the presidency for the Republican party, the first career Republican to do so since Herbert Hoover. However, in the midst of a victory that appeared to compensate for his disappointments in the 1960 presidential election and in the 1962 California gubernatorial election, Nixon failed to achieve the political breakthrough that normally accompanies presidential victories. First, Nixon won the election with the lowest percentage of the vote (43.4 percent) of any president since 1912. Although the Democrats suffered their worst defeat since 1956, Nixon in fact secured less of the vote than he did in 1960 (49.5 percent). It is possible to speculate that because Nixon's positions approximated Wallace's views, Nixon would have won a clear majority had Wallace not run in the election. The notion of a moral victory, however, was no real comfort to Nixon in his official position as a plurality president. His second disappointment was that he had become the first president since 1849 to enter the White House with the opposition party in control of both houses of Congress. The Republicans gained only five and six seats in the House and Senate, respectively. In the process, a number of well-known liberal Senators (Long, Morse, Clark, Brewster) found themselves displaced by Republican challengers. But even these modest Republican gains were not secured by the coattails of the party's national candidate. On the contrary, Nixon ran behind his own party in Congress by more than 4 percent. On the basis of his proportion of the vote, it was difficult enough for Nixon to claim a mandate, but with a Democratic Congress and a Republican party electorally stronger than its president, Nixon found himself in an ambiguous political position.

Finally, Nixon's weak electoral performance was a continual reminder to him that he was not the representative of a majority of Americans. This was perhaps the unkindest cut of all for Nixon because he had always believed in, and had based his campaign on, the notion that he was the embodiment of the "forgotten American" and the mouthpiece of the "silent majority."[122] His identification with the common man was based on his own background of meager beginnings and self-generated elevation, and on his principles of dedicated application, individual enterprise, and self-dependence. He proclaimed his principles to be unfashionable. This was at once an innuendo designed to damage his opponents and a rallying call to Americans to defend their basic values from supposed subversion.

Nixon exploited the mood of anti-Johnsonism but never managed to create a popular impulse toward himself. This was reflected in the public opinion polls at the beginning of his administration. They showed that not only was the level of approval (about 60 percent) significantly lower than that of previous presidents early in their administrations (Kennedy, approximately 70 percent; Johnson, approximately 95 percent), but the proportion of respondents with no opinion at all was registered at an exceptionally high level (about 37 percent).[123] The politician who won the presidency under the banner of the ordinary man's champion had to adjust to the fact that he was not held in great affection or trust by the "silent majority."

It should be noted that Nixon's attempt to represent the average American and to anticipate what he felt was always plagued with problems. Initially, the election itself did not give a clear definition of what the average American really wanted. The electorate certainly did not give Nixon a coherent mandate. The electoral confusion was further compounded by the problem of defining who the average American was, what his attitudes were, and whether the government could respond to these attitudes. Johnson had based his consensus on what he perceived to be the objectives of the average American, only to find that America's amorphous unity tended to break apart when specific policies were at stake. Nixon found that while general statements and broad assertions might be acceptable in an electoral arena, as president he was forced to make substantive policy decisions to the benefit of some and to the detriment of others.

Related to this point of specificity is perhaps the more significant problem of inconsistency. It is now established folklore among opinion pollsters that the public tend to be inconsistent in the logic of their views. For example, most people will agree that more social spending is desirable, yet they will also agree that taxes ought to be cut. The opinions of the American public, to which Nixon attempted to conform, proved to be particularly ambiguous in some areas. Taking Scammon and Wattenberg's division between the "social issue" (crime, race, social disruption) and the "economic issue" (employment, wages, prices), it appeared that Nixon had done especially well in marrying himself to the social issue, in which large opinion-poll majorities were in favor of reasonably clear and feasible proposals to maintain social order and to preserve moral standards.[124] Public attitudes toward the economic issue, however, were by no means as

clear. It is perfectly possible, of course, to argue that a strong position on law and order or racial violence is inherently related to an
equally strong position against social welfare and civil rights. It
seems clear, for example, that Nixon thought that Scammon and
Wattenberg's two issues were implicitly related to each other at most
in terms of philosophy and at the very least in terms of budgetary
priorities. The public, on the other hand, was not as consistent in
its positions. Although there were indications that the "unpoor, un-
young and unblack" had become more skeptical of welfare programs
and black advances, they retained their social conscience, they were
still uncomfortable at the thought of poverty and racism in American
society, and they were therefore loath to press for a reversal of policies in these areas.[125] Criticism was mixed with sympathy, irritation
with embarrassment. The public was wary of Nixon lest he fail to
rationalize their conflicting signals and thereby transform the silent
majority into an anonymous populism.

To a man who claimed to represent middle America, Nixon's marginal electoral victory and ambiguous mandate virtually ensured frustration at the highest levels of government. He was confronted by a
Democratic Congress aided and supported by what he perceived to
be the disproportionate power of other liberal organizations and institutions—press, television, progressive interest groups, bureaucracy,
the Supreme Court.[126] The public supported him but did not hold
him in high esteem. It approved of a political leader who articulated
common anxieties but had misgivings over the capacity of such a
leader to fulfill presidential responsibilities. The burden of incomplete
authority and qualified public support proved to be particularly oner-
ous to a man who was always susceptible to self-pity and a sense
of unwarranted victimization. Indeed, it could be said that Nixon was
one of the least well equipped presidents, in terms of political position
and personality traits, to cope with the problems that confronted his
administration.[127]

To Nixon, the problems with which he had to contend were essentially the problems of the previous Democratic administration.
Like Johnson, he was confronted by inflation, war, crime, growing
domestic expenditures, budget deficits, and a crisis in the welfare
system. Like Johnson, Nixon's executive discretion was heavily cir-
cumscribed by congressional hostility, bureaucratic momentum, previous political commitments, and increasing public skepticism of the

presidency as an institution. If anything was different, it was that the problems were becoming more intractable and the president's capacity to deal with them was becoming progressively more restricted in scope.

In the social welfare field, for example, the administration was not only committed to long-term expenditures but was politically obliged to accept increases in benefits in order to keep payments in line with inflation.[128] A case in point was that of social security benefits, which were increased three times from 1969 to 1972. A more significant constraint on presidential discretion in this field was the Democratic Congress. It still contained many of those Democrats who were closely associated with the Great Society era and who were determined not only to preserve but to increase the scope of the programs enacted in the mid-1960s. Indeed, most Democrats involved in the welfare field proceeded on the assumption that government action in this field, like civil rights, was necessarily expansive in nature—not simply because of inflation, not simply due to the standard congressional maneuver of initial funding and subsequent increases, but because a coherent social welfare policy could only be developed in stages, with each stage reflecting new areas of social concern and governmental assistance. During the Nixon administration, therefore, the Congress became the rallying point for interest groups involved in defending and promoting welfare policies. The Democrats in Congress neither wanted nor needed Republican leadership in this most Democratic of fields. On the contrary, they had become experienced in supervising and refining social welfare policies in 1967 and 1968, when President Johnson's interest in the field had been displaced by the imperatives of war management. Now that they were confronted by a Republican president, congressional Democrats felt no obligations to defer to White House priorities to restrict the scope of their reform proposals.

President Nixon's personal belief was that the welfare system had become a "monstrous consuming outrage"[129] that undermined individual responsibility and moral fiber. Insofar as he could act on this belief, he pressed for efficient Republican management of the diverse programs and as small an increase in their budgets as was politically possible. When congressional Democrats attempted to rearrange Nixon's budgetary priorities by cutting military, space program, and foreign aid funds and increasing expenditure in health, education, poverty, and training programs, Nixon responded by a policy of large-scale vetoes. In 1972, for example, he twice vetoed the enormous $30.5 billion appropriations bill for the Departments of Labor and Health, Education, and Welfare because it contained funds in excess of his original request. In his first term, Nixon vetoed another 27 bills, the majority of which were imposed for reasons of excessive expenditure and fiscal irresponsibility. Nixon's veto strategy sometimes proved to be remarkably effective. As only 4 of the 28 vetoes were overridden, Nixon forced Congress to present bills and funds that were acceptable to the administration on the basis of anticipated presidential reactions. The poverty program in particular proved to be highly susceptible to Nixon's veto tactic. Whereas Congress wanted to enlarge the scope of the Office of Economic Opportunity (OEO), which administered the poverty program, Nixon wanted to restrict its budget and its activities. The dispute came to a head in 1971, when Congress added a $2 billion child development plan to the OEO authorization bill, prohibited the president from transferring programs out of the OEO without congressional agreement, and further reduced the president's administrative discretion by specifically earmarking funds. Nixon vetoed the bill, leaving the OEO still functioning but without legal authority for 14 months. In 1972, Congress passed a "veto-proof" bill that contained none of the controversial passages incorporated into the 1971 bill.[130]

Although Nixon often got what he wanted through these means, it was at the cost of a progressive deterioration in executive–legislative relations. The mutual animosity was quite apparent in Nixon's attempt to seize the legislative initiative in welfare reform.[131] His Family Assistance Plan (FAP) was designed to alleviate the disorder and inequity inherent in the existing welfare system by providing a minimum income to all families suffering financial hardship through unemployment or poorly paid employment. Launched in 1969, the FAP promised to relieve the state and city governments from some of the enormous burden of welfare costs. By 1972, the plan was still languishing in Congress, the victim of conservatives who objected to the expense, and of liberals who resented the "workfare" elements that would have forced employable welfare recipients to take jobs or undergo job training. While Nixon blamed the failure of welfare reform on Senate liberals for their cavalier attitude toward the federal budget, Senate liberals blamed the president for his lack of commitment to the program and for the poor quality of his congressional liaison operations. The failure of the FAP left the welfare system "much bigger and more expensive but in the same framework as when President Nixon took office."[132] In terms of Nixon's relationship with Congress, the rejection of his top-priority bill not only represented an embarrassing defeat but provided him with further proof of the irresponsible partisanship of the legislature.

Nixon was confronted with the momentum of Democratic policies in a number of other areas. In the civil rights field he was expected, as president, to ensure the legal continuity of school desegregation and voting rights.[133] Nixon was in some difficulty here, for he was heavily committed to the South for his nomination and election. His campaign appeals to the southern conservative vote helped Humphrey to secure 95 percent of the black vote and made Nixon the "first contemporary President to be elected without significant black voter support."[134] The southern Republicans expected Nixon to act on his provisional support of neighborhood schools, "voluntary" integration, freedom of choice over schools, and qualified opposition to busing and to federal fund cutoffs. In reality, Nixon's positions on this issue had always been layered with indirection and equivocation. In private, Nixon probably preferred what the southern Republicans publicly demanded—locally determined education programs. To the intense irritation of the southerners, they found that altering civil rights policy was no easy feat. Nixon was their champion but he had to face the full impetus of policies set in motion by Democratic Presidents, enacted by Democratic Congresses, implemented by Democratic administrations, and endorsed by judges appointed by Democrats. The southern Republicans discovered that

> what they had been led to believe would be an easy, immediate and dramatic rollback of school desegregation was absolutely out of the question because *the law would not allow it. . . .* The President could not repeal the *Green* decision; he could not repeal the 1964 Civil Rights Act, with its specific sanctions against de jure segregation and its specific mechanism for HEW guidelines and the cutoff of federal school aid.[135]

However, Nixon was in a position to reduce the momentum toward the full implementation of civil rights reform. So began the long and damaging trail of administrative delays, minimal responses, dilatory enforcement, narrow constructions of court decisions, conservative court appointments, desegregation deadline postponements, and presidential opposition to the principle of busing. Knowing that full presidential commitment to the civil rights course was of crucial importance in maintaining the pressure for reform, civil rights sympathizers and reform groups deplored the regressive posture of the Nixon administration. These opposition forces inflicted several apparently humiliating defeats on the administration, including the Senate's rejection of two Nixon appointees to the Supreme Court.[136] Nevertheless, Nixon's obvious procrastination in the field succeeded not only in encouraging anti-civil rights forces but in establishing himself as a heroic figure in the South. At the same time, he significantly reduced his electoral anxieties by ingratiating himself to the South and by identifying himself with the insecurities of white suburbia. In the process, he became "the President most disliked and distrusted by Negroes since the rise of black political power following World War II."[137]

Previous administrations bestowed on Nixon at least two additional issues of great sensitivity. In the economy, he was faced with the culmination of such long-term trends as the decline in the trading position of the United States and increased pressure on the dollar in the world's money markets. These fundamental problems were made worse for Nixon by "the economic disarray that he had inherited from Lyndon Johnson—especially the inflationarily hot economy triggered by excessive military spending without an accompanying increase in taxes."[138] Between 1968 and 1970, the consumer price index rose by 12.1 points. In the same period, however, industrial production dropped and unemployment increased from 3.6 percent to 4.9 percent.[139] After initially employing traditional Republican methods of counteracting economic recession (increased taxation, reduced expenditure, high interest rates), Nixon conceded the need for Keynesian techniques of economic stimulation. Nixon astounded many in his own party by conceding the necessity for unbalanced federal budgets. Even a $23 billion budget deficit in 1971, however, did not signally affect the inflation or unemployment rates. Ultimately, Nixon was forced into accepting the further indignity of peacetime wage and price controls. As soon as any government introduces such controls, it automatically becomes the natural target for every complaint concerning wages and prices. No matter how independent the decision making bodies may appear to be, the government is always held accountable for every disappointment and is inevitably regarded as biased in its procedures and guidelines. Because it was a Republican administration, rumors were rife that the policy discriminated against wage earners and in favor of major employers. By 1972, these rumors had become substantiated. While wages had been pinned back to 5 percent, prices rose by more than they had risen before the policy, and corporate profits and dividends reached record levels. As a result, the Nixon administration came under even further pressure from increasingly restive labor forces and from congressional Democrats, who were coming to view the president's vetoes on profligate social spending with a good deal of cynicism.

It was the war in Vietnam, however, that proved to be not only the most divisive issue among the public but the issue that revealed the basic antagonism between the Republican administration and the Democratic Congress. In accordance with its election pledge of "peace with honor," the administration was reducing American troop levels and conditioning the American public to the ultimate objective of complete American withdrawal without a communist takeover of South Vietnam. Ironically, as peace was supposed to be approaching, the Indo-China theater was suffering from greater instability as a result of renewed military activity from the Pathet Lao in Laos and Khmer Rouge in Cambodia. In South Vietnam itself the tenacity of the Viet Cong's guerilla attacks continued unabated in spite of massive American bombing campaigns against North Vietnamese installations and supply routes and in spite of the flurry of diplomatic peace initiatives around the world.[140] The Paris peace talks embodied the prevailing sense of frustration as the positions of the respective parties appeared to become more intransigent with each year of intermittent and fruitless negotiations. After the initial optimism of the Nixon administration's hopes for an early resolution to the Vietnam problem, the public's weariness of the protracted nature of both the war and the negotiations tended to find its outlet in the figure of Richard Nixon. Like Johnson, Nixon became the personification of America's war effort and, as a result, he, too, tended to withdraw from an increasingly skeptical public. Given Nixon's personal inclination toward privacy and his sense of unjustified persecution, his retreat was all the more complete. Given his political determination, inflated assessment of presidential prerogative, and vindictive attitude toward political opponents, Nixon's retreat was all the more significant.

The opinion polls at this time show that while the trend toward public disenchantment with the war was well established, the public's view of the precise policy to be followed was as confused as it was in the Johnson administration. For example, in the fall of 1970, 32 percent of those polled wanted American troops pulled out of Vietnam entirely, 32 percent wanted the American troops to stay and to try and end the fighting, and 24 percent wanted a stronger stand to be made, even if it meant invading North Vietnam.[141] In practice, this confusion was often clarified by a widespread sense of irritation with the administration—both for its policies and for its furtive style of operation. Nixon's retreat behind the blanket rationale of "national security" and his assertion of total presidential secrecy in the field of war management served to heighten the mood of skepticism and distrust. When the public was informed, for example, that in the cause of a peaceful contraction of the war, the president had sanctioned the bombing of Cambodia and Laos, the invasion of Cambodia, and the mining of Haiphong harbor, the result was a collective outburst of utter frustration with a government that appeared to be operating under the guidance of insuperable political inertia. It was policies such as these and the public's suspicion of the motives behind them and the methods by which they were arrived at that helped to generate a continuing crisis of confidence in an administration that was becoming increasingly inaccessible at precisely the time when its war policy was becoming more controversial.

Nowhere was the prevailing spirit of distrust and political challenge in greater evidence than in the Nixon administration's relations with the U.S. Senate. After relinquishing so much of its power in foreign policy during the cold war era, the Senate had begun to reassert its constitutional prerogatives during the Johnson administration.[142] The pace of the institution's renaissance in this field quickened noticeably when it was confronted by a Republican president who was even more remote from Congress than Johnson was in his last year in office. The Senate became the major rallying point for political opposition to Nixon's war policy. Indeed, the clash between the Senate and the president was widely regarded as not only a political test that would decide whether the administration could be influenced in its policies, but also as a constitutional test that would determine the relationship between the Congress and the presidency in the field of foreign policy. The Senate's attempt to transform its status from that of a sleeping partner to that of a senior consultant was therefore charged with partisan sentiments, institutional attachments, political divisions, and constitutional convictions.

The most controversial element of the Senate's assault on the administration's authority was its attempt to structure America's role in the war. From 1969 onward, a whole host of resolutions and amendments to bills concerning defense procurement authorization, defense appropriations, foreign military sales, foreign aid, and draft extensions were passed in an effort to restrict the president's avowed discretion in the military conduct of the war.[143] Since legislation in this most complex and sensitive of areas involved the lives of American troops in the field, the Senate was reluctant to give many of its declarations the force of law. It also felt obliged to add so many provisos and qualifications to its policies that in effect the president's field of discretion often remained intact. The Mansfield amendment to the draft extension bill of 1971, for example, urged the president to withdraw all U.S. troops from Indo-China at the earliest practicable date, subject to the successful negotiations for the release of American prisoners of war. Congress hoped that this recommendation would at least be acknowledged, if not accepted, by the president. But because it was only a "sense of Congress" declaration, Nixon dismissed it, claiming that it would in no way change the policies of the administration.[144]

When the Senate attempted to include mandatory language on military policy in legislation, the problems were just as great. In the Cooper–Church amendment to the foreign military sales bill in 1970, for example, the Senate prohibited the use of funds to maintain U.S. forces in Cambodia unless Congress specifically authorized military operations in that country. However, the administration supporters in the Senate succeeded in delaying the vote on the amendment until the president was ready to terminate his incursion of Cambodian neutrality.[145] Moreover, Nixon had an additional safety net in the House of Representatives, which could always be relied upon to vote against any of the Senate's "end-the-war" amendments.

Much of the Senate's weakness in the field of foreign policy derived from its character as a legislative institution. While Congress is limited to either prescription or retrospection, the president, as the officer in the field, has the capacity to alter conditions, thereby rendering legislative judgment irrelevant. Again, as Congress is en-

cumbered by the slow process of devising legal resolutions and en-
acting abstract formulas, it is the commander-in-chief who defines
the real situation and interprets legislative decisions in the light of
external conditions. Consequently, when Congress attempted to exert
an influence in this area of policy, it was confronted not only by a
president accustomed to regarding the field as his natural preserve,
but by the weakness of its own methods. Despite the Senate's apparent failures, however, the very spectacle of the institution attempting
to confront the president in this area not only damaged the administration's public prestige but impugned the reputation of its military
judgment. The Senate's activities forced the president into the embarrassing position of continually having to substantiate his claims
to presidential primacy in the field of foreign and military policy.
Moreover, once the issue was joined, the Senate broadened its attack
and began to challenge other presidential prerogatives in foreign
policymaking (e.g., executive agreements, bilateral compacts, executive secrecy). Yet again, Nixon felt himself to be besieged both by
Johnson's political bequests and by the Democratic party in Congress.

On the basis of this necessarily short review, it can be said that
the period from 1969 to 1972 was characterized by a Republican president convinced that he represented a silent majority of Americans
but that he had been tragically handicapped by freak electoral conditions in 1968, an administration accustomed to Democratic priorities
and programs, and a Congress that contained the remnants of the
Great Society's discredited liberalism. These political conditions, combined with Nixon's exceptionally introspective personality, produced
a concealed presidency—but one that more than made up for its apparent reticence by Nixon's concerted attempt to maximize and centralize political resources within the White House. To many observers
and participants, Nixon "demanded not the support of the other parts
of the government but their total and complete submission."[146] As
Nixon tried to integrate presidential influence and to undermine the
positions of contending centers of political power (e.g., Congress, the
bureaucracy, the press, and various progressively oriented interest
groups), he was increasingly confronted by a gradual decline in respect for the presidential office. Nixon believed that he needed a
strong White House to secure the type of political leverage that had
been wielded by his Democratic predecessors. More significantly,
Nixon had always been an advocate of the need for vigorous and

assertive presidential leadership, especially in policy areas that involved U.S. national security. He also believed that his views intuitively reflected the views of the silent majority. But, as with much of Nixon's domestic and foreign policies, his expansive interpretation of presidential power was not always shared by what he took to be his political constituency. This is not to say that "middle America" suddenly endorsed the claim that Nixon had developed an "imperial presidency," only that it did not identify itself with the chief executive to the same extent as it had in the past. Given the increase in public cynicism toward the political system that occurred during these years, it is clear that if the ordinary voter was becoming more skeptical of presidential power, he was likely to be less than sympathetic toward Nixon's well-publicized efforts to expand executive influence still further.

This movement against the presidency that had been developing since Johnson's administration, which reached its culmination during the Nixon years, represented a significant development in the American political system. Nixon attempted to strengthen the White House not just to insulate the presidency from what he perceived to be the hostility of the Washington establishment, but to maximize his personal influence in as many major policy areas as possible. Nixon's conscious detachment from other power centers, however, only resulted in satisfying the suspicions of each toward the other. It was in Congress that the decline in the presidency's prestige was most evident. Congress was already in the process of an institutional reawakening under Johnson, but in 1969, congressional sensitivities were automatically heightened by the arrival of a Republican president. Nixon's election provided a real tonic to congressional Democrats, for it reduced their internal tensions and integrated the party—and thereby the institution—against a Republican administration. The Senate liberals, in particular, were able to immerse themselves in the occupational therapy of unembarrassed opposition to the White House, a task made easier by their increased seniority in the chamber. The administration condemned them as "radiclibs" whose "pampered prodigies"[147] constituted the "anarchists and communists who detested everything about [the] country and wanted to destroy it."[148] Yet their damaging attacks on executive power only served to emphasize the shift in political attitudes toward the presidency as an institution.

The historical irony that Richard Nixon experienced, therefore, was twofold. First, Nixon, who had always been a devotee of presidential authority, himself provided the personal and partisan catalyst to a process of popular disenchantment with executive authority. Second, the Nixon administration marked a significant turning point in the respective positions of the Senate and the presidency. Just as the Senate had been regarded as a political issue in the early 1960s, so the presidency had become a subject of controversy in its own right during the early 1970s. The Senate, which had been criticized in the past for being insufficiently responsive to progressive executive leadership, was now seen as a body that redeemed the system from the excessive conservatism of the presidency. Changes had occurred in both institutions.

3 American Liberalism and Senate Liberals

In the United States, liberals are almost invariably sensed rather than defined. Liberals do not constitute a party. Neither can they be collectively ascribed to a singular organization. Nevertheless, the term "liberal" is employed habitually—if intuitively—by most political commentators as a useful and substantive mark of distinction. Certainly, this has been the case in respect to the Senate liberals. As chapters 1 and 2 have indicated, liberal senators have been widely regarded as the source of controversy and the vehicle of change. It is precisely this enticing reputation that leads the observer to examine the extent to which it can be justified in substance. Before one reputation can be assessed, however, another must be satisfactorily investigated— that is, the identity of the liberals in the Senate. It is not possible to concentrate on what the liberals actually did until we know who they were.

LIBERALISM: A WAY THROUGH THE QUAGMIRE

One common solution to the problem of identification is simply to determine the Senate's liberal members on the basis of impressionistic evidence. Since the term "Senate liberals" rippled through the pages of the press during the 1960s, it would not be too difficult to devise some list of members commonly referred to as liberals. Although this method need not necessarily be inaccurate, it would fail to preclude the possibility that the final list of liberals might be based upon highly fragmentary, arbitrary, and unverified data. For example, both Senators Edward Kennedy and Mark Hatfield are commonly termed Senate liberals, without regard to their overall legislative records. Popular impressions of members are often based on limited information in limited areas of activity. Just because Edward Kennedy is the brother of John and Robert Kennedy, makes well-publicized speeches on behalf of the underprivileged, and is closely identified

with the liberal wing of his party does not necessarily mean that he
is a liberal to the extent of consistently acting as a liberal within the
Senate. Mark Hatfield's much heralded opposition to President Nixon's
policy in Southeast Asia and his subsequent appearance on the White
House "black list" does not provide real proof of his liberal credentials in such areas as civil rights, social security, or housing—areas
in which being a liberal is at the very least as significant as being a
liberal regarding Vietnam.

To overcome the probable inaccuracies and distortions that threat-
en the validity of such impressionistic surveys, it became necessary
to devise a means of distinguishing Senate liberals that took into
account to the maximum degree possible the political positions and
attitudes adopted by members when operating in the Senate. Specifically, the identity of the liberals should be based on the relationship between their legislative behavior and what could be termed
contemporary liberal causes. Although evidence on members' policy
positions was readily and systematically available through the medium of data on roll-call voting, definite conclusions as to what constituted liberal positions were not so easily obtained.

Inherent in any discussion on liberals and liberalism is the cir-
cular problem of regarding liberal positions as those supported by
liberals, while defining liberals as those who endorse liberal positions.
This problem of circularity is present in all cases where concepts are
being applied to the real world (e.g., democracy, left wing). American
liberalism poses more problems than most, however, for the term is
used in such a variety of diverse and complex ways. In one way,
"liberalism" can be interpreted as simply a term denoting capitalistic
enterprise and the freedom of men "to regulate their own pursuits of
industry and improvement."[1] "Liberalism" can also be used to refer
to a political process in which the competitive interplay of activated
groups leads to a self-regulating form of political justice.[2] Perhaps
most confusing and most damaging to the clarity of the term is the
consensus school of liberalism, which imposes a moral and political
unanimity on American society by emphasizing the organic relationship between the environment of the New World and the declared
existence of liberal values. In this context liberalism is not a set of
abstract principles to be striven for, but a native ideology that ra-
tionalizes and celebrates naturally occurring social values and arrangements. Since "all of America is liberalism,"[3] whatever exists or

develops is predetermined to be liberal, for alternative values and phenomena are automatically excluded. As American conservatism becomes a vehicle for preserving achieved liberal ideals, it thereby becomes indistinguishable from liberalism and completes an amorphous social unity that reduces all internal conflict to problems of adjustments within a ubiquitous liberal framework.[4]

Liberalism in America, therefore, can be everything and it can be nothing.[5] The plasticity of this protean term allows it to be adopted as the "mask of all political positions."[6] In spite of this grave disability, however, the term has not become totally redundant as a means of differentiating positions and ideas in American politics. On the contrary, liberalism and conservatism are traditionally employed to demarcate the chief political divisions in the United States.[7] Political debate is compulsively argued in these terms. Liberals and conservatives address their criticisms to one another; they place responsibilities for social deficiencies on one another; they define themselves in relation to each other; and they interpret almost all social differences as being representative of their own larger conflict.

The relevance of liberalism as a distinctive term has been due largely to the American reformist tradition, which is customarily characterized as liberal, just as its detractors are commonly referred to as conservatives. While subscribing to the basic political and economic framework, their recognition of the size and complexity of society's problems leads liberal reformers to reject the random operations of pluralism and to favor positive action from a strengthened and socially responsible government. By changing politics from a process of self-interested group demands to a quest for humanitarian ideals, reformers believe that it is both possible and desirable to convert government from the position of a neutral umpire to a committed force for qualitative social change. Reform liberals tend to demand substance to America's ideals: a broader distribution of wealth and power; more concern for the realities behind formal political and economic liberties; a greater participation in decision making; and increased attention to the individual's moral worth instead of his material welfare. In their quest for "social justice," reformers continue to publicize society's defects, to recommend improvements, and to attempt to secure to every individual the positive capacity to exercise his freedom.[8]

To most Americans, not least to the reformers themselves, it is

this reformist impulse that characterizes liberalism in modern America
and provides one of the two fundamental approaches to political ideas
and action in American government. Liberalism in the modern context
is generally equated with the reformist's concern for social inequities
and with their support for enlightened governmental intervention.
Conservatives, on the other hand, are seen as those who oppose the
use of government in promoting wide-scale social adjustments and in
restricting the exercise of individual rights and the ownership of private property.[9]

While the reformists give greater clarity to the modern usage of
the term "liberalism," they do not provide it with a systematic theoretical base. In practice, as in theory, there is no completely reliable
and consistent formula of values that can be universally applied to
all political issues. Many of the more statistical studies of legislative
behavior have attempted to use singular characteristics to differentiate
liberals from conservatives, but have done so at the risk of oversim-
plifying, and even distorting, policy positions and individual attitudes.
Randall Ripley,[10] for example, favors the presidential support index,
in which the position of the White House is used as the determining
criterion of liberalism. John Manley,[11] on the other hand, is disposed
toward the *Congressional Quarterly*'s use of the federal role index as
the key to contemporary liberalism. According to this criterion, any
proposal involving the expansion of the federal government's responsibility is presupposed to be liberal in nature. The reliability of both
these popular indices is suspect, because they presuppose that liberalism is a single entity that can be invoked consistently in all cases.
The basic diversity in the use of the term is dismissed as the singular
criterion bulldozes its way through the roll calls. Not surprisingly,
this can lead to some alarming disparities. For example, the federal
role index imputes liberalism to increases in military spending, agricultural subsidies, the space program, and the level of the FBI's
surveillance of citizens. If the same rationale is accepted in the presidential support scale, John Kennedy's early coolness toward civil
rights, Lyndon Johnson's rejection of any restrictions on presidential
war powers, and Richard Nixon's spending vetoes must all be judged
to be valid liberal positions. This is not to say that these indices
never succeed in being accurate guides to current interpretations of
liberalism. It is only that their accuracy in some fields is often
achieved at the expense of gross inaccuracy in others. This is a result

of their basically unidimensional approach, which fails to make any provision for the inherent variation in the nature of liberalism over time and over different issue areas.

Despite the obvious attraction of determining liberal positions deductively from certain given principles, it has to be concluded that a theoretical calculus providing "authentic" liberal positions does not and cannot exist. There can be no "correct" interpretation of liberalism, for it always remains a term that can mean different things to different individuals. For example, some liberals might be concerned about local democracy while others might stress the efficiency of federal intervention. A western populist may disagree with the political priorities of an East Coast progressive. One liberal may be prepared to accept piecemeal revisions while another may refuse to compromise his grander vision of social change. And differences may well exist between a liberal interventionist and a liberal concerned about government encroachment on civil liberties. Given this variety of liberal traditions, values, and impulses, it can be seen that it is impossible to arrive at unequivocal liberal positions.

If we are to avoid having to rely upon impressions and reputations to determine which senators could be regarded as liberal, therefore, it is necessary to work on the basis of some generally accepted and analytically operational standards of liberalism within the context of specific policy areas. This means discounting abstract formulas and depending more upon indigenous and contemporary guides to what Americans regard as liberal positions. No matter how complex the ideological differences might be, the actual divisions between liberals and conservatives become clearer when they apply their principles to actual political issues. As liberals and conservatives are forced to expose the substance of their beliefs in terms of supporting or opposing actual policies, their differences are no longer confined to a stated theoretical plane but are manifested in open political conflict. Under such conditions, it is quite common for distinctively liberal and conservative positions to appear in public debate. It is these positions, generally recognized to be liberal and conservative in terms of the contemporary usage of the labels, that must act as the normative backdrop to any assessment of the direction and intensity of senators' ideological dispositions.

It is appropriate at this stage to leave our acknowledgment of the general problems concerning liberalism and to direct our attention to the Senate, specifically to the ways in which the available voting data can be used to elucidate the divisions within the Senate itself. A very common method of measuring members' liberal attitudes is to assign to each member a simple score based upon the number of occasions he votes in accordance with a stated position.[12] Whether this is expressed as a simple figure or as a percentage of the total responses, this simple index method combines convenience with simplicity. Unfortunately, such indices are excessively insensitive instruments of measurement. Apart from usually being dependent upon such unreliable presuppositions of liberalism as presidential support or federal role characterizations, the index itself provides no statistical assurance that it actually measures what it purports to measure.

The method produces a crude mixture of responses to a variety of policy fields. An appropriate response to a civil rights question is canceled on a one-to-one basis by an inappropriate response to a foreign assistance bill, without any assurance that the two issues involve similar values or that the specific proposals are of comparable significance within the respective fields of policy. Although this type of measurement is quick and easy to follow, it not only fails to differentiate roll calls into degrees of issue content, but makes no attempt to ensure that the attitude responses are related to the same underlying dimension. This shish-kebab approach, whereby different and arbitrarily selected issues are skewered upon a single externally imposed criterion, was rejected for the purposes of this study.

Another common mode of processing roll calls into structures of mutual agreement and disagreement among legislators is the cluster bloc analysis.[13] The single index method proceeded from notions of liberalism and conservatism to statistical data. In complete contrast, the bloc analysis reverses the process and uses statistical data to differentiate groups of legislators to which collective labels can be attached. Although this technique is the more statistically rigorous way of distinguishing levels of agreement, it can suffer from the very comprehensiveness it proffers as its major attribute. That is, cluster bloc analyses generally include the totality of available roll calls, irrespective of the varied significance of different issues. In Aage Clausen's words:

> When a correlational analysis, such as cluster . . . analysis, is applied to the entire set of roll calls in a particular session [or Congress], one is all too often faced with roll call groupings which are a substantive pot pourri. . . . There is the possibility that policy

voting dimensions, which are conceptually distinct, may converge statistically at given points in time. This is to say that policy dimensions can not always be objectively identified in the statistical relationships between roll call votes.[14]

The use of cluster analysis to distinguish the Senate's liberals from its conservatives raises particular problems concerning the nonideological character of many split votes. In other words, since the cluster technique emphasizes the purely statistical patterns of voting behavior, all divided votes would be included in the process, whether or not they actually represented what would commonly be referred to as liberal–conservative divergences. Not all voting splits can by any means be characterized as liberal–conservative confrontations. Nevertheless, when the clustergram technique is employed to distinguish a legislative bloc that is labeled liberal by some outside agency, there are serious risks that the term is being applied to a group on the basis of a conglomeration of nonsubstantive and ideologically irrelevant roll calls.

In an effort to combine the selectivity of the simple index with the statistical advantages of the clustergram's correlational basis, it was thought appropriate to employ the available roll-call data to draw up Guttman scales reflecting the major policy issues of the time. Guttman scaling is a form of bloc analysis, one in which "the criterion of unidimensionality lies not in the views of outside judges, but in the pattern in which the respondents' answers arrange themselves."[15] The method accommodates the relatively crude roll-call responses of "yea," "nay," and "absent" to uncontrolled questions and aggregates them into a cumulative pattern of support and opposition for the total content of the votes included in the scale. Without having the sophisticated information (e.g., agree strongly, agree very strongly, etc.) necessary for other more graduated forms of attitude measurement such as a Thurstone or a Likert scale, Guttman scaling nevertheless succeeds in assessing the direction and intensity of individuals' attitudes to the variable under review. In doing so, it not only distinguishes members in relation to an underlying value but defines the votes by which to assess the attitudes in question. In this way, the scale allows the Senate's liberal members to define themselves through their responses to a series of votes that they and the other Senators have established as unidimensional in issue content and thereby valid as an instrument of attitude measurement.

Before going on to discuss the application of Guttman scaling to senatorial attitudes in detail, it is appropriate to clarify the basic logic and methodology of this particular type of scale. As has already been intimated, Guttman scaling is a system of measurement in which individuals' responses to issues combine to form a cumulative pattern which simultaneously rank-orders both the issues and the individuals in terms of each other. The value content or the degree of significance of each component item—compared to other items in the scale—is therefore dependent upon the level of support given to it. As the items are ranked on the basis of the number of favorable or unfavorable responses, the individuals become similarly ranked by their responses to issues which are graded according to whatever value is being measured. Thus the logic of a Guttman scale is based upon unidimensionality, for without it no cumulative pattern would present itself.

Individual	Distance		
	100 meters	1,500 meters	10,000 meters
Tom	✕	✕	✕
Dick	✕	✕	
Harry	✕		

In this example, it can be seen that the distances and the running abilities of the three individuals have coincided to produce a cumulative pattern of individual capacity. In this context, the 10,000 meters can be regarded as the item of highest rank, since only one individual can run the distance. The 100 meters, on the other hand, is the lowest-ranked item, as all three can manage it. The distribution of abilities conforms to the Guttman pattern for the individual capable of the highest-ranked item (Tom) is also a 1,500-meters and a 100-meters runner. Because Harry cannot keep going for 1,500 meters, it is reasonable to suppose that he could not manage the 10,000 meters, and this is indeed the case. It is fairly safe to assume, therefore, that this scale is actually measuring ability in distance running.

If a new category is introduced, however, this supposition could become questionable.

Individual	Distance			
	long jump: 7 meters	100 meters	1,500 meters	10,000 meters
Harry	✕	✕		
Tom		✕	✕	✕
Dick		✕	✕	

When the long jump is introduced into the scale, the item of highest rank is immediately shared by the 10,000 meters and the long jump. Harry is now in the anomalous position of having the ability to perform the lowest- and one of the highest-ranked events but none in between. When Harry's ability in the long jump is combined with Tom's and Dick's inability in the same event, the result is a total disruption of the previously cumulative pattern of responses. As the scale's symmetry falls apart, it gives graphic proof of the fact that two dimensions of skill and not one have been mixed in a scale designed to measure a single attribute.

Guttman scaling, with its underlying principles of cumulative aggregation and unidimensionality, can and has been used to great effect in assessing the attitudes and policy orientations of legislators on the basis of roll-call data.[16] Bearing in mind the scale's capacity to rank senators and votes simultaneously within a single statistically tested continuum, it was decided to employ this form of measurement to determine the identity of the Senate liberals over the 1959–72 period.

The scales were devised using the following procedures. First, an initial examination was made of contemporary issues and of the general nature of the political debate that surrounded them. In accordance with the point made earlier, close attention was given to whether or not issues were generally recognized and publicly debated, in terms of liberalism and conservatism. Particular reference was made to those papers, journals, and interest groups renown for their liberal or conservative disposition.[17] They were given close attention not because they provided an authoritative guide to "authentic" liberal and conservative positions, but because they indicated the presence or absence of political divisions and the general configuration of such divisions. This type of evidence provided some prima facie evidence of actual political divisions that were characterized as liberal–conservative splits. Since the subject of the study was the Senate, the next stage was to focus attention on the spectrum of issues and attitudes present in the chamber. In addition to the press, information on Senate politics and policies was derived from individual case studies, from interviews, and from surveys provided by the Congressional Quarterly service. On the basis of this research, it was soon evident that the customary federal role indicator of liberalism did not always provide a realistic appraisal of contemporary liberal positions. In some issues, such as civil rights, education, or housing, where American liberalism is traditionally noted for emphasis on universal standards, central direction, and federal resources, the federal role criterion was a useful and generally accurate benchmark of liberalism. In other issues, however, the federal role indicator was either largely irrelevant (e.g., congressional reform, foreign aid), inconsistent (e.g., poverty program), or invalid (e.g., civil liberties, military expenditures). As a result, each issue was studied on its own merits, to determine whether any liberal and conservative dispositions were generally and consistently referred to in political debate and journalistic commentaries. This exercise provided not only an outline of the general criteria of liberalism, but an initial awareness of which political divisions could actually be characterized as liberal–conservative disputes within the Senate. Armed with this general grasp of major Senate issues and ideological dialogue, the next stage was to use the hard-core information of roll-call data and to observe the ways in which the latter was related to the former.

At the outset, it was decided to use the two-year period of a Congress as the basic unit on which to build each scale. This was done mainly because the turnover in membership after elections produced different sets of respondents in each Congress. The two-year unit was also used to allow for a certain flexibility in the issues scaled. It permitted the inclusion and exclusion of subject areas whenever their congressional and political significance warranted such action. The roll-call data on each Congress were obtained from the *Congressional Quarterly* service. This source was selected not only because of the reliability of its information but because of the additional data it provided in the form of pairing arrangements and polled responses. Although some Senators escaped the net or refused to divulge their positions, the *Congressional Quarterly* provided the greatest possible number of responses to each roll call.

Each Congress, therefore, provided an initial pool of roll calls published by the *Congressional Quarterly* service. While these votes covered a wide variety of policy areas, the major political issues during that Congress were generally reflected in groups of roll calls concerned with those issues. In the Eighty-ninth Congress, for example, there were sizable groups of roll calls directly related to such policy categories as civil rights, poverty, housing, and education—all issues in which liberal and conservative inclinations were generally recognized to exist. These roll calls, therefore, provided an initial storehouse of voting data on which Guttman scales could be based.

Before giving the impression of an easily facilitated transition from data to scale construction, it should be pointed out that several problems and necessary refinements were involved in the process. First, not all the roll calls included within a policy category were appropriate for a Guttman scale. Some prospective votes had to be excluded because, while they may have been directly associated with a policy field, they failed to reflect any degree of division. Votes such as 90–0 were dismissed, therefore, as they would not have served any function in differentiating senatorial attitudes. Second, particular care was taken to include those votes that appeared to be innocuously procedural in nature yet actually involved the legislative heart of a policy under consideration. Often the real conflict over legislation was fought on such parliamentary grounds as motions to table bills or motions to recommit bills to committees. Indeed, it is not rare for the type of unanimous or nearly unanimous votes mentioned above to be prefaced by all manner of procedural, yet substantive, floor votes.

A third point to be taken into account in respect to roll-call studies is the number of votes available for analysis. The absolute minimum number of items for a Guttman scale is 3. However, such a low number of responses would hardly have been sufficient to differentiate senatorial attitudes into a graduated pattern of liberal attachment. To obtain a measurement with a greater likelihood of accuracy and sensitivity, the minimum number of roll calls for a scale was set at 6 (most of the scales in fact contained about 10 roll calls). Although the minimum number of roll calls per scale was set at a comparatively low level, occasionally there were an insufficient number of votes even to begin to draw up a scale. The controversial and distinctive issue of gun control, for example, did not generate enough votes inside the Senate to enable a scale to be constructed in any one of the seven Congresses over the 1959–72 period. This deficiency might well be objected to but, given the rationale of roll-call analysis, it is a painful fact of legislative life that not every public issue is translated into an appropriate sequence of recorded floor votes.

A fourth and final point to be taken into account during the initial survey of available roll calls was the question of the issues that the votes were concerned with. In most instances, the roll calls were dominated by a limited number of issues in which clearly recognized liberal and conservative points of view existed at the time. Yet, very occasionally some roll calls were concerned with virtually noncontroversial issues (e.g., space research) or peripheral fields of policy (e.g., minor congressional facilities). These neither ranked as major issue areas nor could be characterized as subjects of liberal–conservative debate. Thus they were excluded from consideration—both on the grounds mentioned above and on the statistical grounds of insufficient roll calls for scale construction.

Despite all the provisos and qualifications that have been discussed in relation to roll calls, in most cases several groups of votes based on different policy fields were clearly evident in the initial pool of roll calls provided by the *Congressional Quarterly* for each Congress. The aim of the voting study was to allow the Guttman scales to follow the number and variety of the roll calls in each Congress—and thereby reflect the major fields of legislative interest and policy division over successive Congresses. In most instances, groups of roll calls fell readily into certain policy "baskets." This grouping of the maximum possible number of appropriate roll calls into major policy fields marked the end of the initial processing of the data.

After this very limited degree of discretion, the roll calls were subjected to statistical testing for scaleability in order to determine each group's unidimensionality.[18] Such testing confirmed or denied whether the senators were voting in reference to the assumed singular criterion. For example, a case could have been made on the grounds of contemporary political debate that the issue of agricultural subsidies and supports could be viewed in terms of liberal and conservative perspectives. Whether or not this was a valid assumption, it could not be supported on the basis of senatorial voting patterns. In other words, while roll calls on agricultural subsidies existed and while this issue might have been initially characterized as a liberal–conservative issue, the senators voted with such inconsistency, and thereby in reference to a number of criteria, that the roll-call responses failed to corroborate the posited prima facie liberal–conservative split. In this way, the scaleability qualification provided the crucial and overriding statistical test on the presence of an attitudinal continuum within each of the initially selected groups of roll calls. After this process of refinement, by which "rogue" votes could be identified and excluded, the senators themselves could then proceed to define their liberal members through the medium of Guttman scaling.

The final voting study, therefore, consists of a number of Guttman scales for each Congress from 1959 to 1972. The score of an individual senator in a scale was based on the number of occasions a member gave a liberal response within the scale. This score was expressed in terms of a percentage of the total universe of roll calls in the scale. If a civil rights scale, for example, comprised 10 roll calls and a senator gave a liberal response to the first seven in sequence and a conservative response to the remaining three in the cumulative scale, he was given a score of 70 percent. Although certain methodological problems remained to be resolved at the operational level and further statistical checks needed to be completed,[19] each scale normally provided a score for every senator included in that particular Congress. To give a clearer definition of the liberal members and to emphasize the differentiation in senatorial attitudes, it was decided to place the qualifying threshold of a liberal score in any scale at the high point of 75 percent. A scale score of 25 percent or below was designated a conservative score, and a score that lay between the two thresholds (25.1 to 74.9 percent) was ranked as a moderate score. The issues scaled in the seven Congresses and the members returning liberal scores in these Congresses are provided in appendix III.

Before going on to analyze the strength and consistency of the senators' liberal responses across different issue areas and over different periods of time, and to distinguish those members who could be classified as representing the core of liberal support during the period, it is necessary to make one final comment on the Guttman scale method. Although it is true that the scaling technique has allowed us to move into the realm of scale scores and averages, this does not mean that the multidimensionality of liberalism has been processed out of the term and replaced by some purely numerical formula. The techniques of measurement may be statistically sound, but what is actually being measured remains inherently subjective and open to dispute. For example, some may criticize the absence of an issue even if there are insufficient role calls to construct a scale. Others may place greater emphasis on one issue rather than another, thereby regarding a liberal in civil rights, for example, as more liberal than a liberal in the social security field. Both these criticisms are reasonable but, given the complex usages of liberalism and the problems of data availability, they cannot be completely rectified. In defense of the voting study, it can be said that exhaustive efforts were made to provide accurate assessments of liberal and conservative dispositions at the time, and to employ a system of attitude assessment that would not only corroborate or deny the presence of ideological divisions but rank-order individual senators in terms of the statistically identified continuum of attitudes. At the very least it can be said that since the study attempted to achieve a far more comprehensive assessment of senatorial liberalism than is usually the case, it can be ranked as a lesser evil than most other studies in the same field.

LIBERALS: THE DIMENSION OF TIME

By examining the average number of liberal, moderate, and conservative scores per scale throughout the 1959–72 period, it is apparent that in the issues covered by the scales, more senators were likely to be liberal than either moderate or conservative in their voting behavior. Although this may initially confirm all the suspicions of right-wing Republicans, it should be pointed out that the liberals normally had a plurality and not a majority. On average, the conservatives were only eight votes adrift from the liberals, and there was an ample pool of moderate members who were often called

Average Number of Liberal, Moderate, and Conservative
Scores per Scale

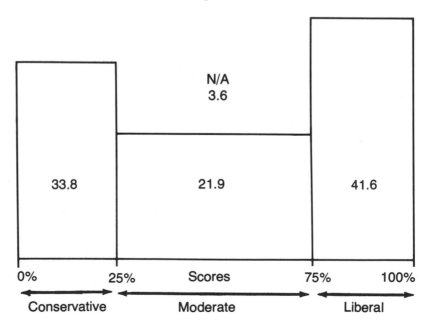

upon to provide roll-call victories for the conservatives. Indeed, it was this moderate sector with its 22 members that could provide the pivotal votes to settle issues one way or the other. Although 75 percent of the senators were concentrated at the polar positions, it was necessary for both liberals and conservatives to court and persuade the minority that did not gravitate toward the two big battalions of the more ideologically committed members.

Although the overall average of the scale scores favors the liberals, they did not always hold such a dominant position over the 1959–72 period. Attitudes and responses varied with time, so the distribution of scores changed with every Congress. In table 3.1 the development of liberal strength in the Senate up to the Eighty-ninth Congress is

Table 3.1 Average Number of Liberal, Moderate, and Conservative Scores per Scale, by Congress

		Liberal	Moderate	Conservative
Eisenhower	86th Congress (1959–60)	48.2	21.5	28.7
Kennedy	87th Congress (1961–62)	44.6	22.0	31.7
	88th Congress (1963–64)	45.8	22.0	31.8
Johnson	89th Congress (1965–66)	49.7	18.8	29.8
	90th Congress (1967–68)	36.5	19.6	40.2
Nixon	91st Congress (1969–70)	34.7	26.0	35.7
	92nd Congress (1971–72)	37.8	23.6	33.6

quite evident. The average liberal group in the Eighty-sixth Congress (1959–60) is probably a little flattering (48.2), as many Republicans forced themselves into uncharacteristically liberal positions (e.g., civil rights) for the sake of their presidential nominee in 1960. The partisanship was matched by northern and southern Democrats who joined forces in 1959 in an effort to amend the Taft–Hartley Labor Relations Act.[20] As a result, the Eighty-sixth Congress featured a high but unstable level of liberal support among the Senate membership.

The real base of liberal strength is probably more accurately represented by the 45 liberal scores per scale during the Kennedy period. This was an era of frustrated optimism when liberal senators could not generate enough momentum to achieve major policy breakthroughs and when many turned their energies toward a critical attack on the Senate as an institution. But the drive for reform was only a temporary distraction for during the early 1960s public attitudes were changing and more liberals were arriving in the Senate. The 1962 election brought Edward Kennedy, Birch Bayh, Abraham Ribicoff, George McGovern, Gaylord Nelson, and Daniel Brewster, and the Johnson landslide brought Joseph Tydings, Walter Mondale, Robert Kennedy, and Fred Harris to join the safely reelected members of the class of 1958. As Republican seats slumped to 32 in relation to the Democrats' 68, the consolidated drive toward liberalism, which had been in progress since 1960, blossomed in the euphoric Eighty-ninth Congress (1965–66). A record 26 senators returned liberal scores in all seven of the issues scaled in the Congress. Although all of them were northern Democrats, the southern wing of the party returned an average of 6 liberal scores per scale, including civil rights. The Democrats crowned their period of complete party dominance with a distribution of scores in which the conservatives registered under 30 votes while the liberals very nearly achieved the status of a self-sustained majority (49.7).

This high level of liberal commitment of the Eighty-ninth Congress made the relative conservatism of the Ninetieth Congress as dramatic a watershed in senatorial attitudes as any experienced in the period. The liberal scores dropped by an average of 13 per scale to 36, and the conservative scores increased from an average of 29.8 to 40.2, thereby achieving a numerical superiority over the liberals for the first time in the series. This configuration of support clearly reflects the overall change in political realities after Lyndon Johnson's great consensus of the mid-1960s. Rising crime rates, campus revolts, black riots, ethnic dissidence, political assassinations, and inflation not only generated public distrust over the long-term social and economic effects of government programs, but produced a widespread fear that Great Society rhetoric had raised expectations to dangerously implausible levels.

The effects of this collapse in liberal confidence are evident in many aspects of the scale data. Direct drops in liberal support were experienced in established issue areas such as foreign aid, social security, and the poverty program. The third great civil rights reform of open housing failed to achieve the margin of the approval that the Civil Rights Act and the Voting Rights Act had secured in 1964 and 1965, respectively. And record low numbers of liberal scores were returned on the sensitive issues of congressional reform (15), civil liberties (22), and military expenditure (17). With this decline in commitment some members returned their first moderate scores (Tydings, Hart, Mondale, R. Kennedy, McGovern) and their first conservative scores (Brewster, Ribicoff, Pell, S. Young, McCarthy, Inouye, Mansfield, Anderson, McIntyre, Church, McGee). As the number of northern Democrats returning at least one conservative score in a Congress increased from 9 in the Eighty-ninth Congress to 29 in the Ninetieth Congress, the total number of senators voting liberal across all the scales decreased from 26 to just 2 (Nelson, Clark).

The first two Congresses under the Nixon presidency represented the tentative beginning of a trend away from the conservatism of the Ninetieth Congress. In the Ninety-first Congress (1969–70) the average number of liberal scores per scale dropped by 2.8, but the average number of conservative scores also declined, by 4.5. The greater emphasis on intermediate scores reflected both the newfound caution of the northern Democrats and the more flexible approach of the Republicans. Several liberally inclined Democrats, for example, had been defeated in 1966 and 1968 (Douglas, Brewster, Morse, Clark, Gruening), and therefore their remaining colleagues became rather more circumspect in their liberal allegiance, especially in such emotive areas as military expenditures and law and order. The same elections, however, changed the composition of the Senate Republican party. The new Republicans, who had defeated a number of the old liberal stalwarts, were not in the Goldwater mold but more in the John Sherman Cooper style of inconsistent progressivism. Members like Charles Mathias, Richard Schweiker, and Mark Hatfield still left Jacob Javits and Clifford Case the lonely job of bearing the standard of Republican liberalism, but they could be relied upon to support the liberal position in a number of issues.[21]

By the time of President Nixon's second Congress (1971–72), the northern Democrats had regained some of their old self-confidence. Having survived Nixon's attempt to defeat many of the most liberal members in the midterm election of 1970, the northern Democratic liberals began to exploit Nixon's minority position. They were assisted in this by the growing public disquiet over the style and tactics of the Nixon administration. Still highly conscious of the popular anxiety over program costs, the northern Democrats advocated no new major welfare projects but tended to concentrate upon defending established Democratic programs from the administration's financial surgeons, proposing defense cuts, and arousing a constitutional controversy over the nature and extent of contemporary presidential power. In these ventures the Democrats were often joined by the new and more progressive Republicans who by now had become disillusioned with the Nixon presidency.[22]

This change in Democratic tactics and Republican support fostered a further recovery for the liberally inclined members. While the average number of conservative and moderate scores fell by 2.1 and 2.4, respectively, the average quota of liberal scores per scale increased by over 3 to 37.8. Although the strength of liberal commitment in no way reached the level that was achieved in the Eighty-ninth Congress, liberal supporters at the end of the period at least reclaimed the distinction of numerical superiority over the conservative supporters.

These figures show that the number of liberal scores varied over time according to conditions both inside and outside the Senate. We have observed a basic pattern of sustained liberal commitment up to the second half of the 1960s, when a sudden slump occurred in support for liberal positions. Definite as these fluctuations may have been, they do not represent the full extent of the variability in liberal scores. The average number of liberal scores in the Eighty-ninth Congress was approximately 50, but this does not mean that there were 50 liberals to each scale in that Congress. In fact, the number of liberals varied from 57 in civil rights to 38 in foreign aid. Clearly, time is only one dimension in the variability of senatorial attitudes. It remains to examine the other dimension, separate issue areas.

LIBERALS: THE DIMENSION OF ISSUE

Presented in table 3.2 is the average number of liberal, moderate, and conservative scores in the policy fields covered by the scales. It can be seen from these figures that the commitment to liberal, moderate, and conservative positions among senators fluctuated substantially from issue to issue. A number of sizable deviations occurred from the average configuration of a plurality of 41.6 liberals over 33.8 conservatives and 21.9 moderates. For example, the number of liberals that could be found in different issue areas varied from 52 in education to just 18.5 in the field of civil liberties. Similarly, the conservative groups varied from 60 in military expenditure to just 18 in consumer and environmental protection. In four fields (i.e., war powers, civil liberties, military expenditures, congressional reform) the average distribution of scale types was disturbed to such a degree that conservative scores actually outnumbered liberal scores. On the basis of the information presented in table 3.2, it is therefore apparent that no obvious pattern existed in the distribution of scale types across the variety of issue areas.

Table 3.2 Average Number of Liberal, Moderate, and Conservative Scores per Scale, by Issue

	Liberal	Moderate	Conservative
Civil rights	51.4	21.8	25.7
Civil liberties	18.5	28.0	48.0
Congressional reform	19.5	36.5	43.0
Consumer and environmental protection	42.5	36.5	18.0
Education	52.0	21.0	22.0
Foreign aid	42.7	18.8	36.0
Housing and urban affairs	47.3	26.6	21.6
Military expenditures	21.0	16.0	60.0
Poverty program	48.6	12.6	35.8
Social security	39.7	23.2	31.5
Social welfare	49.0	19.0	31.0
Union regulation	51.0	16.0	30.0
War powers	35.0	26.0	38.0

Table 3.3 Overall Contributions to Scale Score Rankings, by Party Group

	Proportion of the three score groups supplied by the northern Democrats (%)	Proportion of the three score groups supplied by the southern Democrats (%)	Proportion of the three score groups supplied by the Republicans (%)
Liberal	72.0	8.9	19.1
Moderate	33.3	24.3	42.3
Conservative	6.9	35.7	57.4

The only element of consistency that can be detected lay in the pattern of support given to issues by the three party groups—the northern Democrats, the southern Democrats, and the Republicans. Table 3.3 demonstrates the extent to which liberal support was dependent upon the northern Democratic group. Since the northern Democrats, on average, accounted for 72 percent of all the liberal scores, there was some resemblance in their order of preferences and the overall level of liberal support among the various issues. The northern Democrats' attachment to civil rights, union regulation, and welfare programs, for example, resulted in a high number of liberal scores in these areas. On the other hand, where the northern Democrats' high level of commitment was reduced, the issues involved suffered from a lack of liberal support. In contrast to social welfare, for example, where 96 percent of the northern Democrats returned liberal scores, only 32.4 percent of the group gave similar support to congressional reform. The result of this difference in attitudes was decisive, for while the average number of Senate social welfare liberals stood at 49, the equivalent average for congressional reform liberals was only 19.5.

While it is true that the southern Democrats and the Republicans accounted for 93 percent of all the conservative scores in the scales, the two groups were not totally lacking in commitment to liberal positions. On average, 22 percent of Republicans and 19.5 percent of southern Democrats could be expected to return liberal scores in a scale. In terms of actual members, however, these percentages accounted for only 8 and 4 votes, respectively. Therefore, whenever the customary quota of 30 northern Democratic liberals per issue was appreciably reduced, it was highly unlikely that the other two groups would be able to compensate for the loss and provide the

Table 3.4   Contributions of the Three Party Groups to the Liberal Scores
on Three Selected Issues

	Average number of northern Democratic liberals	Average number of southern Democratic liberals	Average number of Republican liberals
Overall	29.7	4.0	7.9
Foreign aid	26.3	5.7	10.7
Civil liberties	14.0	0.5	4.0
Military expenditures	17.3	1.0	2.7

necessary members to make the liberal scores up to the usual level
of 42.

The three issues of foreign aid, civil liberties, and military expenditures provide an example of the lack of support given to the
northern Democrats by the other two party groups. In the foreign
aid issue the northern Democrats, the southern Democrats, and the
Republicans supported the liberal position in approximately the same
proportions as recorded in their average rate of support for liberal
positions over all the policy fields (see table 3.4). Yet when the northern Democrats' commitment to the liberal position underwent a serious decline in the civil liberties and military expenditures issues, it
was evident that the other two groups did not compensate for the
reduction. On the contrary, their liberal support dropped by an
amount proportionally greater than that experienced by the northern
Democrats, with the result that the number of liberals in the two
areas slumped by large margins.

Another reason why the northern Democrats retained a focal significance in the liberal averages was because both the southern Democrats and the Republicans had different issue priorities and different
patterns of liberal allegiance. The improbability of these two groups
compensating for any northern Democratic lapse was made even
more remote, therefore, by the lack of unanimity between them. Just
as Republicans tended to react against those issues which were
strongly supported by the southern Democrats (e.g., education, consumer and environmental protection), so the southern Democrats
displayed a marked hostility toward issues receiving a high degree
of Republican support (e.g., civil rights, foreign aid, social security).

In fact, no issue succeeded in simultaneously attracting a relatively high number of southern Democratic liberals and a relatively high number of Republican liberals.

As a result, sets of liberal scores in different issue areas never had the same proportion of Republicans and northern and southern Democrats. There were alliances in which the southern Democrats were more prominent than the Republicans (e.g., social welfare, education, union regulation, housing and urban affairs); and groupings in which the Republican liberals outnumbered the southern Democratic liberals (e.g., congressional reform, civil rights, war powers, foreign aid). There were issues that caused splits between the northern and southern Democrats (e.g., congressional reform, civil rights), issues that produced interparty confrontations (e.g., education, poverty program, housing, and urban affairs, social welfare, union regulation), and issues that created divisions within all three groups (e.g., foreign aid). It can be seen from all these variations that the liberal groups in the different policy fields were composed of neither a static number of members nor a uniform formula of Democrats and Republicans. Instead, they were the product of a series of coalitions that fluctuated in size and nature according to the issue areas involved.

LIBERALS: THE DIMENSIONS OF TIME AND ISSUE

In one respect the study has already discovered the identity of the liberals, moderates, and conservatives in different issue areas and over different periods of time. In the Ninetieth Congress, for example, Senator Winston Prouty of Vermont was liberal in the civil rights and social security issues, but moderate in the poverty, housing, and foreign aid issues, and conservative in the congressional reform, civil liberties, and military expenditures fields. Senator Ralph Yarborough of Texas, on the other hand, revealed just as great an inconsistency. In four successive Congresses he responded to the foreign aid issue with a liberal score in 1959–60 (Eighty-sixth Congress), a moderate score in 1961–62 (Eighty-seventh), a conservative score in 1963–64 (Eighty-eighth), and went back to a liberal score in 1965–66 (Eighty-ninth). These two cases are by no means unique, for of all the senators scaled during the 1959–72 period, as many as 76 percent of them received a conservative ranking in at least one scale, while 88 percent made at least one liberal score. In addition, over half the members displayed the maximum variation in score range, so that a number of normally conservative senators had a liberal score, while many liberally inclined members retained a conservative flaw in their otherwise consistent allegiance to the liberal position.

The liberals, moderates, and conservatives may be identifiable in each specific subsection of measurement, therefore, but the positional variation of senators over these units of issue and time generate enormous problems of categorization. Since the scales provide in excess of 4,100 scores from 174 members in 13 policy areas over seven Congresses, they condemn any description of an individual's attitude to a massive compendium of issue strengths and weaknesses, with additional provisos for the possible differences in position over time. In order to arrive at an intelligible assessment of each individual's general ideological orientation, therefore, it becomes necessary to examine the distribution of the scores as a whole. Only through this panoramic perspective is it possible to make any sensible discrimination between senators and to locate those members whose consistency separates them from their colleagues.

The initial step in the method used to arrive at an overall attitude profile for each senator was to exclude those members who had not been scaled over more than one Congress. This time qualification was included to reduce the possibility of classifying senatorial consistency on the basis of an unduly limited amount of scale data. The next stage in the process was to tabulate each senator's scores into liberal, moderate, and conservative subtotals, and then to express them in terms of a percentage of the total number of his scores. To acquire a reasonably coherent typology, a threshold value of 75 percent (the same as used in the Guttman scales) was adopted to isolate the liberals, moderates, and conservatives. Thus:

1. Senators who returned liberal scores on at least 75 percent of occasions were designated liberal.
2. Senators who returned moderate scores on at least 75 percent of occasions were designated moderate.
3. Senators who returned conservative scores on at least 75 percent of occasions were designated conservative.

It must be stated at this point that to assign a senator who occasionally voted conservative to the liberal category did not cancel his conservative scores. His conservatism in particular fields was in no way lessened by his liberalism in 75 percent of the scales. It is only for the purpose of the typology that these exceptional scores were permitted to be outweighed by those scores which were representative of the senator's main philosophical tendencies.

The classification of senators who did not have three-fourths of their responses concentrated in one score group was based upon their two largest groupings. A senator whose top two score types exceeded the threshold point of 75 percent was assigned to the category that embraced the two groups in question. For example, if a senator had 65 percent of his responses in the liberal score group, 25 percent in the moderate score group, and 10 percent in the conservative score group, he would be classified as a liberal-to-moderate. His pool of liberal scores by itself would not qualify him for a liberal classification. However, the liberal score group (65 percent) combined with his second largest score type (moderate, 25 percent) accounted for 90 percent of his scores and therefore qualified him as a liberal-to-moderate. If his moderate score group accounted for 65 percent of his rankings and the liberal group accounted for only 25 percent, he would be classified as a moderate-to-liberal. The first grouping designated a member's primary impulse, while the second grouping represented the direction he tended toward when he was not supporting his usual position.

Occasionally, the groupings did not provide decisive outcomes. For example, a senator's rankings could be apportioned as follows: 40 percent liberal scores, 40 percent moderate scores, and 20 percent conservative scores. Although the two largest subtotals accounted for over 75 percent of the member's scores, there was no way of assigning priority to one or other of them. As a result, the senator would be designated a liberal/moderate. A similar problem was raised when a senator's scores were divided into one superior category (e.g., liberal group with 60 percent of his scores) and two equally inferior categories (e.g., moderate group with 20 percent of the scores and the conservative group with 20 percent). In this case the senator would be classed a liberal-to-moderate/conservative.

Although this framework has certain weaknesses,[23] it does provide a way of reducing the complexities of two-dimensional measurement and arriving at a composite ranking of individual attitudes. A full presentation of assignments to the categories described above is given in appendix IV, but a short summary of the findings is available in table 3.5.

Table 3.5   Average Distribution of Scale Types per Congress

Liberal	24.0
Liberal-to-moderate	16.3
Liberal/moderate	1.6
Liberal-to-conservative	1.3
Liberal-to-moderate/conservative	4.0
Moderate	0.0
Moderate-to-liberal	3.7
Moderate-to-conservative	4.0
Moderate-to-liberal/conservative	2.0
Conservative	17.7
Conservative-to-moderate	16.6
Conservative-to-liberal	2.1
Conservative-to-liberal/moderate	2.4
Nonascertainable	4.3

It can be seen from this breakdown of scale score types that a comparatively high degree of voting consistency existed among the Senate's membership. As the low number of senators who adopted the middle ground indicates, it was a consistency born out of a collective commitment to the liberal and conservative positions. Nearly 18 conservatives, combined with 24 liberals, constituted over 40 percent of the Senate. Most of the remainder tended to gravitate toward either the liberal or the conservative pole. While these members were inconsistent in their support of liberal or conservative positions, the variation in their voting over different issues was usually limited to switching from conservative or liberal groupings to a moderate grouping. Thus most nonconservatives and nonliberals tended to be either conservative-to-moderates or liberal-to-moderates. These two latter groups usually accounted for 33 senators in every Congress. In contrast to these groupings were those senators whose voting on issues was so erratic as to warrant their inclusion in a group spanning the full spectrum of positions (e.g., conservative to liberal, liberal to moderate/conservative). It is a testament to the relatively high level of consistency among the membership that only an average of 12 senators per Congress were sufficiently unpredictable to be ranked under one of these categories.

As for the liberals, they remained the largest Senate grouping, yet one with only a minority of 24 per Congress. Although they could often look to the liberal-to-moderates for assistance, it was the liberals themselves who were most often directly responsible for the support and promotion of liberal propositions inside the Senate. They had to band together before they could expect aid from other quarters. Bearing this in mind, the degree of cohesion displayed by the liberals and their contribution to the general level of liberal support in the Senate over the issues scaled is provided in table 3.6. This table shows the degree to which the liberal positions in various issues were supported by the liberal group, and the impact that the liberals had on the general level of Senate liberalism. In general, the figures show that the liberals remained a relatively tightly integrated group with 88 percent of them, on average, returning liberal scores on the issues presented. In 9 out of 13 issues, their level of liberal support

Table 3.6   Extent of the Liberals' Commitment to Liberal Positions in Various Issue Areas and the Liberals' Share of Liberal Scores in These Areas

	Proportion of liberals (present and voting) returning liberal scores[a] (%)	Proportion of liberal scores provided by the liberal members[b] (%)
Civil rights	97.6 ($n = 166$)	45.0 ($n = 360$)
Civil liberties	62.2 ($n = 45$)	75.7 ($n = 37$)
Congressional reform	55.8 ($n = 52$)	74.4 ($n = 39$)
Consumer and Environmental protection	91.8 ($n = 49$)	52.9 ($n = 85$)
Education	100.0 ($n = 27$)	51.9 ($n = 52$)
Foreign aid	83.3 ($n = 138$)	44.9 ($n = 256$)
Housing and urban affairs	94.7 ($n = 76$)	50.7 ($n = 142$)
Military expenditures	68.1 ($n = 69$)	74.6 ($n = 63$)
Poverty program	96.8 ($n = 125$)	49.8 ($n = 243$)
Social security	90.6 ($n = 96$)	54.7 ($n = 159$)
Social welfare	95.4 ($n = 66$)	42.9 ($n = 147$)
Union regulation	100.0 ($n = 17$)	33.3 ($n = 51$)
War powers	97.8 ($n = 46$)	64.3 ($n = 70$)
Overall	88.3 ($n = 972$)	50.3 ($n = 1704$)

NOTES:
  a. n = total scores recorded by liberal members in each issue
  b. n = total number of liberal scores in each issue area

exceeded 90 percent, and in 2 issues (education, union regulation) all the liberals present returned liberal scores. The effect of the liberal group on the rest of the Senate's liberal scores fluctuated with each policy field. On average, the liberal members could be expected to provide just over half of the Senate's liberal scores in each issue, but this figure conceals a number of interesting variations.

In the more popular areas such as civil rights, education, foreign aid, and social welfare, in which there existed a substantial basis of support in the Senate, the liberals' effect on the overall level of liberal support was relatively low. In civil rights, for example, the liberal group was joined by a substantial number of Republicans who under normal circumstances and in different issues would not be voting with liberals. Thus, while 97.6 percent of the liberal group returned liberal scores in this field, the liberals accounted for only less than half of the Senate's total support for the issue.

In the less popular and more controversial areas of military expenditures, civil liberties, and congressional reform, on the other hand, the liberals became a far more prominent group within the chamber. Although their level of commitment slipped in these issues, their share of the liberal scores increased to as much as 75 percent in the civil liberties field. Paradoxically, it was when the liberals were disunited that their contribution to the overall level of liberal scores was proportionately greatest. This was because the issues were so sensitive that they not only frightened off a number of otherwise liberal members but succeeded in draining away most of the additional support that the liberals might have expected to receive in less controversial areas. Whenever a group of liberals left the ship, therefore, it would coincide with a mass disembarkation by past friends and allies. This would leave the remaining liberals in a prominent, if isolated position on a ship that, if not sunk, was at least in the process of sinking. Thus, when the liberals broke ranks and responded poorly to an issue, the rest of the Senate tended to react to an even greater degree, with the result that the rate of liberal support in that issue suffered accordingly.

All this emphasizes the pivotal position of a group of members who constituted less than a fourth of the Senate at any one time, but regularly delivered over half of the total liberal scores. It was primarily responsible for the conduct of liberal strategies, the viability of liberal legislative campaigns, and ultimately the actual content of liberal legislation in the Senate. Consequently, it is this group which is the chief focus of our interest, the group that the voting study has been dedicated to identifying.

WHO ARE THE LIBERALS?

All that remains is to name the liberals identified by the scales. The average number of 24 liberals per Congress is provided by a total of 37 liberals over the whole 1959–72 period. A simple list of the liberals is given in table 3.7, and the changes in the group's composition over the period is presented in table 3.8.[24] The list includes many of the figures one would expect to find in any gathering of Senate liberals. George McGovern, Eugene McCarthy, Jacob Javits, and Hubert Humphrey are joined by such other readily predictable liberals as Abraham Ribicoff, William Proxmire, Joseph Clark, Wayne Morse, Paul Douglas, and the two Kennedy brothers. The list is notable, however, for those familiar names that fail to appear on it. A number of senators who are widely regarded as liberal do not have the legislative records to fully substantiate their popular reputations. Such well-known "liberals" as Frank Church, Ernest Gruening, Thomas Eagleton, Estes Kefauver, Ralph Yarborough, Daniel Inouye, Charles Mathias, Mark Hatfield, Joseph Montoya, and Richard Schweiker do not, in fact, form part of the bedrock of liberal support within the Senate. Their places are taken instead by a group of members who do not receive the extensive publicity for their activities that is experienced by the more celebrated liberals. Although their public prominence may be low, members like Philip Hart, Lee Metcalf, Alan Cranston, Clifford Case, Frank Moss, Harrison Williams, Walter Mondale, and Claiborne Pell often possess greater leverage within the institution than do their more illustrious colleagues. These quiet but diligent and respected members therefore constitute a distinct but by no means inferior element of the liberal group.

Some of the folklore ascribed to the Senate liberals is substantially accurate. It is true, for example, that 34 of the 37 liberals are provided by that traditional source of progressivism, the Democratic party. Of that 34, all but 1 come from the northern wing of the party, confirming the predictably nonsouthern flavor of the liberal group. Although the South possesses a strong populist tradition and provides the Senate with a number of liberally inclined members (Olin John-

Table 3.7   List of Senators Ranked Liberal in the 1959–72 Period

	Party-State	Term
Wayne Morse	(R/D-Oreg.)	1945–68
Paul Douglas	(D-Ill.)	1949–66
Hubert Humphrey	(D-Minn.)	1949–64, 1971–
Clifford Case	(R-N.J.)	1955–
Pat McNamara	(D-Mich.)	1955–66
John Carrol	(D-Colo.)	1957–62
Jacob Javits	(R-N.Y.)	1957–
Joseph Clark	(D-Pa.)	1957–68
William Proxmire	(D-Wis.)	1957–
Clair Engle	(D-Calif.)	1959–64
Eugene McCarthy	(D-Minn.)	1959–70
Stephen Young	(D-Ohio)	1959–70
Harrison Williams	(D-N.J.)	1959–
Edmund Muskie	(D-Maine)	1959–
Philip Hart	(D-Mich.)	1959–
Vance Hartke	(D-Ind.)	1959–
Frank Moss	(D-Utah)	1959–
Oren Long	(D-Hawaii)	1959–62
Maurine Neuberger	(D-Oreg.)	1960–66
Edward Long	(D-Mo.)	1961–68
Lee Metcalf	(D-Mont.)	1961–
Claiborne Pell	(D-R.I.)	1961–
Edward Kennedy	(D-Mass.)	1963–
Abraham Ribicoff	(D-Conn.)	1963–
Daniel Brewster	(D-Md.)	1963–68
George McGovern	(D-S.Dak.)	1963–
Birch Bayh	(D-Ind.)	1963–
Gaylord Nelson	(D-Wis.)	1963–
Fred Harris	(D-Okla.)	1965–72
Walter Mondale	(D-Minn.)	1965–
Robert Kennedy	(D-N.Y.)	1965–68
Joseph Tydings	(D-Md.)	1965–70
Edward Brooke	(R-Mass.)	1967–
Mike Gravel	(D-Alaska)	1969–
Alan Cranston	(D-Calif.)	1969–
Harold Hughes	(D-Iowa)	1969–
Adlai Stevenson	(D-Ill.)	1970–

ston, Estes Kefauver, Ralph Yarborough, William Fulbright), it has to be satisfied with Fred Harris as its only fully fledged liberal.

The Republicans might have been expected to have furnished more than 3 liberals from their ample stock of members. In spite of the

Table 3.8 Changing Composition of the Liberal Group, from the Eighty-sixth Congress to the Ninety-second Congress

	Congress						
	86th 1959–60	87th 1961–62	88th 1963–64	89th 1965–66	90th 1967–68	91st 1969–70	92nd 1971–72
Morse	✻	✻	✻	✻	✻		
Douglas	✻	✻	✻	✻			
Humphrey	✻	✻	✻				✻
Case	✻	✻	✻	✻	✻	✻	✻
McNamara	✻	✻	✻	✻			
Carrol	✻	✻					
Javits	✻	✻	✻	✻	✻	✻	✻
Clark	✻	✻	✻	✻	✻		
Proxmire	✻	✻	✻	✻	✻	✻	✻
Engle	✻	✻	✻				
McCarthy	✻	✻	✻	✻	✻	✻	
Young	✻	✻	✻	✻	✻	✻	
Williams	✻	✻	✻	✻	✻	✻	✻
Muskie	✻	✻	✻	✻	✻	✻	✻
Hart	✻	✻	✻	✻	✻	✻	✻
Hartke	✻	✻	✻	✻	✻	✻	✻
Moss	✻	✻	✻	✻	✻	✻	✻
Long, O.	✻	✻					
Neuberger		✻	✻	✻			
Long, E.		✻	✻	✻	✻		
Metcalf		✻	✻	✻	✻	✻	✻
Pell		✻	✻	✻	✻	✻	✻
Kennedy, E.			✻	✻	✻	✻	✻
Ribicoff			✻	✻	✻	✻	✻
Brewster			✻	✻	✻		
McGovern			✻	✻	✻	✻	✻
Bayh			✻	✻	✻	✻	✻
Nelson			✻	✻	✻	✻	✻
Harris				✻	✻	✻	✻
Mondale				✻	✻	✻	✻
Kennedy, R.				✻	✻		
Tydings				✻	✻	✻	
Brooke					✻	✻	✻
Gravel						✻	✻
Cranston						✻	✻
Hughes						✻	✻
Stevenson						✻	✻
Totals	18	22	26	28	26	25	23

much vaunted revival of Republican progressivism during the late 1960s, Edward Brooke remains the only recent member to have joined Jacob Javits and Clifford Case in their isolated position on the liberal wing of the party. As a result, the Senate liberal group corresponds to its popular image as a preserve of the northern Democrats.

Another impression validated by the study is the central importance of the class of 1958 to the Senate liberals. In that year a fourth of the liberals were elected to the Senate and even by 1972 the 1958 group was equal to the class of 1962 as the largest surviving class in the liberal ranks. No other class since 1958 has produced liberals on the same scale. The class of 1960 provided 4 liberals and the class of 1962 brought 6 new liberals into the Senate. But the class of 1958 generated 9 liberals, which not only doubled the existing pool of Senate liberals, but by 1972 had provided the liberal group with many of their most senior and influential members (see table 3.8).

While there is a factual basis to the reputed significance of both the Democratic party and the class of 1958, other impressions of the Senate liberals exist which do not correspond quite so well with actuality. The customary stereotype of the Senate liberal is of a member from a large, affluent, northern state which is urban–industrial in nature and which in general is not particularly dependent upon federal resources. Although there is some truth in this caricature, it fails to convey a sufficiently accurate picture of the Senate liberals.

It can be seen from the regional distribution of liberals given in table 3.9 that the East North Central and Middle Atlantic areas predictably account for over one-third (37.8 percent) of the Senate's liberals. New York, New Jersey, Illinois, Wisconsin, Indiana, and Michigan are all confirmed as regular suppliers of liberal senators, with each one providing at least two members to the liberal group. Having acknowledged the contribution of these regions, however, reference must be made to those areas less associated with contemporary liberalism and yet capable of furnishing the Senate with some very liberal members. The West North Central region, for example, is sometimes regarded as a center of conservative Republicanism, but the historical strain of rural populism can emerge to neutralize indigenous caution and to produce a number of highly prominent liberal senators. During the 1959–72 period, the region provided the Senate with George McGovern, Hubert Humphrey, Walter Mondale, Eugene

Table 3.9   Distribution of Liberals According to Region

Region	Number of liberals	Proportion of the 1959–72 liberal group (%)
New England (n = 6)	5	13.5
Middle Atlantic (n = 3)	5	13.5
East North Central (n = 5)	9	24.3
West North Central (n = 7)	6	16.2
South Atlantic (n = 8)	2	5.4
East South Central (n = 4)	0	0.0
West South Central (n = 4)	1	2.7
Mountain (n = 8)	3	8.1
Pacific (n = 5)	6	16.2
Totals (n = 50)	37	99.9

NOTE: n = number of states in each category.

McCarthy, Edward Long, and Harold Hughes, who together constituted 16.2 percent of the liberal group in these years. Another noted
conservative area is New England, but, with the traditional exception
of Massachusetts and with a number of Democratic gains during the
early part of the period (Edmund Muskie, Abraham Ribicoff, Claiborne Pell), the region produced 5 liberals. Finally, the Pacific region
generated more liberals than it is usually given credit for. Moreover,
it is not just California that provides them. Oregon (Maurine Neuberger, Wayne Morse), Alaska (Mike Gravel), and Hawaii (Oren Long)
all sent liberals to Washington. Taken together, these three regions
—West North Central, New England and the Pacific—accounted for
more liberals than did the Middle Atlantic and East North Central
areas. While the latter regions remain the strongest cradles of senatorial liberalism, it should not be forgotten that they do not in any
way monopolize the total group of Senate liberals.

Table 3.10   Distribution of Liberals According to State Population

Population (millions)	Number of liberals	Proportion of the 1959–72 liberal group (%)
Under 1 (n = 13)	7	18.9
1–2.9 (n = 15)	6	16.2
3–4.9 (n = 11)	10	27.0
5–6.9 (n = 4)	4	10.8
Over 7 (n = 7)	10	27.0
Totals (n = 50)	37	99.9

SOURCE: Information on state population levels derived from U.S., Department of Commerce, Bureau of the Census, *Statistical Abstract of the United States: 1968* (Washington, D.C.: GPO, 1968), p. 12.

NOTES: 1966 population figures (average population per state in 1966 = 3.9 million); n = number of states in each category.

Neither were the liberals exclusively from large metropolitan constituencies. Although a fourth of the liberals hailed from such highly populated states as New York, Michigan, Ohio, Illinois, California, and Pennsylvania, just as many came from medium-sized states such as Indiana, Wisconsin, Minnesota, and Maryland (see table 3.10). Most notable, however, is the unexpectedly large number of liberals from the smaller states such as Maine, South Dakota, Rhode Island, Montana, Utah, Hawaii, and Alaska. The liberals from these smaller states succeed in shifting the balance away from the large states and in creating a comparatively equitable distribution of liberals across the variously sized constituencies.

On the other hand, there is a far more pronounced bias toward metropolitan states than there is toward simply large states (see table 3.11). A number of medium-sized states (Maryland, Indiana, Missouri) and some of the smaller states (Connecticut, Rhode Island, Hawaii), all of which provided liberal senators, feature a high degree of urbanization. These have the effect of strengthening the trend toward metropolitan liberal senators set by such states as Massachusetts, California, New York, and Illinois.

Table 3.11   Distribution of Liberals According to the Metropolitan
Composition of Their States

Statewide metropolitan composition	Number of liberals	Proportion of the 1959–72 liberal group
Under 40% (n = 16)	5	13.5
40–59% (n = 10)	6	16.2
60–79% (n = 15)	13	35.1
Over 80% (n = 9)	13	35.1
Totals (n = 50)	37	99.9

SOURCE: Information on the metropolitan composition of states derived from U.S., Department of Commerce, Bureau of the Census, *The American Almanac: The Statistical Abstract of the United States, 1974* (New York: Grosset & Dunlap, 1973), p. 19.

NOTES: 1970 metropolitan area figures (national average = 68.6%); n = number of states in each category.

Tables 3.12 and 3.13 reveal the economic basis of the two major pillars of American liberalism. The rural–agricultural–radical populist strain and the urban–industrial–progressive strain are underlined by the number of liberals from both the farming and manufacturing areas of the United States. Table 3.12 reveals that nearly 38 percent of the liberals came from areas in which the per capita income from agricultural products is very low, while almost a fourth were provided by such agriculturally oriented states as Minnesota, Iowa, South Dakota, Montana, Colorado, Hawaii, and Oklahoma. Table 3.13 confirms the fact that liberals came from both industrial and nonindustrial areas. Thus the 14 liberals from the manufacturing states of Ohio, Connecticut, Indiana, New Jersey, Massachusetts, Rhode Island, Illinois, and Michigan were joined in Washington by senators from Oklahoma, Colorado, Utah, South Dakota, Hawaii, Alaska, and Montana. The balance of cultures and economies clearly favored the manufacturing communities, but this should not obscure the significant contribution made to the liberal ranks of the Senate by the rural areas of America.

Table 3.12   Distribution of Liberals According to the Agricultural Income of Their States

Statewide income from agriculture[a]	Number of liberals	Proportion of the 1959–72 liberal group
Under 25% (n = 6)	9	24.3
25–49% (n = 5)	5	13.5
50–74% (n = 6)	1	2.7
75–99% (n = 5)	4	10.8
100–124% (n =8)	6	16.2
125–149% (n = 5)	3	8.1
150–174% (n = 4)	2	5.4
Over 175% (n = 11)	7	18.9
Totals (n = 50)	37	99.9

SOURCE: Information on the agricultural income of states derived from U.S., Department of Commerce, Bureau of the Census, *The American Almanac: The Statistical Abstract of the United States, 1974* (New York: Grosset & Dunlap, 1973), pp. 13, 589.

NOTE: n = number of states in each category.
[a] Categories denote agricultural income in terms of proportions of the 1969 national average per capita income from agriculture (i.e., $226). Thus the 100–124% group denotes those states which had an agricultural per capita income just over the national average.

Another dichotomy is apparent in the fields of wealth and federal assistance. As shown in table 3.15, a number of poor states, such as South Dakota, Utah, Montana, and Oklahoma, regularly received during the 1960s more federal aid per person than many other states (e.g., federal assistance to Utah in 1966 amounted to 115 per capita dollars). Rich industrial states such as New York, New Jersey, Massachusetts, Illinois, Connecticut, Maryland, Ohio, and Indiana, on the other hand, secured proportionally less assistance from the federal government (e.g., federal assistance to New Jersey in 1966 amounted

Table 3.13   Distribution of Liberals According to the Level of
Employment in Manufacturing

Statewide employment in manufacturing[a]	Number of liberals	Proportion of the 1959–72 liberal group
Under 4% (n = 8)	4	10.8
4–5.9% (n = 8)	3	8.1
6–7.9% (n = 12)	10	27.0
8–9.9% (n = 5)	1	2.7
10–11.9% (n = 5)	5	13.5
12–13.9% (n = 7)	9	24.3
Over 13% (n = 5)	5	13.5
Totals (n = 50)	37	99.9

SOURCE: Information on the manufacturing employment of states derived from U.S., Department of Commerce, Bureau of the Census, *The American Almanac: The Statistical Abstract of the United States, 1974* (New York: Grosset & Dunlap, 1973), pp. 14, 716–7.

NOTE: n = number of states in each category.
[a] Categories denote the proportions of 1967 state populations engaged in manufacturing industries (1967 national average = 9.4%).

to 40 per capita dollars). Exceptions do occur. California and Alaska enjoyed both high per capita incomes and a high level of federal assistance. In contrast, the South, which was the most impoverished region, failed for political and/or ideological reasons to receive a proportionally higher level of aid from Washington.

It can be seen from tables 3.14 and 3.15 that the liberals do tend to come from the richer states. Nearly 60 percent of the liberal group come from states with above-average incomes. Although this leaves 40 percent from the economically weaker states, no liberals have constituencies in the really poor areas of the country (i.e., under 80 percent of the national average). The bias in favor of the richer states is matched by the tendency for liberal constituencies to be relatively more self-sufficient than other states. Well over a third of the liberals come from states that receive under 80 percent of the

Table 3.14 Distribution of Liberals According to the Level of Federal Assistance Given to Their States

Federal assistance[a]	Number of liberals	Proportion of the 1959–72 liberal group
Under 80% (n = 9)	14	37.8
80–99% (n = 11)	6	16.2
100–119% (n = 9)	6	16.2
120–139% (n = 5)	0	0.0
140–159% (n = 7)	5	13.5
Over 160% (n = 9)	6	16.2
Totals (n = 50)	37	99.9

SOURCE: Information on the levels of federal assistance given to states derived from U.S., Department of Commerce, Bureau of the Census, *The Statistical Abstract of the United States: 1967* (Washington, D.C.: GPO, 1967), p. 426.

NOTE: n = number of states in each category.
[a] Categories denote federal assistance in terms of proportions of the 1966 national average per capita level of federal assistance (i.e., $67). Thus the 100–119% group denotes those states which had a per capita income from the federal government just over the national average.

national average of federal per capita expenditure. The less-well-advantaged states, on the other hand, in combination with California and Alaska, collect much higher subsidies from Washington. Although these states provide as much as 29.7 percent of the liberals, they fail to tilt the balance of liberal constituencies toward the areas with disproportionate federal assistance.

As has been observed, the popular stereotype of a liberal as a member from a large, rich, urban, and industrial state in the Great Lakes and eastern region is a distortive oversimplification. It may have been quite accurate in certain individual cases, but there is little justification for it to be employed as a general rule of thumb. Although elements of truth exist in this popular image, sufficient numbers of exceptions and qualifications are present to call its validity into question. Many liberals do come from large and wealthy states (e.g., Javits,

Table 3.15   Distribution of Liberals According to the per Capita
Income of Their States

Statewide per capita income[a]	Number of liberals	Proportion of the 1959–72 liberal group (%)
Under 80% (n = 11)	0	0.0
80–89% (n = 12)	5	13.5
90–99% (n = 10)	10	27.0
100–109% (n = 8)	10	27.0
110–119% (n = 7)	11	29.7
Over 120% (n = 2)	1	2.7
Totals (n = 50)	37	99.9

SOURCE: Information on the levels of personal per capita income in the states was derived from U.S., Department of Commerce, Bureau of the Census, *The Statistical Abstract of the United States: 1967* (Washington, D.C.: GPO), p. 327.

NOTE: n = number of states in each category.

[a] Categories denote statewide levels of personal per capita income in terms of proportions of the 1966 national average personal per capita income (i.e., $2,940). Thus the 100–109% group denotes those states which had personal per capita levels just over the national average.

Case, Williams, the Kennedy brothers, Douglas, Engle, Cranston), but others come from small and relatively poor states (e.g., Metcalf, Moss, Muskie, McGovern, Harris). Just as liberals with industrial constituencies are mixed with liberals from agricultural areas, so eastern liberals are joined by liberals from the Plains and Pacific regions. While a tendency toward a certain model liberal type exists, it remains only a tendency which should not be emphasized to the point of concealing the inherent diversity in the economic and cultural backgrounds of the Senate liberal group.

The aim of this chapter has been to offer a constructive response to the two questions that always arise whenever anyone discusses the Senate liberals. To the question "What is meant by liberals?" the chapter first acknowledged the diffuse nature of the term "liberal" but then went on to offer a method by which liberalism could be usefully defined for the purposes of a voting study. By basing contemporary liberalism on what most Americans took to be the liberal position on political issues, it became possible to assess individual positions and attitudes by their comparability to the series of liberal reference points. In this way, it was possible to respond to the other major question: "Who are the liberals?" Although the roll calls revealed that most senatorial voting varied over time and from issue to issue, a number of members distinguished themselves as consistent and committed supporters of the liberal positions. These were the senators who were ranked liberal in the study.

The identity of the liberals was interesting in an immediate sense because of the names that either were not anticipated, or were expected but did not appear on the final list. In addition, the voting study provided a salutary reminder that liberals do not all come from similar constituencies from the same region of the country. Interesting and important though the adjustment of popular reputation and folklore may be, the main purpose of this chapter has been to provide a systematic base of voting data by which to differentiate the liberal senators from their colleagues. Only by doing this does it become feasible to proceed with an examination of the important areas of liberal attitudes toward the Senate and liberal behavior within the Senate.

4   The Liberals and the Folkways

When a reporter asked Louis Armstrong for the meaning of "soul," the jazz trumpeter replied: "If you've got to ask, you ain't ever going to know." That reply might just as easily have been given by William S. White in response to an inquiry into the necessary qualities of a U.S. senator. To White, the Senate was not just a legislative chamber, but "something unique and fundamentally changeless in American life."[1] Its form of representation, its traditions, and its rules gave it, according to White, a style that was "closer to the artistic than to the business temperament" of most legislatures.[2] An understanding of the Senate, therefore, was dependent upon the standard of an individual's perception and his ability "to sense what cannot be grasped."[3]

Like most romantics, White reveled in the sheer inscrutability of his subject and was reluctant to reduce its mystery to a set of distinguishable features. As there was "no fixed definition . . . of what [was] properly Senatorial,"[4] a member's acceptability to the institution was assessed in terms of his ability to be "in harmony with the forms and spirit of the place."[5] According to White, it was the responsibility of the individual to assume an appearance and a demeanor that was agreeable to the Senate. Since the Senate did not adapt to individuals, it was imperative that individual senators adapt to the Senate.

In the other seminal work on the Senate, Donald Matthews also sensed the importance of continuity and tradition.[6] Unlike White, however, he sought to analyze the necessary prerequisites for acceptance into the Senate's inner life. In his measured and more dispassionate examination, he distinguished six key ingredients of traditional senatorial behavior. These six folkways were (1) apprenticeship, (2) courtesy, (3) specialization, (4) reciprocity, (5) the primacy of legislative work, and (6) institutional loyalty.

In chapter 1 it was shown that both White and Matthews were convinced that a primary function of these folkways was to perpetu-

ate the conservative tenor of the institution and to maintain its position as a center of conservative policy. A conservative committee
hierarchy, a conservative party leadership, a conservative approach
to reform, and a conservative attitude to policy all appeared to confirm their main contention that the Senate's political conservatism
was rooted in an institutional culture that was intrinsically conservative. In this framework the position of the liberal member was assumed to be almost untenable. According to Matthews, for example,
liberals were more likely to transgress the bounds of institutional
etiquette because their heterogeneous, industrial, and competitive
constituencies would force them to react against the pervasive ethic
of gradualism and compromise.[7] Although it was possible for liberals
to adapt to the folkways (e.g., Hubert Humphrey, Theodore Green),
most liberals adopted the approach of Paul Douglas and Herbert
Lehman, who broke ranks and operated from independent but peripheral positions. The protests of such members may have caused minor
disturbances, but these were damaging only to those involved, never
to the Senate as a whole. Since the dissent of the disaffected could
be contained at all times, the folkways remained intact and for most of
the 1950s showed no sign of losing their hold on the Senate's life-style.

The inherent conservatism of the folkways and the intrinsic iconoclasm of the liberal members were endorsed by so many contemporary
writers and observers that the two features rapidly assumed the
status of conventional wisdom on the Senate.[8] In spite of the enduring popularity of the White and Matthews model, the fact remains
that their studies did not take the dramatic result of the 1958 midterm elections into account. *Citadel* appeared in 1957, and *U.S. Senators and Their World* was completed early in 1960. In both cases
the thesis presented was based upon the electoral stability of the
1950s, when the turnover in Senate seats was very low. Therefore,
the effects of the 20 changes in the Senate's membership and the
doubling of liberal seats wrought by the 1958 election were not
assimilated into the studies by White and Matthews.

The purpose of this chapter is to examine the extent to which
the folkways were affected by the greatly enlarged contingent of
liberals that appeared after 1958. If the liberals were lonely and
incongruous figures in the Senate of the early and mid-1950s, what
was their attitude toward the Senate's code of behavior when their
numbers increased in the late 1950s and early 1960s? How did they

actually react to the folkways and to the senior custodians of Senate tradition? Was their reputation for challenge and nonconformity justified? Were the folkways necessarily conservative norms? And how durable did the folkways prove to be in the Senate of the 1960s? The chapter seeks to answer such questions by investigating the liberals' attitudes toward, and direct responses to, each of these central traditions of Senate behavior.

APPRENTICESHIP

One of the most important roots of Senate tradition was the custom of apprenticeship. It was an overt technique in socialization, for its main object was to acclimatize new members to the Senate's legislative style and to orient them toward their expected roles.[9] So complex was the nature of senatorial etiquette that it required a protracted process of learning for a senator to achieve an adequate comprehension and appreciation of their value. According to White, the heightened sensitivity of a mature senator was a work of art that could only be accomplished by a gradual assimilation of senatorial ethics ("all the newcomer needs . . . is the passage of time—but this he needs indispensably").[10]

During his period of training, a freshman was expected to engage in patient and respectful observation of his seniors. He had to seek advice, ask questions, consult elder members, remain diffident in public, and generally be available and willing to assist the senior senators in their legislative duties. The freshman was obliged to assume much of the unattractive work of the Senate (e.g., acting as presiding officer), to refrain from speaking excessively, and to gain prior approval from the senior members for any major legislative maneuver.

Traditional "rules of thumb" existed to guide senators through this difficult process. According to one Senate aide, a freshman was only supposed to speak one word in his first session, two words in his second session, and then—depending on what the words were— his position would be reviewed in his third session. White's advice to freshmen was to comply with the established custom of the Senate—"walk with a soft foot . . . speak with a soft voice, and infrequently."[11] Matthews's formula was similar but stated in more dogmatic terms: "The new senator [was] expected to keep his mouth shut, not to take the lead in floor fights, to listen and to learn."[12] Joseph Clark actually received this sort of advice when he first entered the Senate in 1957. Fellow liberal Hubert Humphrey instructed him as follows: "It's a friendly, courteous place. You will have no trouble getting along. . . . Don't let your ideology embitter your personal relationships. It won't if you behave with maturity. . . . Keep your mouth shut and your eyes open."[13] While the specific instruction may have varied, the basic prescription remained constant. Freshmen were expected to behave as any uninitiated newcomer would in similarly elevated and exclusive surroundings.

Throughout most of the 1950s the apprenticeship folkway remained a noncontroversial piece of Senate tradition. The only exception to this conformity came from a number of northern Democratic liberals (e.g., Clark, Carroll, McNamara), who made a number of vociferous but ineffective complaints against their expected subservience. From this, White and especially Matthews postulated that northern Democratic liberals were more likely than other members to react against the strictures of apprenticeship. Liberals had the reputation of being self-assertive, unreliable, and intransigent, but because there were so few of them, they never seriously threatened the pragmatic style of Johnson's Senate.[14] After 1958, however, the number of northern Democratic liberals doubled (from 9 to 18) and in Senator Ed Muskie's words, "a whole new increment of potentially unruly Senators"[15] arrived in Washington. In contrast to 1957, when Lyndon Johnson could successfully press copies of White's book on three isolated and bemused liberal freshmen, the Senate elders were on this occasion confronted by a large group of highly assertive newcomers who were particularly skeptical of the traditional restrictions on the activities of junior members.

According to White and Matthews, the liberals' response to apprenticeship was a predictable form of behavior given the observed reactions of earlier liberal freshmen. They both tended to regard liberals as the beleaguered representatives of highly industrialized and heavily populated states. The cultural heterogeneity of these areas combined with their competitive party systems not only subjected senators to the most severe cross-pressures, but forced them into a premature prominence within the Senate.[16] Large populations and slim electoral margins may well have accounted for the activism of liberal freshmen earlier in the 1950s, but these two features failed to explain the level of assertiveness within the liberal newcomers of 1958. Indeed, for most of the liberal freshmen, these two factors stressed by Matthews were not generally applicable.

For example, of the 9 liberals in the class, 4 came from states with populations under 4 million:

Edmund Muskie	—	Maine
Eugene McCarthy	—	Minnesota
Frank Moss	—	Utah
Oren Long	—	Hawaii

As for tenuous electoral positions, only 3 had majorities of 52.5 percent or under:

Stephen Young (Ohio)	—	52.5 percent
Harrison Williams (N.J.)	—	52.3 percent
Oren Long (Hawaii)	—	51.4 percent

Most of the remaining liberals won their elections by less critical margins:[17]

Philip Hart (Mich.)	—	53.8 percent
Clair Engle (Calif.)	—	57.0 percent
Vance Hartke (Ind.)	—	57.1 percent
Edmund Muskie (Maine)	—	60.8 percent

Clearly, the liberals' behavior was influenced in ways other than the mere dimension of their constituencies or the size of their majorities. The irreverent attitude of the liberals toward the folkways in general and to apprenticeship in particular was more the product of two sets of factors. The first set includes the various ways in which the liberals were affected by their own success at the polls. The second centers upon the conditions that the liberals encountered when they arrived in the Senate.

The response of the liberals to their own electoral victories was one of confidence and anxiety. The confidence of the liberal freshmen was based not only on capturing so many seats but on securing a number of particularly illustrious seats. Senators McCarthy, Young, and Moss, for example, won their seats by defeating three long-established Republican members (Thye, Bricker, and Watkins). Although Senators Engle and Hartke did not have to defeat incumbents, they succeeded to the seats of two nationally prominent right-wing senators (Knowland and Jenner). So intense was the interest in the 1958 election that some members had become public celebrities before they had even arrived on Capitol Hill. Senators Muskie, Hartke, and Williams, for example, received a particularly large amount of publicity because they were the first Democratic senators from their states for at least 15 years.[18] Even though they were not necessarily their states' favorite sons, senators like Muskie, Moss, Long, Hartke, and Williams were the only national figures in their state Democratic parties. As a result, their senatorial careers were of the utmost importance to the future success of their local party organizations.

A further stimulus to the liberals' impatience with apprenticeship was their concern over the safety of their seats. This anxiety was not attributable to the classic factor of small majorities as much as to the feeling that the liberals' success was the product of freak conditions. Senator Muskie, for example, regarded the class of 1958 "as an accident that was not likely to be repeated."[19] In one respect, the unexpectedness of the victories fostered an attitude of personal achievement and independence among the new liberals. In another respect, it aroused great concern over whether seats won by majorities of even 60 percent would be safe in 1964. A related aspect of this "accidental" element in the class of 1958, which also influenced liberal behavior, was the desire to prevent a reaction against the Democratic party in 1960. Since the war there had been two other large classes—a group of 20 Republican freshmen in 1946 and a group of 15 Democratic freshmen in 1948—but in both cases these impressive gains had been dramatically reduced in the succeeding congressional elections. The Republicans gained 11 seats in 1946 but lost 9 in 1948. The Democrats gained 9 seats in 1948 only to lose 4 in 1950. The class of 1958 did not want these precedents to be followed in 1960. On the contrary, the freshmen wanted 1958 to serve as a springboard for further Democratic victories two years later.[20]

In spite of the variety in their backgrounds and constituencies, the liberal freshmen of 1958 all had a keen sense of how important the class was to the Democratic party in the Senate and in the country at large. They were, after all, the physical manifestation of an unprecedented national swing to the Democrats (i.e., as far as the Senate was concerned). Labels such as "new wave" and "new breed" were attached to them. The class could not really be described as a group of crusaders against the old Senate, but it did contain a large number of buoyant, self-confident, and highly optimistic members who were expected to make some kind of an impact on the

Senate. This attitude, combined with the background of public clamor and controversy that surrounded their celebrated victories, was hardly conducive to the anonymous rigors that Senate freshmen had traditionally been subjected to by their seniors. It became apparent that there was a strong probability that the liberal freshmen of the Eighty-sixth Congress would not submit to being ingested gradually and unobtrusively into the bloodstream of Senate life. This probability only became a certainty, however, when the freshmen received the added stimulus of experience of actual conditions in the Senate.

The style and operation of the Senate in the late 1950s provided the second set of factors in the development of liberal protest. The freshmen quickly perceived that a relationship appeared to exist between the Senate's traditional code of behavior and the power structure within the chamber. To the liberals, the former always appeared to function to the direct advantage of the latter. Like others in the past, the liberal freshmen of 1958 regarded apprenticeship not only as an unnecessary requirement but as a tradition biased against juniors in general and against junior liberals in particular. Yet in contrast to their predecessors, this class was in a position to provide a powerful challenge to the practice.

When the liberals arrived on Capitol Hill, they were immediately confronted by the harsh fact of an institution that was widely regarded to be "the great repository and guardian of tradition."[21] In real terms, this referred not simply to the Senate's conservative leadership, but to the gamut of informal conventions which provided such a fertile environment for the maintenance of conservative control. These conditions produced the additional stimulus to the liberals' sense of active irritation. Consequently, when they became aware of all the obligations that apprenticeship entailed, they reacted against the convention. To the liberals a period of studied meekness was simply asking too much of them. In the elections they had campaigned against conservative senators and against the conservative Senate as a whole. They had succeeded in drastically enlarging the Democratic majority in the Senate. Because of the class, the northern Democrats now outnumbered the patriarchal southerners by 41 to 24. The liberals had come to Washington in a state of high expectation of the opportunities that the Senate would provide for individual achievement. The class was also well aware of its importance to the national Democratic party during the crucial "run-up" period before the 1960 election.

With these achievements and aspirations, the liberals were in no mood to be receptive toward the Johnsonian Senate, which to them was stultifying in terms of both policy and opportunity for the individual legislator. The situation was worsened by the presence of a pronounced age gap between the freshman liberals and their prospective mentors. While the average age of the established southern Democrats (those members who had served at least one full term) was 59 years, the average age of the new liberals was only 49 years, 9 months.

Relations between Johnson and the liberals were further strained by the clash in regional and cultural styles. Before 1958, it was well known that the aristocratic Joseph Clark and the forthright ex-plumber Patrick McNamara could not abide Johnson's imploring and threatening style of persuasion. In 1959, a number of the new liberals (Muskie, Hart, Moss, McCarthy) also discovered that being pressed by the majority leader was a distinctly unpleasant experience.[22] Johnson, in turn, reacted against those northern colleagues who failed to appreciate the subtleties of Texas manners. Perhaps the best example of this mutual irritation was when LBJ attempted to "educate" Senator Edmund Muskie into the pragmatic and compromising style of the Senate. He advised Muskie not to make up his mind on an issue until the roll call had reached the M's. A few days later, when Johnson was earnestly seeking voting commitments to his crucial compromise on the filibuster rule, he asked Muskie whether he would be voting for or against the amendment. Muskie replied—"Well Lyndon, we haven't gotten to the M's yet."[23] Subsequently, Muskie voted against Johnson's compromise and as a result was not only banished to a number of inconsequential committees but pronounced "persona non grata" by the majority leader's office.

If the atmosphere of the Senate represented a provocation to the liberals, it also provided them with the means to avoid the customary obligations of apprenticeship. First, the Senate attracted an unusually high degree of public attention in the Eighty-sixth Congress because it was here that the struggle between the Democrats and the Republicans reached its fullest expression. On the Senate floor the Republican contender for the presidency, Vice-President Richard Nixon, confronted the four Democratic challengers, Senators Johnson, Symington, Humphrey, and Kennedy, in tactical maneuvers over bills and policies.[24] One of these aspirants proved a particularly inspiring model to liberal freshmen. The attraction of John Kennedy was not so much that he was a northern Democratic progressive but because he had become a national figure by the time he had reached his fourth year in the Senate (1956) and a presidential contender by the beginning of his second term. The message was clear to the freshmen: a senator's political career need not necessarily be damaged by failing to serve an apprenticeship. In fact, given the atmosphere of the Eighty-sixth Congress, the liberal freshmen never really had to defy the apprenticeship tradition at all. Intense publicity, presidential politicking, frenetic partisanship, and overt political competition among senators caused the custom to be suspended until conditions might once again be conducive to its reintroduction.

The other aspect of the freshmen's successful evasion of apprenticeship was the sheer force of numbers. The class of 1958 not only provided a large number of uninitiated freshmen, but decreased the number of available senior tutors to instruct them in the ways of the Senate. Since the Senate's conservative elite was already under pressure over the disproportionate degree of influence they held within the chamber, the conservatives' capacity and resolve to insist upon apprenticeship were substantially weakened.[25]

In contrast to previous years, the war of words between intense freshmen and crusty regulars over professional etiquette were not to be heard along the corridors of Capitol Hill. This reduction in mutual hostility was due not so much to any spontaneous sense of conformity among freshmen as to the southern elders giving more license to the junior members. Instead of drawing attention to the provocative extent of their own power by penalizing unorthodox freshmen, the seniors tended to restrain themselves in this area of social education. Given the southerners' political experience and their traditional skills of parliamentary accommodation, it is reasonable to assume that they recognized the impulse for reform and preempted it by dropping the apprenticeship norm, thereby preserving their institutional position for the really important fights that would lie ahead in such areas as civil rights and the filibuster rule.

Matthews' statement in 1960 that freshmen found "the period of apprenticeship . . . very real and very confining"[26] is therefore misleading. It may accurately describe the condition in the Senate before 1959, but after a few weeks of the Eighty-sixth Congress the norm of apprenticeship was no longer vigorously applied to freshmen. Newcomers experienced few limitations on the exercise of their legislative interests. Senator Harrison Williams, for example, became chairman of the Subcommittee on Migratory Labor as early as 1959. Once in that position, he immediately began investigative hearings into the operation of the Fair Labor Standards Act, and used the information he gathered in his committee to prepare bills on the health and education of migrant farmworkers. Williams also exploited to the full his membership of the Housing Subcommittee by adopting and identifying himself with the cause of mass transit. By 1960, the Williams bill proposing $100 million in long-term low-interest loans for transport development in metropolitan areas had been accepted by the Senate.[27]

Senator Eugene McCarthy (Minnesota) provides another illustration of the rapid strides a newcomer could make in the Eighty-sixth Congress. From his base in the prestigious Finance Committee, he successfully engineered a liberal amendment (repealing the 4 percent tax credit on dividend income) through the Senate. But McCarthy's greatest achievement in the Eighty-sixth Congress was his appointment as chairman of the Select Committee on Unemployment. The committee toured the areas of highest unemployment and collected information on the major difficulties involved in alleviating the problem. By mobilizing support for the Youth Conservation Corps, the area redevelopment bill, and for vocational training and retraining courses—an idea that was later to become an integral part of LBJ's war on poverty—the McCarthy Committee succeeded in providing the Democrats with a coherent program on an issue that had been decisive in many of the 1958 races and which would probably be just as crucial in 1960.[28]

Perhaps the best indication of freshman activism at this time was the increased incidence of cosponsorship. The tactic of building support for a bill by offering other senators a share of the limelight became widespread among the liberals of the Eighty-sixth Congress. In this way, freshman members such as Senators Hart, McCarthy, Moss, Engle, Muskie, Young, Williams, and Hartke became publicly associated with some of the most important legislative proposals of the era—medicare, civil rights, aid to education, area redevelopment, and unemployment compensation.[29]

In this context, the well-documented account of Senator Proxmire's open challenge to apprenticeship and his subsequent ostracism by the establishment must be regarded as exceptional.[30] According to

Huitt, Proxmire had begun his senatorial career in 1958 by conforming
to the apprenticeship tradition and maintaining as low a profile as
possible. After 3 months he reacted against the ritual of silent self-
effacement and became vociferously assertive, even to the point of
conducting his own one-man filibuster ("he would talk when he
pleased on whatever he chose and would not worry about his influence in the Senate").[31] His disaffection with the conservatives' control of the Senate and with their demand for unobtrusive freshmen
prompted Proxmire to forgo the customary formalities and engage
in whatever legislative activities he was interested in at any one time.
Although he "unquestionably . . . paid a price for choosing the Outsider role,"[32] he relished the freedom to publicize those issues which
interested him most.

From the Proxmire case, Huitt postulated that a relationship existed between the urgency which liberal members attached to so
many issues and the liberals' propensity to adopt the outsider role.
Owing to the notoriety of the Proxmire case, it is often assumed that
the behavior of the Wisconsin senator represented the authentic liberal response to the restrictions imposed on junior members in the
Senate of the 1950s. While Proxmire was a liberal member, his style
was not reflected in the behavior of his fellow liberal freshmen in
1959–60. During these years Proxmire continued to assert his independence and his refusal to comply with the apprenticeship norm.
Yet his new colleagues were not in sympathy with him. By continually making his point over individual participation, he antagonized
many of his fellow liberal freshmen, who felt uncomfortable in his
presence and regarded his tactics as irresponsible and unnecessary.
Proxmire's attitude and actions were not typical of the freshman
liberal group in the Senate during 1959–60. On the contrary, his style
was determined by his own personal idiosyncrasies and not by his
status as a junior liberal member.[33]

In contrast to Proxmire, it appears that most of his colleagues had
little cause for complaint. On the whole the new members realized
that they were enjoying an unprecedented degree of discretion in
their first term. Even Senator Muskie, who had apparently been forced
into a low profile by a set of disastrous committee assignments, could
remark that "there was a gradual diffusion of power; in the two years
(1959–60) there were not many Senators who had not made out and
got to be on the inside."[34]

By the end of 1960 the liberal freshmen felt that they had fully justified their premature activism. Not only had John Kennedy won the presidential election, but there had been no backlash against the landslide party of 1958. Indeed, the election provided 4 new liberal members (Metcalf, Long, Neuberger, Pell). When these were combined with the 6 new liberals elected in 1962 (Nelson, McGovern, Bayh, Brewster, Ribicoff, E. Kennedy), the result was that by the Eighty-eighth Congress (1963–64) the Senate included as many as 19 liberals serving their first terms. Like the class of 1958, the senators elected in 1960 and 1962 arrived on Capitol Hill firmly resolved to develop their interests, but unlike the 1958 newcomers, they never really encountered any serious suggestions that they should do anything to the contrary.

The thaw that began in 1959 had by the mid-1960s turned into a flood of individual self-expression. After suspending apprenticeship in the Eighty-sixth Congress, the senior members never managed to reimpose it. Their preoccupation with the highly sensitive issues of civil rights, medicare, aid to education, and so on; the embarrassment of continually losing seats to the liberals; and the departure of Lyndon Johnson all contributed toward the establishment's decline.[35] But perhaps the crucial factor was the growth in freshman aspirations. With the numerous precedents of prominent freshmen in the Senate and with the ultimate model of John Kennedy, new senators now came to Washington not only with the belief that they had something to offer the Senate but with the definite expectation that this august body would actively encourage them. As one of the newcomers of 1964 remarked: "We don't feel there's time to waste on that old seen-and-not-be-heard business. . . . After all, if a man manages to get to the Senate, he must have something to contribute."[36] This attitude combined with the liberal advances of the early 1960s and majority leader Mansfield's enthusiasm for wider participation throughout the Senate produced a nearly total collapse of the apprenticeship tradition.[37]

One of the few exceptions was the highly publicized apprenticeship served by Edward Kennedy. It is ironic that the brother of one of the forces behind the tradition's decline should have conformed so diligently to the custom and at the same time conveyed the impression that apprenticeship remained the general practice well into the 1960s. He accepted the chores that other freshmen sought to

avoid (e.g., presiding over the Senate), and through his courtesy and
respect developed close personal relationships with such senators as
John Stennis and James Eastland. It should be noted, however, that
Kennedy's compliance with the apprenticeship norm was not despite
his family's success but rather because of it. As one Kennedy aide
put it: "Senator Edward Kennedy was one of the last Senators to
serve an apprenticeship. Since John Kennedy had become President
and Robert Kennedy had become Attorney General, he felt he had
to serve an apprenticeship in order to allay fears of a Kennedy takeover."[38] Although Edward Kennedy's was the most publicized example of continued apprenticeship in the Senate, there were a number
of other individuals who preferred the gradual and inconspicuous
road to senatorial prominence. Included in this group were a number of liberals and liberal-to-moderates (Hartke, Dodd, Bartlett, Randolph) who opted to serve an apprenticeship either because it helped
them to acquire some sense of a role as a legislator or because they
believed that it was the most effective method of achieving political
power. But the majority of apprentices were conservative freshmen
who were drawn toward it as a custom and as a method of assimi-
lating the many other principles of Senate life.

For most liberals, however, the early 1960s had witnessed the
evaporation of apprenticeship. To some extent the void was filled by
ad hoc allegiances to personally chosen mentors. Senator Proxmire,
for example, was much influenced by the style, attitude, and policy
interests of Senator Paul Douglas. Senator Fred Harris, on the other
hand, had three father-confessors in his first term. He developed a
close working relationship with Senator John McClellan and then
he sheltered under the wing of Robert Kennedy before finally join-
ing Walter Mondale as Hubert Humphrey's second protégé in the
Senate.[39] Such instances provided some semblance of education by
experienced members, but they in no way amounted to apprentice-
ships in the old sense of a compulsory period of formal training. Inconspicuous conformity to a set group of members and a set pattern
of behavior was at an end.

By the late 1960s the tendency of freshmen to be, in the words
of one prominent conservative senator, "young bucks who from the
start go right down the line to make a name for themselves"[40] was
no longer confined solely to the liberal ranks. The attraction of this
role was beginning to prove too great even for conservatives. By 1968

and 1970, the Senate was receiving new conservatives like James Buckley, Robert Dole, and Howard Baker, who dismissed most forms of ceremonial induction and made their presence felt at an early stage. Whether their initial prominence was motivated by constituency demands for visible and active members, by their intention to equal the liberals in personal assertion and political commitment, or just by the absence of so many of the old conservative patriarchs, these conservatives moved quickly to acquire personal reputations and notoriety. However, it should be noted that not all conservative freshmen were by any means in the same mold as Buckley or Dole. Traditional gradualism and diffidence still appealed to the conservative nature, and therefore apprenticeship has remained a mark of differentiation between liberal and conservative freshmen. In Senator John Tower's words: "There are just fewer 'grandstanders' among the conservatives. . . . They show more deference to their elders."[41] Whether or not the conservatives can long resist the pressures of freshman activism and individual aspiration is open to conjecture.

In this section we have devoted a good deal of space to an examination of apprenticeship both before and after the liberal classes of 1958, 1960, 1962, and 1964. The scale of the study was partly a reflection of apprenticeship's central importance as a technique in socializing new members into an acceptance of all the remaining folkways. But the main reasons for such an extensive analysis were (1) that drastic change in the Senate's life-style had occurred, and (2) that this change could not be explained in the simple terms of more liberals with demanding constituencies and slender majorities. The impulse of the liberals to abandon many of the old restrictions on freshman behavior and the conservatives' decision to sanction this irreverence were derived from a complex process in which abnormally large numbers of confident liberal freshmen changed not only the political composition of the Senate but the whole atmosphere within the chamber. The result was an active reassertion of the notion that a variety of senatorial roles could exist and that it was within the discretion of each member to select the one most appropriate to his interests and character. Although apprenticeship in a rudimentary form still existed for those who wanted a period of voluntary training, structured apprenticeship had collapsed under the weight of liberal freshmen with strong policy commitments and high political aspirations. Given the increased level of individual participation within the

Senate over the 1960s and the establishment of numerous precedents for freshman activism, it is difficult to foresee a period in the future when young lights will once again be hidden by old bushels.

COURTESY

After the liberals' assault on the apprenticeship tradition, one might have predicted that the rest of the folkways would have been in jeopardy. Without the initial period of training during which newcomers might learn how to savor the subtleties of Senate tradition, it seemed possible that all the old customs might fall before the iconoclasm of the liberals. This proved to be a false assumption, for the liberals both attacked tradition and adapted to it. The folkway of courtesy provides an example of adaptation.

Like most legislatures, the Senate maintains a set of rules and conventions that attempt to regulate the formal relationships between members.[42] Custom prescribed that senators refrain from personal attacks that impugned the motives of other senators and transgressed the bounds of gentlemanly conduct. Senators were also expected to address each other with the most lavish references to their backgrounds and reputations (e.g., the most distinguished, learned, able, and gallant senior senator). This form of courtesy probably made a functional contribution to the legislative process. By obliging senators to refer to each other in the third person and through the presiding officer, the custom reduced the possibility of deep personal antagonism. As long as differences were expressed formally, politely, and impersonally, they were less likely to lead to a serious dislocation in legislative cooperation.

Senators were supposed to, and actually did, go to great lengths to maintain the chamber's decorum by moderating political attacks and by concealing profound personal antipathies from the public. Senators Ralph Yarborough and Strom Thurmond, for example, always provided each other with the usual laudatory compliments even though their personal disagreements were so intense as to prompt them to a violent fight outside the Commerce Committee room in 1964.[43] An indication of the lengths that senators went to keep their ranks closed was the practice of "correcting" the *Congressional Record*. If a senator made an indiscreet remark or an intemperate attack on a colleague, the offender had the right and the moral obligation to rephrase his verbatim remarks for the *Congressional Record* or have them struck completely.[44]

At the very least the courtesy folkway fostered an environment in which the lines of communication could remain open no matter how deep the political divisions may be. It must also be conceded that the institution's style of extravagant flattery and grandiose expressions of admiration did appear to satisfy a genuine need among senators. Although many of them perceived its superficiality, nearly all of them accepted the folkway as one of the perquisites of membership. They may not have been affected by courteous approaches, but they were likely to resent being selectively excluded from the general norm of mutual respect. Senator George McGovern particularly resented Norris Cotton because he once referred to him as simply "McGovern" on the floor of the Senate.[45] The courtesy folkway remained relevant to members because it created the best atmosphere for working out agreements and because it reflected the fact that "legislative support was mobilized on a highly personal basis"[46] in the Senate.

The Senate liberals had very little effect on this tradition; liberals and conservatives could not be differentiated on the basis of their conformity to this norm. Conservative senators have always had the reputation of mixing professional competence with charm and affability. According to Leon Shull, National Director of the Americans for Democratic Action (ADA), most conservatives were sufficiently courteous to receive the ADA's lobbyists and to listen carefully to their arguments.[47] And liberals tended to respond to the example set by the conservatives. Whatever their level of frustration and indignation, they normally recognized the futility of discourtesy. Their distaste of personal criticism was an important element in the liberals' disapproval of Proxmire, who not only publicly criticized Johnson's leadership on the Senate floor, but did so when the majority leader was out of town.

The delicacy of liberal susceptibilities was also revealed by their reluctance to investigate the personal and financial rectitude of fellow members. In the Thomas Dodd case of 1967, for example, allegations were made by the press that Dodd had (1) accepted money from people who had been given official appointments through pressure from the senator; (2) intervened in the federal government on behalf of clients from his private law firm; (3) took money and gifts from industries that were being investigated by committees whose membership included Senator Dodd; (4) took government-paid vacations by classifying trips as essential congressional business; (5) used campaign contributions for his own personal expenses; (6) included persons on his payroll who did not fulfill any official congressional duties; and (7) claimed expenses from the government when they had already been paid by private organizations. In spite of the gravity of these charges, no member of the Senate was willing to mobilize support for an investigation. Even the many liberals who were committed to internal reform that would counteract just these types of abuse refused to break ranks and turn against Dodd. It was only when Dodd himself pressed for an inquiry that the Senate Ethics Committee began to examine the charges. The committee started by reprimanding the four staff aides who had divulged information about their employer to the press. It not only refused to consider documents removed by Dodd's staff as evidence, but severely criticized their action in breaking the traditional trust between a senator and his aides. Eventually, the committee recommended that Dodd should be censured, but on the less sensitive counts of the misuse of campaign funds and of double-billing. As a mark of charity and tolerance, the Senate chose to censure him (94–5) on just the first charge. With all the other complaints left unanswered, Dodd rejoined his colleagues as a normal member, served out the remaining three years of his term, and nearly managed to gain reelection to the Senate in 1970.[48]

To many liberals, courtesy most certainly extended to the privacy of members' financial and business interests. Disclosures of personal resources has always been a subject that has divided congressional reformers and traditionalists. However, it is an issue that also tends to split any group of liberal senators. For example, during the 1960s Senators Clark and Case attempted to persuade the Senate to accept a comprehensive reporting requirement for senators' financial interests. The failure of their efforts illustrates the difficulty of their campaign. Senators Clark and Case not only failed to attract the support of the more moderate members but could not prevent a hemorrhage of votes from their own liberal group. Of the 26 liberals sitting in the Eighty-eighth Congress (1963–64), nearly one-third (8) opposed the proposal.[49]

The Clark–Case amendment, which was rejected 25–62 in 1964, failed to gain acceptance in the succeeding years. By 1968 the sponsors reluctantly accepted a very weak compromise which obliged senators to give the Ethics Committee details of their income, assets, debts, and tax returns. These would remain secret unless the committee voted to divulge them to the public. The only open reports would be those containing details of honoraria, political contributions, and gifts.[50] Since the personal records of senators' financial interests remained secret and since the public disclosures were often distorted by legal loopholes, the cause of full and candid information on the interests of senators did not progress very far.

The courtesy folkway thus involved far more than the habitual use of appropriate titles or the exchange of pleasantries. It included a general appreciation of the problems and pressures on other senators and a reluctance to capitalize on colleagues' weaknesses. Collective trust, discreet behavior, gentlemanly agreements, privacy, consistency, and a dislike of duplicity were all hallmarks of senatorial courtesy. A member's conformity to these norms was not dependent upon his ideological inclination. It was essentially a matter of character and personality. This fact was confirmed by the number of close working relationships that developed in the 1960s on the basis of courtesy between the liberal group and some of the Senate's most established conservatives (e.g., Ervin, Bennett, Mundt, Dirksen, Eastland, and Stennis). The importance of individual attitudes was also substantiated by the wide variety of senators who did not comply with this folkway, and who in White's phrase failed to "get on" with their colleagues. This group included those who publicly embarrassed the Senate (e.g., Mike Gravel), those whose partisanship was regarded as excessive and offensive (e.g., Robert Dole), and those seen as highly unpredictable and inconsistent (e.g., William Langer, Charles Goodell, William Proxmire).

Although it is true that liberalism was not a distinguishing characteristic of nonconformism in this field, developments in the early 1970s tended to associate the liberal group with senatorial discourtesy to a far greater degree than ever before. This was due to the increase in the number of presidential aspirants among the ranks of liberal senators and to the increase in the number of presidential primaries. These fratricidal encounters not only bred divisions between members but provided the opportunity for private antagonism to be translated into public abuse on the hustings.

In 1968, the acrimony between Senators Robert Kennedy and

Eugene McCarthy was veiled, but very thinly. By 1972, as many as 8 liberals and liberal-to-moderates were in contention and it was not long before they began referring to each other's voting records and policy positions and criticizing each other's personal capacity for office. Henry Jackson, for example, showed little restraint in describing George McGovern as "the spokesman for some of the most dangerous and destructive currents in American politics . . . amnesty, acid and abortion."[51] As the primary elections reduced the main contestants to George McGovern and Hubert Humphrey, the latter launched a vitriolic attack against his colleague from South Dakota by describing him as "a fool."[52] He continued, "McGovern is a practitioner of the oldest kind of politics and the worst kind: promising things you can't deliver."[53] The Senate code of seniority and apprenticeship was clearly an influence on Humphrey's attitude: "If you want a doctor you don't go to the kid who just got his internship. You go and see the guy who has done a few operations."[54]

Since George McGovern was the front-runner he had less cause to engage in public recriminations, but he did react violently to Humphrey's challenge to the credentials of his crucial California delegates: "It's an incredible, rotten, stinking political steal. I'm not going to support anyone who is elected by crooked and unethical procedures. . . . If a bunch of old established politicians gang up to prevent me from getting the nomination . . . I would repudiate the whole process. I would run as an independent."[55] Humphrey's response was equally provocative: "The party is weary of temper tantrums of juveniles who, if they don't get their way, are going to bolt."[56]

Although these remarks were made in public, they were uttered under the strain of electioneering well away from Capitol Hill. Personal divisions may have persisted after the end of the primary season, but there was very little indication that these electoral squabbles seriously disturbed the inner tranquility of the Senate or established its liberal members as any less courteous than their colleagues.

RECIPROCITY

To William S. White, "the greatest political raison d'être of the Institution"[57] was reciprocity or compromise. The spirit of accommodation in combination with the folkway of courtesy was supposed to encourage legislative cooperation by reducing conflict and fostering a framework within which agreements could be arrived at. A senator who isolated himself from this conciliatory environment could not expect to receive the same degree of cooperation as could those who subscribed to its ethos of pragmatic accommodation. If an individual persistently refused to compromise he could not "remain a good, or effective, member."[58]

Although the folkway of mutual accommodation could be regarded as a euphemism for logrolling, White made no apologies for this. To him, logrolling was an essential form of cooperation within the Senate.[59] As the institution's system of representation was founded upon states, communities, and minorities, the Senate was expected to make its decisions on the basis of negotiation, not on the "crude" principle of simple majority rule. Senators represented distinct regional entities and therefore were obliged to work toward legislative outcomes that took into account, to the greatest degree possible, all the constituent interests embodied in the membership. In the ultimate sense of the "concurrent majority" doctrine, senators were expected to refrain from endorsing policies that were intolerably prejudicial to a minority's vital interests. Whether it was expressed as logrolling or as the convention of "concurrent majority," tradition decreed that the Senate be a chamber in which bargaining and conciliation were to be preferred to dogma and inflexibility.

Despite the custom of reciprocity, liberal senators acquired a reputation for intransigence during the 1950s. Of the 37 liberals identified in the voting study, only 9 (i.e., Javits, Case, Douglas, Morse, Carroll, Clark, Proxmire, McNamara, Humphrey) were operating in the Senate before 1959. Much of this small minority felt both estranged from the mainstream of Senate politics and frustrated by the chamber's rules, which tended to favor the obstructionist strategy of the dominant conservative group. Since legislative compromise is always based upon the numerical strength of the respective protagonists, the liberal group had very few resources with which to enter into a real bargaining relationship with the conservative coalition. To avoid being swallowed up in the mainstream of Senate politics, most liberal members tended to adopt a position of publicized obduracy.

The strategy adopted by the liberals was the unorthodox one of attrition through a continual process of innovation, education, and persuasion. Remaining on the periphery, they sought not only to preserve the integrity of their positions but to attract colleagues to their cause. They used the ample opportunities for expression in the Senate to raise divisive issues (e.g., civil rights, medicare, cloture, congressional reform), to present their own policies, to challenge the leadership's positions, to criticize the administration, and to denounce the stultifying practice of compromise that pervaded political operations in the Senate.[60] The individualistic campaigns of such liberals as Morse, Douglas, and Clark represented an open rejection of Matthews' and White's criterion of legislative "effectiveness." In place of the enactment of bills and resolutions, their aim was to publicize alternative proposals and to manage the long-term process of mobilizing support for the enactment of measures in the future.

The liberals who played this role were heavily criticized for undermining Lyndon Johnson's fragile packages of legislation, for exacerbating the political differences among senators, and for emphasizing the internal inconsistencies within the Democratic party. Their rejection of the moderate bipartisan approach and their endorsement of confrontation tactics were interpreted as a negative and provocative form of self-righteousness—"the old liberals had a flaming sword in their hand. . . . They were the heirs of the New England puritans and had a Calvinistic element to their attitudes."[61] In this way, liberal senators quickly acquired the image of being an isolated minority that rejected any responsible role in legislative decision making in order to indulge in a sterile adherence to principles.

After the 1958 and 1960 elections the liberals achieved a stronger base on which to operate. Not only had the liberals increased their numbers from 9 to 22, but the ranks of the liberal-to-moderates had grown from 10 to 16. This latter group of members, who were more likely to vote with the liberals than against them, represented a substantial reservoir of possible support for the liberals. With their own improved strength and with assistance from the liberal-to-moderates and from President Kennedy, the liberals sensed that substantial legislative achievement was at least within their grasp.

Some of this potential was fulfilled in the successful campaigns for New Frontier programs such as area development, manpower development and training, and aid to dependent children. But the liberals failed in their attempts to secure effective legislation in the really controversial areas of aid to education, medicare, civil rights, poverty, and congressional reform. The intensity of their disappointment and frustration was such that it discounted any sense of achievement they might have derived from their minor legislative successes. As a result, the liberals' resentment of the Senate's rules and the Senate conservatives continued unabated. The liberals did not abandon their aggressive posture. If anything, the pungent aroma of possible legislative success on a major scale induced them to become more intransigent in their attitudes and more critical of the Senate.

It should be pointed out that the assertion of liberal intransigence is not meant to convey the impression of suicidal tendencies on the part of liberal senators. Liberals were able to compromise. They would never have won their elections if they had not had the capacity to accommodate themselves to diverse interests and expectations. Furthermore, liberals did compromise in the Senate when they felt that they were in a reasonably equable negotiating relationship. Liberals could and did compromise initial policy positions for the sake of legislative achievement in those areas where they were politically strong in the chamber. In the fight for the manpower development and training bill in 1962, for example, the bill had been given a good deal of momentum by the active support of the president and by the endorsement of the liberally inclined Labor and Public Welfare Committee.[62] The favorable reception that the bill experienced in the Senate, however, was not matched in the House, where the measure was passed in more restrictive terms and with a reduction in the proposed funding. Joseph Clark was the bill's sponsor. Since he wanted the strongest possible bill for President Kennedy, he pressed for the initial Senate version of the bill in the conference committee. Despite his reputation for intransigence and inflexibility, Clark accepted a one-third reduction in the program's financial authorization (i.e., from $655 million to $435 million), a cut of one year in the duration of the training program (i.e., from four years to three), and a number of other weakening amendments, to secure passage of the bill.

Where the liberals were noted for their intransigence was on those occasions and in those policy areas in which the terms of trade were overwhelmingly against the liberal position. Whether it was a policy in the jurisdiction of a conservative-dominated committee or a proposal that did not attract widespread sympathy, the liberals gained notoriety by prolonging disputes with their opponents in committee and bringing them onto the floor itself. Instead of conceding to the obvious voting strength of the opposition and to the institutional momentum of committee decisions, the liberals often refused to make floor votes into nearly unanimous acclamations. On the contrary, they sometimes used the opportunity to attempt to reassess committee reports and to offer uncompromising floor amendments. Although these tactics were normally doomed to failure, they did serve to highlight the legislative position of many liberal policies in the Senate and to dramatize the institutional position of the liberal members.

A prime exponent of the liberals' tactic of pressing for "no-loaf" rather than "half-a-loaf" floor amendments in the early 1960s was Joseph Clark. In addition to his famous condemnation of the "Senate establishment" in 1963,[63] he was noted for making proposals that did not take into account the views and probable objections of the leadership, the specialist members, the ranking senators of relevant committees, or the key moderate members. Contrary to the advice he received to opt for voice votes that would conceal the weakness of his position, he preferred roll calls on issues he raised. In the words of one legislative assistant: "Clark would insist on roll call votes even if he knew he was going to lose. He would rather go for all and lose. It was a measure of his influence that he was usually supported by 16 to 18 members."[64] Whether it was Joseph Clark advocating congressional reform, Paul Douglas proposing tax reforms, or Wayne Morse championing educational aid, the strategy of publicity and education was the same. It was in controversial policy areas like these, in which the liberals felt their proposals to be of the utmost importance but in which their institutional leverage was weakest, that the liberals established their reputation for overt intransigence.

By the mid-1960s, however, the liberal group had expanded to 28 and the liberal-to-moderates had increased to 18, giving the Senate 46 members oriented toward liberal positions. More significantly, political conditions (see chapter 2) were now more conducive to the acceptance of liberal policies. In short, Kennedy's assassination, Johnson's legislative skills, combined with persistent pressure from within Congress, a weakening of the conservative coalition, and a profound shift in public opinion all contributed toward the landslide of legislation during the Great Society era. The liberals' strategy of a determined adherence to established positions in the hope of long-term victory had been vindicated. They had provided "the cutting edge of change"[65] and it had remained relatively sharp despite all the customary congressional entanglements of delays, deferments, and outright obstruction. The liberals had stood their ground and waited for a change in the political climate. By the mid-1960s, the terms of political trade had swung decisively in their favor. Other members now gravitated toward the liberals. As a result, the liberals were forced to make only minor concessions in order to achieve major successes in such fields as regional development, medicare, housing, urban renewal, aid to education, mass transit, consumer protection, and poverty.[66]

Perhaps the most controversial and symbolic victory came in the campaign for the civil rights bill in 1964. Rejecting all attempts to emasculate the strongest civil rights legislation since reconstruction, the liberal group was instrumental in the movement to invoke cloture on the southern Democrats' filibuster. The forcible limitation of debate represented a cultural shock of the deepest kind to the Senate. Cloture had always been more than a simple device to end a filibuster. It had been a psychological barrier in itself that had only been breached on one minor occasion since 1927. Therefore, when the liberals spearheaded the movement to overrule the fundamental objections of a minority group of senators, they raised a number of basic questions concerning the legitimacy of the liberals' role in the Senate.

The debate was not so much concerned with the question of cloture and minorities as with the type of action which the majority of senators was intending to take against the minority. It became evident that, when an effective majority was controlled by a liberal group, it represented a danger to the Senate's traditional form of decision making. In any normal democratic chamber it is accepted that majorities can be as insistent and as uncompromising as their numerical strength warrants. Not so in the Senate. Again, in any normal legislative encounter it is the intransigent minority which is customarily condemned as provocative and unreasonable. Not so in the Senate. According to the "concurrent majority" doctrine, changes in public policy should only be made when they are basically congenial to all the constituent sovereignties represented. Consequently, intransigent positions are only to be tolerated in the Senate when they are held by a conservative majority, or a conservative minority, or a liberal minority. The folkway of reciprocity, the Senate rules, and the concurrent majority tradition militate openly against the presence of a liberal majority, because this configuration has the power to enforce changes and to dismiss objections.

An intransigent conservative minority is acceptable because it conforms to the classical pattern in which groups are permitted to obstruct those proposals which they regard as intolerable. An inflexible conservative majority is also acceptable because it would usually be opposed to any major changes. Even in those cases where the conservative majority demands change, it will probably be an attempt to recapture a past situation by removing the controversial elements of a contemporary policy.

An intransigent liberal minority is not really within the Senate tradition because its strategy is based upon improvization and initiation and not on objection and defense. As such a minority is usually ineffective in producing change, it does not give the Senate serious cause for concern. A liberal majority, on the other hand, represents a direct challenge to the concurrent majority doctrine. As a majority motivated by the desire for change, it is the one Senate force that will not give protection to those who are confronted with intolerable changes in policy. The invocation of cloture and the mass rejection of all the southerners' amendments, therefore, appeared to herald the capture of the Senate by an unsenatorial force—one that did not defer to minority objections, one that preferred the Senate to be an integrated part of a national democratic framework.

After this high-water mark of legislative success in the mid-1960s, however, the integration of the liberal group and its political leverage within the Senate began to decline. Just as exceptional public support had precipitated a cluster of major reforms, so the public's increased skepticism of government policies reduced the momentum of liberal advances. It is not possible to attribute the shift in popular sympathies to a single event or trend. It was more the product of a complex series of interacting anxieties over government policies and social phenomena that, more often than not, were characterized by the president and the liberal Congress. Program costs, for example, became a major cause of concern after the mid-1960s. It was damaging enough for liberals that the public was beginning to speculate over whether various social welfare projects were in fact aggravating the problems they were designed to resolve. Great Society programs, however, were not only seen as failing to correspond with President Johnson's grandiloquent assurances, but prompted public disquiet over the alarming increases in their costs. The innocuous $33 million allocated to the food stamp program in 1965, for example, had burgeoned to $550 million by 1970. Federal spending on health expanded over the same period from $1.7 billion to $12.9 billion.[67] Perhaps most alarming was the dramatic rise in the scale of the federal government's contribution to public assistance programs. In 1967, 5 percent of children under 16 were receiving welfare benefits under the Aid to Families with Dependent Children scheme. By 1972, the proportion had doubled to 10 percent. The costs had nearly tripled, from $2.3 billion to $6.7 billion.[68] Traditionally, Americans have always regarded public assistance as a form of temporary readjustment that would "'wither away' as an expanding economy drew more and more people back to work and social insurance programs were expanded."[69] When they were confronted by large increases in welfare rolls at a time of economic expansion and of high rates of taxation, they began to resent the prospect of further increases in public assistance expenditure and to question the need for further experimentation in social policies.

Opinion polls show that in the late 1960s, Americans became more skeptical of government policies, more distrustful of decision makers, and more cynical of the system itself.[70] They also became less liberal. Whereas 49 percent of the public regarded themselves as liberals in 1963, only 33 percent ranked themselves as liberals in 1969.[71] It is true that the public still retained its traditional duality of ideological conservatism and operational liberalism that Free and Cantril first analyzed in a polling study that appeared in 1964.[72] That is, Americans tend to react against liberalism in terms of broad statements of ideological principles but to sympathize strongly with liberal positions on poverty, race discrimination, education, health care, and so on. Although these attitudes constitute a core of liberal convictions that would seriously impede any radical attempt to reduce the infrastructure of established social programs, it does not necessarily follow that Americans always respond to issues and vote on the basis of their operational liberalism. On the contrary, given that the nation's most important problems during the late 1960s were classified as inflation, race, crime, Vietnam, and law and order, and given that the President had come to personify the frustration of the various failures in foreign and domestic policy, the Senate liberals could no longer depend on the operational liberalism of their constituents in the same way as they had done in the mid-1960s.[73]

In effect, the political temperature had changed. The liberals were not dead, but they were wounded. They were still committed, but they had fewer friends than before and, as a result, were more vulnerable to legislative failure. Moreover, for the first time in a decade, liberal senators began to suffer defeats at the polls. Between 1966 and 1972, Edward Long, Daniel Brewster, Paul Douglas, Joseph Clark, Wayne Morse, and Joseph Tydings all lost their seats.[74] As they were not replaced in sufficient numbers by new liberal freshmen, the turning of the political tide had a direct effect on the size of the liberal group. From 1966 to 1972, the liberal contingent declined from 28 members to 23.[75]

Although the liberals suffered setbacks after 1966, they did not return to their earlier posture of aggressive criticism and intransigent policy positions. Evidence suggests that in the late 1960s, the liberals became less inflexible and more accommodating than they had been before. In Senator Gale McGee's words: "Liberals had suffered in the past because of their ideals. They were less inclined to compromise; to take half a loaf. They would rather go down in defeat and not get anything. This changed after the mid-60's. Liberals felt it was better to get something than nothing. Better to get ahead."[76] The days of the passionate liberal outsider had effectively ended after the Great Society era. By the late 1960s the liberals were no longer as "homogeneous as they had once been . . . for within the liberal group varying strains of philosophy"[77] had begun to appear.

The shift toward a more accommodating spirit is reflected in the voting study. Taking the 17 liberals who were present from the Eighty-ninth Congress (1965–66) to the Ninety-second Congress (1971–72), it is possible to see a marked reduction in their level of commitment. Whereas the group returned liberal scores on 93 percent of available occasions in 1965–66, their rate of liberal scores had dropped to 81 percent during 1971–72.[78] The increase in the liberals' flexibility was apparent in a number of areas (e.g., revenue sharing, foreign aid), but it was nowhere more marked than in the civil liberties field. In the late 1960s and early 1970s liberals were voting in favor of restraints on civil liberties that they would never have tolerated in the early and mid-1960s. The 1968 Long amendment to Johnson's omnibus crime bill, for example, would have deleted the wiretapping title, which gave federal, state, and local enforcement officers wide discretion in electronic surveillance. This civil libertarian proposal only attracted 12 votes, as 15 of the 26 liberals either abstained or voted against.[79] One of the most controversial parts of the Nixon administration's 1970 D.C. crime control bill was the proposal to hold dangerous suspects in preventive detention to protect the community. Philip Hart led the campaign to weaken the measure by requiring proof beyond all reasonable doubt before a person could be established as an especially dangerous offender. On this occasion the civil libertarian position only attracted 11 votes, as half the liberals opposed Hart's measure.[80]

The general change in political conditions, the decline in liberal seats, and the loss of a Democratic administration all contributed to the relaxation in liberal attitudes. Yet these were not the only causes. At least four other major factors were in operation after the mid-1960s.

First, the liberals lost one of their key motivating forces through their own increased power inside the Senate. In the late 1960s the liberals were no longer a group of juniors, but a set of members at advanced stages in their senatorial careers. For example, by the mid-1960s the liberals had achieved high levels of representation, in terms of seats and seniority, in the Labor and Public Welfare Committee, the Banking and Currency Committee, the Government Operations Committee, the Judiciary Committee, and the Public Works Committee (see table 4.1). In contrast to the early 1960s, the liberals no longer had the feeling of being excluded from power or frustrated by unfair means at vital moments in the legislative process. By the late 1960s their keenly developed sense of victimization and discrimination began to fade and, as a result, the liberals began to lose some of their old fighting spirit.

Second, the liberals had achieved a great deal in a short space of time. Not only had they finally secured passage of policies that had a 20-year pedigree behind them (aid to education, civil rights, medicare), but they had passed brand new policies such as the poverty program and the model cities project. If all this legislative activity did not exactly exhaust the liberals, it certainly gave them an overwhelming sense of achievement. They had proved to themselves and to the public that they could defeat the South and the conservative coalition and that they could shift the policy bias of the Senate. The immensity of the liberals' success had wiped the great social issues of the postwar era off the legislative calendar and, as a result, the liberals of the late 1960s tended to concentrate on consolidation, oversight, and the simple defense of programs against a critical Republican administration.[81]

Table 4.1 Distribution of the Liberals' Committee Assignments and Growth in the Liberals' Seniority from 1959 to 1972

	Congress						
Committee	86th 1959– 60	87th 1961– 62	88th 1963– 64	89th 1965– 66	90th 1967– 68	91st 1969– 70	92nd 1971– 72
Aeronautical and space sciences	2	2	2	3	3	1	0
Agriculture and forestry	4	5	4	2	2	1	2
Appropriations	0	1	2	2	3	2	3
Armed services	1	1	3	1	2	2	1
Banking and currency	6	8	8	7	6	7	6
Commerce	3	3	3	4	4	4	3
District of Columbia	2	2	2	3	3	1	1
Finance	3	3	4	4	5	4	4
Foreign relations	2	2	2	4	5	3	4
Government operations	2	3	6	6	6	6	6
Interior	2	4	4	4	4	5	4
Judiciary	2	3	4	6	5	4	3
Labor and public welfare	6	7	7	9	8	8	9
Post office and civil service	1	1	1	2	2	2	1
Public works	5	6	8	7	4	4	3
Rules	0	1	2	2	2	1	1
Veterans	—	—	—	—	—	—	3
Total number of liberal seats	41	52	62	66	64	55	54
Number of upper-level seats held by liberals[a]	6	12	16	16	13	19	19

[a] Upper-level seats refer to seats in the top half of the Democratic and Republican hierarchies in each committee.

Third, the liberals became more defensive as a group. Although the Vietnam war could in no coherent and consistent manner be regarded as a specifically "liberal war," liberals in general suffered from both the war itself and the social disturbance associated with it. The war became bound up with the Great Society not only in terms of budgetary competition and inflationary spending but in terms of political disaffection and social dislocation. In many ways, Johnson's Great Society backfired on the president when the contemporary syndrome of cultural and moral dislocation became increasingly associated with the social experimentation of liberal reform. Vietnam merely compounded the liberals' problems, for it was not long before the public had to encounter the even more discomforting phenomena of open opposition to the armed forces, the commander-in-chief, and the war effort. The president was condemned not only for being responsible for the war itself, but for spawning the conditions that permitted contempt for such a key component of social authority as the presidency. The Senate liberals also became doubly vulnerable in this shift in historical circumstances. They, too, were closely associated with the Great Society. In addition, they assumed the delicate, and largely thankless task, of organizing congressional efforts to intrude upon the previously hallowed preserve of presidential discretion in foreign policy. The liberals' commitment to continuous social legislation lost its earlier edge as they circumspectly redirected a sizable portion of their energies and resources away from the sensitive field of Great Society–style reform and toward the even more politically charged fields of war management and international commitment.

The final element in the relaxation of liberal attitudes was the increase in the liberals' senatorial experience. Whether this is seen in terms of pragmatism, disillusionment, institutional socialization, or complacency, the fact remains that the liberals gained a reputation for "mellowing" in office. The view is widespread that the longer a liberal is in office, the more likely he is to tolerate the views of his opponents and to appreciate the value of compromise. This mellowing effect was referred to by many senators. Senator Thomas McIntyre, for example, thought that senior liberals had undergone a mellowing process because they had become "disillusioned over the way legislation was enacted and implemented . . . especially at the level of regional and town administrations."[82] Senator Quentin Burdick believed that because the "hard core liberals had learnt to compromise," the Senate had become "more and more practical"[83] as an institution. Such views are echoed by the liberals themselves. According to Senator Edmund Muskie: "There is a mellowing effect, but this is not surprising. . . . You have to make a positive effort to jolt yourself out of ideas that were acceptable in 1958. Since then, there have been changes in public values and needs. You have to keep aware of the meaning of progress in current times."[84]

Although Senator Gaylord Nelson was one of the most liberal members of the Senate in the 1960s, even he found that he was not immune to the sobering effects of long experience and increased seniority. "If you are an outsider, you may not accept the compromises that those with responsibility accept. . . . I do not think that you should go around compromising all over the place. [Nevertheless] when you have responsibility there is a feeling that you have to accomplish something—to maximize what you can get."[85] But perhaps the best commentary on this mellowing of attitudes comes from a liberal senator's (Lee Metcalf) administrative assistant: "Older liberals know how to move toward social progress in the direction which they want. . . . They are pragmatists who know how to achieve their aims by compromise and by knowledge of the mechanics of government. With experience you realize that you cannot get everything . . . so you should take what you can get."[86]

The effect of this mellowing phenomenon on the Senate's liberal group would not have been so significant if the group had continued to be supplemented with a regular intake of young liberal freshmen. But this was not the case. The number of new liberals coming into the Senate declined after 1966. In addition, the situation was aggravated by the fact that many of the new liberals elected in the late 1960s did not show the same streak of intransigence and idealism that had pervaded the earlier classes. After experiencing the failures and expense of the Great Society programs from outside, the new liberals tended to be more skeptical of the traditional issues and the approaches of the old guard.

According to one of Senator Adlai Stevenson's assistants: "The newer liberals appeared to be interested in substance but they were really concerned with process and with the reform of the congressional structure. Less effort was put into programs because New Deal policies had not been popular with the new liberals."[87] To many senior liberals, mellowed or not, this interest in procedure represented a diversion that only succeeded in distracting the Senate's attention from important issues concerning society and the economy. The effect of this generation gap is perhaps best summed up by one of the 1958 veterans, Senator Harrison Williams: "The young liberals have not been exposed to many of the hardest periods of our national history, as we were. The Depression implanted certain emotional and intellectual 'indelibles' in your mind that you relate to events today. If you don't have these, your reactions are different. The younger [liberals] do not have the same feeling of urgency. There is no passion for substantive issues."[88] It should not be thought that as the result of these developments the Senate has been devoid of a strong and occasionally intransigent core of liberal members since the mid-1960s. The 20-vote roll call continued to be regarded as a great educative instrument. The crucial difference between the 20-vote group in the early 1970s and the liberal minorities of the earlier period is that they had contrasting objectives. While the old liberal minority groups used to press for new programs like medicare and educational aid, the later liberal groups tended to fit more into the concurrent majority framework by assuming the role of policy objectors. They would adopt intransigent positions and engage in filibusters in order to object to the maintenance of a policy (e.g., military budget) or to counter administration attempts to cut old liberal programs (e.g., busing).[89]

Nevertheless, it is true to say that the liberals were generally less averse to compromise in the 1970s than they used to be in the early and mid-1960s. They were more prepared to trade votes and to modify their positions. Even William S. White acknowledged this change in a recent interview: "The old and new liberals can be distinguished by the principle of compromise. The liberals in the late 1960s and early 1970s have not been so inflexible as the old liberal senators used to be. They have been pretty pragmatic and have moved around a bit."[90]

As has been seen, the liberals' more relaxed posture in the late 1960s was the result of a complex set of factors. Adverse political conditions, liberal defeats, the pragmatic approach of younger progressives, overachievement during the Great Society, and the growth of issues which combined both liberals and conservatives in an overall congressional framework (e.g., impoundment, executive privilege) all played a part. Not the least significant factor, however, was the liberals' own transformation in attitudes by which they learned to accept their past mistakes and to acknowledge the arguments of their opponents. They were no longer distracted by neuroses over senatorial discrimination or legislative ineffectiveness. As a result, they came down from the elevated plane of high principles and intransigent positions to the traditional Senate lowlands of intimate bargaining and infighting between equals—who know themselves to be equals. In contrast to their earlier detachment, the liberals had finally developed a genuine appreciation of the value and function of compromise.

SPECIALIZATION

In a chamber that provides plentiful opportunity for personal involvement and lengthy debate, the specialization folkway was valued by White and Matthews for reducing inputs and expediting the flow of legislative business.[91] By encouraging concern for and expertise in restricted fields of policy, this folkway was supposed to foster the type of specialized approach necessary to the efficient operation of the committee system. According to White and Matthews, a member's reputation and political leverage within the Senate would always be in inverse proportion to the number and variety of his legislative interests. In their view a senator was obliged to concentrate his "attention on the relatively few matters that [came] before his committees or that directly and immediately affect[ed] his state."[92] White and Matthews believed that only by members disciplining themselves in this way would the committee system remain efficient and the Senate continue to fulfill. its legislative obligations.

This view of the Senate was very much the product of the "end of ideology" era, in which comparatively few political issues were regarded as really urgent. Consequently, senators were free to concentrate their energies on one or two essentially limited areas of government. It was also a time when a larger number of problems and issues were peculiar to one state or a limited group of states. Therefore, a senator was expected to have expert knowledge of these specific problems and was generally given the opportunity to advance what he perceived to be the welfare of his home state.

During the 1960s and early 1970s this format of limited interests and specialization was transformed by a large increase in both the number and scale of political issues. Problems such as poverty, civil rights, housing, environmental protection, urban renewal, crime, and consumer rights were fully national issues which were apparent in most centers of population. As a result, all senators to some extent became generalists. In order to serve their increasingly large and complex constituencies, senators had to master a wide range of issues and to spread themselves over the full gamut of their state's problems. Senator Alan Cranston, for example, had the largest state in the union as his constituency and he found that "there was seldom a problem which did not concern California."[93]

But the pressure on senators was not solely the result of constituency interests. The overall enlargement of the government sector, the increase in Congress's oversight obligations, and the revival in congressional policy formulation after 1965 all created additional demands. The increase in the workload was reflected in the growth in the Senate's subcommittees. Whereas in 1959, 85 subcommittees existed in the Senate, by 1972 the number had increased to 116 (i.e., by 36.5 percent). Even more significant than the increase in subcommittees was the growth in the number of subcommittee places, which rose from 590 in 1959 to 903 in 1972 (i.e., by 53.1 percent). The irony was that, while the increase in subcommittees gave the impression of greater specialization, the limited membership of the Senate meant that individual members were, in fact, forced to diversify their interests and resources to a greater degree than before. Although the number of subcommittee assignments varied from members like John McClellan (17), Jacob Javits (16), Robert Byrd (15), Edward Kennedy (14), and Henry Jackson (4) to members like Abraham Ribicoff (2), Fred Harris (2), and William Fulbright (1), the fact remained that on average each member had nine distinct areas of responsibility within as many as three standing-committee jurisdictions. When select and joint committee assignments were taken into account, the contrast between the workload of a senator and a congressman with only one major committee assignment was even greater.

Despite this extra pressure, the tradition of developing specialized fiefdoms of knowledge for political ends remained a powerful force in the life of the Senate. Expertise based on committee jurisdictions continued to be recognized not only as a source of political leverage but as the foundation of leadership in most issue areas. Policy leaders still emerged from the relevant committees and subcommittees. The motivating force behind specialization was well described by Senator Proxmire's legislative assistant: "Concentrate on your committee area . . . become well versed in the subject matter. Pay no attention to apprenticeship but make an issue for yourself as quickly as possible."[94] This strategy was exactly what many liberals had in mind when they entered the Senate in the late 1950s and early 1960s. For this reason the Judiciary and the Labor and Public Welfare committees were particularly attractive, not just because of their subject areas but because it was well known that the chairmen (i.e., Eastland and Hill) were generous with subcommittee chairmanships and staff facilities. In these and other committees, many liberals quickly established themselves as proficient and influential figures in a number of specialized areas.[95]

However, a sizable proportion of the liberals undermined their internal status in specific fields by too often casting their eyes upon the treasured subject areas of other members. Traditional specialization had always been confined to one or two limited fields per member. Accordingly, the individual member was not obliged to immerse himself very deeply in the subject matter of all his subcommittees. After all, in the case of a senator like Jacob Javits, his official positions would have required an active interest in as many as 16 different fields of policy. It was generally accepted, therefore, that a senator permitted the subcommittees' senior members and staff to assume much of the day-to-day monitoring of the subject area. (The problem of overzealous attendance and interest was often resolved satisfactorily by the many clashes in committee schedules.[96]) In short, a senator had no real justification for broadening his area of personal commitment on the basis of official committee duties.

Although the Senate's workload undoubtedly increased in size and variety throughout the 1960s, the fact remained that the committee framework and the specialist convention generally succeeded in orienting members to the micro dimension. The exceptions to this rule were those members who were distracted by the galaxy of issues considered in the Senate. Such senators either failed to develop expertise in a particular field altogether (the "gadfly"), or else damaged their reputation in an initial area of competence by branching out into other policy fields and arousing interest in the public at large (the "national senator"). Although exceptions occurred, evidence suggests that gadflies and national senators were represented so strongly in the liberal group during the 1960s that the latter became almost synonymous with these two senatorial types.

The liberal gadfly never spent enough time and resources to commit himself to any one field. He preferred to move freely from issue to issue, arousing public concern, highlighting immediate problems, and attracting media attention. Included in the gadfly category were such members as Mike Gravel, William Proxmire, Fred Harris, and Charles Goodell. When Senator Gravel's legislative assistant described his boss's style in the following terms, he was in effect defining the role adopted by all the members mentioned above: "He is a fast mover. He is not regarded as a good soldier for a committee chairman. He pricks people's consciences. He is interested in almost all issues and channels his energy into this style. Gravel sees his own role as a gadfly; as an abrasive Senator."[97] Probably the best example of Gravel's abrasive style was when he ignored all advice to the contrary and plunged into the controversy of government secrecy by exposing unpublished and classified sections of the Pentagon Papers through his own Public Works Subcommittee on Public Buildings.[98] As Ralph Huitt has correctly pointed out, the maverick gadfly is a legitimate senatorial role with a fine pedigree stretching back at least to Robert LaFollette (1906–25). Nevertheless, this did not prevent other members—including fellow liberals—from being irritated by the activities of gadflies in highly controversial and sensitive areas. General opinion on the unrestrained and unpredictable style of the liberal gadfly was perhaps captured best by Senator McGee's legislative assistant, who was commenting on William Proxmire's active intervention in such diverse areas as taxation, consumer credit, housing, transportation, foreign aid, congressional reform, and military expenditure: "His attitude to legislation was like a man knocking in a bunch of nails with a hammer—once in a while and all over the place. He shot his mouth off but most people were not with him. Liberals were sympathetic to his causes but not with his methods."[99] Another less extreme but no less significant form of liberal generalism was the national senator, who developed a political base outside the chamber. Such members tended to specialize in distinct areas (e.g., Muskie in air and water pollution, McGovern in military expenditures and poverty, Kennedy in health), but they did not accept that their interests and activities should be limited to their committee responsibilities. A national senator saw himself as having a roving commission that permitted him to expand the area of his activism in response to personal interests and public demands. He was less concerned with cloakroom politics and internal status and more with publicizing issues, making direct appeals to national audiences, and mobilizing forces to pressure the government (including the Senate) into action. Although less unpredictable than the gadfly, the national senator nevertheless embraced a wide range of policy fields. In fact, it was their general competence in diverse problem areas and their established relationships with the outside groups that made national senators so attractive as presidential material during the 1960s and early 1970s.

Generalized activity, however, was not just confined to these two fairly distinctive types of liberal senator. Broad interest and commitment at the macro level were widely regarded as a characteristic common to almost all liberals. While the involvement of the rank-and-file liberal was not of the same order as the gadfly or the national senator, the fact remained that even the ordinary liberal member had the reputation of traversing his committee boundaries and encroaching on the preserves of his colleagues. In the words of one conservative aide: "Senators have only the sketchiest knowledge of subjects outside their committee specializations. Nothing annoys Senator Dole so much as to hear a non-expert on agriculture talking on *his* subject. Liberals are generally the guilty ones in this respect."[100] Many reasons exist for this distinctive style of operation. Some of them must evidently be derived from such elusive variables as personality traits and perceptions of constituency interest. However, it is possible to distinguish at least three factors that have had a profound impact on liberal attitudes and that have been closely related to the liberals' generalist strategy in the Senate.

First is the simple fact that the nature of liberal activism is inherently expansive. Concern in one field tends to lead onward and outward to concern in other areas. This macrodimensional interest is born out of the liberals' motivation to investigate issues and seek out areas of distress and injustice. Once immersed in these activities, the liberal soon recognizes that social problems are interrelated and that government action in one field will often be ineffective without action in others. Conservatives, on the other hand, "do not inject themselves into issues and future planning because they are still only interested in the best way of saying 'no'."[101] While the conservative has no real motivation to identify new problems, the liberals' desire for continued social improvement automatically extends his interests beyond his immediate committee responsibilities.

The second factor is based upon the liberals' early sense of ineffectiveness as a legislative force. The generalist posture of many of the liberals was fostered by their junior status and their minority position. The weakness that irritated the liberals most was their poor position in the committee system. As table 4.2 reveals, the liberals were not evenly distributed throughout the committee system in the 1960s.

The attraction of the three middle-ranking committees—Judiciary,

Table 4.2   Liberal Composition of the Senate's Standing Committees
in the Eighty-ninth Congress, 1965–66 (the median unit
in the 1959–72 period)

Committee	Size of the liberal component in the committee membership (%)
Labor and public welfare	56.2
Banking and currency	50.0
District of Columbia	42.9
Government operations	42.9
Public works	41.2
Judiciary	37.5
Interior and insular affairs	25.0
Finance	23.5
Commerce	22.2
Rules	22.2
Foreign relations	21.0
Aeronautical and space sciences	18.7
Post office and civil service	16.7
Agriculture and forestry	13.3
Armed services	11.8
Appropriations	7.4

Labor, and Banking—could be partly explained by their jurisdictional
fields, which embraced so many of the liberals' favored programs (e.g.,
civil rights, civil liberties, urban renewal, housing, welfare). In addition, the substantial liberal influence on these committees during the
first half of the 1960s tended to create its own momentum. While
liberals claimed that they were discriminated against in assignments
to high-status committees, they were nevertheless content to capitalize
upon their institutional strengths by progressively expanding their
membership levels on the three "liberal committees." In contrast to
liberals such as Proxmire, Hughes, and Douglas who fought solitary
campaigns in the Appropriations, Armed Services, and Finance committees, respectively, most liberals preferred to follow the pack and
to gravitate toward the established enclaves of liberal power in the
institution.

The concentration of liberals in a limited number of committees
may have maximized their political potential in one respect, but in
another respect it weakened their institutional position. This paradox

hinged upon the apparently conservative bias of the specialization folkway. While conservatives did not expect to be questioned or challenged in their stronghold areas of finance and foreign and military policy, they retained the right to criticize the conclusions of the strong liberal committees. The rationale underlying this double standard was the assertion made by conservatives that the subject matter of their committees was technical in nature, like that of the Post Office or Public Works committees. The jurisdiction of the Banking, Judiciary, and Labor committees, on the other hand, was overtly ideological in nature, and this enabled outsiders to dispute the committees' judgment on the basis of generalized attitudes about government and society. In effect, while the conservatives concealed their political bias behind the mystique of technical competence, they dismissed the expert knowledge of specialists in the civil rights and welfare fields on simple ideological grounds. By offering external aid and comfort to the conservative minority on these liberal committees, the conservatives not only fostered ideological conflict within the committees but undermined the committees' position in respect to the chamber as a whole.

Both Matthews and Fenno have acknowledged that the integration and subsequent prestige of the appropriations committees in particular benefited from the impression that a technical budgetary decision is noncontroversial.[102] In Fenno's view, an appropriations committee makes decisions on the same controversial issues as a legislative committee but a "money decision—however vitally it affects national policy—is, or at least seems to be, less directly a policy decision."[103] The conservatives exploited this fact not just by skillfully presenting financial, military, and foreign policy decisions as "apolitical" in nature, but in attributing the unity of their committees to the noncontroversial nature of the subject matter.

So the specialization folkway by which members limited themselves to a few constituency and committee matters was never quite complied with to the extent imagined and described by White and Matthews. Both the liberals and the conservatives operated on a broader front than custom prescribed. But it was the liberals who had the reputation of policy generalists, while the conservatives won respect as career specialists. The conservative seniors achieved this by running a closed shop in legislative expertise within their own "technical" committees at the same time that they declared areas such as civil rights and welfare to be fair game for any interested member.

The liberals realized that this double standard existed, but were either unwilling or unable to make a concerted effort to increase their seats in what were for the most part unspectacular and anonymous committees (Foreign Relations excepted).[104] Instead, they enhanced their reputation for generalism by adopting a strategy of floor challenges to the conservative committees. The liberals learned from past experience that they could not effectively argue with the Armed Services or Finance committees on the basis of generalized concepts about military policy or the tax structure. The subject may have been contentious, but it was also very complex—as the conservatives had always claimed. As a result, the liberals developed their own knowledge on subjects unrelated to their main committees and improved their relationships with outside groups and institutions that offered alternative sources of information. Ultimately, the liberals were able to offer their own proposals in such areas as military affairs (e.g., the anti-ballistic missile debate of 1969), foreign policy (troop commitments and bombing halts in Indo-China), budgetary procedures (revenue sharing, military procurement), and taxation (campaign finance, depletion allowances, student tax credits).

Such activities contributed to a generally less deferential attitude among senators toward the prestigious committees. Senator Edmund Muskie's legislative assistant summed up the mood: "The Finance and the Armed Services Committees had a stronger solidarity but even they were consistently opposed over defense spending and tax bills in the late 1960s and early 1970s; this reflected an overall erosion of structural discipline in the Senate."[105] In effect, the liberals had been forced to become proficient generalists in order to be in a position to give a liberal perspective to many areas of previously undisputed policy. They were not always successful on the floor with their counterproposals, but they were sufficiently effective to dispel some of the mystique of the military and financial fields and to force relevant committees to take account of new alternative centers of expertise.

The growth of national issues and the corresponding increase in the demand for national solutions represent the third factor in the diversification of liberal activities. It was the liberals who were particularly responsive to new or continuing social and economic problems, so much so in fact that a bandwagon effect often occurred whereby a number of senators claimed a new subject area for their own committees. By 1972 the wave of enthusiasm to fight pollution and protect the environment, for example, had led to a grand total of five environmental subcommittees.[106]

The inclination to respond to new problems, and to associate themselves personally with them, was so great that many liberals were led to expand the field of their formal committee responsibilities. In his position as chairman of the Subcommittee on Executive Reorganization, a unit of the Government Operations Committee, Senator Abraham Ribicoff, for example, exploited his brief to "study the operation of government activities at all levels with a view to determining its economy and efficiency" by holding hearings into controversial aspects of automobile safety. These nationally televised hearings were probably most noted for the dramatic confrontation between Ralph Nader and the management of General Motors, but their long-term significance lay more in the public pressure and support that the hearings mobilized in favor of improved safety regulations.[107]

Senator William Proxmire provided another example of what an activist could do with an apparently innocuous committee. As chairman of the little known Joint Economic Committee's Subcommittee on Economy in Government, Proxmire began a series of dramatic and controversial investigations into the cost overruns of weapon system projects in the late 1960s. He used this committee as a base from which to develop a highly sophisticated and damaging critique of the Pentagon's procedures for program estimates, cost control, procurement planning, and project testing.[108]

But probably the best example of an elastic jurisdiction is the Administration Practice and Procedure Subcommittee of the Judiciary Committee. Its official duty is to "make a full and complete study and investigation of administrative practices and procedures within the departments and agencies of the United States in the exercise of their rule-making, licensing, investigatory, law enforcement, and adjudicatory functions."[109] In effect, this charge gives the subcommittee a free rein over the procedures of the entire executive branch. When Edward Kennedy became its chairman, the ambiguity of the distinction between process and substance became evident. During the hearings on the efficiency of presidential commissions in 1971, Kennedy was presented with the opportunity not only to criticize the health commissions in general but the American Medical Association and the Nixon administration's position on improved health facilities in particular. An investigation into the procedure for imposing quotas on Canadian oil imports in 1970 provided the platform from which Kennedy publicly discussed the issues of energy, inflation, and consumer prices. Finally, in June 1972, the Kennedy subcommittee was the only committee prepared to investigate the Watergate burglary. It was not until January 1973 that the Select Committee under Senator Sam Ervin was formed, at which point the Kennedy subcommittee submitted all the information that it had collected in the case.[110]

Another aspect of the liberals' close relationship with the broader external framework of politics was their central role in the debate during the late 1960s and early 1970s over the question of priorities in national spending. With increased public awareness of the direct interrelationship among programs in terms of costs and resources, demands arose for adjustments in budgetary allocations. In contrast to the first half of the 1960s, programs and projects were viewed as demands within a framework of increasingly limited resources. A new defense system, therefore, was seen as directly responsible for a reduction in child care centers or in hospital construction. As a result, liberals became more restive about corporation immunities, tax privileges, and defense waste. Ultimately, their aim was to restrain the enormous inertia of the budget in order to effect a substantial readjustment in priorities and a significant redistribution of resources. Assisted by increased congressional staff and by powerful outside research groups such as Common Cause and Nader's Center for Study of Responsive Law, the liberals were able to develop a strong and independent basis of expertise with this overall aim in mind. Despite the inherent difficulties involved in budgetary redistribution, the liberals became sufficiently competent in defense strategy and foreign policy by the early 1970s to be a real thorn in the flesh of both the Nixon administration and the official congressional committees.[111]

In conclusion, it can be said that the liberals were distinctive in the scale of their concern and in the breadth of their commitments. The specialization folkway was always something of a mirage because it permitted conservative/"technical" specialists on financial and military affairs to intervene in the liberal/"nontechnical" subjects of civil rights and social welfare. In a way, the liberals just reversed the process. However, this reversal involved far more than the mere motivation to criticize the tax structure or the Pentagon. It necessitated the development of a hard core of real expertise and a high level of commitment. In this way the liberals combined their competence in traditionally liberal issues with a newly acquired expertise in the more complex fields of financial and military policy. The net result was a "broader base of knowledge" that reflected "the liberals' broader base of interest and concern."[112]

While the liberal was always probably more of a generalist than the conservative, the difference between them became progressively less sharp during the 1960s. As society in every state became more complex, the old limited-interest conservatives could no longer survive by simply attending to their states' key industries (cattle, corn, textiles, etc.). In the late 1960s and early 1970s the conservatives were having to acknowledge the heterogeneity of their states and to recognize the relationship between their economies and national economic problems such as energy and inflation. Like the liberals, the conservatives were also having to accustom themselves to government programs so complex in nature that they had to be administered by a variety of departments at a variety of governmental levels. In this context, conservative senators were increasingly drawn into political, economic, and administrative fields that were wider than most conservatives were accustomed to operating in. Although the liberals in the early 1970s still had the reputation for possessing broader-based and more diversified interests, their conservative colleagues had also made a significant contribution toward developing the Senate into a body which, in Fenno's words, combined "high participation with low specialization."[113]

LEGISLATIVE WORK AND INSTITUTIONAL LOYALTY

As the folkways of legislative and institutional loyalty are so strongly related, it is appropriate to examine them together. These two folkways provided the hallmarks of the authentic senatorial type, for they not only prescribed what a member's primary legislative role should have been but determined the direction that his political career ought to have followed.

According to White and Matthews, each senator was obliged to concentrate most of his time on the "highly detailed, dull, and politically unrewarding"[114] activities of lawmaking. By applying himself to these largely anonymous activities, the member would win respect and status where it mattered to White and Matthews—within the chamber.[115] Popular appeals or highly publicized work were acceptable only as long as they truly reflected a senator's status in the Senate and as long as they did not interfere with the member's primary obligation of hard legislative work. Those members who persistently courted public attention, therefore, were not approved of, even though their activities might be well supported outside. The difference in publicity coverage between senators led, in Matthews' words, to "a puzzling disparity between the prestige of senators inside and outside the Senate."[116]

The traditional Senate distrusted its highly publicized members not only because they disturbed the cloistered deliberations of the institution, but because they were suspected of having higher ambitions. According to White and Matthews, the true Senate type regarded the institution as "a career in itself, a life in itself and an end in itself."[117] White and Matthews both acknowledged that an authentic senator would be so committed to the institution's corporate interests that he would view his own career as secondary to its reputation and position. His affinity to the Senate would lead him to recognize the presidency as an office wholly foreign to the Senate because of its northern orientation, its basis of simple majority rule, and, in White's words, its proclivity for "always tinkering about with things that might well be left alone."[118] The true senator, therefore, would have no desire to sacrifice his position in the Senate to seek elevation to an institution that was traditionally alien to the upper chamber.

According to White, the public recognition of such Senate celebrities as Richard Russell, Robert Taft, and Lyndon Johnson was won through solid legislative achievement. The notoriety of Senators Douglas, Clark, and Morse, on the other hand, was purely the result of their publicized nonconformity with the Senate's policy positions and with the institution's traditional forms of activity. The conservative bias of the Senate was quite evident in this aspect of internal and external prestige. As the liberals were not only in a minority but usually constituted a junior group of members, their position both inside and outside the Senate should have been one of quiet and hardworking anonymity. It was only the senior senators and the committee barons who were legitimately entitled to publicity, as they alone were capable of achieving legislative results in the relatively centralized Senate of the 1950s. Accordingly, any liberal exposure represented a short-circuiting of the established power relationships and resulted in public reputations that were automatically out of proportion to the senators' institutional muscle.

With the greater diffusion of Senate power in the 1960s, the liberals had increased opportunity to participate in the legislative process and to build solid legislative records. Despite these developments, the liberals still retained their reputation as members who did not commit themselves totally to the institution or to its primary function of legislation and oversight.

First is the simple point of attendance. Because of their outside interests and obligations, liberals were more likely than other members to be unavailable for committee meetings, party caucuses, or floor votes. During the Ninety-second Congress (1971–72), for example, three conservatives were absent for more than 25 percent of all roll calls. The number of liberals with a similar attendance rate was eight, six of whom had worse attendance figures than the most absent conservative.[119] The absenteeism of some liberals caused severe problems to their colleagues who were endeavoring to pass legislation through the Senate. Senator Alan Cranston, one of the liberal organizers in the Senate, experienced the effects of this absenteeism at first hand: "We have lost a lot of votes by small margins because of a lack of attendance by liberals; attendance has always been very tough to achieve with liberals because they have wanted to be elsewhere."[120]

Associated with their attendance rate was the liberals' reputation for not applying themselves fully to their committee responsibilities. In a recent interview, William S. White gave the traditional conservative viewpoint: "A Senator used to need a capacity for committee work. Senators did not rush around going to television shows. Today there is too much clamor and too many not doing their homework."[121] The notion that liberals refused to immerse themselves in the detailed and often mundane grind of committee work was widespread on Capitol Hill during the 1960s. Liberals were not regarded as committee team members because they were unwilling to devote themselves to achieving a thorough comprehension of the subject matter or to protecting the jurisdictional fiefdoms of their committees. Even some liberals accepted this point. According to Senator Claiborne Pell: "Conservatives do not move about the country so much; they are closer to the Senate. Conservatives have their noses a little more to the grindstone than the liberals."[122] While the liberals received much of the publicity, it was the conservative "workhorses" who were usually the most successful in terms of actual legislative achievement and internal power. Thus a strong disparity existed between the prestige of liberals outside the Senate and the reputation of liberals within the institution.

Another complaint concerning the liberals' lack of commitment to legislative work was that they had undermined the Senate's status as a great debating chamber. Because of their orientation toward the public and their interest in diverse issue areas, the liberals were thought by some to be not only personally unable to debate a subject in depth, but unwilling to regard the floor debate with the same respect as the conservatives. For example, liberals were reputed to have started the practice of issuing press releases of pending Senate speeches—and of changing the content in response to editorial comment. Liberals were also reputed to have begun bringing large numbers of staff members onto the floor for information and advice during Senate debates.[123] Whether or not liberals were solely responsible for these changes, the impression remains that the standard of Senate debate deteriorated over Senate's liberal era in the 1960s. By the early 1970s most members were prepared to concede what they had been reluctant to admit before, that, in Senator Gaylord Nelson's words, "the Senate [was] no longer a very good debating body . . . and certainly not the greatest deliberative body in the world."[124]

While the complaints over the liberals' legislative diligence were legion, perhaps the most intense criticism leveled against the liberals concerned their open quest for higher office. To many, presidential ambition and all the related aspects of national politics both encapsulated and emphasized all the worst features of liberal behavior inside the Senate.

When White issued his "unwritten law of politics . . . that being Senatorial all but disqualifie[d] a man to be Presidential,"[125] he based it upon the known commitment of the southern Democrats and the conservative Republicans to the Senate. Their adherence to the norm that a Senate career should be an end in itself was unremarkable

simply because the Senate was the highest electoral office that any
southern Democrat or conservative Republican was ever likely to
attain. Self-interest therefore assisted the "authentic" senator to recognize the presidency as an office of intemperate innovation, presidential ambition as an open rejection of the Senate, and presidential
campaigning as a vulgar distraction from legislative obligations and
responsibilities. Difficulties arose over senators like Lyndon Johnson,
Richard Russell, Robert Taft, and Barry Goldwater, who all made
attempts on the presidency from the vantage point of the Senate.
White dismissed these exceptions by the rather tortuous and uncon-
vincing rationalization that they regarded the presidency "as only
another and not as really a *higher* ambition."[126] A lesser but more
significant defense, however, was the fact that these notable senators
"did not campaign in a frenetic way . . . and did not allow the campaign to interfere with their Senate work."[127] This is an important
qualification and one that cannot generally be applied to liberal senators who have sought the presidency. It was in this particular aspect
of style and tactics that the liberal aspirants engendered most irritation among their colleagues.

Such were the demands of presidential campaigning in the 1960s
and early 1970s that the many liberal runners were forced to spend
a good deal of time away from the Senate. In 1972, which was a
vintage year for presidential politics in the Senate, the average attendance rate for roll calls was 82.2 percent. The average attendance
for the main liberal contenders for the White House, on the other
hand, was 40.5 percent. They were:

George McGovern	—	22 percent
Hubert Humphrey	—	53 percent
Fred Harris	—	39 percent
Edmund Muskie	—	48 percent

These figures do not compare very favorably with the liberal-to-moderate candidate (Henry Jackson, 75 percent), or with the attendance
rate of Lyndon Johnson in 1960 (95 percent).[128]

The widely publicized activities and policy positions of the presidential hopefuls did tend to create internal stress on the esprit de
corps of the Senate. Ordinary members became suspicious of the
motives behind aspirants' proposals, less prepared to support aspirants
in their legislative ventures, and jealous of their public esteem. In
Senator Abraham Ribicoff's words: "Senators always tend to under-

estimate the ability of their colleagues to be President. Political egos are aroused when a colleague becomes a Presidential hopeful. The reaction is—'I am better than that guy'."[129] Perhaps the best example of a "prophet not being without honor except in his own land" was Edward Kennedy. An archetypal national politician and a perennial chunk of presidential timber, Kennedy nevertheless lost the majority whip position in 1971 after only two years precisely because he had spent so much time away from the Senate and too little time attending to the mundane activities of scheduling, vote counting, and party mobilization. The public celebrity who did not do his "homework" was replaced by the anonymous and respected member who did— Robert Byrd.[130]

While many liberal senators continued to strive for the ultimate elevation to the White House, it is probably true to say that by the early 1970s a majority of their fellow liberals were becoming increasingly irritated by their extramural activities. The additional workload, the loss of votes, and the generation of intraparty conflict were beginning to take their toll. In the secret vote on Kennedy's post, for example, it was thought that a number of his liberal colleagues had turned against him on the simple grounds of dereliction of duty.[131] The liberals who tended to stay at home in the Senate had begun to develop an appreciation of legislative work and institutional commitment. Their heroes were not so much George McGovern and Edward Kennedy, but Philip Hart, Walter Mondale, Alan Cranston, and Lee Metcalf, who were not well known to the public yet were four of the most influential liberal members in the institution. Their success was due not so much to strong official positions but to their willingness to act as full-time members and to work quietly and competently with their Republican and Democratic colleagues. They were always available, they did their homework, they had numerous contacts with other senators, and they were highly respected. Even the unlikely figure of William Proxmire was praised by colleagues for his record of not having missed a roll call from 1965 to 1972.[132]

This did not mean that a deep cleavage existed in the liberal ranks between the presidential contenders and the liberal workhorses. It was that a majority of the liberal members had come to acknowledge that the old folkways of legislative work and institutional loyalty did possess some functional value after all.

Given the Senate's comparatively centralized format and its conservative disposition during the 1950s, White and Matthews believed that the independent behavior of many liberal senators was an indication of their fundamental political incongruity with the institution and a reflection of their social ostracism from the Senate's culture. The two writers saw no reason to suppose that things would change. The conservative establishment was in a position to fulfill its own assertion that the inherent role and philosophy of the Senate was fundamentally conservative. It controlled the recruitment of leaders to the party hierarchy and to the prestigious committees. It also defended the Senate's traditions that preserved the institution's operational style and not least the form of its political structure. It was these traditions that stimulated a most profound reaction among the liberal members, for they believed that the Senate's well-known customs were directly related to the institution's more private network of personal status, internal reputation, and collegiate influence. According to many disaffected liberals, it was this network of individual relationships that represented the foundation of the more visible superstructure of formal party and committee power. Most liberals felt that they had only two alternatives. Either they could acquiesce in the politically charged process of socialization, or withdraw and face the isolation preserved for any declared nonparticipant in the pluralist framework of congressional politics. Most selected varieties of the latter option and dissociated themselves from the folkways and thereby from the Senate as a whole.

When the elections of the late 1950s and the early 1960s converted the handful of liberal dissidents into a substantial group of legislators, the attitudes of the liberals became that much more significant. Initially, the liberals confirmed predictions and reacted indiscriminately against the folkways. They criticized the apprenticeship norm as an overt form of conservative socialization. The folkways of specialization and compromise were perceived to be politically biased in operation because the conservative seniors applied them selectively in favor of their own objectives. The liberals also reacted against the folkways of legislative work, institutional loyalty, and in some respects, courtesy. All three customs appeared to the liberals to be intrinsically conservative in effect, for they resulted in a functionally limited institution that remained insulated from national political trends and divorced from the democratic and progressive centers of political power.

The liberals' early disenchantment with the folkways generated the long-lasting impression that the liberals were radical nonconformists who had permanently undermined the Senate's code of honor. Although it is true that the large liberal classes of the late 1950s and early 1960s effectively disabused the elders of their expectations of freshman humility and self-restraint, the liberals by no means proved to be as iconoclastic as they were sometimes portrayed. The strident tone of their impatience tended to become less strident and less impassioned with the passing of each year in the 1960s. Even by the middle of the decade they had become far less aggressive toward the institution's cultural norms. By the end of the 1960s, the liberals had begun not only to rediscover the value of some of the folkways, but to assess colleagues in traditional terms.

This fundamental shift in attitudes was caused by a number of factors. First, the liberals lost their self-consciousness as a minority of purposely disadvantaged freshmen. As the number of liberal seats progressively increased, as the liberals' seniority ratings rose, and as their representation in the party organizations grew, the liberals were divested of the stimulus of their earlier neurosis over being systematically excluded from the Senate's mainstream.

Second, death, retirement, and electoral defeat decreased the number of conservative elders and further undermined the influence of the conservative coalition in the Senate.

Third, as liberals became increasingly compartmentalized into the committee system, they became less interested in wholesale reform of the internal distribution of power. While the liberal normally remained more generalist in his policy interests than did the conservative, he nevertheless developed a protective instinct toward his committee fiefdom and the specialized subject matter that lay in its jurisdiction.

Fourth, the passage of so much liberal legislation in the 1960s made the liberals less convinced that a conservative conspiracy was in operation or that the Senate was inherently hidebound by its rules, precedents, and customs.

Fifth, and possibly related to the development of the liberals' integration within the Senate, was the notion of liberal attitudes toward the institution and the conservatives mellowing with time and experience. Inside knowledge of the need for good personal relationships with opposing groups combined with liberal–conservative friendships, committee responsibilities and loyalties, a developed appreciation of opposition arguments, a disillusionment with the effects of reform, and an embarrassment over the costs and defects of past liberal programs all contributed to the experienced liberal becoming more accommodating and less intransigent in his attitudes.

Sixth, the liberals elected since the late 1960s experienced neither the stimulus of a conservative establishment nor the early optimism of liberal programs. Having already realized the failures and expense of the Great Society policies before they entered the Senate, they arrived in Washington more skeptical and less committed than the earlier classes of liberal zealots.

Seventh, liberal senators were strongly associated with the controversial Great Society programs, they were becoming increasingly responsible for their continuation and improvement, and they were simultaneously adopting the even more sensitive role of war critics. The delicate nature of the liberals' field of operations no doubt contributed to the more cautious and more circumspect posture that they adopted in the late 1960s.

Finally, the liberal impulse in the mid-1960s was to create as strong a link as possible between the traditionally insulated and independent Senate and a progressively inclined presidency. Many liberal senators ran for the presidency, as this office appeared to be the focal point for the national progressive wing of the Democratic party. In the early 1970s, however, many Senate liberals began to react against the presidency and the presidential aspirants inside the Senate. The latter tended to irritate their fellow liberals by encroaching on their specialist jurisdictions, by excessively personalizing issues, and by absenting themselves from the chamber. By the early 1970s, liberals were criticizing liberal presidential aspirants in traditional folkway terms for failing to do their homework, for being too general in their interests, and for not being committed to their senatorial obligations. As for the presidency itself, many liberals had reacted against the office so strongly that by 1972 they were invoking the classical notion of greater senatorial independence from the White House. Political detachment and a distinct institutional culture, which were such outmoded notions in the mid-1960s, had begun to be reinstated in the 1970s by liberals who had originally denounced the cleavage between the presidency and the Senate.

After a period of hostility toward the folkways, therefore, the liberals gradually developed a new appreciation of compromise, legislative diligence, specialization, and institutional loyalty. Of course, these folkways were now different in interpretation and in effect. Since the liberals had already undermined apprenticeship, diversified individual responsibilities, exploited cloture, and generally increased participation, Senate life was far more flexible and informal than it had been in the 1950s. Nevertheless, most of the folkways survived in a modified, yet identifiable form. They were now more qualified expectations of behavior than politically charged cultural prescriptions. Absenteeism, generalism, intransigence, and personal ambition were all tolerated more than before, but they were still forms of behavior that were expected to be moderated for the good of the chamber.

In the 1970s, the folkways became commonly interpreted once again as adjuncts to the corporate identity of the Senate as an institution. It is in this respect that the liberals' greater receptivity toward the folkways is significant, for it demonstrated that it was possible for a young Turk to be transformed from a committed liberal to a hybrid figure in which political liberalism became combined with institutional conservatism (e.g., Harrison Williams, Hubert Humphrey, Frank Moss, Philip Hart, Walter Mondale, George McGovern). The liberals may have moderated the folkways, but they were also influenced by them. They came to appreciate their functional value and to perceive that institutional tradition need not necessarily be related to political conservatism.

Matthews and White, therefore, were both wrong and right. They were incorrect in supposing that liberals would always be led to challenge all the folkways all the time. They were wrong in thinking that the folkways were necessarily conservative in content and in effect. And they did not foresee that it was possible for the liberals to influence the operation of the folkways. Despite these deficiencies, White and Matthews were accurate in emphasizing the durability of much of the Senate's system of values and its general life-style. Maybe the form of the folkways in the 1970s was not quite what White would have wished for or Matthews would have predicted, but their general form was still distinguishable. Certainly, the Senate had retained its intimate atmosphere, its group identity, and its clublike spirit, which continued to temper the effects of indiscipline or intransigence by its tone of quiet persuasion, discreet bargaining, and private accommodation.

5   The Liberals as
a Legislative Force

We have already noted how the influx of liberal members undermined one old Senate tradition and modified others. The liberals initially rejected most of the folkways but then found that they were not necessarily conservative in nature or deficient in functional value to the legislative process. After addressing ourselves to the relationship between the liberals and the institutional culture, it remains to study the relationship between the liberals and the system of internal power.

According to White and Matthews, a symbiosis existed between the Senate's indigenous culture and its internal power structure which perpetuated both the conservative tenor and policy bias of the institution. In this context, liberals were to remain in peripheral and ineffectual positions. We have already noted that, contrary to White and Matthews's expectations, liberals readily gained positions of formal power and quickly accumulated seniority in the period of high membership turnover during 1958–64. Indeed, the accession to internal power probably contributed to the mellowing of liberal attitudes toward some of the folkways. However, individual advancement within the committee structure did not give the liberals parity with the conservatives' traditional skill. Just because the formal power of individual liberals had increased, this did not necessarily mean that the liberal group was more than a composite of middle-level but isolated committee members. On the contrary, the centrifugal nature of Senate politics raised the whole question of whether the conservative group was still the only force that could operate effectively in the Senate. Its impulse to oppose was perhaps the only generating force that could neutralize the inherent diffusion of power within the Senate. In this context White and Matthews's notion of a natural affinity between conservatives and the Senate's rationale of objection and reassessment could still have been as valid in the liberal 1960s as it appeared to be in the 1950s.

While the voting study revealed the existence of a liberal group that tended to vote together, it could not give any information on whether the liberals represented a coherent and integrated group that made its presence felt both before and after roll calls. Legislators do not live by voting alone, and roll calls do not account for all the available information on legislative activity. Although voting may be the final act on a proposal, it does not necessarily represent the climax of a legislative operation or present an accurate assessment of the political skills possessed by the groups involved. Roll-call analysis cannot distinguish a spontaneous collection of voters from a conscious and organized bloc of members. No matter how systematic a pure voting study may be, it cannot discriminate between legislators who just respond to presented questions and those who organize themselves into a parliamentary force, engage in prevote bargaining, and actually affect the terms in which a question is put to the chamber. This is certainly the case in the voting study presented in chapter 3, for while a liberal group was apparent in the voting figures, no evidence was produced to show whether or not the liberals had overcome the centrifugal forces of Senate politics and become an internal unit of political leverage.

It is the purpose of this chapter to discover whether the liberals' voting unity was matched by an ongoing political unity. It will not only study the form and style of the cooperation among liberal members, but will examine the ways in which the Senate both stimulates and deters group cohesion. In its aim to provide an assessment of how adept the liberals were in maintaining a strong basis of support, the chapter will examine the degree to which the liberals developed such key attributes as (1) group identity, (2) internal communications, (3) group mobilization, and (4) group organization.[1]

GROUP IDENTITY

In the House of Representatives a number of liberals formed an organization called the Democratic Study Group (DSG) in an attempt to counteract several of the classic deficiencies inherent in the congressional system.[2] Party disunity, committee fragmentation, poor leadership techniques, weak channels of communication, inadequate methods of mobilization, inconsistent and ambiguous guidance, and limited access to leadership groups all contributed to the atmosphere of dissatisfaction among the liberal northerners, who found that they were persistently unable "to marshal the potential forces that they did have"[3] in the House. When these perennial defects of congressional life were combined with an observed lack of internal power and a perceived conservative bias in the institution, the stimulus was complete, and during the mid-1950s liberal northern Democrats organized themselves into a mutually consultative grouping. As the DSG developed into a permanent organization with regular procedures, staff assistants, and a whip system, it could sometimes assume the position of a "countervailing force to committee or party loyalty."[4] To many, the DSG represented a model of what could be achieved by the liberals in the Senate. Indeed, a number of congressmen and senators expected that a comparable organization would be formed in the upper chamber after the 1958 elections.[5] But while the political conditions may have appeared similar to those in the House of Representatives, the Senate's internal structure and culture were sufficiently dissimilar to deter most efforts at creating a DSG-style organization among its membership.

The Senate was a smaller and more intimate chamber than the House of Representatives. With a memberhip less than one-fourth that of the House, the potential level of personal interaction among senators was much higher. The access of members to one another was facilitated by the committee system, which involved as many as 17 standing committees (i.e., only 3 less than the House). Although the committees were smaller in size, individual assignments were more numerous because of the shortage of available senators. The intimacy of the Senate compared to the House can be seen in table 5.1 In this table personal interaction means simply the number of contacts a member of either the Senate or the House had with other members of the same chamber through the medium of his committees.

Table 5.1   Personal Interaction in Senate and House through Committee Memberships (1972)

	Senate	House
Average membership per committee	14.6	31.9
Average number of committee assignments per member	2.5	1.5
Average degree of personal interaction	33.7	47.6
Average degree of personal interaction as a percentage of the total membership	33.7%	10.9%

It can be seen from the table that while the average senator was acquainted with fewer colleagues (33.7) through his committee work than was a congressman (47.6), the level of interaction was, in fact, proportionately greater. The individual congressman was likely to mix with nearly 11 percent of the House membership through his committee duties, whereas the senator came to know nearly one-third of the Senate through comparable committee activities. Even allowing for the greater likelihood that a senator would meet the same colleague on more than one committee, the level of formal interrelationship within the Senate was still very high. On the surface this appeared to provide an excellent environment for group formation and integration.

In spite of the intimate atmosphere and the close proximity of members to each other, senators were nevertheless reluctant to incorporate personal talents and influence into effective group organization. In some ways this was due to the fissiparous tendencies inherent in congressional politics—constituency pressures, committee compartmentalization, party weakness, seniority system, and so on. The DSG demonstrated, however, that such conditions were by no means insuperable barriers to some rudimentary group mobilization. But what existed in the upper chamber and not in the House, and which the DSG never had to contend with, was the Senate's tradition of maximum individual discretion.

Ironically, the phenomenon of individual atomization was in part caused by the high level of personal interaction within the Senate. Given the large number of committee assignments and the high rate of committee obligations, some senators tended to retreat to the relaxed privacy of their inner offices whenever possible. A certain "tower block" mentality existed in the Senate which caused members to exploit all available opportunities for excluding themselves from any additional exposure to the variegated demands and cross-pressures of life outside in the congested corridors and cloakrooms. Eugene McCarthy, for example, is statistically ranked among the liberal group, yet he was a member who preferred to keep his colleagues at arm's length and who delegated as much of his legislative work as possible to his staff assistants.[6] There are other cases of senators who found that they had neither the time nor the motivation to mix much with members who were not on their committees. For example, when George McGovern nominated Thomas Eagleton as his vice-presidential candidate in 1972, it was revealed that they did not know each other well. They were both members of the Senate Democratic party but because they belonged to separate committees, the two senators had in fact conversed together on only one occasion—and this conversation took place in the Senate steam bath.[7] The excessive and diversified workload of a senator fostered a counterbalance of individual detachment in a way that was quite foreign to the congressman, whose work and loyalty were focused on one career committee.

Senators were aware that they personified the sovereign entities of the several states, and never made serious attempts to substitute anonymous collaboration for personal activism. On the contrary, the Senate not only gave each of its members a certain individual rarity value, but actively encouraged individual political expression. The senatorial cult of personality flourished in an environment that accommodated maximum participation and tolerated nongermane and unlimited debate. Whereas congressmen needed to form into groups in order to be heard above the throng, a senator had only to rise from his desk to address the floor. In Garry Wills's words: "[P]ower in the House of Representatives is agglutinative; but the senators like to open up interstellar spaces, pushing each other off with mutually adoring gaze."[8] While the House sported the Chowder and Marching Society, the DSG, the Black Caucus, the Boll Weevil group, various state delegations, and its assorted breakfast and prayer groups, the Senate regarded itself as a single corporate club in which the formation of permanent and highly organized subgroups appeared to be both unnecessary and unseemly.

Even attempts to strengthen the party structures had to be carefully qualified by assurances that reforms would not reduce the discretion of the individual senator. In William Proxmire's famous address on the need to improve the operation of the Democratic caucus, for example, he had to go to such lengths to allay the fears of senators who sensed a restriction of freedom that he virtually contradicted his own arguments. After declaring the desperate need for an effective and representative party caucus, he went on to state that such an organization ought not to restrict senatorial discretion. "In no way do I mean to imply or to suggest that this [a reformed caucus] would entail submission of the individual Senator's conscience to the will of the majority of the caucus. . . . I want to emphasize my deep conviction that the primary, fundamental responsibility of an elected representative must be to his own conscience."[9] Proxmire's difficulty was by no means unique in a chamber so fluid and informal in its organization. In relation to the Senate, the House appeared to be a tightly structured and centralized unit. While it seemed that no man was an island in the House, the Senate looked like an archipelago. In the words of Senator Philip Hart's legislative assistant: "There was a strong tendency for each Senator's office to be a law unto itself; Senators valued their freedom of movement and protected it."[10]

It was precisely because party and committee allegiances were so weak that unofficial and informal groupings appeared to have so much potential in the Senate. Such forms of cooperation seemed not only the most viable method of collective enterprise but in many ways the only form possible within the Senate. It is in this respect that the liberals were consistently viewed as just the type of ideological and programmatic group that might override the debilitating effects of congressional decentralization, constituency distraction, and senatorial individualism. The levels of optimism and expectation were in fact so high that many people believed that the liberals did actually operate as a cohesive legislative bloc in the Senate. Certainly, the Senate liberals became so deeply embedded in journalistic terminology that at first sight they appeared to be a more conscious and organized a group than the DSG. On closer examination, however, the liberals had a very mixed record in overcoming the centrifugal forces of congressional politics.

Even after the 1958 election, when the liberal group was probably at its most self-conscious because of its minority and junior role, no unified and coordinated bloc of liberal members existed. The liberals were highly enthusiastic over the opportunity to present a clear alternative program to the Eisenhower administration, but they were also frustrated over their inability to project themselves effectively as a legislative force. Much of the blame for this was attributed to the majority leader, who preferred party unity to liberal integration and pragmatic negotiation to provocative assertion. Lyndon Johnson's determination to avoid contentious issues, to keep his party's ranks closed, and to achieve limited but solid legislative results produced widespread complaints from the liberals, who demanded bold proposals and uncompromising tactics (see chapter 2). The liberals came to regard the Senate itself as a major political issue and accordingly pressed for reforms in the Senate rules, the policy and steering committees, and the party leadership.[11] But even with the additional stimulus of perceived discriminatory practices against them, the liberals still found it difficult to operate as a unit.

For example, the liberals failed to fulfill their potential level of support for the crucial cloture reform campaign in 1959. Under the direction of Paul Douglas, the liberals attempted to amend the cloture rule, which at that time stated that the votes of two-thirds of the membership (67) were necessary to close debate. The Douglas amendment proposed that cloture be invoked when a majority of the membership (51) demanded it. This liberal measure, however, did not even secure the support of all the liberals. Hartke and Young voted against the rest of their colleagues.[12] The Johnson–Dirksen compromise, which offered cloture whenever two-thirds of those members actually present occurred, divided the liberals to an even greater degree. The liberals were hopelessly split between voting for a minor improvement and registering their disapproval by voting with the southern Democratic opposition. Ultimately, the measure passed the Senate by 72 to 22, with the liberals divided 5 to 12.[13]

When Johnson left the Senate and the Democrats recaptured the presidency, the liberals still found themselves unable to combine on a regular and systematic basis. Indeed, the absence of the Texas impressario served only to confirm that the liberals were not immune to the myriad distractions of senatorial politics. The conditions of the 1960s appeared to favor the formation of a liberal group; but not even a Democratic administration, a weaker majority leader, a greater number of liberals, an increase in their seniority, and a growth in public support were sufficient to overcome the many diversions that members traditionally experienced in the Senate.

Innumerable reasons exist to explain why a liberal might be deterred from combining with his fellow liberal members. Committee loyalties, pleas or threats from party leaders, an approaching election, local party commitments, different perceptions of legislative roles, personality clashes, vulnerable seats, and so on, can all be sources of stress and strain within an outwardly homogeneous group. Constituency interests, for example, could be a particularly important focus of senatorial commitment. Contrary to popular impression, liberal senators were not national ideologues, especially resistant to provincial concerns. Like any other senator, the liberal was well aware that his constituency represented his political base and he knew that he might be forced to compromise his principles when a legislative measure was unequivocally related to his state's major interests.

George McGovern, for example, consistently supported the liberal position in the major issue areas of the era, including the reduction of tariff barriers. In 1964, however, constituency interests were clearly in conflict with his declared position on free trade. The importation of beef was damaging South Dakota's beef industry, and this led McGovern to compromise his earlier stand on free trade. He felt obliged to protect one of his state's major industries by pressing successfully for stricter controls on beef imports.[14] Another case is provided by Wisconsin, the home of both the American dairy industry and William Proxmire, the arch foe of military waste and overspending. In 1960, the Navy proposed to amend the Naval Ration Act of 1902, which stipulated that each serviceman had to be supplied with 1.6 ounces of table butter per day. The Navy wanted to save $1 million in the military budget by introducing a one-third margarine component into the prescribed ration. Although Proxmire would normally have been an enthusiastic supporter of any such cut, he deferred to constituency interests in this case and led a successful move against the amendment inside the Senate.[15]

Constituency interests represent the Achilles heel of every senator, and some local pressures are more embarrassing than others. Whereas few have heard of McGovern's and Proxmire's "local difficulties," it is well known that southern progressives such as Fulbright, Kefauver, Yarborough, and Gore were not able to give such enthusiastic support to civil rights as to many other equally controversial causes. Liberals from oil-rich states (Gravel of Alaska, Harris of Oklahoma) were similarly embarrassed by the need to join the conservatives over the "gut" issue of the oil depletion allowance. Gun control was another national issue that stimulated wide interest at the constituency level and tended to split the liberal ranks. The 1968 Kennedy amendment prohibiting the interstate mail-order sale of rifles and shotguns, for example, was generally supported by liberals from the eastern urban states. But for those liberals from the West (e.g., Metcalf of Montana, Moss of Utah, Morse of Oregon) and the Midwest (e.g., Proxmire of Wisconsin, Bayh of Indiana, Hart of Michigan, McGovern of South Dakota, Nelson of Wisconsin) constituency sensitivity over the traditional right to bear arms was seemingly sufficient to override any concern for the urban crime wave or for the possibility of future assassinations.[16]

While constituency interests represented a powerful distraction, they were not the only significant factor in the liberal group's internal tensions. Conditions inside the Senate itself were as much to blame as pressures from outside. Apart from the more dramatic incidents of liberal disruption such as Proxmire's precipitous and divisive attack on the party leadership, much of the liberals' disunity was due to the more consistently debilitating features of Senate life. The sheer scale of the workload placed on members, for example, left little time and resources for regular group activities. Senator Philip Hart, in particular, regarded the pressure of legislative work as a key factor in the failure of even a DSG-like organization to materialize in the Senate. When he arrived in 1959, Hart was optimistic that a stable consultative group of liberals was a feasible undertaking, but as other commitments increased, so the enthusiasm for extra legislative activities declined: "The more work we got the less likely we came to ask each other things, and how we could be spending our time as constructively as we could. At the beginning we used to have talks and meetings about it every few days, but then it became every week and then every month. It gradually died out by the inescapable day to day chores. People would begin not to show up."[17] An additional feature of Senate life that also tended to cause disarray among the liberal ranks was the increased incidence of senators with presidential aspirations. By 1972 nearly one-half of the liberal group had been recognized in one form or another as presidential material.[18] Senator Lee Metcalf, who was one of the founders of the DSG when he was a congressman, regarded this development as the *chief* cause of the liberals' failure to organize a DSG in the Senate. In Metcalf's words: "Kennedy, Mondale, Muskie and Jackson were analogous to the DSG, but they were prevented from acting as a group because of their Presidential aspirations. Just look at how many of the liberals are or have been running for President. Cooperative effort is hampered by each of them trying to get ahead of the other."[19] Unfortunately, the ramifications of the rivalry between presidential hopefuls was not confined to the relationship between the immediate contenders. The efforts that members with White House wanderlust made to distinguish themselves from one another tended to generate a sense of suspicion and distrust between

themselves and the nonpresidential liberals. Since the latter did not
"want to be led down the primrose path by a senator running for the
Presidency,"[20] they tended to be very cautious in their commitment
to those plans and projects proposed by colleagues running for that
office.

While all these aspects of Senate life were relevant to the liberals'
problems in group organization, the fundamental difficulty was that
of senatorial individualism. The Senate's diminutive membership, its
idiosyncratic form of representation, its aristocratic heritage, its tradition of concurrent majority, its accommodation of individual positions, and its custom of unlimited and nongermane debate all supported an institutional culture that centered upon personal discretion
and individual participation. While the House liberals formed the
DSG to provide a degree of compensation for the deficiencies in
organized communications and guidance, the Senate liberals continued to revel in the confused fluidity of the upper chamber. Like
their more conservative colleagues, the liberals were more than willing to accept and to savor the traditional Senate perquisites of personal power and privilege.[21] In contrast to the congressman who
tended to join unofficial groups in order to secure the type of influence
that he could not otherwise gain through individual means, the senator was never really confronted with the stimulus of anonymity. In
a chamber that was more intimate and informal and had a more
diffused distribution of internal power, the Senate liberals did not
have the same motivation to value collective influence above individual discretion. This point was stressed most forcibly by Senator
Gale McGee: "In the Senate each member is immediately sucked into
the mainstream of Senate responsibility and power. There is no need
to mobilize groups to cry on each others' shoulders."[22]

This sensitivity about freedom of maneuver deterred conservatives
and liberals alike from forming into highly organized subgroups.
Most liberal senators, for example, would have regarded a permanent
structure in the Senate as an impediment to legislative accommodation and compromise. It would have unnecessarily divided group members from nonmembers and increased the degree of mutual suspicion
between senators; it would have produced a cumbersome voting bloc
that would have drastically reduced the scope for individual compromises, personal favors, and unilateral communications; and it
would have undermined the Senate's characteristic style of intimate
discussion, discreet negotiation, and overall collegiate trust.

The Monday Morning Meeting (MMM) provides a good example of the way in which this preoccupation with personal discretion served to weaken any attempt to organize a permanent liberal grouping within the Senate. The limited aim of the MMM project was merely to provide a regular form of communication and consultation between the chief staff assistants of the liberal members. Even so, the MMM group soon began to experience the emasculating force of senatorial disapproval. Senator Philip Hart's chief staff officer explained the problem in the following terms. "Senators began to feel that there was too much information being circulated about their positions. There was a great deal of embarrassment as Senators' private strategies became known. This was compounded by the knowledge that the coalition on one issue would differ on the next, thereby enlarging the audience for information about his pressures and weaknesses."[23] The senators' sensitivity over their individual strategies and bargaining flexibility imposed severe inhibitions on the group of staff assistants. Ultimately, the pressures were too great and the MMM group was disbanded in 1972 after only one year's intermittent operation.

At first sight it seemed as if constituency pressures, party obligations, committee loyalties, personal maneuverability, and so on, precluded even the possibility that the liberals could have developed any sense of group identity or cohesion. And yet the 20 or so members classified as liberal in each Congress by roll-call analysis did indeed constitute a conscious group with a strong sense of mutual awareness and reciprocal support. The liberals were recognized by senators and staff alike as a distinct force in the chamber. Even Senator Philip Hart's chief staff assistant, who earlier described the debilitating effect of senatorial individualism on liberal cooperative enterprise, had to acknowledge that "the twenty or so consistent liberals identified very well in the Senate; they spearheaded the liberal vote in the chamber."[24] Although it may have suffered from the diversity in its members' legislative role orientations and from the general absence of any central focus of leadership, the liberal group nevertheless constituted an element of permanent substance amid the swirling mists of senatorial alliances and coalitions.

In some areas the general esprit de corps was translated into permanent and highly organized pockets of liberal activity. Although the Wednesday Club and the Members of Congress for Peace through

Law (MCPL) were not exclusively composed of liberal senators, they were liberally oriented enterprises. The MCPL was originally formed in 1959 by Senator Joseph Clark.[25] By 1972 the membership had grown to 105 congressmen and senators, including Gravel, Hartke, McGovern, Nelson, Proxmire, Hughes, Mondale, and Goodell. This bicameral and bipartisan group of liberal representatives was dedicated in general to examining constructive alternatives to contemporary U.S. defense policy and in particular to providing in-depth analyses of the costs and effectiveness of major weapons systems. The MCPL maintained its own independent staff and was organized into several subcommittees that concentrated on a variety of military and international areas (e.g., East–West trade, U.S.–China relations, military spending). The extent of the members' commitment to this unofficial agency was perhaps best revealed by the MCPL's 1969 project, in which each member of its military spending committee adopted a weapons system or a specific Pentagon policy to examine personally. The result was a highly perceptive and damaging critique of over 20 major military projects and policies.[26] Although the group failed to secure the recommended military cuts in Congress, the MCPL's reports provided the legislature with much valuable information, educated the public in alternative military policies, and, according to some sources, succeeded in stimulating the armed services committees into making their own budgetary reductions.[27]

The Wednesday Club was another permanent yet unofficial group; but, unlike the MCPL, its membership was limited to the Senate.[28] It was formed in 1966 to strengthen and coordinate the liberal wing of the Senate Republican party. It really developed into its present form, however, in 1968, when a substantial number of new liberal and moderate Republicans entered the Senate. Included in that class were Senators Richard Schweiker and Charles Mathias, who had been members of the liberal group in the House of Representatives. It was they who gave the real impetus to the Wednesday Club although at the very beginning they met with some opposition within the Senate: "When we wanted to set up a group we were told that we should not do it because the Senate is a club. You should not have a club within a club. However, that attitude did not stop us."[29] The Senate purists need not have concerned themselves, however, for the Wednesday Club remained a typically senatorial grouping with little discipline and few commitments. It was important in some issues, but it did not attempt to provide a comprehensive service of information and voting cues for each and every vote, nor did it try to ensure unanimity on all issues. In Senator Mark Hatfield's words: "The Club does not try to force its members into one bloc, it relies more on a natural basic philosophy."[30] Although the club was in no way a tightly organized unit, it did provide a means by which views could be exchanged, positions confirmed, and strategies planned.

The liberal group as a whole was just as sensitive over organizational rigidity and collective commitment. In contrast to the DSG, the Senate liberals did not have a whip system, nor a formal communications structure, nor any established framework of personal interaction. The liberals were too immersed in the Senate's tradition of collective reciprocity to attempt to create a detached and disciplined clique of members. In whatever ways the liberals may have been drawn together by the common stimulus of national party proposals, White House positions, or interest-group suggestions, their sense of group awareness was developed in their own personal terms. External conditions and forces were highly significant, but liberal interaction inside the Senate was more often than not based on personal bonds, friendships, mutual accessibility, and a semideveloped sense of group commitment. These methods preserved the liberals' sense of individual discretion but at the same time bound them together in terms of personal interaction, past favors, similarity in positions, and group nostalgia over past campaigns.

A general empathy among the group, however, was insufficient by itself to produce a continuously functioning legislative force with bloc voting potential. Despite the self-consciousness of the liberal group, tendencies still had to be confirmed, leanings had to be checked, and past loyalties had to be made relevant to the present by a perpetual process of appeals and assurances. The mobilization of the liberal group may not always have been an arduous task but it was a necessary one, for the group was insufficiently integrated to materialize spontaneously in response to issues. A general state of group identity would have been irrelevant had it not been exploited and used to produce hard commitments and real voting strength.

An important factor in arousing group instincts and in converting group consciousness into political muscle was the standard and frequency of the members' contacts with one another. No matter how loose the liberal group was in structure, it could not function effectively without some form of internal communications. The purpose of the next section, therefore, is to examine the communications of the liberal group and to assess how far these were effective in galvanizing the liberals into a legislative unit.

INTERNAL COMMUNICATIONS

Like the American governmental system in general, the Senate is noted for its multiple centers of decision making authority. Given the atomized character of its internal organization, communication can be regarded not just as a useful contribution toward information exchange among members, but as an essential prerequisite to a minimal form of institutional integration. In many ways, it is only through effective communication that a rudimentary framework, linking together the individual cells of political influence, can be achieved in an institution like the Senate. Having acknowledged in general terms the potential of communication as a countervailing force against the compartmentalization of institutional power, attention should be drawn to the enormous diversity in the sources, types, quality, and significance of information given and received. In short, communications can foster pockets of legislative integration, but they do not guarantee them. Much depends on the information, the channels, and the receptivity of the individuals involved.

When discussing a group such as the Senate liberals, it is all too easy to work backward from the accepted presence of the group and to infer all manner of causal relationships between it and liberal interest groups, the congressional liaison offices of liberal presidents, liberal constituencies, and so on. However, just as the Senate liberals did not spontaneously gravitate toward one another in response to some singular vision, so they were not directed to collective effort by a common set of external information points. The Senate liberals may have had a notional sense of group identity based on general policy inclinations, but they were also individual senators who were exposed to an extraordinary variety of information. Like any other member, a liberal was part of a society festooned with parties, agencies, governmental institutions, constituencies, and politically active groups, clubs, and associations. Different senators were exposed to, and were affected by, different political and electoral conditions in different ways. Each individual senator was personally drawn to some of these political forces, obliged to others, electorally dependent on others, and legislatively reliant on others for research data, ideas, and arguments. His individual perspective was likely to become even more idiosyncratic inside the Senate. There, he would have been given a nearly unique permutation of committee assignments and left to comprehend and to respond to literally thousands of bills from a personal but often isolated base without the assistance of systematic party guidance.

With this multiplicity of obligations, perspectives, and dispositions, the Senate liberals can in no way be seen as a homogeneous and regimented unit of members. Their diffuse esprit de corps provided the possibility of cooperation, but converting possibility into actuality depended upon accommodating their inherent diversity to a sense of active purpose. In other words, the liberals' mutual awareness only became relevant to themselves and to the Senate when they were actively and consciously in contact with one another as a liberal group, or at least as part of a liberal group.

Given the nature of coalition building in the Senate, any potential group required at least two important types of communicative channels: first, a link between the legislative group and associated groups and interests outside the institution, and second, a linkage between members of the group itself. The first channel yielded information on issues, political attitudes, constituency positions, and so on, while the second and perhaps more significant channel in the Senate provided information to the group members about each other.

Clearly, the communications between the liberals and related interest groups could not be structured and standardized by the liberals themselves. Whether he liked it or not, each liberal was subjected to a haphazard variety of information on issues and on other senators. Any attempt to integrate the Senate liberals, therefore, by creating a uniform relationship between the group and external political activities would have been impossible. Whatever sense of corporate identity among the Senate liberals was derived from their connections with a group like the AFL-CIO, this common factor was not enough in itself to draw the liberals actively together inside the Senate. The overlap in sources of information among the liberals may have been significant in reducing the inconsistencies in their political positions and in creating the groundwork for cooperation, but it did not remove the atomization of individual senators. In short, the lib erals may have had relationships with particular groups and adopted similar political positions, but they would have been unable to make this count in legislative encounters unless they were sufficiently aware of each other and of one another's political positions.

If the liberals were going to exploit their common links and to maximize their legislative strengths, a secondary and more direct form of communication was absolutely imperative. Each liberal needed to know about his fellow liberals before he would commit himself to an issue and involve himself in a legislative campaign. The organizational barriers that divided many liberals from each other therefore had to be circumvented by improvised lines of communications. Senators could always discover something about each other by collecting one another's newsletters and press releases, by listening to cloakroom rumors, and by close attention to the media. Information derived from these sources, however, was often irregular in supply, inaccurate in quality, and presented to audiences other than those found inside the Senate. There was no real substitute for direct two-way interchanges between senators. As far as the liberals were concerned, the opportunities for discussion, negotiation, and planning were often provided by third parties such as interest groups, national party organizations, and the White House. Liberals like Harrison Williams, Philip Hart, Hubert Humphrey, Birch Bayh, Lee Metcalf, and Harold Hughes, for example, were drawn into closer contact with one another more than they would possibly otherwise have been through their developed relationships with the labor movement. The same was true for liberals like Frank Moss, Gaylord Nelson, Edmund Muskie, Abraham Ribicoff, and again Philip Hart, who were closely engaged with such groups as Common Cause, the Consumer Federation of America, Friends of the Earth, and Nader task forces in legislative campaigns for environmental and consumer protection.

While the forums provided by outside parties could be of great significance in increasing the interaction among senators, they could not normally provide the final linkage among members of a group like the liberals. Notwithstanding all the position papers received, the outside interests listened to and White House breakfasts consumed, the Senate liberals ultimately had to sort things out for themselves inside the institution. Internal senatorial politics tended to complicate the clearest of policy stances made outside Capitol Hill. Committee jurisdictions, personality clashes, political ambitions, and previous commitments, in addition to senatorial sensitivity over institutional independence and legislative individualism, necessitated an effective communications network among the liberals inside the institution itself. If the liberals were going to assert themselves collectively in this shrouded regime of fluctuating coalitions and multiple transactions, at the very minimum they needed the capacity to discuss legislative issues among themselves.

The high number of committee assignments in the Senate, together with the overlap in committee memberships, produced an excellent basis for regular contact between senators. In a committee environment, liberal members could react to the same stimuli, exchange ideas and information at first hand, and come to some agreement over future strategy. The level of interaction among liberal committee members was particularly high because the liberals were concentrated in a limited number of committees.[31] During the median Congress in the 1959–72 period (i.e., Eighty-ninth Congress, 1965–66), 64 percent of the liberals were located in three committees (i.e., Labor and Public Welfare, Judiciary, and Banking committees). Members like Edward Kennedy and Jacob Javits, for example, knew, worked with, and shared committee responsibilities with as many as a dozen of the 18-member liberal group. Ironically, this concentration of liberals in three committees tended to counteract the very atomization that had so often led liberal members to object to the committee system. With this potential for group contact, it was to the liberals' enduring advantage that Joseph Clark failed in his campaign to disperse the liberals more widely throughout the system.

Important as the committee system was to the liberal network, however, it was not sufficient to provide the liberals with a comprehensive communications system. First, the "liberal committees" only covered a limited number of issue areas and, therefore, several policy blind spots existed within the liberal network. Second, the committees did not provide a formal link between the liberal committee members and the remainder of the Senate liberal group. Committees may have had great potential as centers of communication, but for that potential to be fulfilled, they had to depend upon additional supportive apparatus.

During the 1960s, many liberals regarded the Senate Democratic party as the organization with the greatest potential for providing an arena within which the liberal members could exert real political influence.[32] The composition and performance of both the Steering and Policy committees were criticized and presented as suitable cases for reform by the liberals. It was the party caucus or conference, though, which was of particular interest to the liberals. Many of them regarded it as an institution that would not only provide much-needed debate over party platforms and legislative programs, but would draw the liberals together in a united front against their opponents in the party. The disuse of the caucus, and the jaundiced view of its position taken by a majority of its members, served only to spur liberal protest and to increase liberal optimism over the caucus's potential capacity. In a speech given by William Proxmire in 1959, for example, he endorsed Woodrow Wilson's interpretation of the caucus as an antidote to the committees and as a "cohesive principle which the multiplicity and mutual independence of the committees so powerfully tend to destroy."[33] Mindful of their junior and minority status at this time, the liberals came to regard caucus and party reform as a final solution to their problems.

To an extent the liberals succeeded in enlarging the scope of the caucus. Whereas caucuses used to meet once a year under Lyndon Johnson, the party was convening several times a session by the early 1970s. Under pressure from Senator Fred Harris, Majority Leader Mike Mansfield agreed in 1971 to hold a caucus whenever any member requested a meeting and to permit the caucus to reject any committee assignment made by the Steering Committee.[34] In spite of these changes, the caucus did not become the panacea that so many liberals had predicted in the early 1960s. The liberals' later indifference toward the caucus was partly a reflection of their advanced penetration into the power structure of the committees, and their general submission to the seductive forces of senatorial individualism. It was also due to a recognition that the conference was "awkward and inefficient as a communications device."[35] Caucus meetings attracted either small groups of senators who were already involved in a particular issue, or large groups of members who were wary of foreclosing their personal options in front of such a wide audience.

Finally, the liberals' general lack of enthusiasm over the caucus must also have been related to their general belief that the party organization as a whole had remained largely insensitive to their presence in the Senate. This attitude was not just derived from the fact that the voting preferences of Mansfield and his chief whip

(Robert Byrd) had too often been at variance with the position of the liberal group. It was also based on the liberals' perception of continued discrimination against them on the part of the leadership. Although the liberal presence on party committees had grown since Senator Joseph Clark's reform campaign in the early 1960s, it was still disproportionately low by the end of the decade. Taking the 1959–72 period as a whole, the liberal Democrats on average made up 37 percent of the Democratic party in the Senate. The average liberal component of the Democratic Steering Committee, however, was 25 percent, and on the Democratic Policy Committee the liberal element accounted on average for only 9 percent of the membership. The tiny group of Republican liberals had always had to accept minority status inside the minority party, but the Democratic liberals had some justification in expecting greater leverage within their party structure. Their unfulfilled expectations combined with their increased institutional power produced an attitude of both cynicism and suspicion toward the party hierarchy. While Mansfield called for more caucuses and attempted to revitalize the Policy Committee,[36] the liberals at most remained unimpressed and at worst believed that the leadership was "buying off the insurgents through measures which [were] only cosmetic."[37]

In the absence of an effective formal system of internal communication, the liberals often relied on an incoherent network of informal channels that might best be termed the "bush telegraph." In its literal sense, a bush telegraph is a form of communication between individual jungle posts which to the outsider consists of barely audible and incomprehensible reverberations, while to the initiated it exchanges information with an efficiency that belies its apparent disorder. The term is particularly appropriate for the mode of communication among Senate liberals. Bearing in mind the variety of information sources and dispersal of liberals throughout the chamber, the bush telegraph was the chief means by which the varied subgroups of liberals were effectively linked together. It was the most informal and yet the most effective part of the liberal network. In fact, its very informality was probably the key to its success, for the bush telegraph managed to link liberals and to arouse a group identity among them in a way that still acknowledged each senator's status as a free trader in political capital. In an unstructured and inconsistent fashion, information between senators was actively relayed through such available and interested intermediaries as congressional liaison officers, interest-group lobbyists, party and senatorial staff assistants, and even the president. The liberals themselves supplemented the limited opportunity for information exchange provided through established legislative groups (e.g., Wednesday Club, Members of Congress for Peace through Law) and through the formal committee and party apparatus by relying on friendships, regular contacts, and mutual acquaintances. Of course, some liberals were more socially prominent than others. Senators Walter Mondale and Gaylord Nelson, for example, were both well known in the Senate for their availability to other members. They regularly took lunch in the dining room reserved for senators and developed a reputation for being two of the most important points of contact for the liberal members.[38] But the cultivation of personal linkages probably reached its fullest development in the person of Senator Alan Cranston. He devoted his senatorial career to developing one kind of relationship or another with every other member of the chamber. As Cranston himself explained: "It is almost a game and a challenge to find an area in which I can be in agreement with every Senator. Through this I encourage the movement toward compromise. This is the basis of my work around the Senate."[39] While the hand of friendship was extended to all, Cranston's endeavors were made primarily on behalf of the liberal group. In fact, his role in linking members to one another caused him to be known as the "liberal whip." It was through brokers like Cranston, Mondale, and Nelson that the full complement of liberals could become part of a generalized chain of information and views.

Much of the time, the role of this diffuse community was limited to the exchange of Washington rumors and the discussion of overall policy objectives. When a specific issue was at stake, however, the bush telegraph was transformed into a comparatively efficient system of communication. Those channels that had originally been formed through friendships, corresponding interests, and matching committee responsibilities were exploited to furnish the liberal group with substantive information over bill content, voting intentions, and legislative strategy. In the battle over the military budget in 1969, for example, the liberals and their supporters organized opposition on the basis of informal contacts and unofficial negotiations. Since the liberals were hardly represented in the Armed Services Committee and had taken very little interest in military expenditures up to that point, they had no established framework of communications in the policy area. As a result, they relied upon the bush telegraph technique of staff messengers, working lunches with cosponsors, and private briefings with interest-group representatives to organize a concerted attack upon various military projects. For example, George McGovern's office became the clearinghouse for information and strategy concerning the Air Force's new supersonic bomber. And the offices of Philip Hart and John Cooper became the nerve center for the movement against deploying the massive anti-ballistic missile system. While these campaigns met with only very limited success, the liberals did succeed in mobilizing themselves into an organized force in the absence of any formal committee or party network.[40]

Although the bush telegraph could become highly activated by precise issues, it nevertheless maintained its normally restrained and unstructured style of operation. No matter how urgent a matter may have been, liberal communications remained strictly within the senatorial code. Contacts were made and developed on the basis of tentative suggestions, courteous requests, and private arrangements. Information was exchanged and compromises were reached in groups small enough to assemble in a senator's office or around a lunch table. The liberal network operated through a profusion of multilateral contacts that appeared to be a hopelessly entangled maze of communicative channels. Yet the sheer multiplicity of these capillaries did provide the liberals with an initial form of group contact.

An aspect of the bush telegraph that should be acknowledged separately was the staff network. Unstructured and confused, it nonetheless provided a crucial element of linkage between senatorial offices and contributed toward closer contacts among senators themselves.[41] Although no official staff organization operated on behalf of the liberal group, senators exploited personal and committee staff facilities in an effort to compensate for the "sheer lack of time that Senators [had] to communicate with one another."[42] Staff units were habitually called upon to make contacts to engage in bargaining, to mobilize support, and even to act as senators' alter egos. This civil service function of the staff was well described by an administrative assistant: "After despatching the normal 'dear colleague' letters, the legislative assistant will phone all the relevant staff assistants and ask for reactions. After 4 to 5 days he will be able to count votes.

If there are any 'don't knows' he will ask his Senator to find out their positions by buttonholing them in the corridors or cloakrooms."[43]

Although the combination of senatorial authority and staff operations was a common feature within the Senate, the exact relationship between members and their staffs varied enormously. Some preferred to deal directly with other senators (e.g., Alan Cranston). Others, like Edmund Muskie, tended to "work alongside their staffs thereby benefiting from the knowledge that there [were] more people in support."[44] Some ran "loose ships," in which the staffs were generally given a wide degree of discretion. The model for this system was provided by Eugene McCarthy's office, which was given substantial leeway in controlling the nature and flow of communications to other senatorial offices. In contrast, some senators operated "tight ships," where the level of staff independence was carefully restricted. Such a senator would check and countersign all the major communications leaving his office and would not always divulge everything to his chief aides. A case in point was Senator Lee Metcalf, whose sense of caution and even secrecy was captured by his administrative assistant: "It is all hit and miss. Metcalf may mention that he has spoken to another Senator on a matter. At other times he won't tell his staff whether he has or not."[45] Finally, some members maintained a hybrid form of senator–staff operation in which the staff's position could change from that of first lieutenants to mere infantry support, depending on the issue and interests involved. Senator Gaylord Nelson, for example, exploited both avenues of communication. As his administrative assistant explained: "Nelson alternates between personal and staff intervention. On the latter I often commit the Senator's vote to others. It is a case of 'if you don't hear from me in an hour you can consider it settled'."[46] Despite the variety of tight and loose ships in the liberal flotilla, it did not prevent the staffs from performing the vital role in informing and in linking together the offices of the liberal senators.

The liberal network inside the Senate, therefore, consisted of a variegated combination of formal and informal communicative channels. While the committee and party organizations represented the formal skeleton of the liberals' internal communications, it was the unofficial components that provided much of the connective ligament between the liberal members. The bush telegraph offered liberal members an opportunity to convert their basic group empathy into a substantive and viable organization that could exist in the hard world of legislative campaigns and roll calls.

GROUP MOBILIZATION

The liberals had something of a group spirit; they had a communications network, albeit a largely informal one. But clearly they needed indigenous leaders if they were to function effectively as a legislative group.

This is not to deny the importance of external coordinators, who often assisted the momentum of legislative campaigns. A lobbyist like Andrew Biemiller of the AFL-CIO, for example, could provide a legislative group with research data, supportive arguments, political information, procedural advice, and a whole range of managerial skills. Presidents could also facilitate senatorial cooperation. In an active sense a president could adopt a brokerage role among senators by which he stimulated or confirmed their interest in a policy and then through his intermediary position obliged them to convert their interests into legislative effort. In fact, a president could often generate or strengthen a supportive group in Congress simply by providing it with an "administration position" that acted as a common source of reference to the group's constituent members. With or without the benefit of a brilliant political strategist like Biemiller or the reflected glory of a national leader like President Johnson, the Senate liberals needed indigenous leaders to mobilize support among senators inside the Senate. Outside coordinators could be of great value but, ultimately, whatever the merits or demerits of such a process, coalitions were formed inside, not outside, Congress. Whatever political support they were receiving from the outside, liberal leaders were necessary to maximize the institutional potential of the liberal group.

No two legislative campaigns are ever exactly the same, nor did the Senate liberals mobilize themselves in a specific way from issue to issue. The development of the liberal group proceeded by different methods under a variety of conditions. This diversity reflected the multiplicity of potential and actual influences involved in congressional decision making. Once again, it is necessary to acknowledge the individuality of a senator's personal, institutional, electoral, political, and party circumstances. The purpose of this study, therefore, is not to present a deceptively simple construction of the complex interactions occurring within the liberal group. It is rather more an attempt to identify and examine a number of features that have generally been evident on those occasions when the liberals formed themselves into a distinctive group.

Like other legislative groups, the liberals did not operate under one leader or even a limited group of leaders. The focal point of a liberal legislative campaign could just as easily be a freshman as a party whip. The factors that usually determined the leadership's identity were the issues involved and the units of the committee system relevant to those issues. The authority of a leader was usually based on the classic attributes of a congressional committee. Specialist knowledge, long-term experience, and developed relationships with interested parties all contributed toward committees being the primary source of leadership recruitment within the liberal ranks. In the words of Senator Joseph Tydings: "Liberal leadership tended to come from the committees involved in an issue; the Judiciary Committee liberals for example dealt with and led the fights over the civil rights bills."[47] Whether it was Harrison Williams advocating mass transit from the Banking and Currency Committee, or Edward Kennedy mobilizing support for health measures from the Labor and Public Welfare Committee, or Philip Hart pressing environmental issues from the Commerce Committee, their leadership positions were due largely to their strategic places in the committee framework.

Initially, a liberal leader on an issue had first to persuade some of his immediate colleagues on the committee involved to lend their support to his position. This provided him with a nominal power base in the institution. Such a base was mostly significant in a negative sense, for if he failed to engage the support of at least some of his fellow committee members, his position as leader and probably the position of the issue concerned would become almost untenable. Given the status of committees in affording the chamber basic judgments on policy, a minority of one or two on a committee would find it very difficult to combat the institutional inertia against them. Singular liberals who were not even members of the appropriate committees have led minority campaigns in the Senate. However, such occurrences have been comparatively rare and normally unsuccessful.[48] In general, a liberal leader had to develop the credibility of both the policy and himself within the relevant committee.

After establishing a primary nucleus of support, the liberal leader would then exploit the bush telegraph in order to circulate his position and to fathom the possibilities for additional support. This would involve contracting a large number of individual senators on a separate basis—either directly or through staff assistants and colleagues. As has already been acknowledged, a president's congressional liaison office, an executive agency, or an interest group might, separately or in combination, constitute part of the bush telegraph and might well have completed some of the initial groundwork by alerting senators to a particular proposal. Whatever the level of presidential, bureaucratic, or private interest, however, the liberal leader attempted to capitalize upon the activated communications circuitry running inside and outside the Senate that he himself had helped to prime. Whether or not he was receiving much in the way of external assistance, the leader's function was to engage in the delicate process of securing firm commitments to his position and of widening the pool of support inside the Senate.

The task of group building was by no means an easy one, for the Senate contained "one hundred very individualistic people who [did] not easily adhere to a particular line."[49] Liberals were certainly no exception to this rule, and often their behavior served to exemplify it. Senator Abraham Ribicoff, for example, led many legislative campaigns on behalf of the liberals, but he openly revealed his displeasure when the roles were reversed and he became the respondent and not the canvasser. As he explained: "I do not like being buttonholed; every Senator should make up his own mind."[50] Given the highly developed personal and political sensitivities among Senators, any liberal leader had to arouse the interest of his immediate liberal colleagues in a proposed policy. The ways in which liberal leaders did this were many and varied, but generally they could be reduced to variants of two basic approaches.

The first type was the "liberal publicist," who supplemented his persuasive efforts inside the Senate by taking issues to the public. In this way he attempted to gain support by generating public interest in his policies. His tactics included addressing national audiences, publicizing issues through the press and television, and encouraging external groups to lobby fellow senators in the interest of a cause. Leaders in this mold (Robert and Edward Kennedy, George McGovern, William Proxmire, Mike Gravel) sought to exploit their celebrity status by presenting issues to the nation, stimulating popular concern and assuring colleagues of public support for their positions.

An example of this strategy is provided by George McGovern, who, in 1968, established himself as the chief Senate spokesman on the emotive and controversial issue of hunger and malnutrition in the United States.[51] The issue had come to the public's attention only the year before, when Robert Kennedy and Joseph Clark used the Employment, Manpower and Poverty Subcommittee of the Labor and Public Welfare Committee to conduct investigations on nutritional deficiencies in children and on the inadequacies of federal programs such as food stamps, food distribution, and school lunches. As Kennedy and Clark began to concentrate more on electoral politics in 1968, George McGovern adopted the issue and pressed successfully for the establishment of the Select Committee on Nutrition and Human Needs. As chairman, McGovern exploited his past experience as President Kennedy's Food for Peace director and a Democratic critic of the Agriculture Department, to embarrass the Nixon administration. His most controversial move was to dramatize the issue by shipping the committee to areas of poverty and by undertaking field investigations on his own initiative. The televised tours of McGovern's committee witnessing some of the worst housing conditions in the country, combined with the alarming statistical reports of the National Nutrition Survey (set up by Congress in 1967), succeeded in generating public outrage. Despite the disapproval of conservatives such as Ellender and Dole, McGovern's tactics enabled him to take the initiative in the issue.

At a time when the Nixon administration was more interested in its family assistance program than in direct relief in food supplies, McGovern pressed the issue so hard that the administration increased its food stamp proposals from under $100 million to nearly $600 million in 1970 and to $1 billion in 1971. To McGovern even this was not enough, and he persuaded a majority of the Senate to accept a major reform in the structure of the food stamp program and to pass additional funds for the project. McGovern continued to plague the administration, stir the public's conscience, and pressure his colleagues on such issues as housing, environmental conditions, and the nutritional value of foods. His position as chairman of the Select Committee and the use he made of it not only stimulated the Nixon administration into tripling its food stamp budget and doubling its school lunch program, but gave McGovern the national platform he needed to become a serious contender for the Democratic presidential nomination in 1972.

In contrast to the liberal publicists were what could be termed "liberal insiders," who preferred to concentrate on the careful cultivation of support inside the chamber. Although members like Philip Hart, Clifford Case, Walter Mondale, Jacob Javits, and Alan Cranston were not prominent public figures, they were just as much leaders as were Kennedy or McGovern. Their influence was founded upon the more traditional base of private negotiation and discreet prompting. This type of leader was usually an expert on colleagues' idiosyncracies, a keen judge of internal atmosphere, an exponent of strategic timing, and an affable but tough infighter.

Probably the best example of this leadership style was Philip Hart. In the course of conducting interviews with senators and assistants, Philip Hart was continually spoken of as one of the most respected members in the institution. His name always evoked sighs of admiration from secretaries and never failed to generate a strong note of approval from liberal and conservative members alike. Hart's personable character and internal stature enabled him to exert the type of pressure in the Senate that belied his low political profile outside Washington. In no issue was Hart's prestige more evident than in the fight for open housing legislation in 1968.

After the great advances made in 1964 and 1965, the momentum of civil rights reform slowed down in 1966, when the Congress refused to pass President Johnson's open housing legislation. Although a majority favored a bill to bar racial discrimination in the sale and rental of housing, it did not amount to the two-thirds majority necessary to break the customary conservative filibuster. With Johnson's subsequent preoccupation with Vietnam and the public's increased disenchantment with the civil rights issue, open housing appeared to be a lost cause by 1968. Contrary to popular expectations, however, a group of Senate liberals suddenly resurrected the open housing measure and began to reawaken the old northern Democratic–Republican civil rights coalition. The group believed that if the bill was ever going to be secured, it would have to capitalize upon what remained of the momentum toward civil rights reform. Against the advice of the president, the Justice Department, and the Senate leadership and with very little external support, a small group of Judiciary

Committee liberals (Edward Kennedy, Joseph Tydings, Philip Hart, and Walter Mondale), in conjunction with Edward Brooke, took it upon themselves to make 1968 another landmark year for civil rights.[52] Hart, after some initial reluctance, decided to apply his considerable status in the civil rights field to the open housing issue. He assumed the leadership of the liberal group pressing for the measure, whose chief cosponsors were Walter Mondale and Edward Brooke.

By the first cloture vote Hart had not only mobilized the liberal group but almost completely renovated the old northern Democratic–Republican civil rights coalition. Even though Hart's liberal group failed to secure a two-thirds majority (53–37) of those present and voting, the margin represented a significant improvement on the last cloture vote in 1966, which the civil rights forces won by only 52–41. In contrast to the great civil rights victories of 1964 and 1965, however, the liberals did not have the advantage of the support and active participation of the party leaders. On the contrary, Mike Mansfield opposed the amendment because he believed that it would jeopardize other minor but nevertheless significant civil rights proposals (e.g., the protection of persons exercising their civil rights). The redoubtable Everett Dirksen, whose virtuoso performance had successfully mobilized Republican civil rights majorities in 1964 and 1965, opposed open housing on the grounds of individual property rights. Philip Hart knew that Mansfield would eventually come to support the liberals once they had defeated his attempts to table their amendment, and the liberals sensed also that the turnover in Republican members made Dirksen's position in 1968 far more tenuous than it had been in 1966. Both suppositions proved correct, for Mansfield was soon sucked into the growing vortex, and Dirksen found himself in a minority within his own party. The minority leader moved quickly to compromise with the liberal leaders, none of whom held formal party positions.

The liberals succeeded not only in maintaining their internal cohesion while they engaged in negotiations, but in achieving an agreement heavily weighted toward the liberal position. In the words of one of the group, the liberals had been prepared to "give Dirksen just about anything he wanted; we were astounded at how well we came out."[53] It was indeed a famous victory, for while the original Mondale–Brooke proposal planned to cover 91 percent of all housing, the compromise measure covered as much as 80 percent of housing.

It was this proposal which, with President Johnson's long-awaited support, was finally passed by the Senate on the fourth cloture vote.

In the open housing case in 1968, Hart provided the liberals with leadership that was sufficiently experienced and respected to conduct a forceful campaign in a major issue area. While the liberals had provided the main thrust to the civil rights victories in 1964 and 1965, they had always been led by party leaders like Hubert Humphrey and Everett Dirksen. In the open housing measure, senior liberals assumed responsibility for leading the large bipartisan coalition of northern Democrats and liberal and moderate Republicans. In spite of their limited power base (i.e., Judiciary Committee), the lack of assistance from both the White House and party hierarchies, the absence of mobilized mass support, and the unfavorable political climate, Philip Hart and his colleagues nevertheless succeeded in securing a measure that was regarded as lost.

In many ways these two types of leader could complement one another. As the publicist educated and stimulated public opinion, the insider acted as program manager and carried out much of the internal groundwork that effectively combined the two roles through a successful demonstration of legislative support. This symbiosis of the two different styles within two different political arenas was personified by the close relationship between Senators Mike Gravel and Alan Cranston. As Gravel's legislative assistant explained: "Gravel is closer to Cranston than any other Senator and often follows his lead. Cranston has a nonabrasive personality, but Gravel sees his role as a gadfly, as an abrasive Senator. They are effective as a pair because Gravel often makes the challenges while Cranston smoothes the feathers. Cranston is more of a vote-getter while Gravel pricks people's consciences."[54] The relationship between publicists and insiders was not always so well developed as in this case, but the example shows that the two leadership styles were by no means incompatible with one another. The differences between the two styles was significant but essentially one of degree, not of kind.

Whether an issue leader was a publicist or an insider, he would have to apply himself in one way or another to the time-consuming task of direct or indirect negotiation and persuasion. One very important way by which leaders built up internal liberal support was through the practice of cosponsorship.[55] This senatorial device permitted a bill to be sponsored by any number of members. A liberal leader could capitalize upon this privilege by offering fellow liberals the opportunity to lend their names to a measure. The leader retained his prominent position as first among formal equals and had the comfort of at least receiving a number of declared supporters publicly associated with his position.

In the quest for cosponsors leaders often attempted to negotiate the support of what were termed *pivotal* or *swing* senators. Such members were regarded as sufficiently prestigious or powerful to influence the attitudes of other senators. It was part of Senate folklore in the late 1960s and early 1970s that in the Republican party Margaret Chase Smith and George Aitken could each turn the votes of about five fellow Republicans. The notion of pivotal senators was also widely held inside the liberal group. In interviews it was regarded as quite important—although not absolutely crucial—to secure the allegiance of a respected senior liberal. This was thought to give a campaign greater political weight and to enlarge the number of commitments, as several liberals would follow the guiding cue of a prestigious and trustworthy colleague. A staff assistant explained: "There are a number of liberal swing men who will decide the case for other Senators. Staffers phone Senator X's office and ask which way he is voting and then they will inform their boss."[56] Senators like Hubert Humphrey, Walter Mondale, Philip Hart, Clifford Case, Jacob Javits, and Paul Douglas, for example, were reputed to have particularly strong coattails.

To gauge the substance of some of these reputations, it was decided to take a sample of the roll-call data from the central voting study and see how well the "influential liberals" were supported by their colleagues. The sample selected was the set of roll calls from the Ninetieth Congress (1967–68). Since the liberal group was split on more occasions in this Congress than in any other during the 1959–72 period, it was possible to determine which individual liberals appeared to be pivotal within the liberal group.

The figures revealed that those liberals with the reputation for coattails did indeed attract greater support than those without the reputation. Walter Mondale's position was supported by a majority of liberals on 94 percent of occasions. The rate at which the positions of Jacob Javits, Philip Hart, and Clifford Case received majority support from the liberal group was 92 percent, 90 percent, and 89 percent, respectively. The rate at which Stephen Young, Birch Bayh,

William Proxmire, and Daniel Brewster attracted majority liberal support, on the other hand, was 69 percent, 64 percent, 59 percent, and 57 percent, respectively. The fact that more liberals tended to join Mondale than to join Brewster does not, of course, prove that Mondale's influence was the main reason for their support. After all, Mondale could have come into the liberal majorities at the end of the day and played no role in swinging anyone's vote. Nevertheless, the figures do indicate that there may at least be something to the reputation of such swing men.

The staff assistants and the senators themselves seemed to think that the liberal heavyweights could make a significant difference. For example, when Harrison Williams was developing support for his mass transit bill in the early 1960s, he regarded the cosponsorship of such senior liberals as Humphrey, Javits, Morse, and Douglas as crucially important to the bill's chances.[57] It was no surprise to him, therefore, that when the bill came to a vote in 1963 it was supported by almost all of the liberal fraternity. In general, endorsements and cosponsorships were not necessarily seen as the key to legislative success. But in the difficult process of gaining an initial momentum for a campaign, they were often thought to provide an important political and psychological boost when campaigns were at their most vulnerable.

In the effort to mobilize the liberal group into an effective unit of leverage, the issue leader was sometimes forced to sacrifice his own position in the interests of a policy. This was caused by a leader recognizing that he was inappropriately positioned or insufficiently qualified to maintain a credible and forceful leadership. For example, Edward Brooke originated the initial movements against the nominations of both Clement Haynsworth and Harold Carswell to the Supreme Court in 1969 and 1970, respectively. Once the opposition was in motion, however, he had to relinquish control of the campaigns to Birch Bayh, who was strategically placed in the Judiciary Committee.

In spite of all the Senate traditions of self-dependence and individual atomization, many members were prepared to ask colleagues to assume responsibility for their campaigns. Senator Gaylord Nelson's legislative assistant witnessed this phenomenon at first hand: "Liberals do ask each other to lead them. Senator Nelson has asked Edward Kennedy to assist him in the past. . . . Many members in turn come to Nelson and tell him that they are having trouble in getting a campaign off the ground and would he take over."[58] Often it was a junior member who would be forced to renounce his leadership in favor of a better qualified and more experienced colleague. In 1969, for example, Senator Charles Goodell attempted to marshal the liberals behind an amendment to cut off all funds for military operations in Vietnam after December 1, 1970. In a humiliating floor defeat, he failed to secure the support of even half the liberals. Conditions certainly prevailed against him but not the least of these was his inexperience and his lack of stature in the Senate.[59] The junior member for New York, who had only been appointed to Robert Kennedy's seat the year before, found he could make very little headway on his own in such a major policy area. In the succeeding year, however, George McGovern took charge of Goodell's amendment. Goodell himself was quite willing to become second in command, but McGovern wanted a Republican with greater pulling power as the chief cosponsor. Ultimately, Goodell had to accept the position of an assistant manager alongside Alan Cranston, Harold Hughes, and Fred Harris as the Goodell amendment of the previous year was transformed into the McGovern–Hatfield measure.[60] Although the amendment was defeated, the improved organizational management and the greater experience of the sponsors had had their effect for the amendment collected the support of all the liberals in a respectable floor vote of 39.[61]

It was always possible that a senior liberal would reverse the process and permit a junior to assume responsibility for a campaign. This happened in 1966 when the senior liberal in the housing field, Paul Douglas, agreed to let Edmund Muskie take command of the model cities bill in 1966.[62] Douglas did this because he felt that Muskie's shorter and less controversial record would be less likely to alienate other senators in such a sensitive issue area. Although such magnanimity did occur, it was exceptional. In general, it was the credentials of the senior liberals that led them into the positions of group authority.

An important part of a senior liberal's attraction lay in the relationships he had developed with outside political groups. Such organizations as the AFL-CIO, the League of Women Voters, Common Cause, the National Governors' Conference, the U.S. Conference of Mayors, the Consumer Federation of America, and the United Auto

Workers often provided valuable assistance in legislative fights. Group activity is a ubiquitous phenomenon in American politics and therefore no legislative leader was able to operate in a political vacuum even if he wanted to. Group activity and influence was present whether or not it was requested or recognized by an issue leader in Congress. Given this political context it was important for a leader to have the confidence of the relevant progressive groups; otherwise, they were likely to shift their attention away from him toward an alternative leader. This occurred in 1960, when the major lobbies in favor of federal aid to cities (the U.S. Conference of Mayors, the American Municipal Association) became so disillusioned with the efforts of their chosen champion, Senator Warren Magnuson, that they developed a closer liaison with Senator Harrison Williams.[63]

It can be seen that the legislative leader had to operate with regard to two areas of reference. In one he had to retain the confidence of his colleagues, and in the other he had to assure the external forces that he could translate their views into hard votes. The expectations of these progressive groups certainly inflicted pressures upon a leader, but if he could satisfy them, he could exploit their allegiance to strengthen his own position within the Senate. On this positive side, groups could provide the liberal leader with a number of benefits. They could impose pressure on him, but they could also assist him in stimulating his colleagues' interest and in marshaling them around a focal project. Whether it was by appeal, by bargaining, by promises, or by cajolery, the groups could publicize an issue and circulate the relevant information more quickly and comprehensively than any senator's office. On many occasions the feasibility of a legislative campaign and the credibility of a leader were almost totally dependent upon the research facilities of outside groups. The momentum of the campaign against the anti-ballistic missile project in 1969, for example, was to a large extent maintained by such groups as the Americans for Democratic Action, the National Committee for a Sane Nuclear Policy, the Council for a Livable World, the Southern Christian Leadership Conference, and the Federation of American Scientists. They furnished Senators Hart and Cooper with scientific data and strategic information that enabled them to challenge effectively the most complex and expensive weapons system ever devised by the Pentagon.[64]

Other aspects of group assistance could be just as valuable to a struggling leader. Aid in drafting proposals was a group specialty and one that was often appreciated by senators. A leader did not usually regard a draft bill as a definitive and final proposal to be defended at all costs. Nevertheless, he did value a draft as a beginning to the process and a basis for discussion and negotiation. This was especially so in those cases where a senator's staff was inexperienced or where no established agency existed to provide him with authoritative proposals. In 1972, for example, it was a citizen action group, Common Cause, that drew up detailed proposals for the public financing of presidential elections. These were adopted by Senator Walter Mondale, who disclosed to the Senate that he owed a "great deal to the experience, research and good counsel of Common Cause."[65]

In addition to information and proposals, groups could provide a Senate leader with tactical advice based on their long-term experience of agency positions, opposing group strategies, and congressional politics. It was not uncommon, in fact, for a Senate leader to come to rely upon the expert guidance and political influence of a lobbyist. David Cohen of the ADA, for example, acted as an aide de camp to Robert Kennedy and Maurine Neuberger during their campaign to require a government health warning to be included in all cigarette advertisements.[66] In the early 1960s one of the most valuable lobbyists to the liberal group was High Mields of the U.S. Conference of Mayors. He not only helped to draft clean air and clear water legislation for Senators Ribicoff and Muskie, respectively, but acted as an important link between the senators and the environmental groups.[67] But perhaps the best known example of a close relationship between a liberal leader and a private troubleshooter was Ralph Nader's association with Senator Abraham Ribicoff. Although officially employed at the Department of Labor at the time of Ribicoff's investigations into automobile safety, Nader was in fact acting as an unofficial staff member of Ribicoff's Subcommittee on Executive Reorganization. His efforts at obtaining information, collating research results, refining legislation, mobilizing outside groups, and publicizing the issue were largely responsible for the National Traffic and Motor Vehicle Safety bill becoming law in 1966.[68]

This last example underlines the role of senatorial staffs in facilitating linkages between the issue leader and the supportive apparatus outside the Senate. Both personal and committee staffs were politically relevant organizations, for they provided significant access points for groups and agencies interested in congressional policymaking. They often acted as communications centers where information was processed and guided toward the senator, where relationships with political groups were cultivated, and where the number and content of the communiques to other senators were controlled.[69] Whether or not staff assistants entered the profession as activists, they naturally assumed policy interests in the highly charged political climate of the Senate. Over and above the simple development of political sympathies were the opportunities for involvement and activism available to the average staffer. Even on the tightest of tight ships, the decentralized structure of the Senate was reflected in its staff organization. As a result, there was great scope and sometimes even encouragement for initiatives to be taken by committed individuals within the staff system.

The degree of staff discretion varied, of course, according to differences in committee rules, staff structures, policy areas, and in senators' interests, sensitivities, and political perspectives. At the highest level of its development, however, a staff organization could provide an individual member or a committee not just with a ready-made communications network but with a politically active suborganization. Among the individual liberal members who benefited from such assistance were Harrison Williams, whose initial interest and advance in the mass transit area was stimulated by his legislative assistant Ardee Ames; Wayne Morse, who had the benefit of Charles Lee's experience and initiative in the issue of federal aid to education; and Joseph Clark, who utilized the policy expertise and legislative drafting skills of James Sundquist in the manpower development field.[70] But perhaps the best example of an activist staff appeared in the Commerce Committee, within which so much consumer and environmental protection legislation was developed. The operational discretion and political rationale of the staff in this committee is described by Michael Pertschuk, the committee's chief counsel.

> Any staff man worth his salt will augment his own resources by reaching out to establish a core of contacts and resources, from public interest groups to Universities to the Library of Congress to the bowels of the agencies where committed workers are found. . . . Staff members . . . are characterized by a strong public com-

mitment; a delight in taking independent initiatives; a taste for achieving through indirection that which could not be achieved by confrontation [and] an ability to tread gingerly upon conflicting lines of loyalty.[71]

While such comments may seem audacious, they do serve to indicate the extent to which senators depended upon their staffs for so many legislative functions. Many liberal leaders expected their staffs not only to provide them with technical assistance, but to help generate issues that they would then adopt in the Senate.

In addition to group and staff assistance, the liberals could also benefit from presidential leadership. According to much of the popular folklore concerning legislative–executive relationships, congressional liberals were totally dependent upon activist presidents to formulate progressive policies; inspire public opinion; organize supportive executive agencies, interest groups, and party organizations; and to manage the requisite legislation through the Congress. In many ways, there is more than a grain of truth in such a grossly simplified view of the president's role in progressive legislation. A chief executive like Lyndon Johnson could maximize the opportunities for reform legislation through the careful marshaling of political forces outside Congress and through the circumspect cultivation of legislative support within Congress. In respect to proposals with which he was personally identified, Johnson was prepared to exploit the full force of his pivotal position in order to gain clearance from both the interests, parties, agencies, and governmental units involved in prospective legislation and from the relevant congressional elites before he was prepared to submit bills to the legislature. His strategy of task forces was based on this emphasis on consultation. Through these, he attempted to reduce open political dispute by permitting the maximum number of interested and involved parties to come to some agreement on a policy before it was released into the legislative process. Once in Congress, an attentive but discreet president like Johnson could assist the bills' sponsors in a whole variety of ways—recommendation of appropriate procedures, advice on timing, optimum scheduling of presidential proposals, assistance in congressional persuasion, and so on.[72] It was presidential services such as these that helped Johnson achieve congressional passage of major administrative proposals in such areas as civil rights, aid to education, medicare, poverty, and urban renewal. One small but significant example of legislative management undertaken by Johnson is provided by the campaign for the model cities bill in 1966.

This ambitious program, which proposed to inject $2.3 billion into the cities for the purpose of replanning and redeveloping depressed urban areas, was sufficiently expensive and controversial to arouse widespread opposition to it in Congress. Despite intense administration pressure, it appeared in October 1966 that the program might just fail to win approval in the House of Representatives. The bill's overall sponsor, Edmund Muskie, suggested that if the bill could gain more support from the business sector, its chances of securing passage would be greater. The administration responded to this point and within days 22 leading corporation executives had issued a joint statement of support for Johnson's program.[73] It was Johnson's capacity and motivation to immerse himself in the minutiae of congressional mechanics that raised the general standards of legislative liaison to an unprecedented level during the Great Society era.

Although presidents necessarily devoted most of their resources to major administration proposals, they could provide very useful assistance to members of Congress who were sponsoring their own legislation. The presidency's sheer potential as a political mobilizing force in fact often led liberal senators to seek presidential support of their policies. When Harrison Williams was attempting to increase the political momentum behind his mass transit legislation in 1963, he regarded President Kennedy's declared interest in the area to have been crucial in gaining him additional support. "The bill had the support of numerous metropolitan groups and of the urban Senators, but we wanted Presidential support. We went to the White House and eventually turned them around. After that things really began to happen."[74] Although Kennedy had only agreed in principle to the aims of Williams's bill and did not specifically endorse it, his acceptance of the need for a future mass transit program was sufficient to change the political status of the proposal.[75] The prominence and momentum given to bills associated with the president was appreciated by a number of liberals, who invited the White House to help straighten their paths inside the Senate.

Philip Hart, for example, had been introducing truth-in-packaging proposals throughout the first half of the 1960s.[76] He also regarded presidential support of his bill, or at least administrative acceptance of the need for reform in the area, as crucial to the success of the measure. In 1966, Johnson specifically endorsed the principle of fair packaging and made it known that Hart's bill was an acceptable method of achieving the objective. The truth-in-packaging bill was enacted in the same year. Another long-term campaign was fought by Paul Douglas for the truth-in-lending measure.[77] First introduced in 1959, Douglas gained qualified and low-priority support from Presidents Kennedy and Johnson from 1961 to 1966. In 1967, however, after Douglas had left the Senate, the bill's new sponsor (William Proxmire) gained a signficantly more enthusiastic and specific endorsement from the president. This gave an extra boost to the campaign and by 1968 the truth-in-lending measure had been enacted. Hart, Douglas, and Proxmire all found that administration support of their measures was of great value in terms of both technical consultation between executive agencies and related interest groups, and political communication among the relevant parties inside and outside Congress.

Bearing in mind the strategic brilliance of Johnson and his congressional liaison office under Larry O'Brien, it is possible to relax into the comfortably simplistic notion that the congressional liberals relied for their policies, organization, and legislative achievements on executive leadership. Before succumbing to this seductive interpretation, it is necessary to acknowledge a number of important provisos to this particular facet of presidential leadership. To begin with, not all liberal policies were directly derived from the presidency. Given the multifarious roots of public policy, it would be more accurate to say that no liberal policy was provided in totality by the presidency. Any presidential policy would be the result of a long-established interchange of ideas between and among administrators, intellectuals, interest groups, parties, the media, previous presidents, the courts, and not least, members of Congress.[78] During the Great Society era, in fact, Congress could claim to be a significant source of several pieces of reputedly Johnsonian legislation. For example, Johnson's famous "poor schools" formula for federal aid to education had been suggested in principle by Wayne Morse well before Johnson adopted the stratagem. Members of Congress could exploit their position in the policymaking process and not always have to rely on presidential inspiration and direction. This was certainly true in the case of Hart, Douglas, and Proxmire with their consumer legislation. Without presidential encouragement or assistance, they became focal points of political interest for those groups concerned with consumer protection and, in conjunction with those groups, formulated the policies for which they then attempted to mobilize support.

Senate liberals also showed that they could wrest the initiative from a president. The Hart–Mondale campaign for open housing in 1968 mentioned earlier (pp. 196–98) provides one of the best examples in this field. A minority of senators mobilized a coalition behind a policy formulated by a Johnson task force but which had been permitted to stagnate by the president after he had failed to secure its passage in 1966. The efforts of liberals like Hart and Mondale were reflected in a number of other domestic policy areas between 1966 and 1968. It was during this time that President Johnson came to devote an increasing amount of his resources and energies to the Vietnam war. This left many of the Great Society programs relatively unattended by the White House just at the time when they needed renewed political support to move them into their secondary phase of development. It was often the Senate liberals who provided an organized defense of the programs and fought for the necessary increases in expenditure.[79]

If the Senate liberals sometimes showed that they found sympathetic presidents to be very useful in their legislative campaigns, they also revealed that they were not totally dependent on presidential leadership. They could set up their own policy formulation networks with private and governmental centers of influence. They also revealed that they could effectively mobilize themselves as a group in the face of reduced presidential interest and even presidential indifference. But perhaps the greatest test of all came with the Nixon administration when the liberals demonstrated that they could adopt a position and marshal their forces in support of it—even when they were being confronted by a hostile president. The most dramatic example of the liberals' ability to withstand not only intense presidential opposition but also the institutional inertia of a presidential appointment came in 1970, when Judge Harold Carswell was appointed to the Supreme Court. Because this case illustrates many of the points discussed so far in this chapter, it will be examined next in some detail.

Case Study: Liberal Mobilization and the Carswell Nomination

After Judge Clement Haynsworth's nomination to the Supreme Court had been rejected by the Senate in 1969, it was generally felt that President Nixon's second choice would be accepted.[80] The Senate's authority to refuse to confirm a president's court appointee had almost become a constitutional dead letter until Senators Birch Bayh, Walter Mondale, and Edward Brooke began a long campaign to challenge the previously accepted convention of uncontested presidential preference.[81] By asserting itself in this way, the Senate believed that it had created an effective deterrent against another ill-considered appointment.

The Senate received the second nominee in an almost apologetic mood. It knew that it had seriously embarrassed the President over the Haynesworth nomination and was therefore anxious to make a reconciliation with the White House. In the words of Evans and Novak: "One rejection was a serious blot on any President's record: two rejections would be out of the question . . . an unimaginable humiliation."[82] Senators reiterated that they had no objection to the selection of another southern conservative judge for the Supreme Court. Although the liberals deplored Nixon's southern strategy and the administration's retrogression in the civil rights field, they accepted the notion that appointments should not be openly disputed on philosophical grounds. Thus when Judge Harold Carswell was presented to the Senate as a nominee clear of all conflict of interest charges, he was initially regarded as a thoroughly acceptable candidate for the Court. Civil rights groups complained about his decisions in Florida, but since the liberals knew that it would be impossible to mount an effective opposition campaign on this type of complaint, they were generally prepared to acquiesce in the appointment.

It was only when reports on Carswell's private demeanor, professional competence, and political activities began to filter through into public debate that some senators experienced their first doubts over the appointment. As each story emerged concerning Carswell's treatment of black lawyers in court, his bias against civil rights litigants, his speech on white supremacy, and his assistance to a golf club in resisting desegregation, the group of skeptics grew larger. The liberals quickly seized the opportunity for opposing Carswell's philosophy on the acceptable grounds of personal and professional competence. Once again it was Senator Edward Brooke, a liberal in the president's own party, who initiated the first serious opposition to the Carswell nomination. After the strain of conducting the campaign against Haynsworth, Birch Bayh was reluctant to take up the new cause, but with persistent pressure from Brooke he eventually agreed to exploit his position on the Judiciary Committee to lead the anti-Carswell group.[83]

Bayh became the leader and his first job was to secure the support of the rest of his liberal colleagues on the Judiciary Committee. If he could not persuade them, there would be no point in continuing the campaign. In this case Senators Edward Kennedy, Joseph Tydings, and Philip Hart readily fell into line and provided Birch Bayh with all the assistance he needed. With this initial momentum, Bayh began to make it known through the bush telegraph that the Judiciary Committee liberals were going to make a fight of it. Friends were contacted, views were exchanged, and voting commitments were given on a totally informal basis. At a very early stage in the campaign the liberals had galvanized themselves into a solid core of opposition. The liberal bloc materialized apparently so effortlessly that very little persuasion, bargaining, or lengthy appeals were necessary. Although such an organization proved a valuable rallying point, it could not by itself arrest the tidal inertia of another presidential appointment. If the liberals were ever going to succeed in winning the support of their less easily convinced colleagues, they needed time more than anything else.[84]

Back in the Judiciary Committee, Bayh and the liberals knew that they could not persuade the whole committee to oppose Carswell, yet they did manage to delay the final recommendation long enough for investigations to be made, colleagues to be persuaded, and outside forces to mobilize themselves. Gradually, the political leverage of the AFL-CIO, the United Auto Workers, the NAACP, the National Education Association, and the Leadership Conference on Civil Rights began to move votes over to the liberals. Most damaging of all to the Carswell cause was the opposition of his own legal profession, whose objections became increasingly vociferous as the debate progressed.[85]

Information, support, and pressure not only snowballed outside the chamber but also inside the Senate. Bayh was now assisted in the coordination of the campaign by the Republican Wednesday Club, the staff of the Democratic Policy Committee, and the staff of various liberal senators, but Bayh remained the center of the operation. After additional delays on the floor of the Senate, the Carswell supporters suffered a continual series of defections until the liberally inspired minority revolt approached the size of a majority. Right up to the actual vote, Bayh was drawing previously uncommitted senators (e.g., Cook, Smith, Prouty) and previously pro-Carswell members (e.g., Dodd, Packwood, Fong, Percy) to the opposition camp.[86] These represented the crucial hemorrhage of votes from the administration and the Carswell nomination was rejected 51 to 45.

Despite the fact that the president had staked his reputation on the nomination and that a majority of the Judiciary Committee favored confirmation, the liberals succeeded in resisting the institutional inertia long enough to deny the president's second selection for the Court. From an initial platform inside the Judiciary Committee, Senators Bayh, Kennedy, Hart, and Tydings exploited the opportunities for delay and obstruction to allow time for greater pressure to develop within both the chamber and the country at large. Even when the nomination finally emerged from the Judiciary Committee, the liberals still managed to subject the final vote to a number of postponements. By carefully coordinating the release of new information and new statements of opposition, Bayh managed to give the impression of an accelerating movement away from Carswell: "They subjected the loyalists to a . . . drop by drop water torture, engineering one by one announcements of new anti-Carswell Senators."[87] Even desperate White House lobbying could not prevent the president from losing the initiative. With each delay came new defections timed to inflict maximum damage on the administration's confidence. Eventually, the opposition group, which had started with only two senators and very little credibility, succeeded in obtaining the necessary 51 supporters.

In conclusion, it can be said that the organizational coherence of the liberal group was very dependent on the internal and external status of its leaders. The liberals were molded into a legislative force when they were guided by authoritative leaders. No single way existed by which leaders brought them together. As one legislative assistant remarked, "liberal support [was] mobilized in different ways on different issues."[88] The leader's techniques varied according to the technicality of the proposals, the operational style of the external support, the president's position, constituency pressures, and the personalities of fellow senators. But one factor that remained constant was leadership quality. The leader activated the liberal members and translated generalized liberal attachments into specific legislative commitments. Some liberals were only too willing to support the leader, whereas others lent their support grudgingly. On some occasions, liberals rallied around an issue and a leader almost as a reflex action, but on others any liberal cooperation was the result of extensive deliberation and negotiation. Once a reasonable degree of mutual support had been achieved, by whatever means and at whatever speed, the leader was in a position to provide the liberal members with some of the benefits that should accrue to any community.

First, he provided a focal point of communications and information. Second, he was responsible for the effective coordination of internal and external resources. Third, he gave organizational cohesion to the liberals' efforts. Fourth, he was able to satisfy the liberals' expectation that there should be a recognized liberal position on the issue involved. George McGovern was not the only senator who used to respond to issues in which he was inexperienced with the question, "What are the liberals doing?"[89] Most liberals expected that the communal spirit they experienced as a cultural group ought to yield dependable guidance and trustworthy voting cues when the group was operating as a political force.

Finally, the leader had to be able to inspire optimism among the liberals by working to expand the initial pool of mainly liberal support. The leader was expected to attract the maximum level of internal support for the measure endorsed by the liberals. This was a difficult problem for a leader because even when the liberal group was mobilized in a cooperative effort, it remained very much an informal coalition of individual members. At no point did the group constitute a self-contained organic unit. On the contrary, it remained a heterogeneous conglomerate with dozens of hairline fractures—each one affording immediate escape for the anxious defector. The leadership, therefore, not only had to conserve this delicate group structure but had to attract the type of additional nonliberal support that could well weaken the already limited cohesion of the original liberal group.

Perhaps the leadership's most difficult problem lay in maintaining internal consistency during legislative campaigns of ever-increasing specificity. Unlike the simple Carswell question of acceptance or rejection, most legislative issues involved not just building support for a rigidly defined measure but changing proposals to match the available number of votes. Since initial liberal formations were usually based upon provisional and qualified support for generalized policy positions, the resultant groups were highly susceptible to division when abstract issues matured into detailed measures that aroused public attention.

These two problems of nonliberal recruitment and the maintenance of group integration involved questions of group priorities and collective strategy. These types of problem made the most stringent demands upon any embryonic liberal organization. They tended not only to reveal the leadership's ability in closing the group's ranks but to expose the group's capacity to resolve internal conflict, to decide priorities, and to make collective responses. To arrive at any accurate assessment of the liberals as a legislative force, therefore, it is necessary to examine the degree of cohesion that existed when the liberal group was actually subjected to the stress of legislative campaigns.

GROUP ORGANIZATION

In some issues on some occasions the rigors of mobilization and organization did not present much of a problem to the liberals. Where strong public support was activated in favor of a specific form of legislative action, the liberals inside the Senate might well find themselves with a large number of unsolicited friends. Whether it was the Civil Rights Act of 1964, the poverty program (1964), the Elementary and Secondary Education Act of 1965, or the Medicare Act of 1965, the combination of aroused interest-group activity, intense media coverage of the proposals, vigorous presidential support, and general public sympathy ensured plentiful support for the Senate liberals. Many of the liberal measures of the Great Society had been formulated and developed over the past 20 years. Liberal senators continually pushed these proposals in Congress until in the mid-1960s the liberals were swamped with support from previously reluctant and even obstinate colleagues. The liberals exploited this exceptional receptivity to reform and played no small part in channeling the progressive impulse into floor victories. Much of the necessary legislative organization was effectively done for them by the declared urgency and general acceptability of the proposals. At times it was difficult to determine whether the Senate liberals represented the vanguard of congressional progressivism or just the vehicle by which Johnson's consensus was converted into legislative measures.

As was the case with mobilization, the liberals succeeded in organizing themselves into a particularly cogent legislative force when they were aided and supported by a popular president with popular policies. However, such favorable circumstances were not always present, even in the liberal atmosphere of the mid-1960s. Apart from the major administration bills, the liberals were often left to fend for themselves, to develop direct relationships with executive agencies and external interest groups, and to build up their own political momentum inside the chamber. If the liberals could not always rely on the committed support of a President Kennedy or a President Johnson, they could by no means expect any substantial assistance from President Nixon. Yet during the Nixon years, liberal activity in the Senate increased somewhat in scale. Clearly, there is more to the study of the Senate liberals' legislative campaigns than the support of major presidential measures. Furthermore, one is likely to arrive at a more balanced perspective of the liberals' capacity as a legislative force by deliberately avoiding those occasions when the liberals acted as frontline troops for the centerpiece policies of progressive presidents. For this reason, it would perhaps be better to begin the analysis from the opposite perspective by studying the liberals when they appeared as a distinct minority and examining the ways by which they attempted to keep together but at the same time increase their support within the chamber.

It should be acknowledged at the outset that it was always possible for the liberals to reduce the problems involved in maintaining group coherence simply by confining the group to a limited number of members. As the group concentrated on strengthening internal bonds, it was relieved of the strain of negotiation and compromise with outside elements. This strategy was associated particularly with the liberal group because liberal members used to present unequivocally progressive proposals to the Senate on such sensitive subjects as gun control, congressional reform, military expenditures, and taxation. Although it was customary for these proposals to be decisively defeated on the floor, they could serve several useful functions on behalf of the liberal position. A minority proposal not only established a group commitment to a policy but placed it on the agenda for public discussion. The very act of raising the issue led to heightened public awareness of the problems involved and of the plans being presented to resolve them. In the words of David Cohen of Common Cause, the "twenty vote roll call often made an issue and got it talked about."[90] By continuing to press for votes in the face of adversity, the liberal minority could begin to embarrass the opposition groups and force them to consider ways of accommodating the new issue. As the public became conditioned to the possibility of legislation in the field, the minority could sometimes press home its advantage and ultimately achieve a long-term victory.

This combination of positional intransigence and incremental increases in support was much in evidence in the liberals' long campaign against the oil depletion allowance. Throughout the 1950s and 1960s, the liberals pressed for reductions in the allowance. In 1951 a proposal sponsored by Hubert Humphrey was defeated by the massive margin of 9 to 71. The liberals continued to raise the subject, in spite of the apparently hopeless odds. By the middle of the 1960s, Paul Douglas and William Proxmire had succeeded in attracting 35 members to the cause. The increased support, coupled with the growth in public disquiet over tax inequities, shifted attitudes in the Finance Committee. In 1969, the liberals' strategy was vindicated when they secured Senate approval for a 4½ percent reduction in the allowance.[91]

The strategy of minority detachment did not, however, always yield results; it could prove counterproductive. As the liberals luxuriated in self-indulgent rigidity, they could alienate colleagues who might otherwise have looked favorably upon some aspects of their position. A sequence of major defeats might have illustrated ideological authenticity but might also have been regarded as indicative of an overall lack of support. This was certainly true in the areas of military expenditures, civil liberties, and congressional reform, where the liberals adhered to persistently unattractive minority positions.[92] In general, humiliating failures could occasionally serve to publicize issues and build up long-term support, but the liberals could not afford to employ this strategy indefinitely.

Like any other legislators, liberals were concerned with maximizing their resources in order to influence public policy. To achieve this they had to establish themselves as a major institutional force that could either win roll calls or at least attain respectable levels of solid support (i.e., 35–50 votes). It was an unfortunate fact of liberal life, however, that even if the group was in absolute agreement on an issue (which was unlikely), without outside support it was only possible for them to secure about 25 votes. To win a respectable degree of support, they had to draw what the voting study termed liberal-to-moderates and moderate-to-liberals into the liberal camp. This could be a difficult task, for, as their rankings indicate, these members were not as consistent in their policy positions as were the liberal members. Legislative advances for the liberals, therefore, depended very much upon the attitudes and activities of these less predictable colleagues.

While the Senate's individualistic form of coalition building could be affected by innumerable factors, not the least of these was the degree to which the liberal group was prepared to work with the less committed and more skeptical moderate members. These senators could hold the key to legislative success, for a shift of 10 moderates either way would disturb a majority margin by 20 votes. When the liberals wanted help, they therefore appealed to moderate members such as Carl Hayden, Frank Church, Stuart Symington, Mike Mansfield, Clinton Anderson, Warren Magnuson, John Cooper, Mike Monroney, and William Fulbright. The nature of the appeal, the response of the moderates, and the subsequent reaction of the liberals to the moderates' positions tended to vary from case to case.

On some occasions it was possible for the liberals to attract additional support at very little cost to their initial position. When the liberals took the initiative in an issue that had suddenly achieved public prominence, they could provide a political rallying point to all those who were disturbed by the issue and who wanted some political action in response to it. Under these conditions, the liberals could catch the conservative opposition forces unprepared and thereby attract a sizable number of more moderate colleagues to their cause. In this case the movement would be very much one of liberal-to-moderates and moderate-to-liberals moving to the liberal camp with few questions asked. When the president failed to respond to an apparent crisis and was in fact the cause of the public's disquiet, the position of the liberals could be even stronger. These conditions prevailed in 1970 when President Nixon ordered the invasion of parts of Cambodia to seek and destroy enemy mobilization areas and supply bases. This provocative action, taken at a time when the public's tolerance of the Vietnam war was already stretched to the limit, led to widespread criticism and demands not only for a retreat from Cambodia but for a definite plan for the complete withdrawal of U.S. troops from Southeast Asia. The liberals responded to the outcry with the McGovern–Hatfield amendment, which would have limited the use of funds to facilitate a complete phasing out of troops from Vietnam by December 31, 1971.[93] This radical attempt to circumscribe the President's discretion as commander-in-chief in a theater of war was a liberal proposal from its very inception. Yet its sponsors found little difficulty in securing the support of most of the more moderate senators, who were similarly disturbed by the Cambodian invasion and impressed by the public's attitude toward it. Apart from some minor modifications, the basic proposal to end financial support for the war in 1971 remained intact and ultimately attracted an impressive tally of 39 votes. In this case the liberals were afforded the luxury of positional consistency and additional support. The transformation from a small minority to a sizable voting bloc, however, was not always achieved with such ease.

In contrast to the controversial and much publicized McGovern–Hatfield amendment, a coalition strategy on the part of the liberals could well have involved them in extensive negotiations and group adjustments. Unlike an antiwar measure, most proposals were developed over a long period of time, during which various forms of the basic proposal would come to be presented. In the case of the wholesome meat bill of 1967, the liberal group was not in the type of sellers' market that was evident in the McGovern–Hatfield case.[94] With this bill, which proposed to raise the standards of meat hygiene in state slaughterhouses, the liberal group had its position and the more moderate members were grouped around an alternative measure of their own. The liberals supported the Mondale plan, which would have extended federal inspection to all meat-processing plants unless states could demonstrate that they had already achieved standards equivalent to the federal norm. The less liberal members, on the other hand, were attracted to Joseph Montoya's weaker bill, which would have given federal funds to the states to improve their own inspection standards. Since Mondale was determined to maximize the level of support for legislation in the field, he was willing to compromise on a number of points. He successfully persuaded his liberal colleagues to support a bill that would assist state governments in implementing federal standards of inspection. If the states failed to achieve federal standards of inspection in two years, then, and only then, could the federal government intervene in the way Mondale originally wanted and assume direct responsibility for meat hygiene. The result of this compromise was the Mondale–Montoya bill, which passed the Senate in 1967 without any liberal defections. It showed that the liberals were both willing and able to conduct negotiations and resolve differences as a collective group. Although they failed to secure their bill in toto, they did not renounce all interest in the alternative measure. Instead, they maintained the initiative and achieved a significant input to the final policy by establishing joint control of the compromise legislation at an early stage.

On some occasions the demands of a coalition strategy with more moderate members could cause such internal stress among the liberals that they would cut their losses and revert to their traditional posture of minority dissenters. The price of additional support could impose such an intolerable strain on the group that the liberals might seek to reject a cooperative venture in order to retain some positional integrity. This hardening of opinion would become particularly apparent when the liberals sensed that they were having to move too far to meet the demands of their nonliberal colleagues. As the liberals faced a serious loss of control over the terms in which a bill was considered, they might try to arrest the momentum toward unacceptable legislation which they themselves may have started through their original support for legislative intervention.

This occurred in 1965, when the liberals came to the defense of the Federal Trade Commission (FTC) over the issue of cigarette advertising.[95] The FTC made a ruling that required a health hazard warning to be given on cigarette packaging and in cigarette advertising. Although the FTC gave a one-year period of grace for the tobacco manufacturers in the sensitive area of advertising, intense political pressure arose for the moratorium to be extended to three years. Most liberals supported the FTC ruling and pressured many nonliberals into taking an interest in the issue. But it was the highly skilled tobacco lobbyists who took the initiative by actively mobilizing support for the weaker proposal. The tobacco interests successfully isolated the liberals by capitalizing upon the public pressure for reform to secure passage of a bill that would appear to be a consumer victory and which would hopefully forestall further regulation or legislation in the future. By the time the liberals came to realize that the momentum that they had helped to create had slipped out of their control, it was too late. They attempted to arrest the flow of votes away from their position, but in a vote to remove the three-year ban the liberal group emerged as a detached minority with only 29 supporters.

Finally, the strain involved in securing additional support could ultimately create so much internal tension that the liberals' group cohesion could begin to break down. This is not to say that the liberals normally maintained a highly integrated organization. In fact, it was common for the liberals to suffer from one or two defections in most floor votes. In contrast to these minor irregularities was the deep and debilitating division over an important policy issue. This is a perennial problem in any bargaining relationship, but it was particularly relevant to the liberals, who were traditionally renowned for forsaking pragmatism in favor of intransigence. The bruising process of negotiating principles and values for numerical support could produce a damaging split between those liberals who were prepared to make concessions and those with the more traditional liberal characteristics of withdrawal and detachment. The problem of keeping members with these differing inclinations inside an already fragile group framework could sometimes prove insuperable. It has been noted elsewhere that the liberal ranks could be deeply divided by such issues as gun control (see pp. 177–78), Rule XXII (see p. 176), the poverty program (see p. 224), military expenditures (see p. 224), and the disclosure of senators' financial interests (see p. 134).

In the civil rights field, for example, the liberals were continuously confronted in the late 1950s and early 1960s with demands for compromise in return for additional support and a viable legislative base. Occasionally, this frustration broke through and the liberal group split between those who rejected marginal reforms and those who preferred to persevere on the inside and achieve reform by accretion. In 1961, for example, Jacob Javits offered an amendment which cut through all the prevarication and detailed provisos that normally characterized civil rights legislation. It proposed the prohibition of all federal contract funds for airport terminal buildings containing segregated facilities. This provocative amendment in the sensitive area of public accommodations aroused great controversy among liberals, for many thought that such a proposal would undermine the carefully nurtured framework of the bipartisan coalition in civil rights. While some defended the move as a definite statement of liberal intent, others condemned it as a counterproductive ploy which would aggravate their less liberal allies and jeopardize future

civil rights advances. Predictably, the amendment was defeated and
the liberals' internal dispute was publicly exposed in the process, for
while 17 liberals supported the measure, 5 of them did not.[96]

It is probably true that by the early 1970s the liberals were less
inclined to abandon ship for the sake of their principles. As chapter
4 revealed, the liberals developed from a collection of mostly inexperienced juniors to a group of senators who achieved some remark-
able legislative advances. In contrast to the late 1950s, the liberals
had a number of major Senate leaders and committee chairmen
within their ranks. It was this growth in institutional power, in political confidence, in legislative achievement, and in positional flexibility
that largely dispelled the liberals' old neurosis over their systematic
exclusion from senatorial influence. Nevertheless, liberals could still
find negotiation with nonliberals to be a strain that could occasionally
lead to rejection and to detachment. Since liberals continued to revere
the image of themselves as the "cutting edge of change, innovation
and liberalism"[97] in an environment of veto points and negativism,
they remained naturally susceptible to keeping the blade away from
the snagging undergrowth of compromise. This was a problem that
remained insoluble in a system that demanded group cooperation
for positive action but simultaneously facilitated individual objection
and secession.

Another problem that confronted the liberal group lay in the
liberals' competence in using the Senate's rules. Any group that
wanted to develop into a credible legislative force needed to possess
parliamentary expertise. The conservatives always had a reputation
for procedural mastery because they "realized better than anyone
that knowledge was power."[98] The liberals, on the other hand, tended
to be preoccupied with the nature of legislation to such an extent
that they sometimes neglected the machinery by which it could be
brought into effect. While liberals were carried on a wave of enthusiastic concern for goals and ends, the conservatives were left unattended to exploit the myriad opportunities for procedural delay. In
the words of one liberal's senior staff assistant: "Liberals tend to be
more interested in the substance of legislation. . . . Conservatives are
far better parliamentarians because their role is to block proposals."[99]
Another liberal aide put the point more graphically:

> So many liberals go on their asses because they are either unwill-
> ing or unable to learn procedures. . . . Parliamentary knowledge

and tactics are qualities that are lacking among the liberals. They are concerned with broad global issues and have no time to mess around with this nitty gritty. . . . The intricacies of the legislative process escape them or they do not regard it as important. Consequently they sometimes get clobbered."[100]

As crusading initiators, liberals were not willing to permit their grand strategies to be deflected by the minutiae of procedure. In many ways they believed that their commitment to the substance of legislation compensated for any deficiencies they might have in parliamentary skills. An example of the liberals' cavalier attitude toward the rules was given by Senator Gaylord Nelson: "In the Senate it is possible to be successful without knowing much about the rules. Rules are only really useful when you want to block something. They are of no great consequence to liberal legislators."[101] It was this attitude that sometimes led liberal legislative efforts to be seriously compromised. The example selected by the assistant parliamentarian to illustrate the liberals' weakness in this area concerned "unanimous consent agreements." Under Rule 40, the Senate is permitted to suspend the rules to facilitate business and plan schedules. To do this, all the senators had to do was to consent to an agreement containing specific stipulations over subject matter, debate rules, and voting times. On numerous occasions liberals consented, or at least chose not to object, to such agreements without being fully aware of what they contained. The liberals "often got caught out"[102] on these agreements because while they arrived on the floor expecting a smooth flow of business, they also expected to retain their customary privileges. Often, they discovered that the debates were rigidly structured, with restrictions on the admissibility and timing of amendments, discussions, and votes. The liberal who tried to exercise his traditional right of offering a nongermane amendment would be ruled out of order.

In response to these and other failures, the liberals began to show a greater interest in the rules and precedents of the Senate. By the late 1960s and early 1970s, such individuals as Jacob Javits, Philip Hart, Lee Metcalf, and Alan Cranston had become widely recognized as skilled parliamentary operators. But perhaps the most significant indication of the liberals' newly acquired proficiency in this area came with a number of organized filibusters. Not without irony and even a trace of hypocrisy, the liberals reversed their attitude toward Rule XXII and used it to frustrate some of the Nixon administration's policy proposals that they regarded as unacceptable.[103] Senator Alan Cranston rationalized the *volte face* in the following terms: "I came to support the filibuster in response to its use by others who used it as a weapon to prevent something from happening. I supported it while Mr. Nixon was abusing power and remolding the Presidency."[104] Liberals helped to organize filibusters and extended debates in such areas as the anti-ballistic missile system (1969), the supersonic transport plane (1970), the Lockheed loan (1971), and the draft (1971). On occasion, their employment of the filibuster technique led to some notable victories. In the busing debate of 1972, for example, civil rights supporters used the filibuster against the higher education bill, which contained numerous restrictions over the busing of children to achieve integration in schools. Although the bill had been passed by the House and had majority support in the Senate, the liberals held firm in three cloture votes and eventually killed the measure.[105]

By the early 1970s the liberals had certainly improved upon their earlier undistinguished record in procedural competence. Experience from the salutary lessons of the past had led to a much greater interest and proficiency in parliamentary mechanics. Liberals were more disposed not only to avail themselves of the facilities provided by the parliamentarian's office, but to resort to procedural maneuvers by which to obstruct objectionable proposals. A senior staff assistant summed up the new mood of the 1970s: "There is now more attention to details and to the floor. We are less apt to go down in flaming defeat. We fight tougher."[106]

In spite of all the improvements, however, the liberals had yet to conquer their own feeling of inferiority in this field. Liberal experience may have increased but it had not reached the level of parliamentary craftsmanship achieved by the conservatives. Serious doubts remained over the liberals' aptitude for procedural gamemanship. According to the assistant parliamentarian: "The liberals do not get outmaneuvered as much as they used to, but they still get snookered on a greater number of occasions than the conservatives do."[107] For example, it was not long before the conservatives began to counter the liberals' newfound regard for filibustering through a newly developed appetite for cloture. As the conservatives' traditional antipathy for cloture had long since been buried, they were prepared to use it "for purposes that it was not supposed to be used for—i.e., to facilitate efficient business."[108] A successful cloture vote did not just limit subsequent debate but eliminated all opportunities for proposing nongermane amendments or any amendment that had not been presented before the cloture vote. As a result, the conservatives began to press for cloture on liberal measures (e.g., opposition to the Lockheed loan, 1971) at an early stage in floor consideration, thereby restricting the liberals' freedom of manoeuvre on their own legislation.[109] Although the liberals had become more competent in procedure, they had still to emulate the conservatives in this area of legislative activity.

To the liberals, the conservatives' proficiency in parliamentary maneuver was an intrinsic part of their overall strategy of obstruction. Since the conservatives were normally in the position of policy objectors, they were naturally inclined toward the numerous veto points afforded by the Senate rules. When this abiding interest in procedure was combined with their already limited legislative agenda, the result was highly conducive to group consensus and integration. It was in this field that the liberals felt they were most disadvantaged. The liberals saw their conservative counterparts as "better integrated and better organized"[110] because their strategy was "obstructive and non-constructive." Since conservatives were invariably on the defensive, they had a garrison mentality that responded favorably to requests for unanimity and discipline. As a result, conservatives had "no alternative ideas" and "few internal tensions."[111]

The liberals looked enviously upon the conservatives' organizational strength, yet believed that their own diffuse philosophy was necessarily incongruent with developed and stable cooperation. As Senator Gale McGee explained: "The Senate liberals are fragmented by the very nature of their philosophy which makes it difficult for them to close ranks. Whereas conservatives react spontaneously together in reaction to change, the liberals will be split two or three ways over the type of change they want. It is difficult for them to have the same discipline."[112] Differences between western populists and East Coast intellectuals, urban machine liberals and rural progressives, junior freshmen and senior chairmen, old New Dealers and new activists, and between liberal Republicans and liberal Democrats could all lead to disagreements over methods and priorities. As a result, the liberals benefited from a wealth of ideas and options, but they often suffered from a lack of direction which the conservatives were only too ready to exploit.

The internal tension within the liberal group could lead to conflict over procedural strategy. In 1968, for example, a movement against excessive Pentagon spending developed within liberal circles. As this issue concerned the sensitive area of national security, some liberals wanted to build up a well-researched and responsible critique of military expenditures that would attract nonliberal support. Others believed that the liberals should capitalize on both the Vietnam debacle and the emergence of excessive cost overruns on several projects, and press forward with wholesale cuts in the military budget. One of the occasions when this intraliberal dispute came to a head was when Senator Joseph Clark proposed a series of amendments that would have reduced army, navy, and air force funds by a flat 10 percent. This successfully split the liberals between those who accepted the proposals and those who regarded them as embarrassing, indiscriminate, provocative, and irresponsible. The depth of the division was revealed in the vote on the air force funds, which split the liberals 12 to 10.[113]

Finally, divisions could occur over the implementation of policy. For example, when the liberals were pressing the poverty program through the Senate in 1964, they were constantly subjected to opposition efforts to include state governmental control of community action groups. As a compromise, the Johnson administration accepted a proposal whereby a governor could veto those community action projects contracted with private organizations. A majority of the liberals (18) accepted this amendment, but nearly one-third (8) opposed it on the grounds that it would detrimentally affect the implementation of the poverty program in the field.[114]

When this propensity for internal division was combined with the liberals' problems in dealing with nonliberal support and their weakness in parliamentary craftsmanship, the group's effectiveness as a legislative unit might be called into question. Certainly, the liberals themselves tended to think that they were not well versed in the requisite arts of internal agreement, group coordination, and strategic bargaining. While they believed that their strong kindred spirit could be effectively exploited into legislative activism, they remained frustrated that their enthusiasm for innovation often failed to be translated into group cohesion and bloc voting. In their minds the result was that "liberal legislation was seldom well planned and coordinated."[115] Before the liberals are dismissed as an organized legislative group, however, it should be pointed out that many of their problems were not limited to them alone but were experienced throughout the Senate. In many ways the liberals drew attention to and exaggerated their own deficiencies by assuming that they had an exceptional potential for close and continuous group cooperation. Numerous observers and commentators proceeded on the same premise. The Senate liberals were expected to act as a bloc simply because they were Senate liberals. But if the Senate liberals are viewed less as liberals and more as senators operating in the dissonant atmosphere of manifest individualism, the intermittent and rudimentary form of their organization becomes quite significant. It has been the purpose of this section to examine the liberals in relation to their inflated reputation as a rigid group of committed ideologues. On some occasions, the liberals did emerge as a group unable or unwilling or not needing to compromise to achieve their objectives. On many other occasions, the liberals revealed that just like any other group of senators, they were vulnerable to internal disagreements and open policy splits. The net result of the liberals' experience, therefore, has not been a spectacular record of group unity and collaboration. On the other hand, neither has it been a disaster insofar as collective effort is concerned. Given the multifarious deterrents to consistent group activity in the Senate, the liberals showed not only that they could organize themselves into an effective legislative force in support of a presidential program, but that they could devise their own proposals and develop a legislative coalition capable of seeing them into law.

This chapter has proceeded to examine the liberals' behavior as a legislative group on the premise that they were inherently incapable of organizing themselves into an effective political unit inside the Senate. This assumption was widely subscribed to in the 1950s and early 1960s. As late as 1964, for example, President Johnson told Hubert Humphrey, in unequivocal terms, that the fight for the civil rights bill in 1964 would probably fail because Humphrey would be unable to control his own liberals. Humphrey recalled the incident: "He [LBJ] said that liberals had never worked to understand the rules and how to use them, that we never organized effectively and would therefore go down to defeat. . . . He shook his head in apparent despair, predicting that we would fall apart in dissension. . . . I would have been outraged if he hadn't been basically right and historically accurate."[116]

Nevertheless, the liberals showed that they could operate as a disciplined unit not only in the civil rights field but in a whole host of other campaigns for Great Society reforms. The astonishing scale of progressive legislation enacted from 1964 to 1966 appeared to repudiate the liberals' reputation of being peripheral and ineffectual members. They often provided the central thrust to legislative campaigns in terms of strategy and management. Of course, the liberals were operating in optimum conditions for reform legislation. Most of the proposals had been on the political agenda for some time and had become familiarly acceptable to the public by the mid-1960s.[117] Others were devised in response to specific and urgent problems in a political climate that condoned and even demanded rapid action. These conditions, in conjunction with Kennedy's assassination, President Johnson's commitment to maximizing the potential for reform, the president's sophisticated techniques in congressional liaison, the Democrats' landslide election in 1964, and the public's expectation of legislative action generated a political momentum personified in the Senate by the liberal members. They had always presented and advocated the policies of the national party. With the assistance and inspiration of Johnson, the liberals now reaped the whirlwind of the public's liberal mood and received and organized the support of many of their colleagues whose assistance they had been seeking for years.

After 1966, the position of the liberals changed. While government action had attempted "to eliminate, or at least mitigate, the social, economic and legal foundations of inequality and deprivation,"[118] liberal policies increasingly appeared to be associated with social disharmony and political disaffection. Liberal optimism turned to defensiveness. To many liberals, contemporary social discord was not a reflection of the failure of reform programs, as conservatives claimed, but an indication of the necessity to expand and improve the services provided by the federal government. Nevertheless, the budgetary capacity and political motivation of the administration to maintain the momentum of social reform were severely curtailed by the demands of the Vietnam war. The liberals moved intermittently and inconsistently, yet remorsefully, to a position opposed to Johnson's war posture. They did so not only on the grounds of foreign policy and of constitutional prerogatives, but on the basis of contested financial priorities. The liberals were insistent upon preserving the scale of social programs and, as a result, were increasingly prepared to assume the initiative in domestic policy. In doing so, they came to depend less upon an increasingly beleaguered presidency and more on the expertise and political leverage that they had developed during the euphoric period from 1964 to 1966. When Richard Nixon replaced Lyndon Johnson in the White House, the pattern of increased liberal self-dependency in an era of ambivalent public attitudes toward the costs and efficacy of liberal programs became a firmly entrenched feature of policymaking in the late 1960s and early 1970s.

It is established that the Senate liberals operated most effectively and most productively during the Great Society era. Given the sheer scale of liberal legislation enacted in the mid-1960s, it is all too easy to dismiss the liberals as a legislative force in those years when the success rate for liberal proposals was much lower than it was in the Eighty-ninth Congress. This chapter has attempted to show that the Senate liberals over the period under review were not a wholly consistent and integrated bloc, but neither were they a fortuitous amalgam of maverick progressives. They were rather more a collaborative operation of varying intensity and size—with weaknesses and strengths, failures and successes.

As an informal legislative organization, the liberal members suffered from the lack of a permanent and organized structure. They were never able to provide a framework of regular consultation, a structured network of communications, or a focal unit of internal decision making. Instead, they relied upon a number of irregular and haphazard techniques by which to arrive at a common understanding and a joint commitment to the immediate future. Although the liberals were "cohesive on a great many questions . . . it could take a long time for this cohesion to build up."[119] Even when the liberals succeeded in transforming their sense of group identity into a conscious collective effort, there was no guarantee that the resulting unit would be sufficiently durable to withstand the counterpressures that inevitably arose in open legislative conflict.

The organizational problems inherent in such external stresses as presidential positions, constituency pressures, party requirements, and regional attachments were compounded by several internal flaws: poor attendance, a weak command of parliamentary procedures, a fascination with presidential politics, and a propensity to forgo compromise for ideological authenticity and positional consistency. But probably the most debilitating defect was the liberals' lingering enchantment with the seductive forces of senatorial individualism, which reduced their impulse to form a permanent and disciplined voting bloc. Since power was much more diffused in the Senate than the House, a senator did not experience a congressman's need to achieve influence through some form of collective enterprise. The aim of attaining political power by collegiate discipline and bloc voting was not widely subscribed to in the Senate, where the individual was fully aware that he already had a disproportionate degree of political influence. To the continuing detriment of their organization, the Senate liberals remained first and foremost children of the Senate, with an inherent suspicion of permanent structures, group obligations, and personal restrictions.

Although the liberals were prepared to operate as a group only within a loose framework of provisional agreements and cautious commitments, they nevertheless formed a distinct if disjointed group of members. By surface and underground tributaries they remained in contact, exchanged views, and marshaled themselves into ad hoc and temporary groupings. Because of the lack of any permanent and comprehensive liberal structure, the liberal groups that did materialize tended to be centered upon specific areas and problems. As a result, they had a task force style of operation that focused upon a limited aim with a sense of urgency and enthusiasm. While the conservatives were "only interested in the best way of saying 'no',"[120] the liberals were primarily responsible for introducing new issues, discussing future planning, and providing the driving force for so many innovatory proposals. Liberal organization may not have been as sophisticated as that of the conservatives, but it could amount to a formidable force that could not only place opposing groups in uncomfortable public positions, but could pressure them into making accommodating concessions.

It is true that to some extent the liberals had a disordered approach to their cooperative enterprises. Yet their unorthodox and often improvised forms of legislative collaboration were not totally devoid of organizational skills. First was their capacity for maintaining the momentum of reform through the mire of veto points within the Senate. One of the great problems connected with innovatory legislation in these conditions was the task of keeping the political pressure up to the requisite level to ensure the survival of proposals. "It was a question of constantly hammering away and developing support,"[121] and the liberals often proved themselves equal to the task by their stubborn persistence in raising problems and by their tenacious pursuit of reforms. Although the liberals' procedural strategy may sometimes have left something to be desired, their collective commitment was sufficient to secure several long-term programs through the labyrinth of the congressional process.

Associated with the theme of internal pressure was the political leverage exercised by outside forces. In this field of institutional and public liaison the liberals revealed another of their strengths. They were particularly proficient in "mobilizing political forces outside"[122] the Senate and in harnessing the resultant pressure to their own efforts inside the Senate. Whether this took the form of a close working partnership or a general mutuality of interest, the liberals' relationship with progressive interest groups often determined the viability of their proposals and the strength of their organization. Therefore, the liberals sought to appeal to a broad constituency with the well-founded expectation that public pressure would provide additional support that would have been unattainable through the traditional methods of discreet personal persuasion.

A later addition to the liberals' repertoire was their increased skill in the internal mechanics of legislative campaigns. Procedural expertise, intragroup liaison, vote counting, and group leadership had all improved since the early 1960s. Although the Nixon administration probably provided the main stimulus to better liberal organization, the liberals themselves contributed to the improvement by a gradual realization of the importance of effective cooperation with the Senate.

While these acquired legislative skills were significant, perhaps the liberals' most impressive achievement was simply their capacity to act and think together as liberals. The nature of their formations may have differed from issue to issue and their performances may have fluctuated from week to week, but the liberals remained a remarkably cohesive entity in an environment hostile to genuine cooperation. This is not to say that the liberals were in some way divorced from the normal atomized framework of the Senate. On the contrary, they were regarded as being just as sensitive over their individual rights and privileges as were the most capricious of senators. The differences between such members as Mike Gravel and Philip Hart bore testimony to the fact that the liberals were not a homogeneous group of regimented and anonymous members. Indeed, the liberals might be said to be more heterogeneous in their ideas, positions, and priorities than were any other comparable group of senators. Therefore, it was in spite of both the Senate's individualist culture and their own inherent divisions that the liberals succeeded in establishing a clearly discernible legislative grouping in the Senate. Its structure may have been skeletal, its services may have been partial, and its activities may have been episodic, but it fulfilled several of the functions normally attributed to informal legislative groups. It not only provided a focal point of reference for the liberals, but determined group positions and voting cues, coordinated information and resources, and finally established an alternative center of authority and leverage to the dispersed power of the committee and party organizations.

6   The New Senate: Change and Tradition

The purpose of this study has been to ask two questions: first, what, if anything, happened to the Senate over the reputedly turbulent era of the 1960s?; and second, did anything that could be termed a new Senate come into existence during this period? It will be recalled that the 1950s marked a time when the Senate became widely regarded as an institution insulated against social changes and political demands by a cocoon of self-perpetuating conservatism. White and Matthews presented the mechanics of the Senate's apparent continuity in specific, and highly plausible, terms. They asserted that the institution's conservative norms and traditions interlocked with the chamber's conservative power structure to produce a constant conservatism in policy and leadership personnel that automatically reduced any liberal members to peripheral and ineffective positions in the institution. To White and Matthews, the internal dynamic between the two mutually supportive frameworks of internal culture and formal institutional power was so durable that it could not fail to produce a generally conservative Senate. The presence of so few liberal members, who were more likely than not dismissed as irrelevant "outsiders," served merely to emphasize the conservative tranquility of the Senate during the 1950s. Of course, much of the Senate's conservatism at this time was the result of the contemporary social and political conditions referred to in chapter 2. While White and Matthews were aware of the limited number of salient issues on the political agenda and the lack of urgency with which they were viewed, they were not prepared to permit their view of the Senate to rest on such a tenuous basis as transient external conditions. On the contrary, they assumed that the close relationship between internal structure, institutional norms, senatorial elites, and policy output would ensure that the Senate would remain conservative and certainly more conservative in relative terms than either of the other two elected bodies at the federal level.

Clearly, the liberal senator was the rogue element in this neat political and institutional equation. He was seen as the representative of large, urban, industrial, and electorally unstable states with severe problems and attentive constituents. As such, he was not usually able to adjust well to the rural pace and to the regional bias of the Senate's decision-making process. While the urgency with which the liberals interpreted so many contemporary problems often led them to breach the norms of self-restraint, sobriety, and seniority, the substance of the liberals' issues more often than not provoked active hostility from the Senate elders. Liberals either annoyed conservative Republicans by advocating social welfare programs over and against President Eisenhower's budgetary recommendations, or they irritated the southern Democrats by persistently raising the sensitive and divisive issue of civil rights. The situation was made even worse by the fact that so many social welfare proposals (e.g., housing, education) involved the civil rights issue. Although majority leader Johnson was sufficiently incensed by the liberals' presence in the chamber to refer to them as "troublemakers," "extremists," and "bombthrowers,"[1] he joined the majority of members in dismissing the liberals as a small and tiresome minority of senators dedicated to the national Democratic party in an institution resolved to resist the nationalization of party politics. The liberals for their part complained of discrimination against them on the basis of region, numbers, style, policies, and junior status, and presented not only Johnson's leadership but the Senate itself as suitable cases for reform. The liberals' sense of exclusion, their political weakness, and their failure in achieving most of their policy aims therefore appeared to endorse the notion of a structural conservatism within the Senate during the 1950s.

To determine the extent to which the Senate had changed over the 1960s, it was decided to examine the behavior and achievements of the institution's liberal members—those members who had been written off by much of the conventional wisdom of the Senate; those members who most wanted change and were most prominent in attempting to secure it; and those members who could not succeed in improving their political effectiveness in the Senate without upsetting the declared relationships that sustained senatorial conservatism.

As the material presented in chapters 3 and 4 shows, the liberals reacted against the Senate very much in accordance with the predictions of White and Matthews. Where the liberals deviated from the classic model of the Senate was in the ultimate effect that this reaction had on the institution, and on them. Initially, the liberals felt their presence to be almost incompatible with the declared philosophy and style of the Senate. Despite the dramatic infusion of liberals into the Senate during the late 1950s and early 1960s, the liberals' anxiety over their minority and junior status appeared to lead to the predictable break with the Senate's traditions and customs. During these frustrating years, the liberals moved against the Senate's culture and subjected the value and operation of the institution's folkways to the most rigorous scrutiny. At first, the liberals tended to discuss all the folkways as politically biased constructs that supported and maintained the institution's conservative elite. Apprenticeship was regarded as a means by which a lag was imposed on new ideas and new policies from new members. The customs of specialization and compromise were derided as false norms because they were selectively applied by conservatives to the benefit of conservatives. Finally, the specialization and institutional loyalty folkways were interpreted by the liberals as yet further proof that the conservatives wished to confine the horizons of both the institution and its members.

Although the liberals' critique of the Senate's culture led to a substantial loosening in the operation of the folkways—even the abandonment of the old custom of apprenticeship—the liberals themselves also underwent a change during the heady days of legislative triumph in the mid-1960s. Whether it was due to their increased institutional power, the decline in conservative leadership, a mellowing of attitudes, electoral insecurity, political overachievement, or a combination of these, the liberals became more tolerant and even appreciative of the remaining folkways. They began to perceive that the folkways were not necessarily related to a conservative elite, to conservative policies, and to a politically conservative perspective of the Senate. The fact that the Senate conservatives had become less prominent during the 1960s, of course, encouraged the liberals to take a much more benign view of the Senate's culture. Whatever the reason, the liberals began to regard the folkways more as the informal concomitants to the institution's basic structure and to its activities. Since they were now an integral part of that structure, the liberals developed an appreciation of the folkways' functional value to the legislative's operations. In short, the liberal senator came to accept over the 1960s that cultural conformity need not necessarily be associated with political conservatism or elitist manipulation. The liberals, therefore, not only changed the nature and status of the folkways but underwent a certain transformation in their own attitude toward them which in turn ensured the survival of the folkways in a changed, yet recognizable form.

The liberals also changed their attitude toward the more formal power structure of the Senate. Once again, the liberals' early disaffection with the party and committee system was derived from a sense of exclusion and discrimination. They believed that the Senate as a whole was unrepresentative of the country and that this deficiency was made even worse by the fact that the Senate's leadership cadres were unrepresentative of the overall membership. According to the liberals, the formal power structure, like the folkways, operated to the continuing advantage of the senior conservative ranks. For example, the liberals suspected, with some justification, that recruitment to important committees was dependent upon various philosophical and behavioral prerequisites which tended to exclude qualified liberals from major assignments. Whether or not the liberals experienced an organized form of conscious discrimination, it is clear that they did suffer from two severe handicaps in the early 1960s. The first was the liberals' simple lack of seniority. Numerically, they accounted for 25 percent of the Senate's membership, yet they remained an essentially junior group of senators serving their first terms. The second feature of Senate life that detrimentally affected the liberals was the exceptional degree to which institutional power had become centralized during the preceding decade. This concentration of resources in a chamber normally noted for the atomization of its power was the result not just of Johnson's majority leadership but of a large number of conservative chairmen fortuitously thrown up by the seniority rule. Thus the liberals labored under their own lack of seniority and their opponents' surfeit of continuous service.

This dual condition, which fueled so much of the liberals' early resentment, changed quite dramatically within a few years. To begin with, the liberals quite simply gained power. They did not necessarily become committee chairmen, but they did begin to climb up the seniority ladder to middle-ranking committee positions. It is true that they failed to make an impact on the top-flight committees, but they compensated for this by concentrating on those committees most closely related to their major interests (civil rights, housing, urban affairs, social security, poverty, education, health). Such concentrations of liberal members probably made the liberals more influential than they would have been if they had been evenly distributed throughout the committee system. Most important of all was that these committees offered their members some of the best opportunities for subcommittee responsibilities. A subcommittee could provide the new member with a chance to jump clear of the normal seniority hierarchy and develop an individual, and largely independent, power base. According to Randall Ripley: "By the mid-1960s a new situation had emerged in which a number of moderately senior and very junior Democrats, virtually all liberals, had begun to develop significant impact on important legislative matters. They began to make impressive records of their own in their subcommittees."[2] Liberals had begun to realize that opportunities for individual advancement were available and that the Senate's distribution of power was not as restrictive as they initially believed it to be.

This progression in the legislative careers of several liberals represented a crucial stage in the general process of internal fragmentation that liberals had contributed so much toward in the post-Johnson era. The benign inactivity of Mansfield's leadership, the liberals' reaction against strong leadership, the high number of liberal first-termers, the decline of apprenticeship, the weakened position of the conservative seniors, the increasingly high expectations of freshmen, the multiplication of subcommittees, and the sheer pressure of large members of liberals all served to undermine the old Johnson structure. The liberals had gained power and in the process had contributed toward transforming the whole framework of power distribution in the institution.

Moreover, the liberals used the power they had gained to great effect. While the 1950s had led White and Matthews to dismiss the liberals as isolated figures languishing on the periphery of the Senate, the 1960s bore testament to the fact that liberal members were not inherently condemned to remain a permanently detached and ineffectual group of dissidents. In David Broder's words, the mid-1960s "destroyed a generation of theoreticians' strictures about the inability of Congress to keep pace with the country's needs."[3] As the Senate yielded power and status to its steadily growing liberal contingent, the liberals themselves demonstrated that they could rise above their own divisions and the atomized culture of the Senate, to make a collective impact on legislative decision making.

The liberals did suffer some disappointments. They were basically unsuccessful in such areas as military expenditures, congressional reform, foreign aid, and tax reform. In these fields the subject matter was either too complex or too sensitive for them to build up any sustained momentum both inside and outside the Senate. But in the less technical and more visible and salient issues of civil rights, poverty, housing, social security, consumerism, environmental protection, medical care, and minority causes, it is generally agreed that the liberals have been highly successful. In these issues, the liberals were able to exploit the favorable conditions for reform and to convert public interest and expectation into political pressure inside the Senate. In this way, the liberals were often instrumental in developing and maintaining the momentum for innovation, necessary to negotiate reform proposals through the labyrinth of senatorial veto points.

After their initial disaffection, in which they threatened to become an anti-Senate protest group, the liberals were quickly mollified by the increase in their power, status, and achievement. The liberals demonstrated that they could accustom themselves to the Senate's idiosyncrasies and its perquisites. They showed the Senate, the public, and not least themselves that they could be "effective," in the strict sense of legislative output, without necessarily undermining the Senate's culture and without always offending the institution's traditionalists. However noteworthy and significant as all this evidence of socialization on the part of the liberals is, it should not permit us to be deluded into the comfortable assertion that nothing much has changed in the Senate as a whole over the 1960s. The late 1960s and early 1970s may have seen a decline in the intensity of the liberals' activity, but the Senate had in no way reverted back to the mold of the late 1950s. On the contrary, according to a liberal member (Frank Moss), the liberals had "gained an ascendancy in the Senate and had changed the institution from a defense of the status quo to the cutting edge of innovation."[4] Furthermore, statistical studies confirm that the Senate had become more liberal than the supposedly activist and impulsive House of Representatives.[5] It appeared that what had been billed as a confrontation between a resistible force (i.e., the liberals) and an immovable object (i.e., the Senate) turned out to be a process of mutual accommodation between two adaptable phenomena.

The liberals had adjusted themselves in various ways to the Senate, but the institution itself had not been immune from change. The impact of a large liberal membership, liberal policies, and external liberal pressures produced a different type of Senate than the one which had been witnessed in the Eisenhower era. Although the liberal members themselves were not solely responsible for all the changes experienced during the 1960s, they played a major role in directly inspiring and precipitating much of the Senate's transformation. As the embodiment of political trends, public attitudes, and policy expectations, and as the manifestation of dissident forces inside the institution, the liberals came to characterize what could be termed a new Senate.

Before going on to review and to appraise what can justifiably be called the new Senate, it should be acknowledged at the outset that there will be many who will strenuously object to the very notion of a new Senate. Because social anthropological modes of studying human organizations have become widely accepted as tools of political analysis over the past 20 years, a tendency has developed for observers increasingly to see a political organization in terms of the integration and continuity of the underlying social subculture.[6] More often than not, the social system is viewed as a self-adjusting framework that accommodates a variety of behavioral roles while retaining its operational and functional integrity. Certainly, the interplay of mutual expectations and reciprocal obligations in terms of such concepts as norms, roles, socialization, and integration can be of enormous value in explaining the operation of a legislative system. This study itself has depended heavily upon such informal and social factors in analyzing the behavior of the Senate liberals. Despite the value of these concepts, they can lead the observer to lose a sense of perspective regarding the extent to which a social organization has in fact changed in nature over a period of time. In respect to the Senate, it is perfectly plausible to argue that given the system's presumed capacity to assimilate change and to remain qualitatively the same institution, neither the liberals nor the institution underwent very much change over the 1960s. According to this argument, there was nothing that compelled liberals to become outsiders, but if some did decide to adopt the role, they would be absorbed into a framework that was tolerant and flexible, yet somehow remained inert. Nelson Polsby approaches this position when discussing the work of Ralph Huitt on the Senate: "The reality, as Huitt saw, contained elements of White's description but other things in addition, and what emerges from Huitt's account is a picture of a social organization capable of containing diversity, conflict, and even change, while maintaining a core of values and expectations."[7] If one goes too far down this road, either the Senate has to be seen as an amorphous body that ingests anything into its protean state, or one will have to resort to employing colorful, yet descriptively sterile oxymorons such as "uniform diversity" or "static transformation."

Clearly, in any organization certain continuities will no doubt exist. Yet if these continuities are stressed to the point of persistently subordinating diversity and change to them, any modification of the organization becomes homogenized in accordance with the stated limits and criteria of adjustment. Just as the changes lose significance, so the defining characteristics of the organization can lose their distinctiveness—thereby rendering the continuities meaningless, as one is never quite sure what is being continued. By stressing consistency as a primary factor in organizational development, it is possible to lose all sense of the way small but significant changes can build up by accretion to produce large-scale shifts in the operation and function of an organization. The Senate provides a good example of the need to stress the positive aspects of institutional development, as much as its negative aspects. In the 1950s the organizational characteristics and operational style of the institution were defined to the satisfaction of almost all contemporary observers and participants. The material presented in chapters 4 and 5, however, revealed that various changes had occurred by which the institution deviated from what it had been in the 1950s. Certain continuities persisted, but the degree of change that had taken place was sufficient to conclude that the Senate of the 1970s was not quite the Senate of the 1950s. In that sense, one can be justified in referring to the Senate as the new Senate.

The Senate of the 1970s differed from the Senate of the 1950s in a whole variety of respects—from membership changes to institutional facilities and from policy concerns to senatorial salaries. On the basis of the analysis presented in preceding chapters, however, it does not seem unreasonable to conclude that the major changes experienced by the Senate over the 1960s can be reduced to three significant and prominent developments. First, the institution had been modified in terms of its structure. Second, the Senate's culture had undergone a transformation. Third, the chamber's operational style and political function in the early 1970s had shifted in relation to what it had been during the Eisenhower era. These three changes will now be considered and reviewed in turn.

STRUCTURE

During the late 1950s and early 1960s, the most prominent feature of the liberals' discontent was their attack on the Senate's structure and, in particular, on the committee system, which many of them regarded as biased in favor of the senior conservative members. According to one of the system's most vociferous critics at the time, Joseph Clark, committee assignments were manipulated to the benefit of conservatives and of those liberals who were prepared to accommodate themselves to the conservative cause; committee membership ratios insufficiently reflected the surge in northern Democratic seats; and liberals in general were discriminated against in respect to committee preferences.[8] Because of the disproportionately high degree of power held by a disproportionately low number of exclusive committees, Clark claimed that the Senate was incapable of functioning in accordance with the preferences not only of a majority of senators but a majority of the country as embodied in the program of the Democratic president. Liberals like Clark, Proxmire, and Douglas suggested that since the problem of institutional influence was rooted in the distribution of power inside the Senate Democratic party, the liberals' plight could be alleviated by party reform. Tentative and heavily qualified proposals for more regular and more assertive caucuses, for compositional changes in the party organization, and a more rigorous policy committee were floated during this early period, when the liberals' discomfort was most acute. However, as the liberals themselves realized, attempts to change the rules and organization of the party risked opening a Pandora's box of party splits and coalition breakdowns that could endanger the party's capacity to organize Congress. Given the high stakes of party control and the self-interest and political resources of those who benefited from the contemporary distribution of party power, apart from some inconsequential changes, the liberals failed to exploit their party membership and make the party provide the sort of influence they were striving for at the time.

Liberal attempts to force themselves and their policies onto the committee structure through the party organization only served to underline the validity of Froman's observation that it is "easier to change the rules and procedures of Congress rather than to change the rules and procedures within the party."[9] To a number of liberals, a change in the Senate itself appeared initially to be the only alternative available to progressively inclined northern Democrats. As the liberals became increasingly identified as congressional reformers, so the Senate became a political issue in its own right. Among the many proposals presented by reformers were restrictions to the seniority rule, changes in committee jurisdictions, the establishment of uniform committee procedures, caucus ratification of committee assignments, and easier ways to discharge bills from committees. These ambitions and broad-scale attempts at legislative reorganization all failed, however, not just through the concerted opposition of the committee elites, but ironically enough through the liberals' own increasing disinterest in challenging the committee system. Far from assuming the position of anticommittee radicals who wished to wrest power from the committees and to centralize and coordinate internal influence within some integrated and accountable locus, most liberals came to see that their political potential was more likely to be fulfilled at an individual level *within* the existing structure. Thus, at the climax of senatorial reform in 1967, when the Senate passed the first major legislative reorganization bill since 1946, the changes were notable for their emphasis on the opportunities and rights of committee members rather more than for any movement toward reducing committee autonomy. The bill restricted the influence of committee chairmen, for example, by permitting a majority of a committee to convene meetings without the chairman's permission, by authorizing a committee majority to report a bill out of a committee if it had already been adopted by it and by restricting the use of proxy votes. The less-senior members benefited in a more positive way by the limitation of major committee assignments—thereby allowing for a wider distribution of pivotal committee places to less senior members. Furthermore, the potential resources available to junior members were further increased by the provision of additional staffs and improved information facilities to the committees.[10] A handful of liberals wanted more far-reaching reforms. Most liberals, however, were highly satisfied with the reorganization and provided the main political thrust for its acceptance. By pressing for the reorganization, the liberals in effect revealed themselves to be highly senatorial insofar as they conformed to Randall

Ripley's dictum that "every Senator's instinct is to seek power and the way to power lies in maximizing individualistic tendencies in the Senate."[11]

In terms of the Senate's structure, therefore, most liberals believed that the best way to intrude more effectively into the decision-making processes was not by attempting to centralize power in some form of invigorated party apparatus, but through enhancing and extending preexisting forms of decentralization. This was seen to good effect in the feast of individual opportunities provided by the reorganization that finally passed both houses in 1970. The burgeoning spirit of structural individualism, fired by the aspirations and self-assertion of the Senate's young liberals during the 1960s, was most dramatically exemplified, however, by the growth in subcommittees. Junior senators had always valued subcommittees because of their small size, their specialist jurisdictions, and their ability to afford junior members with an institutional power base. During the early 1960s, young liberals were particularly enthusiastic over subcommittees, not just as a way of circumventing the seniority hierarchy in the main standing committees, but as a means to promote and publicize new policy proposals. Indeed, the freedom of operation given to subcommittees by such chairmen as James Eastland and Lister Hill was an important reason why so many liberals applied for the Judiciary and the Labor and Public Welfare committees. Having gained places on these committees, liberal members were not usually disappointed over the provision of subcommittee opportunities. Birch Bayh, for example, was given the chairmanship of the Judiciary Committee's Subcommittee on Constitutional Amendments soon after he entered the Senate in 1963. From this base he promoted the constitutional proposal on presidential disability and succession that was ratified as the Twenty-fifth Amendment in 1967. Such were the social interests and policy aspirations of liberal senators that many of them succeeded in persuading the relevant chairmen and the standing committees involved that new subcommittees were necessary to reduce the load on existing units and to provide an adequate response to new areas of political concern. As a result of this sort of pressure, Philip Hart, for example, was given the chairmanship of the Commerce Committee's Subcommittee on Environment and Edmund Muskie was made chairman of the Air and Water Pollution Subcommittee in the Public Works Committee.

The Senate liberals, therefore, were not merely the passive recipients of subcommittee resources and facilities. They consciously oiled the engine of centrifugal force in the Senate by pressing for greater numbers of compartmentalized units. This feature of liberal activism was quite apparent in the expansion of subcommittees inside the "liberal committees" during the period under review. The overall increase in subcommittees during these years was 36 percent, but in the five committees with the highest liberal representation the rise was 43 percent.[12] In the Labor and Public Welfare Committee, which contained more liberals than any other committee, the number of subcommittees doubled from 7 in 1959 to 14 in 1972. The number of liberal subcommittee chairmen also underwent a significant increase over the 1960s. Thirteen subcommittee chairmanships were held by liberals in 1959, at a time when there were 18 liberal members in the Senate. In 1972, liberals held 40 subcommittee chairmanships when their overall membership stood at 24. In this way, the liberals succeeded in forcing the committee to respond to their policy interests and personal ambitions on its own terms of political atomization.

As a result of the dilution of the seniority principle and the growth in activist subcommittees, the Senate became far less structured as an institution than it had been in the 1950s. Although it can be argued that Lyndon Johnson may have contributed toward this new fluidity through the "Johnson rule" in committee assignments and by taking some of the initiative from the committee leaders, it is generally agreed that the Senate was nevertheless a closely controlled and managed institution under Johnson in the 1950s.[13] So frustrated were the liberals with Johnson's leadership that when he left the Senate, his successor never even attempted to develop the same sort of influence that Johnson had cultivated as majority leader. Mansfield's style of benign partisanship and minimal intervention was derived partly from his personal distaste for the sort of flamboyant exhibitionism that colored Johnson's leadership. It was due partly to Mansfield's conviction that senators were coequal and responsible individuals who should be left to arrive at broad decisions through full discussion and consultation—free from unwarranted interference by party leaders who had no responsibility for engineering certain forms of policy outcome. In addition, Mansfield's reticence was derived from the fact that the Senate would simply not tolerate another legislative impressario. On the contrary, such was the reaction against Johnson in the early 1960s that Mansfield positively had to accommodate the leadership to the new spirit of collective license and individual ambition that prevailed in the 1960s. After the relatively constricted and hierarchical structure of the 1950s, therefore, the Senate of the 1970s was noticeable for a decline in the political homogeneity and institutional leverage of its committee elders, and for a changed leadership style that disclaimed power, advocated individual participation, and merely suggested, and registered areas of agreement instead of fashioning elaborate legislative transactions.[14] This is not to say that the new Senate was an institution in which the theoretical legislative principle of membership coequality had been achieved. The committee system still distributed power unevenly. Seniority rankings and party affiliation still discriminated against some to the benefit of others. Nevertheless, the 1960s had witnessed a rapid diversification and atomization of the Senate's formal structure to such a degree that the institution was no longer noted for integration and direction so much as for compartmentalized power centers, maximized personal influence, and "leaders" without command structures.

CULTURE

The modifications to the Senate's structure over the 1960s were accompanied by several related changes in the institution's informal code of behavior. In any social grouping, collective principles or norms always provide much of the supportive apparatus to the more visible and formal distribution of influence. In a legislative organization like the Senate, social roles and expectations are closely related to the internal framework of the committee system and its functions. In the 1950s it appeared that the Senate's power structure and its folkways were mutually supportive to such an extent that each would prevent the other from ever changing in terms of form and operation. By the early 1970s, however, not only did the Senate's structure look different from what it had been in the 1950s, but the Senate's culture, which was once regarded as an impregnable feature of the institution, had also undergone a significant alteration.

Given the liberals' traditional resentment of the folkways, the dramatic infusion of new liberal members at a time of heightened public consciousness over the institution was almost bound to take its toll on the Senate's life-style. In the words of one noted com-

mentator on legislative behavior: "[Norms] are not immutable. . . .
New people are rarely socialized perfectly into an institution. . . . The
greater the number of newcomers to an institution the more likely
that the norms will change."[15] In respect to the Senate, the conscious
reaction against the folkways from the inflated ranks of liberal members during the early 1960s effectively changed the form and significance of the Senate's culture. The new Senate has become noted
for the complete absence of any formal period of apprenticeship for
junior members. The personal and political drive of large numbers
of new liberal members in the early 1960s, together with the atmosphere of individual expression and the expanded opportunities for
personal power bases, allowed members to develop institutional leverage and public prominence—immediately and effectively. Mansfield's
accent on broad participation, the relaxation of the seniority principle,
and the proliferation of subcommittees had given the freshmen of
the late 1960s greater license to involve themselves in the decision-
making process. By the early 1970s, the heights to which senior eye-
brows were raised when a new senator intervened in a debate on
his own initiative were significantly lower than they would have
been in the 1950s. Indeed, it has not been unknown for freshman
senators to enter unembarrassed into disputes with party leaders on
the floor during the first few days of their senatorial careers. Informal
types of apprenticeship still existed whereby a junior member would
adopt, or be adopted by, a senior senator who would then provide
guidance for the freshman in terms of procedure, legislative tactics,
and even voting decisions.[16] The formal apprenticeship of muted personal adjustment, however, was at an end.

The absence of any established expectation of deference toward
fully socialized senior members did not mean that there were no
longer norms with which senators had to familiarize themselves. It
was more that the Senate was less integrated as an organization and
less the center of patterned behavior than it had been in the 1950s.
Norms still existed in the 1970s, but they tended to be cast in a less
definitive form and were maintained more by mutual consent and
perceived self-interest than by the convention of apprenticeship which
liberal members had always attacked as an artificial contrivance. Insofar as traditional apprenticeship tried to process senators into pre-
conceived roles within a static structure, the absence of the latter in
the 1970s rendered apprenticeship an irrelevant vestige of the Senate's lost past.

The two folkways of specialization and legislative work also underwent something of a transformation in the 1960s. Although these two norms did not suffer the same fate as the apprenticeship convention, their role in the Senate's style of operation was significantly reduced during this period. At one level, the two folkways appear to have survived the turbulence of the 1960s simply through their obvious functional contribution to a legislative organization characterized by a committee-style division of labor. Commitment to committee duties, the development of subject matter expertise, the sharing of the overall workload, and the provision of cues to a membership generally deferential to committee authority continue to be based upon the senators' acknowledgment of the specialization and legislative work folkways. Senatorial interest in these norms is not so much born of an abstract regard for successful conflict management as out of the personal rewards accrued from a system of virtually autonomous political subunits. The elixir of individual political opportunity, however, led not only to more subcommittees but paradoxically to a transcendence of the committee rigors of microdimensional policy interests and compartmentalized authority. The paradox is in part explained by the fact that the Senate has never been as committee-dominated as has the House of Representatives, where an individual literally sinks or swims on the basis of his committee position and reputation. In the Senate, committees are smaller, members are more pivotal, assignments more numerous, structures less hierarchical, peronnel overlaps more common, and individual career opportunities more diverse.[17] A senator, therefore, could become a prominent figure either by closely identifying himself with a particular committee, or by maximizing the political potential from all his committee assignments, or even by concerning himself with a whole range of policies and subject-matter specialties irrespective of committee expertise or obligations. During the 1960s, the incidence of senators who spread themselves over a broad sweep of policy areas increased substantially over the previous decade. Their internal status had also changed. While policy generalists would have been denounced as charlatans in the 1950s, they had become largely legitimized by the early 1970s.

On one level, therefore, the specialization and legislative work folkways still provided the normative backbone to the Senate's committee system. At another level, however, the two folkways had come to accommodate the sorts of senatorial activity not normally associ-

ated with the central precepts of committee politics. Initially, it was
the liberals who, in their chase for progressive policies through the
chamber, were noted for treading on the jurisdictional toes of other
senators. Liberals not only experienced the urgency of social problems but sensed the interrelationship of issues and, as a result, tended
to move in both the micro dimension of policy technicalities and the
macro dimension of broad social assessment. By the end of the 1960s,
practically every senator had a complex constituency experiencing
national problems and demanding greater assistance from an increasingly centralized framework of political decision making and economic
direction. While it was the liberals who were regarded as the policy
generalists in the early and middle 1960s, no real difference existed
between liberals and conservatives by the early 1970s. Both had their
committee specialists and both achieved institutional leverage through
them. Yet both would not hesitate in intervening in any problem area
that involved their constituencies, their personal and political ambitions, their policy interests, or their committees' field of discretion.
Given the perceived interdependency of issues and the conspicuously
zero-sum nature of an increasingly limited budgetary capacity, it was
not surprising that so many senators came to have a direct or indirect
interest in so many issues.

This enhanced political awareness of senators, together with the
customary personal competitiveness within the institution, tended to
diversify senators' legislative activities. Under the folkway of legislative work, senators were expected to devote themselves to the
process of legislative draftsmanship. A Senate type was literally a
bill technician whose reputation was built on subject-matter expertise,
committee experience, and legislative enactments. Like the specialization folkway, the norm of legislative work was still in evidence in
the new Senate but not to the same extent or in the same form as it
had been in the 1950s. By the 1970s, senators not only took an active
interest in areas outside their committee responsibilities, but did things
other than process detailed legislation.[18] Again, it was the liberals who
really began the Senate's transformation from a gray honeycomb of
legislative units to a more functionally varied institution. In the 1960s,
liberal senators were renown both for taking issues out of committees
and into the country and for responding to issues and introducing
them into Congress. Liberals often used their position to investigate
social and economic deficiencies, publicize the need for reforms, gather

information from external sources, mobilize support for measures, force issues onto the agenda of public debate, and condition the public to the possibility of future policy changes in sensitive areas. During the 1960s, many liberal senators became major political figures outside the Senate. Although liberal members in general retained the reputation for being less committee- and legislation-oriented than their more conservative colleagues, most senators came to acknowledge the legitimacy of various activities not explicitly related to the often mundane tasks of fashioning legislation.

The newly developed degree of discretion in the apprenticeship, specialization, and legislative work folkways meant that the folkway of institutional loyalty was no longer quite what it used to be. When White and Matthews were observing the Senate in the 1950s, members were expected to regard the institution as an exemplary political organization beyond the reproach of any critic. A Senate seat was seen as the apogee of any member's political career and no senator was expected to spoil the triumphant experience of senatorial status either for himself or his fellow incumbents by criticizing the institution in any way. The institutional loyalty folkway, in conjunction with the courtesy norm, presupposed the existence of a bedrock of shared values in respect to the institution and its form of operation. It was disloyal and discourteous, therefore, to call into question either the institution or any of its members. To the liberals, the institutional loyalty folkway appeared to be the central norm that bound the other folkways together in a self-contained system of obligation and deference. In other words, while apprenticeship served to socialize members as to the nature of the folkways, institutional loyalty was the final reminder to them to defer to Senate tradition and, in so doing, conform to the remaining folkways. Since the liberals initially regarded the folkways as an integral feature of an inequitable distribution of institutional power, they reacted against the institutional loyalty folkway both indirectly and directly.

In indirect terms, the liberals were guilty of contravening the institutional loyalty folkway by changing and even disregarding some of the other folkways to which loyalty was implicitly related. In direct terms, the liberals were well known for their overt criticism of the Senate—from the committee structure to the party leadership, from Rule XXII to conservative elitism, from unrepresentative obstructionism to anachronistic procedures. While such controversial attacks on the Senate's integrity achieved great notoriety, perhaps the most overt assault on the institution came through what could be claimed to be the liberals' habitual attempts to reject it altogether in favor of the White House.

John Kennedy's elevation from the Senate to the presidency began the quadrennial stampede of senators searching for presidential candidacies. While some of the subsequent presidential aspirants have included both conservatives (Goldwater) and more moderate members (Jackson), presidential ambition among senators has been most closely associated with the liberal members. The executive ambitions of all these senators were fired not just by Kennedy's crucial precedent but by the Senate's prominent position in a federal institution, at a time when the American system was becoming progressively more centralized in terms of policy management and economic resources. Senatorial advantages in national politics were further enhanced by a decline in the status and capacity of state government and by the increased salience of foreign policy issues with which the Senate was closely involved. When these advantages were combined with the institution's statewide constituencies, its six-year terms, its extensive staff and research facilities, its generous provision of time and opportunities to develop national constituencies, and its culture of individual self-advancement, the Senate began to assume the status of being the center with the greatest potential for producing presidential timber in the American system.[19] This development is quite evident in the figures on presidential recruitment from 1920 to 1972. Whereas the proportion of presidential runners who came from the Senate was 29 percent during the period from 1920 to 1956, it had increased to 46 percent in the 1960 to 1972 period—thereby eclipsing the state governors' traditional primacy in this field. From being the institution commonly regarded as most divorced from the presidency, therefore, the Senate in the 1960s achieved the position of being the chief source of presidential material and the most promising political springboard for presidential aspirants.

In many ways, the inflated personal competition and even mutual suspicion between fellow senators involved in presidential politics has tended to have a detrimental effect on the Senate's esprit de corps. Far from personally identifying themselves with the institution and with their colleagues, some members have been suspected of gaining a Senate seat merely as a prior step to a campaign for the presidency. Whatever the original motives may have been, the fact remains that large numbers of senators have disturbed the collegiate identity of the membership and the working operations of the institution. Nevertheless, the picture of membership loyalty in the new Senate is not totally black. Ironically, while the presidency may have been the cause of so much internal disruption at the level of personal ambition, it has also provided the stimulus to increased senatorial integration at the general level of institutional consciousness. The realization during the late 1960s that the contemporary presidency had expanded in power at the direct expense of senatorial prerogatives led to a regeneration of collective identity and to a renaissance in senatorial assertiveness with regard to the executive.[20] If the folkway of institutional loyalty attempted to reduce internal conflict by developing shared experiences and values among the membership, the new Senate was not devoid of such communal allegiance. Senators' commitment to the institution may not have been of the same nature as White and Matthews observed in the 1950s, but at least it existed sufficiently to offset the explicitly divisive influence of presidential ambition.

The folkways, therefore, have changed in form and effect over the past 20 years. At the basic level of committee authority, the folkways of specialization, courtesy, and legislative work were still very much in evidence in the new Senate. Congressional traditionalists from both the conservative and liberal camps continued to assess members in precisely these terms. However, at another level it was evident that these norms could be summarily dismissed as readily as the apprenticeship tradition had been in the early 1960s. A senator might object if another member intruded on his committee jurisdiction, yet he would not be shocked, for in the new Senate it had become comparatively common for such incursions to take place. The aggrieved party might call attention to the specialization and legislative work principles, but he could not claim that they were definitive, all-inclusive norms. Norms denote cultural "oughts" which are related to social actuality; otherwise, they are not norms. In the case of the new Senate, norms tended to embody qualified expectations among members. In contrast to the 1950s, when the folkways were seen in terms of orthodoxy and occasional deviance, the folkways of the early 1970s could best be seen in the light of provisional and intermittent operation. Indeed, such was the degree of personal license in the Senate that the institution's culture could legitimately be characterized as mutual tolerance of nonconformity toward the folkways.

It was precisely this phenomenon of behavioral diversity that highlighted the crucial significance of the one folkway that maintained, and even increased, its effect in the Senate. Given the increasingly atomized structure of the institution, the proliferation of individual power points, the innumerable opportunities for individual objection, and political aspirations and appetites of the members themselves, any concerted legislative action could only be achieved through the medium of mutual accommodation. It has never been easy to bind groups of senators together under any kind of formal arrangement. In the 1960s, the disaggregate nature of the Senate was never more evident.[21] It was precisely because of this type of loose framework, however, that members found more functional value than ever before in the custom of reciprocity. Individual senators were aware that they often maintained a pivotal position in the institution and that the Senate's culture and formal procedures almost encouraged members to maximize their positional advantage, even to the point of legislative obstruction. But senators were also aware of the real possibility of legislative stasis and of all the features associated with it— personal antagonism, frustration, intransigence, and reprisals. The reciprocity folkway, therefore, tended to be subscribed to by common consent, in order to keep the channels of communication open and to foster an environment of cooperation and accommodation.

The reciprocity folkway provided the essential convention of sociability in a chamber notorious for separating members from each other. As has already been noted, senatorial individualism had been rekindled in the 1960s. Many of the old social conventions, such as apprenticeship, specialization, legislative work, and institutional loyalty, had declined in importance and had changed in nature to suit contemporary circumstances. The reciprocity tradition, however, increased in status by counteracting individual atomization and by cultivating the conditions of compromise, cooperation, and trust, necessary for most kinds of legislative action. It is in this perspective of mutual assistance that the other folkways should be seen. The Senate's culture has traditionally been informal in nature. In the absence of a highly structured code of rules, members' behavior has been regulated by the social structure of the folkways.[22] By the end of the 1960s, it had become exceptionally diffuse. The folkways, which had provided a form of social regulation in the absence of a highly structured code of rules, appeared to give way under the weight of so many new members. Nevertheless, the folkways survived the 1960s. They were no longer quite as well defined as they had been in the 1950s. They were no longer expected to produce a consistent and predictable form of behavior for senators. Yet on the basis of mutual agreement among members increasingly aware that they were not obliged to concur with each other, the members of the new Senate had retained a modicum of social control and direction through the central folkway of informal accommodation.

STYLE AND FUNCTION

The changes in both the Senate's culture and structure have produced a very different institution to the one acclaimed and criticized in the 1950s. During that period, it was generally accepted that a symbiosis existed between the Senate's structure and its norms that not only maintained a conservative elite but ensured conservative outcomes to policy decisions. This equation had many roots. The low turnover in membership during most of the 1950s, the rural bias in the Senate's representational system, the seniority principle, Johnson's relatively centralized leadership, and the institution's rules and traditions tended to restrict participation in general and limit freshman liberal participation in particular. Not the least of the factors in the Senate's conservatism, however, was the presence of numerous conservative members elected by a generally conservative public.[23] The sustained electoral success of many conservative members over the 1940s and 1950s produced a conservative elite in the committee system and thereby in the Senate as a whole. The existence of conservatives in the higher echelons of the committee system was due mostly to electoral circumstances, yet once the conservatives had achieved dominance they began to be seen as philosophically and operationally consistent with the institution. In some respects this declared relationship was valid. The Senate's decentralized structure and its emphasis on generalized agreement and minority accommodation has generally favored those objecting to policy changes rather than those pressing for reforms. Conservatives, therefore, could and did exploit with great effect conservatively biased procedures and structures made available to them in the Senate. As such, it appeared that conservatives and conservative policies were an intrinsic part of the Senate.

Where the thesis of a conservatively disposed institution became strained and distortive was when the notions of institutional traditionalism, system maintenance, and structural stratification were introduced into the analysis, in order to substantiate the notion of an implacable and self-perpetuating conservatism in the Senate. Many observers in the 1950s were much influenced by the complaints of liberal senators, who perceived the existence of an inner conspiracy that actively discriminated against them through the operation of reputedly biased rules and norms. As a result, the Senate tended to be analyzed in terms of deductive reasoning from the assumed presence of conservative control. Having asserted the existence of a conservative clique, everything else tended to flow from that central principle. Thus the folkways were seen as a series of social norms supporting and maintaining those conditions that produced conservative leadership and conservative policies. Conformity to the folkways was doubly conservative. It led not only to the maintenance of the system, but also to the continuation of the conservative elite and policies produced by that system. The same deterministic rationale was employed with the Senate's formal rules and precedents. Given that a conservative elite existed and given that the rules of the Senate, like any other organization, were beneficial to one set of interests and not to others, it was concluded that the rules actually established the conservatives as an elite. Being conservative, the Senate leaders would not wish to change the rules by which they prospered in power. Being an elite, the leaders would ensure that those rules were not changed in political effect. In this way, the Senate of the 1950s came to be widely regarded as an institution literally tied to a predetermined role through the inbred and insuperable nature of its structural conservatism.

Despite the professed durability of the Senate's conservative character and its unidimensional role in the political system, the institution was transformed by the mid-1960s. The normal pattern of predictable policies arrived at by uniform means under the same leadership was acutely disturbed by the events and demands of the 1960s. The dramatic changes in the membership, combined with Johnson's departure, Mansfield's accent on participation, the increased provision of institutional facilities to individual members, the relaxation of the folkways, the advent of progressive and assertive Democratic administrations, and the shift in public attitudes toward policy reforms, all helped to modify the character of the institution.

It was the massive influx of liberals in the late 1950s and early 1960s, however, that embodied the changes in public opinion and precipitated so many of the changes that occurred inside the Senate. In terms of the general life-style of the Senate, it is generally agreed that the liberals introduced "a greater informality of general demeanor and relaxed the stuffiness in the chamber."[24] In the process, the liberals made the Senate a less cocooned and cloistral institution, they reduced the mystique of its introverted and private operations, and they undermined the whole notion of a structured hierarchy of personal status and privilege. Distinctions between juniors and seniors became blurred as the atmosphere within the institution became one of individual assertion. The liberals' disparate ideas and high expectations enlivened the Senate, made it more heterogeneous in composition, and brought it more into the mainstream of national political pressures and trends.[25]

It is possible to speculate that the Senate always had the potential for amplifying liberal opinion in the country. In the early 1960s, however, that potential looked at best a long way from being realized and at worst an unrealizable attribute. The Senate still appeared to be locked securely into its own ingrown conservatism. As late as 1963 Joseph Clark was denouncing the Senate's conservative establishment.[26] Yet by 1965 the same member was proclaiming the end of the establishment and the inauguration of internal democracy.[27] Conservative chairmen still existed, the conservative coalition was still prominent in legislative roles, but the notion of an inner ruling clique of conservative seniors no longer had the attraction that it did in the 1950s. Liberals began to feel that they were not being discriminated against by some manipulative conspiracy and that their policies were not necessarily doomed to failure through rules and practices that worked in favor of their opponents. While the conservatives declined in numbers, the liberals increased their seats, their seniority, and their institutional power. They were not slow in exploiting their political leverage. In conjunction with the White House and with the whole apparatus of external political support, the liberals were able to mobilize themselves into an effective legislative force and to secure the sort of progressive legislation that would have been unthinkable a few years earlier. By the late 1960s, the Senate had reversed its previous reputation and was widely recognized as more liberal than both the House of Representatives and the presidency. The issue of the Senate's intractable and encapsulated conservatism was dead.

Although it is appropriate to stress the dramatic change in the Senate's policy decisions during the 1960s, the new Senate is notable not just for responding to White House initiatives and passing presidential policies. The old dictum of "President proposes—Congress disposes" that normally characterizes discussions on the legislative process has always imposed a deceptively simple construction on a complex and interdependent set of relationships. Congress has always been "one of the major intersections of a policy communications network that extends across most policy domains."[28] Even so, in the 1950s and early 1960s it was generally accepted that Congress was, and could only be, the passive partner in a stimulus–response interaction between the White House and the legislature.[29] To some observers Congress was so politically out of touch and so functionally ill-suited to policy initiation that it ought not even to try and participate in policymaking. More often than not, therefore, Congress's role as a passive receptor was seen not only as a fact but as a normative principle. Samuel Huntington even went so far as to suggest that since "[l]egislation had become much too complex politically to be effectively handled by a representative assembly,"[30] Congress ought to abandon its putative role in this area and concentrate on executive oversight, which was what it was organizationally equipped to perform. Despite the underestimation in the potential capacity and actual influence of Congress in policy formulation, the fact remains that in the 1950s Congress did indeed appear to be an institution whose important policy outcomes were decisions on presidentially inspired and produced proposals. The Senate, in particular, appeared to match the public mood of tranquility and the general congressional image of an institution gently deliberating on the very limited number of policy issues presented to it.

By contrast, the 1960s witnessed an explosion in the number, variety and urgency of political issues. Given the scale and general salience of these issues and the liberals' disposition toward governmental solution to problems, the Senate massively expanded its role as a positive participant in policymaking—a role barely perceptible in the 1950s. The new Senate came to assume a prominent position in the general flow of problems and policy ideas.[31] Increasingly, senators appeared in the front line of political controversy—investigating problems, highlighting inequities and injustices, arousing public concern, mobilizing interest-group support, formulating innovatory proposals, tapping the political resources of the White House, and forcing issues onto the agenda of public debate. In some cases, senators made indirect, yet significant contributions to final White House policies.[32] In other cases, however, senators made highly visible and direct contributions, occasionally to the point of being primarily responsible for new reforms.[33] So much active initiative was being shown in the Senate by the late 1960s that Nelson Polsby was prompted to make the following observation:

> The Senate is in some respects at a crucial nerve-end of the polity. It articulates, formulates, shapes and publicizes demands, and can serve as a hot-house for significant policy innovation. . . . Its organizational flexibility enables it to incubate policy innovations, to advocate, to respond, to launch its great debates, in short, to pursue the continuous renovation of American public policy through the hidden hand of the self-promotion of its members.[34]

Whatever the motives for their actions, senators were renown in the 1960s for moving in to plug the "policy gaps" in such areas as campaign financing, urban renewal, and environmental and consumer protection.

While the Senate had gone some way toward restoring its credibility as a policymaking participant in the 1960s, it had also improved its capacity for performing the function that many observers regarded as its only true role. Executive oversight was no longer just the careful monitoring of administration and budgetary changes. By the Ninetieth Congress (1967–68), executive oversight had become almost indistinguishable from policymaking, as the Senate in particular assumed the mantle of protector of the Great Society. While Johnson became increasingly distracted by the Vietnam war, the Senate carefully reviewed recently enacted social programs, suggested reforms, and pressed for increased resources. Furthermore, as the Senate began to restore its constitutional prerogatives in the foreign policy field, it increasingly subjected the administration's war policies to critical review. In the Nixon years, the Senate became a focal point for the support of social programs that the administration was attempting to curtail and a center of opposition to the war. As a result, the Senate's oversight function came to be seen less as a device for technical readjustment in policy administration, and more as a means to restrain the apparently arbitrary discretion of the modern presidency.[35]

Far from being restricted in its activities through its organizational inadequacies and through the incapacity of its members, the Senate of the 1970s has demonstrated enormous versatility in its operations. The oversight role, prescribed for the Senate by observers like Huntington, has been developed to such a sophisticated degree that it has far surpassed expectations in terms of political effect and institutional self-awareness. The Senate's advances in executive control, however, have not displaced those roles that had been questioned by observers in the early 1960s. In respect to policymaking and legislative deliberation, the Senate has not only maintained its position but has increased its contribution in these fields. As has been acknowledged, senators investigate, evaluate, and publicize policies. They also formulate policy innovations, circulate policy ideas, and enact policies.

To assist themselves in this variety of functions, senators have done as much as possible to accommodate the needs of the modern communications media.[36] In addition to their already substantial advantages in gaining publicity, senators have opened up their communities to media coverage to a far greater degree than has the House of Representatives. As a result, it has been the Senate which has presented the glamorous television hearings; it has been the Senate which has made congressional–executive confrontation into great popular entertainment; and it has been the Senate which has given the best after-sales services in the form of readily available members for backup interviews, television debates, and chat shows. The publicity generated by such means, however, has not only aided the Senate in executive oversight, problem investigation, policy deliberation, and so on, but has enhanced the political careers of individual senators to such a degree that it has led to a further extension of the Senate's long list of functions. Given the vast opportunities for personal prominence and political leverage in the Senate, the institution has become established as the single most significant hatchery for potential and aspiring presidential and vice-presidential candidates. The role of leadership recruitment has in turn served to increase the already strong pressures on the Senate to become a more visible, assertive, and active institution.[37] In contrast to the 1950s, therefore, when the Senate was cast as an insular, inhibited, and rather drab organization dedicated to detailed legislative engineering, the new

Senate appeared as a highly flamboyant, heterogeneous, and publicity-conscious body with all its fingers stuck firmly into every available pie.

The style of the new Senate has not been without its detractors. The shift toward a less integrated membership broken down into greater numbers of units without any form of central direction to contain individual participation or to regularize legislative business is reflected in the views of those who witnessed the Senate in the 1950s. White, for example, has lamented that the description of the Senate in his book *Citadel* bears little relation to the Senate of the 1970s.[38] According to White, the Senate has never recovered from the departure of such stabilizing figures as Lyndon Johnson, Robert Kerr, Everett Dirksen, and Robert Taft—"big men who got things done."[39] In the absence of high-caliber leaders, the Senate has become vulgarized by "too much clamor, too many running for the Presidency and too many not doing their home-work."[40] According to other observers, the cacophony of so many active participants among the membership has not only obstructed the efforts toward cooperative enterprise between senators, but has undermined the whole framework of effective leadership in the institution. The exasperation induced by the stress of unrestrained inputs was well captured in the following sentiments recorded by *Newsweek* in 1971: "Some see a virtual breakdown of the legislative system in the endless delays, hot-and-cold running filibusters and unwonted displays of contrariness where compromise used to be king. The Senate . . . has degenerated into a bunch of ego-tripping, fuss-budgety prima donnas."[41] Given these complaints, it is not surprising that by the early 1970s a certain nostalgia had developed for the direction and clarity of the conservative establishment era.

On the other hand, it can be argued that it is precisely because of the absence of the old conservative leadership that the Senate has improved in various respects. In place of friction and detachment, the junior and senior members have developed a greater understanding between one another in the more informal and relaxed atmosphere of the modern Senate. This increase in the actual tolerance of diverse roles has meant that far less energy has been directed toward internal disputes than there used to be in the days of the "inner club" and the "liberal outsiders." Legitimate legislative operations have no longer been distracted by the presence of a large reservoir of frustrated and resentful freshmen.

On the contrary, the boom in participation has both liberated the Senate from its earlier inhibitions and expanded its operations and political roles. The point is made strongly by one noted staff assistant: "When the inner club was in control, the Senate was not operating as it should. It functions best when there is chaos. When there is fighting and commitment the Senate is really focusing on problems. There should be a hundred inputs to policy formulation."[42] It should be pointed out that the new emphasis on individual-member involvement need not necessarily preclude the possibility of effective leadership. It can actually improve the basis for leadership and cooperation. Whereas leadership in the 1950s used to be a matter of manipulation and inducement, the leaders' authority by the early 1970s had become accepted more on the basis of arguments and facts. Less leadership may have existed in the Senate during the 1960s, but where it did exist it was stronger and more resilient than it used to be under Johnson. Since each senator tended to gain recognition more on the basis of his legislative contribution than on the duration of his incumbency, he was more likely to be personally receptive to the idea of cooperating with his fellow senators. With honor satisfied and status assured, freshmen and liberals were more likely to combine with senior members to form effective and durable coalitions. This element of tolerance and collective license was caught well in Senator Philip Hart's comment on the new-style Senate: "We are all constructively free-wheeling individuals."[43]

The relative merits or demerits of the new Senate clearly depend upon one's individual view of what the institution's role should be and the degree to which it conforms to that role. Whether the Senate is or is not representative, efficient or inefficient, and whether the Senate produces good or poor legislation are all matters for personal evaluation. What is certain is that the new Senate has clarified the nature of the underlying relationships among the institution's structure, culture, ideology, personnel, and policies. In effect, the new Senate has forced us to make a number of revisions to the traditional interpretation of these central relationships upon which so many of the theories concerning the old Senate were based.

First, while the Senate's structure and culture are closely associated with one another, they do not form a symbiosis that produces and maintains a particular set of leaders with a particular form of policies. Second, institutional traditionalism cannot be equated with political conservatism. Whether it be on the basis of an appreciation of a group identity or of the folkways' functional value, or whether it be a case of political self-interest or just social conformity, liberals can and have become orthodox folkway members without losing their liberal values or their commitment to liberal causes. Third, the Senate's structure may once have been dominated by conservative members, but it is not in itself oriented to raising conservatives to positions of formal leadership. The seniority rule, for example, can cut both ways. As personal longevity and electoral circumstances fostered the conservative leadership of the 1950s, so death, retirement, and defeat allowed liberals with safe seats to fill the vacuum. Fourth, while the Senate's rules exemplify the American system's disposition toward consensus as a precondition to change, they are not predetermined to preserve the status quo and to preclude liberal policy decisions. Given new conditions and substantial dissatisfaction among the membership, the rules can be changed (e.g., Legislative Reorganization Act of 1970). Given public support and sufficient numbers of well-organized members, the political effect of the rules can be changed (e.g., the Great Society reform program). And given preexisting liberal policies, the obstructionist capacity of the rules need not be conservative in political terms (e.g., liberal filibusters). Finally, the Senate as a whole is not subject to inviolable and self-perpetuating conservatism. On the contrary, this study has attempted to demonstrate that the institution has experienced sufficient change to warrant the title "new Senate."

List of Persons Interviewed

Senators

Quentin Burdick (D – N.Dak.)	22 March 1974
Clifford Case (R – N.J.)	26 March 1974
Alan Cranston (D – Calif.)	23 September 1975
Thomas Eagleton (D – Mo.)	24 September 1975
Philip Hart (D – Mich.)	28 March 1974
Vance Hartke (D – Ind.)	29 March 1974
Mark Hatfield (R – Oreg.)	16 September 1975
Daniel Inouye (D – Hawaii)	23 September 1975
Mike Mansfield (D – Mont.)	5 September 1975
Charles Mathias (R – Md.)	24 September 1975
Gale McGee (D – Wyo.)	18 March 1974
Thomas McIntyre (D – N.H.)	28 March 1974
Lee Metcalf (D – Mont.)	8 March 1974
Edmund Muskie (D – Maine)	28 March 1974
Frank Moss (D – Utah)	21 March 1974
Gaylord Nelson (D – Wis.)	27 March 1974
Claiborne Pell (D – R.I.)	21 March 1974
William Proxmire (D – Wis.)	29 March 1974
Abraham Ribicoff (D – Conn.)	18 September 1975
Richard Schweiker (R – Pa.)	19 September 1975
Joseph Tydings (D – Md.)	12 September 1975
John Tower (R – Tex.)	13 March 1974
Harrison Williams (D – N.J.)	25 September 1975

Staff Assistants

Verda Barnes, Administrative Assistant to Senator Frank Church of Idaho, 18 March 1974

Michael Baroody, Administrative Assistant to Senator Robert Dole of Kansas, 20 August 1975

William Cochrane; Senior Staff Counsel, Senate Rules Committee, 4 September 1975

Richard Cook, Administrative Assistant to Senator Gale McGee of Wyoming, 25 August 1975

George Cunningham, Administrative Assistant to Senator George McGovern of South Dakota, 17 September 1975

Merill Englund, Administrative Assistant to Senator Lee Metcalf of Montana, 26 August 1975

Gerry Frank, Administrative Assistant to Senator Mark Hatfield of Oregon, 11 March 1974

Michael Franks, Assistant to Senator John Tunney of California, 16 September 1975

Gene Godley, Administrative Assistant to Senator Thomas Eagleton of Missouri, 9 September 1975

Roy Greenaway, Administrative Assistant to Senator Alan Cranston of California, September 1975

Louis Hansen, Administrative Assistant to Senator Gaylord Nelson of Wisconsin, 22 August 1975

John Hardy, Counsel to the Senate Commerce Committee, 25 February 1974

Frances Henderson, Administrative Assistant to Senator Clifford Case of New Jersey, 26 February 1974

William Hoffman, Legislative Assistant to Senator Mike Gravel of Alaska, 24 September 1975

James McKenna, Legislative Assistant to Senator John Pastore of Rhode Island, 21 March 1974

John Nolan, Policy Adviser to Senator Edward Kennedy of Massachusetts, 5 March 1974

Courtney Pace, Administrative Assistant to Senator James Eastland of Mississippi, 16 September 1975

Michael Pertshuk, Chief Counsel, Senate Commerce Committee, 7 March 1974

Eugene Peters, Executive Director, Joint Committee on Congressional Operations, 25 February 1974

Howard Shuman, Administrative Assistant to Senator William Proxmire of Wisconsin, 3 September 1975

Antony Smith, Press Secretary to Senator Barry Goldwater of Arizona, 24 September 1975

Maynard Toll, Administrative Assistant to Senator Edmund Muskie of Maine, 22 August 1975

Gerry Udell, Executive Officer to Senator Mike Gravel of Alaska, 26 August 1975

Sidney Woolner, Administrative Assistant to Senator Philip Hart of Michigan, 12 March 1974

Party and Interest Group Representatives

Martin Clancy, Deputy Staff Director, Senate Republican Policy Committee, 6 March 1974

David Cohen, Director of Operations, Common Cause, 25 March 1974

Charles Ferris, Staff Director, Senate Democratic Policy Committee, 12 March 1974

Joseph Lipman, Director, Congress Watch, 28 February 1974

Knox Pitts, Electoral Research Officer, Democratic National Committee, 1 March 1974

Leon Shull, National Director, Americans for Democratic Action, 20 March
  1974

Journalists/Authors

William S. White, author of *Citadel: The Story of the U.S. Senate,* 29
  March 1974
Paul Wieck, political columnist for the *New Republic,* 15 March 1974
Harold Wolman, author of *The Politics of Federal Housing,* 24 September
  1975

Senate Officials

Floyd Riddick, Senate Parliamentarian, 4 September 1975
Murray Zwebin, Assistant Senate Parliamentarian, 18 March 1974

Notes on the Methods Used in the Construction of Guttman Scales in the Senatorial Voting Study

Having obtained at least the minimum number of appropriate roll calls, the different responses (i.e., "yeas," "nays," polled affirmative responses, polled negative responses, paired for, and paired against) were standardized in terms of favorable and unfavorable attitudes to the posited liberal disposition. For example, an affirmative vote in one roll call for an expansion in a housing program and a negative vote in another roll call against cutbacks in a housing program would both be standardized as liberal votes for the purposes of scaling.

Before any votes could be used to construct a Guttman scale, however, they had to be tested for scalability—whether or not they were related to each other through a single underlying variable. The method used to determine the existence of scalability was the Yules Q coefficient recommended for Guttman scaling by Anderson, Watts, and Wilcox in their standard text *Legislative Roll Call Analysis.*[1]

The coefficient is based upon a fourfold table framework in which pairs of roll calls are cross-tabulated in terms of the consistency of responses.

Roll Call y

		Yeas	Nays
Roll Call x	Yeas	a	b
	Nays	c	d

The coefficient can be expressed in the following way:

$$Q = \frac{ad - bc}{ad + bc}$$

The value of Q can range from -0.1 to $+0.1$, depending on the strength of the relationship between pairs of roll calls. The adopted threshold point of scalability, therefore, is an arbitrary one. The level of $+0.6$ can be regarded as high enough to ensure substantial homogeneity. However, to ensure a fairly high degree of scalability in this analysis, the threshold point was set at $+0.7$. Accordingly, every suitable roll call that reached a Yules Q value of $+0.7$ or over with every one of the other roll calls in an issue area was included in the final set of roll calls for a Guttman scale.

At this point, the individual respondents and the votes could be arranged in the familiar cumulative pattern of the Guttman scale. In an idealized form, six individuals and six roll calls would appear in the following pattern:

Individual	Roll Calls						Score
	1	2	3	4	5	6	
A	×	×	×	×	×	×	6
B	×	×	×	×	×	—	5
C	×	×	×	×	—	—	4
D	×	×	×	—	—	—	3
E	×	×	—	—	—	—	2
F	×	—	—	—	—	—	1

The six roll calls constitute what is called the universe of content within the scale. In this example, it refers to the total liberal attitude or to the total conservative attitude, depending on whichever is being considered. As mentioned in chapter 3, it should be possible in a Guttman scale to infer, from an individual's total score, on which roll calls he voted liberal and on which roll calls he voted conservative. Assuming that the liberal responses are denoted by ×, senator D scored 3, as he consistently supported the three items of least liberal value and consistently opposed the three items of greatest liberal value. Ideally, therefore, responses should contain a minimum of one change within a single sequence, when a continuous series of affirmative responses meets a continuous set of negative responses.

However, very few Guttman scales achieve this form of perfect accumulation. When dealing with multiple individual responses, inconsistencies are bound to occur. In a 10-item scale, for example, it is possible to experience the following sequence:

	1	2	3	4	5	6	7	8	9	10
Senator A	×	×	×	(=	×	×)	—	—	—	—

The underlined response which disrupts the continuity of the series is known as a nonscale response. In order to assign a scale score to a sequence containing a nonscale response, it is necessary to convert the imperfect pattern into a perfect sequence by a process which involves the least number of changes (i.e., *minimum-error criterion*).

1	2	3	4	5	6	7	8	9	10			
×	×	×	×	×	×	—	—	—	—	= 1 change	= score of 6
×	×	×	—	—	—	—	—	—	—	= 2 changes	= score of 3

The first rearrangement assigns error to response number 4, whereas the second readjustment identifies responses 5 and 6 as the erroneous votes. Under the minimum-error criterion, this member would be assigned a score of 6.

Difficulties arise when the least number of changes produces a situation in which a senator could be given more than one score. The following sequence, for example, could be rearranged in two ways, both of which would comply with the minimum-error rule.

	1	2	3	4	5	6	7	8	9	10
Senator B	×	×	(−	−	×	×)	−	−	−	−

One adjustment produces a score of 6, while another produces a score of 2.

1	2	3	4	5	6	7	8	9	10
×	×	×	×	×	×	−	−	−	− = 2 changes = score of 6
×	×	−	−	−	−	−	−	−	− = 2 changes = score of 2

One method of resolving this difficulty is to assign to such sequence the mean score of the two possible results (i.e., 4). Other methods of assigning scores include *extreme weighing*, in which an ambiguity is resolved by giving greater weight to those responses in the more extreme columns. In the example, error can either be assigned to items 3 and 4, or to 5 and 6. Under extreme weighing, error would be allocated to 5 and 6, thereby producing a score of 2. Extreme weighing minimizes the number of errors on the more extreme items and helps to maintain the scalar purity of the marginal votes. *Middle weighing*, on the other hand, emphasizes the middle-item responses and therefore ascribes error to the more extreme responses at the end of the scale. In the example, middle weighing would apportion error to items 3 and 4 to produce a score of 6.

Among the many methods of assigning nonscale responses in Guttman scales, the one finally selected was a variation of the method of *distribution of perfect scale types*. This process resolves the ambiguity caused when a sequence can be given more than one scale score under the *minimum-error criterion*. It assigns an ambiguous pattern according to whichever one of the possible scores has the greatest number of perfect examples in the rest of the scale. Such a method assigns an ambiguous sequence to the scale type "from which it had the greatest probability of deviating."[2] When there are a large number of scale score categories, however, there may not be a sufficient number of perfect scale types to provide a solution. C. F. Andrain has overcome this difficulty by assigning ambiguous types to the score "that most nearly approaches the mean score of the total number of Senators voting consistently."[3] This refinement succeeds in distributing nonscale responses according to the distribution of pure types in the Guttman scale. The sequences that contained nonresponses equal to, or exceeding, half the number of total items in a scale were considered to have too many unknown responses to be assigned a definite score. Such patterns were therefore designated as nonascertainable.

Once the ambiguous response sequences had been resolved and inserted into the appropriate score classifications, the Guttman scale was complete. The final check on the scale was a test to determine its accuracy as a scale. Guttman's *coefficient of reproducibility* was used to determine the degree to which the items and the responses had built up into a cumulative framework.

$$\text{Coefficient of reproducibility} = 1 - \frac{\text{total number of errors}}{\text{total number of responses}}$$

The coefficient assesses the "proportion of responses that can be correctly predicted from the individuals' total scores."[4] Where the value of the coefficient exceeded the threshold point recommended by Guttman[5] (i.e., 0.90), the scale was regarded as possessing an acceptable degree of scale perfection.

Issues Scaled through the
Guttman Technique, by Congress

86th Congress (1959–60)
Civil rights
Social welfare[a]
Union regulation
Foreign aid

87th Congress (1961–62)
Civil rights
Social welfare[a]
Foreign aid

88th Congress (1963–64)
Civil rights
Social welfare[a]
Poverty program
Congressional reform
Foreign aid

89th Congress (1965–66)
Civil rights
Social security
Poverty program
Housing and urban affairs
Education
Consumer and environmental
  protection
Foreign aid

90th Congress (1967–68)
Civil rights
Social security
Poverty program
Housing and urban affairs
Congressional reform
Civil liberties
Military expenditures
Foreign aid

91st Congress (1969–70)
Civil rights
Social security
Poverty program
Housing and urban affairs
War powers
Civil liberties
Military expenditures

92nd Congress (1971–72)
Civil rights
Social security
Poverty program
Consumer and Environmental
  protection
War powers
Military expenditures
Foreign aid

[a] It should be pointed out the number of roll calls in certain well-defined areas (e.g., social security, education, housing, etc.) was occasionally insufficient to devise Guttman scales. In these circumstances, roll-call data from related areas—where scalability permitted—were combined to form a composite, yet relatively distinct policy field scale. The social welfare field is the only example of this ad hoc arrangement. While education, housing, and social security could be regarded as major issue areas in their own right during the late 1950s and early 1960s, they nevertheless generated very few roll calls in Congress. Therefore, in the 86th, 87th, and 88th Congresses these issues were collectively grouped under the broader, and admittedly more diffuse category of social welfare. In later Congresses, social welfare issues became more important in the business of the legislature. In accordance with the large rise in the number of available roll calls, the increased differentiation among the issues, the growing lack of scalability among them, and their salience in public debate, the rationale of the study's Guttman scaling reverted to the principle of maximizing the number of policy areas scaled. Where possible, Guttman scales on each of the major areas were introduced to reflect the issues' contemporary prominence and to measure degrees of senatorial support and opposition with greater accuracy.

Distribution of Liberal Scores among the Scaled Issues, by Congress

L   denotes a liberal score
—   denotes a nonliberal score
N/A   denotes a nonascertainable score

86th Congress

	Civil rights	*Social welfare*	*Union regulation*	*Foreign aid*
Engle (D – Calif.)	L	L	L	L
Carroll (D – Colo.)	L	L	L	L
Douglas (D – Ill.)	L	L	L	L
Hartke (D – Ind.)	L	L	L	L
Muskie (D – Maine)	L	L	L	L
Kennedy (D – Mass.)	L	L	L	L
Hart (D – Mich.)	L	L	L	L
McNamara (D – Mich.)	L	L	L	L
Humphrey (D – Minn.)	L	L	L	L
McCarthy (D – Minn.)	L	L	L	L
Hennings (D – Mo.)	L	L	L	L
Symington (D – Mo.)	L	L	L	L
Williams (D – N.J.)	L	L	L	L
Young (D – Ohio)	L	L	L	L
Morse (D – Oreg.)	L	L	L	L
Clark (D – Pa.)	L	L	L	L
Jackson (D – Wash.)	L	L	L	L
Moss (D – Utah)	L	L	L	L
Randolph (D – W.Va.)	L	L	L	L
Proxmire (D – Wis.)	L	L	L	L
Hayden (D – Ariz.)	—	L	L	L
Church (D – Idaho)	—	L	L	L
Cooper (R – Ky.)	—	L	L	L
Mansfield (D – Mont.)	—	L	L	L
Murray (D – Mont.)	—	L	L	L
Monroney (D – Okla.)	—	L	L	L
Gore (D – Tenn.)	—	L	L	L
Kefauver (D – Tenn.)	—	L	L	L
Johnson (D – Tex.)	—	L	L	L
Yarborough (D – Tex.)	—	L	L	L
McGee (D – Wyo.)	—	L	L	L
O'Mahoney (D – Wyo.)	—	L	L	L
Neuberger (D – Oreg.)	N/A	L	L	L
Pastore (D – R.I.)	L	L	L	—
Magnuson (D – Wash.)	L	L	L	—
Gruening (D – Alaska)	L	L	L	—

86th Congress (*continued*)

	Civil rights	Social welfare	Union regulation	Foreign aid
Case (R – N.J.)	L	—	L	L
Anderson (D – N.Mex.)	L	L	L	—
Javits (R – N.Y.)	L	—	L	L
Kuchel (R – Calif.)	L	—	L	L
Bartlett (D –Alaska)	L	L	—	L
Smith (R – Maine)	L	L	—	L
Long (D – Hawaii)	L	L	N/A	L
Bible (D – Nev.)	—	L	L	—
Cannon (D – Nev.)	—	L	L	—
Green (D – R.I.)	—	L	L	—
Byrd (D – W.Va.)	—	L	L	—
Hill (D – Ala.)	—	—	L	L
Sparkman (D – Ala.)	—	—	L	L
Aiken (R – Vt.)	—	—	L	L
Langer (R – N.Dak.)	N/A	N/A	L	L
Bush (R – Conn.)	L	—	—	L
Beall (R – Md.)	L	—	—	L
Saltonstall (R – Mass.)	L	—	—	L
Dodd (D – Conn.)	L	L	—	—
Scott (R – Pa.)	L	—	—	L
Fulbright (D – Ark.)	—	—	—	L
Smathers (D – Fla.)	—	—	—	L
Dirksen (R – Ill.)	—	—	—	L
Capehart (R – Ind.)	—	—	—	L
Hickenlooper (R – Iowa)	—	—	—	L
Carlson (R – Kans.)	—	—	—	L
Morton (R – Ky.)	—	—	—	L
Young (R – N.Dak.)	—	—	—	L
Case (R – S.Dak.)	—	—	—	L
Mundt (R – S.Dak.)	—	—	—	L
Bennett (R – Utah)	—	—	—	L
Wiley (R – Wis.)	—	—	—	L
Ellender (D – La.)	—	—	L	—
Long (D – La.)	—	—	L	—
Johnson (D – S.C.)	—	—	L	—
Kerr (D – Okla.)	—	L	—	—
Chavez (D – N.Mex.)	—	L	—	N/A
Keating (R – N.Y.)	L	—	—	—
Goldwater (R – Ariz.)	—	—	—	—
McClellan (D – Ark.)	—	—	—	—
Allott (R – Colo.)	—	—	—	—
Williams (R – Del.)	—	—	—	—

Holland (D – Fla.)	—	—	—	—
Russell (D – Ga.)	—	—	—	—
Talmadge (D – Ga.)	—	—	—	—
Dworshak (R – Idaho)	—	—	—	—
Martin (R – Iowa)	—	—	—	—
Schoeppel (R – Kans.)	—	—	—	—
Butler (R – Md.)	—	—	—	—
Eastland (D – Miss.)	—	—	—	—
Stennis (D – Miss.)	—	—	—	—
Curtis (R – Nebr.)	—	—	—	—
Hruska (R – Nebr.)	—	—	—	—
Bridges (R – N.H.)	—	—	—	—
Cotton (R – N.H.)	—	—	—	—
Ervin (D – N.C.)	—	—	—	—
Jordan (D – N.C.)	—	—	—	—
Lausche (D – Ohio)	—	—	—	—
Thurmond (D – S.C.)	—	—	—	—
Prouty (R – Vt.)	—	—	—	—
Byrd (Sr.) (D – Va.)	—	—	—	—
Robertson (D – Va.)	—	—	—	—
Frear (D – Del.)	—	—	N/A	—
Fong (R – Hawaii)	—	N/A	N/A	—
Brunsdale (R – N.Dak.)	—	N/A	N/A	N/A
Lusk (D – Oreg.)	—	N/A	N/A	N/A

87th Congress

	Civil rights	Social welfare	Foreign aid
Engle (D – Calif.)	L	L	L
Dodd (D – Conn.)	L	L	L
Long (D – Hawaii)	L	L	L
Douglas (D – Ill.)	L	L	L
Hartke (D – Ind.)	L	L	L
Muskie (D – Maine)	L	L	L
Smith (D – Mass.)	L	L	L
Hart (D – Mich.)	L	L	L
McCarthy (D – Minn.)	L	L	L
Humphrey (D – Minn.)	L	L	L
Long (D – Mo.)	L	L	L
Symington (D –Mo.)	L	L	L
Williams (D – N.J.)	L	L	L
Case (R – N.J.)	L	L	L
Javits (R – N.Y.)	L	L	L

87th Congress (*continued*)

	Civil rights	Social welfare	Foreign aid
Young (D – Ohio)	L	L	L
Morse (D – Oreg.)	L	L	L
Neuberger (D – Oreg.)	L	L	L
Clark (D – Pa.)	L	L	L
Moss (D – Utah)	L	L	L
Randolph (D – W.Va.)	L	L	L
Gruening (D – Alaska)	L	L	—
Carroll (D – Colo.)	L	L	—
Burdick (D – N.Dak.)	L	L	—
Hill (D – Ala.)	—	L	L
Sparkman (D – Ala.)	—	L	L
Bartlett (D – Alaska)	—	L	L
Hayden (D – Ariz.)	—	L	L
Church (D – Idaho)	—	L	L
McNamara (D – Mich.)	—	L	L
Mansfield (D – Mont.)	—	L	L
Metcalf (D – Mont.)	—	L	L
Anderson (D – N.Mex.)	—	L	L
Chavez (D – N.Mex.)	—	L	L
Kerr (D – Okla.)	—	L	L
Pastore (D – R.I.)	—	L	L
Pell (D – R.I.)	—	L	L
Kefauver (D – Tenn.)	—	L	L
Jackson (D – Wash.)	—	L	L
Byrd (D – W.Va.)	—	L	L
Hickey (D – Wyo.)	—	L	L
McGee (D – Wyo.)	—	L	L
Cooper (R – Ky.)	L	—	L
Wiley (R – Wis.)	L	—	L
Kuchel (R – Calif.)	L	—	—
Allott (R – Colo.)	L	—	—
Bush (R – Conn.)	L	—	—
Boggs (R – Del.)	L	—	—
Fong (R – Hawaii)	L	—	—
Dirksen (R – Ill.)	L	—	—
Capehart (R – Ind.)	L	—	—
Carlson (R – Kans.)	L	—	—
Morton (R – Ky.)	L	—	—
Smith (R – Maine)	L	—	—
Beall (R –Md.)	L	—	—
Keating (R – N.Y.)	L	—	—
Lausche (D – Ohio)	L	—	—

Scott (R – Pa.)	L	—	—
Mundt (R –S.Dak.)	L	—	—
Prouty (R –Vt.)	L	—	—
Proxmire (D – Wis.)	L	—	—
Long (D – La.)	—	L	—
Bible (D – Nev.)	—	L	—
Cannon (D – Nev.)	—	L	—
Yarborough (D – Tex.)	—	L	—
Magnuson (D – Wash.)	—	L	—
Fulbright (D – Ark.)	—	—	L
Monroney (D – Okla.)	—	—	L
Gore (D – Tenn.)	—	—	L
Goldwater (R – Ariz.)	—	—	—
McClellan (D – Ark.)	—	—	—
Williams (R – Del.)	—	—	—
Holland (D – Fla.)	—	—	—
Smathers (D – Fla.)	—	—	—
Russell (D – Ga.)	—	—	—
Talmadge (D – Ga.)	—	—	—
Dworshak (R – Idaho)	—	—	—
Saltonstall (R –Mass.)	—	—	—
Eastland (D – Miss.)	—	—	—
Stennis (D – Miss.)	—	—	—
Curtis (R –Nebr.)	—	—	—
Hruska (R – Nebr.)	—	—	—
Cotton (R – N.H.)	—	—	—
Ervin (D – N.C.)	—	—	—
Jordan (D – N.C.)	—	—	—
Young (R – N.Dak.)	—	—	—
Johnston (D – S.C.)	—	—	—
Thurmond (D – S.C.)	—	—	—
Case (R – S.Dak.)	—	—	—
Bennett (R – Utah)	—	—	—
Aiken (R – Vt.)	—	—	—
Byrd (Sr.) (D – Va.)	—	—	—
Robertson (D – Va.)	—	—	—
Miller (R – Iowa)	—	—	—
Ellender (D – La.)	—	—	—
Schoeppel (R – Kans.)	N/A	—	—
Butler (R – Md.)	N/A	—	—
Bridges (R – N.H.)	N/A	—	—
Hickenlooper (R – Iowa)	N/A	—	—
Tower (R – Tex.)	—	N/A	—

88th Congress

	Civil rights	Social welfare	Poverty program	Congress reform	Foreign aid
Engle (D – Calif.)	L	L	L	L	L
Ribicoff (D – Conn.)	L	L	L	L	L
Douglas (D – Ill.)	L	L	L	L	L
Hartke (D – Ind.)	L	L	L	L	L
Brewster (D – Md.)	L	L	L	L	L
Hart (D – Mich.)	L	L	L	L	L
Williams (D – N.J.)	L	L	L	L	L
Javits (R – N.Y.)	L	L	L	L	L
Neuberger (D – Oreg.)	L	L	L	L	L
Clark (D – Pa.)	L	L	L	L	L
McGovern (D – S.Dak.)	L	L	L	L	L
Moss (D – Utah)	L	L	L	L	L
Nelson (D – Wis.)	L	L	L	L	L
Inouye (D – Hawaii)	L	L	L	—	L
Muskie (D – Maine)	L	L	L	—	L
McNamara (D – Mich.)	L	L	L	—	L
Humphrey (D – Minn.)	L	L	L	—	L
McCarthy (D – Minn.)	L	L	L	—	L
Mansfield (D – Mont.)	L	L	L	—	L
Metcalf (D – Mont.)	L	L	L	—	L
Monroney (D – Okla.)	L	L	L	—	L
Pastore (D – R.I.)	L	L	L	—	L
Pell (D – R.I.)	L	L	L	—	L
McGee (D – Wyo.)	L	L	L	—	L
Bayh (D – Ind.)	L	L	L	—	L
Bartlett (D – Alaska)	L	L	L	—	L
Kennedy (D – Mass.)	L	L	L	—	L
McIntyre (D – N.H.)	L	L	L	—	L
Proxmire (D – Wis.)	L	L	L	L	—
Morse (D – Oreg.)	L	L	L	L	—
Symington (D – Mo.)	L	L	L	L	—
Young (D – Ohio)	L	L	L	L	—
Dodd (D – Conn.)	L	L	L	L	—
Kuchel (R – Calif.)	L	L	—	L	L
Smith (R – Maine)	L	L	—	L	L
Case (R – N.J.)	L	L	—	L	L
Keating (R – N.Y.)	L	L	—	L	L
Burdick (D – N.Dak.)	L	L	L	—	—
Magnuson (D – Wash.)	L	L	L	—	—
Gruening (D – Alaska)	L	L	L	—	—
Jackson (D – Wash.)	L	L	L	—	—
Anderson (D – N.Mex.)	L	L	L	—	—

Randolph (D – W.Va.)	L	L	L	—	—
Fong (R – Hawaii)	L	L	—	L	—
Church (D – Idaho)	—	L	L	—	L
Gore (D – Tenn.)	—	L	L	—	L
Yarborough (D – Tex.)	—	L	L	—	—
Bible (D – Nev.)	—	L	L	—	—
Cannon (D – Nev.)	—	L	L	—	—
Johnston (D – S.C.)	—	L	L	—	—
Byrd (D – W.Va.)	—	L	L	—	—
Boggs (R – Del.)	L	—	—	—	L
Aiken (R – Vt.)	L	—	—	—	L
Dirksen (R – Ill.)	L	—	—	—	L
Fulbright (D – Ark.)	—	—	L	—	L
Smathers (D – Fla.)	—	—	L	—	L
Long (D – Mo.)	L	L	—	—	—
Saltonstall (R – Mass.)	L	—	—	—	L
Hayden (D – Ariz.)	N/A	L	—	—	L
Scott (R – Pa.)	L	—	—	L	—
Edmonson (D – Okla.)	L	—	L	—	—
Hickenlooper (R – Iowa)	—	—	—	—	L
Cooper (R – Ky.)	—	—	—	—	L
Morton (R – Ky.)	—	—	—	—	L
Sparkman (D – Ala.)	—	—	—	—	L
Holland (D – Fla.)	—	—	—	—	L
Hill (D – Ala.)	—	—	—	—	L
Carlson (R – Kans.)	—	—	—	—	L
Prouty (R – Vt.)	L	—	—	—	—
Miller (R – Iowa)	L	—	—	—	—
Allott (R – Colo.)	L	—	—	—	—
Beall (R – Md.)	L	—	—	—	—
Goldwater (R – Ariz.)	—	—	—	—	—
McClellan (D – Ark.)	—	—	—	—	—
Dominick (R – Colo.)	—	—	—	—	—
Williams (R – Del.)	—	—	—	—	—
Russell (D – Ga.)	—	—	—	—	—
Talmadge (D – Ga.)	—	—	—	—	—
Jordan (R – Idaho)	—	—	—	—	—
Pearson (R – Kans.)	—	—	—	—	—
Ellender (D – La.)	—	—	—	—	—
Long (D – La.)	—	—	—	—	—
Eastland (D – Miss.)	—	—	—	—	—
Stennis (D – Miss.)	—	—	—	—	—
Curtis (R – Nebr.)	—	—	—	—	—
Hruska (R – Nebr.)	—	—	—	—	—
Mechem (R – N.Mex.)	—	—	—	—	—
Ervin (D – N.C.)	—	—	—	—	—

88th Congress (*continued*)

	Civil rights	Social welfare	Poverty program	Congress reform	Foreign aid
Jordan (D – N.C.)	—	—	—	—	—
Young (R – N.Dak.)	—	—	—	—	—
Lausche (D – Ohio)	—	—	—	—	—
Thurmond (D – S.C.)	—	—	—	—	—
Mundt (R – S.Dak.)	—	—	—	—	—
Tower (R – Tex.)	—	—	—	—	—
Bennett (R – Utah)	—	—	—	—	—
Byrd (Sr.) (D – Va.)	—	—	—	—	—
Robertson (D – Va.)	—	—	—	—	—
Simpson (R – Wyo.)	—	—	—	—	—
Cotton (R – N.H.)	—	—	—	—	—
Walters (D – Tenn.)	—	—	—	N/A	—

89th Congress

	Civil rights	Social security	Poverty program	Housing and urban affairs	Education	Consumer and environmental protection	Foreign aid
Bartlett (D – Alaska)	L	L	L	L	L	L	L
Dodd (D – Conn.)	L	L	L	L	L	L	L
Ribicoff (D – Conn.)	L	L	L	L	L	L	L
Inouye (D – Hawaii)	L	L	L	L	L	L	L
Douglas (D – Ill.)	L	L	L	L	L	L	L
Bayh (D – Ind.)	L	L	L	L	L	L	L
Muskie (D – Maine)	L	L	L	L	L	L	L
Kennedy (D – Mass.)	L	L	L	L	L	L	L
Tydings (D – Md.)	L	L	L	L	L	L	L
Hart (D – Mich.)	L	L	L	L	L	L	L
McCarthy (D – Minn.)	L	L	L	L	L	L	L
Mondale (D – Minn.)	L	L	L	L	L	L	L
Long (D – Mo.)	L	L	L	L	L	L	L
Mansfield (D – Mont.)	L	L	L	L	L	L	L
Metcalf (D – Mont.)	L	L	L	L	L	L	L
Montoya (D – N.Mex.)	L	L	L	L	L	L	L
Kennedy (D – N.Y.)	L	L	L	L	L	L	L
Young (D – Ohio)	L	L	L	L	L	L	L
Neuberger (D – Oreg.)	L	L	L	L	L	L	L

Clark (D – Pa.)	L	L	L	L	L	L	L
Pastore (D – R.I.)	L	L	L	L	L	L	L
Pell (D – R.I.)	L	L	L	L	L	L	L
McGovern (D – S.Dak.)	L	L	L	L	L	L	L
Yarborough (D – Tex.)	L	L	L	L	L	L	L
Nelson (D – Wis.)	L	L	L	L	L	L	L
McGee (D – Wyo.)	L	L	L	L	L	L	L
Gruening (D – Alaska)	L	L	L	L	L	L	—
Hartke (D – Ind.)	L	L	L	L	L	L	—
Brewster (D – Md.)	L	L	L	L	L	L	—
Burdick (D – N.Dak.)	L	L	L	L	L	L	—
Morse (D – Oreg.)	L	L	L	L	L	L	—
Magnuson (D – Wash.)	L	L	L	L	L	L	—
Proxmire (D – Wis.)	L	L	L	L	L	L	—
Symington (D – Mo.)	L	L	L	L	L	L	—
Anderson (D – N.Mex.)	L	L	L	L	L	—	L
Williams (D – N.J.)	L	L	L	L	L	—	L
Case (R – N.J.)	L	L	L	L	L	—	L
Javits (R – N.Y.)	L	L	L	L	L	—	L
Church (D – Idaho)	L	—	L	L	L	L	L
Monroney (D – Okla.)	L	—	L	L	L	L	L
Moss (D – Utah)	L	—	L	L	L	L	L
Jackson (D – Wash.)	L	L	L	L	L	—	—
McIntyre (D – N.H.)	L	L	L	L	L	—	—
Gore (D – Tenn.)	L	L	L	—	L	L	—
Randolph (D – W.Va.)	L	L	—	L	L	L	—
Bass (D – Tenn.)	L	—	L	L	L	L	N/A
Long (D – La.)	—	L	L	L	—	L	—
Fulbright (D – Ark.)	—	N/A	L	L	L	—	L
McNamara (D – Mich.)	L	N/A	L	L	N/A	L	—
Hayden (D – Ariz.)	—	N/A	L	L	N/A	L	L
Harris (D – Okla.)	L	—	L	L	L	—	L
Smathers (D – Fla.)	—	—	—	L	—	L	L
Cannon (D – Nev.)	—	L	—	L	L	—	—
Aiken (R – Vt.)	L	L	—	L	—	—	—
Byrd (D – W.Va.)	—	L	—	—	L	L	—
Boggs (R – Del.)	L	L	—	—	—	—	—
Long (R – Hawaii)	L	L	—	—	—	—	—
Smith (R – Maine)	L	—	—	L	—	—	—
Scott (R – Pa.)	L	—	—	L	—	—	—
Ellender (D – La.)	—	—	—	L	—	L	—
Kuchel (R – Calif.)	L	—	—	—	—	—	—
Allott (R – Colo.)	L	—	—	—	—	—	—
Dominick (R – Colo.)	L	—	—	—	—	—	—
Saltonstall (R – Mass.)	L	—	—	—	—	—	—
Prouty (R – Vt.)	—	L	—	—	—	—	—

89th Congress (*continued*)

	Civil rights	Social security	Poverty program	Housing and urban affairs	Education	Consumer and environmental protection	Foreign aid
Bible (D – Nev.)	—	—	—	—	L	—	—
Hill (D – Ala.)	—	—	—	—	L	—	—
Holland (D – Fla.)	—	—	—	—	—	—	L
Fannin (R – Ariz.)	—	—	—	—	—	—	—
McClellan (D – Ark.)	—	—	—	—	—	—	—
Murphy (R – Calif.)	—	—	—	—	—	—	—
Williams (R – Del.)	—	—	—	—	—	—	—
Talmadge (D – Ga.)	—	—	—	—	—	—	—
Jordan (R – Idaho)	—	—	—	—	—	—	—
Dirksen (R – Ill.)	—	—	—	—	—	—	—
Hickenlooper (R – Iowa)	—	—	—	—	—	—	—
Miller (R – Iowa)	—	—	—	—	—	—	—
Carlson (R – Kans.)	—	—	—	—	—	—	—
Pearson (R – Kans.)	—	—	—	—	—	—	—
Cooper (R – Ky.)	—	—	—	—	—	—	—
Morton (R – Ky.)	—	—	—	—	—	—	—
Eastland (D – Miss.)	—	—	—	—	—	—	—
Stennis (D – Miss.)	—	—	—	—	—	—	—
Curtis (R – Nebr.)	—	—	—	—	—	—	—
Hruska (R – Nebr.)	—	—	—	—	—	—	—
Cotton (R – N.H.)	—	—	—	—	—	—	—
Ervin (D – N.C.)	—	—	—	—	—	—	—
Jordan (D – N.C.)	—	—	—	—	—	—	—
Young (R – N.Dak.)	—	—	—	—	—	—	—
Lausche (D – Ohio)	—	—	—	—	—	—	—
Thurmond (R – S.C.)	—	—	—	—	—	—	—
Mundt (R – S.Dak.)	—	—	—	—	—	—	—
Tower (R – Tex.)	—	—	—	—	—	—	—
Bennett (R – Utah)	—	—	—	—	—	—	—
Robertson (D – Va.)	—	—	—	—	—	—	—
Simpson (R – Wyo.)	—	—	—	—	—	—	—
Sparkman (D – Ala.)	—	—	N/A	—	—	—	—
Russell (D – Ga.)	—	—	—	—	N/A	N/A	—
Russell (D – S.C.)	—	—	—	—	N/A	N/A	—
Byrd (Sr.) (D –Va.)	—	N/A	—	—	N/A	—	—
Griffin (R – Mich.)	N/A	—	N/A	N/A	N/A	N/A	N
Byrd (Jr.) (D – Va.)	N/A	—	N/A	N/A	N/A	N/A	N

90th Congress

	Civil rights	Social security	Poverty program	Housing and urban affairs	Congress reform	Civil liberties	Military expenditure	Foreign aid
Clark (D – Pa.)	L	L	L	L	L	L	L	L
Nelson (D – Wis.)	L	L	L	L	L	L	L	L
Hart (D – Mich.)	L	L	L	L	L	L	—	L
Case (R – N.J.)	L	L	L	L	L	L	—	L
Javits (R – N.Y.)	L	L	L	L	L	L	—	L
Hartke (D – Ind.)	L	L	L	L	L	L	L	—
Proxmire (D – Wis.)	L	L	L	L	L	L	L	—
Morse (D – Oreg.)	L	L	L	L	L	L	L	—
Mondale (D – Minn.)	L	L	L	L	L	—	L	L
Moss (D – Utah)	L	L	L	L	L	—	L	L
Brooke (R – Mass.)	L	L	L	L	—	L	L	L
McCarthy (D – Minn.)	L	L	L	L	—	L	—	L
Metcalf (D – Mont.)	L	L	L	L	—	L	—	L
Williams (D – N.J.)	L	L	L	L	—	L	—	L
Gruening (D – Alaska)	L	L	L	L	—	L	L	—
Burdick (D – N.Dak.)	L	L	L	L	—	L	L	—
Young (D – Ohio)	L	L	L	L	—	L	L	—
Tydings (D – Md.)	L	L	L	L	—	—	L	L
Kennedy (D – Mass.)	L	L	L	L	L	L	N/A	N/A
Inouye (D – Hawaii)	L	L	L	L	—	—	—	L
Brewster (D – Md.)	L	L	L	L	—	—	—	L
Pastore (D – R.I.)	L	L	L	L	—	—	—	L
Pell (D – R.I.)	L	L	L	L	—	—	—	L
Yarborough (D – Tex.)	L	L	L	L	—	—	—	L
Jackson (D – Wash.)	L	L	L	L	—	—	—	L
McGee (D – Wyo.)	L	L	L	L	—	N/A	—	L
Kuchel (R – Calif.)	L	L	L	L	L	—	—	—
Ribicoff (D – Conn.)	L	L	L	L	L	—	—	—
Magnuson (D – Wash.)	L	L	L	L	L	—	—	—
Bayh (D – Ind.)	L	L	L	L	—	—	L	—
Kennedy (D – N.Y.)	L	L	L	L	—	L	N/A	N/A
Cooper (R – Ky.)	—	—	L	L	—	L	L	L
Dodd (D – Conn.)	L	L	—	L	—	—	—	L
Mansfield (D – Mont.)	L	L	—	L	—	—	—	L
Montoya (D – N.Mex.)	L	L	—	L	—	N/A	—	L
Randolph (D – W.Va.)	L	L	L	L	—	—	—	—
McIntyre (D – N.H.)	L	L	L	L	N/A	—	—	—
Harris (D – Okla.)	L	—	L	L	—	N/A	—	L
McGovern (D – S.Dak.)	L	N/A	—	L	—	N/A	L	L
Aiken (R – Vt.)	L	—	L	L	—	—	—	L
Muskie (D – Maine)	L	L	L	N/A	—	—	—	L

90th Congress (*continued*)

	Civil rights	Social security	Poverty program	Housing and urban affairs	Congress reform	Civil liberties	Military expenditure	Foreign aid
Bartlett (D – Alaska)	—	L	L	L	—	L	—	—
Hatfield (R – Oreg.)	L	—	L	N/A	—	L	L	—
Monroney (D – Okla.)	L	L	—	L	—	—	—	—
Gore (D – Tenn.)	L	L	N/A	L	—	—	N/A	N/A
Symington (D – Mo.)	L	—	L	L	—	—	—	—
Scott (R – Pa.)	L	—	L	L	—	—	—	—
Anderson (D – N.Mex.)	L	—	—	L	—	—	—	L
Percy (R – Ill.)	L	—	L	—	—	—	—	L
Long (D – Mo.)	L	N/A	L	—	—	L	N/A	N/A
Church (D – Idaho)	L	L	—	—	—	—	L	—
Fong (R – Hawaii)	L	—	—	—	L	L	—	—
Sparkman (D – Ala.)	—	—	—	L	—	—	—	L
Hayden (D – Ariz.)	—	N/A	—	L	—	—	—	L
Fulbright (D – Ark.)	—	L	—	L	—	—	N/A	N/A
Cannon (D – Nev.)	—	L	—	L	—	—	—	—
Griffin (R – Mich.)	L	—	L	—	—	—	—	N/A
Prouty (R – Vt.)	L	L	—	—	—	—	—	—
Hill (D – Ala.)	—	—	—	L	—	—	—	—
Talmadge (D – Ga.)	—	—	—	L	—	—	—	—
Ellender (D – La.)	—	—	—	L	—	—	—	—
Long (D – La.)	—	—	—	L	—	—	—	—
Stennis (D – Miss.)	—	—	—	L	—	—	—	—
Cotton (R – N.H.)	—	—	—	L	—	—	—	—
Young (R – N.Dak.)	—	—	—	L	—	—	—	—
Baker (R – Tenn.)	—	—	—	L	—	—	—	—
Spong (D – Va.)	—	—	—	L	—	—	—	—
Byrd (D – W.Va.)	—	—	—	L	—	—	—	—
Allot (R – Colo.)	L	—	—	—	—	—	—	—
Dominick (R – Colo.)	L	—	—	—	—	—	—	—
Boggs (R – Del.)	L	—	—	—	—	—	—	—
Pearson (R – Kans.)	L	—	—	—	—	—	—	—
Smith (R – Maine)	L	—	—	—	—	—	—	—
Lausche (D – Ohio)	L	—	—	—	—	—	—	—
Hollings (D – S.C.)	—	L	—	—	—	—	—	—
Fannin (R – Ariz.)	—	—	—	—	—	—	—	—
McClellan (D – Ark.)	—	—	—	—	—	—	—	—
Murphy (R – Calif.)	—	—	—	—	—	—	—	—
Williams (R – Del.)	—	—	—	—	—	—	—	—
Holland (D – Fla.)	—	—	—	—	—	—	—	—
Russell (D – Ga.)	—	—	—	—	—	—	—	—

Jordan (R – Idaho)	—	—	—	—	—	—	—
Dirksen (R – Ill.)	—	—	—	—	—	—	—
Hickenlooper (R – Iowa)	—	—	—	—	—	—	—
Miller (R – Iowa)	—	—	—	—	—	—	—
Eastland (D – Miss.)	—	—	—	—	—	—	—
Curtis (R – Nebr.)	—	—	—	—	—	—	—
Hruska (R – Nebr.)	—	—	—	—	—	—	—
Bible (D – Nev.)	—	—	—	—	—	—	—
Ervin (D – N.C.)	—	—	—	—	—	—	—
Thurmond (R – S.C.)	—	—	—	—	—	—	—
Tower (R – Tex.)	—	—	—	—	—	—	—
Bennett (R – Utah)	—	—	—	—	—	—	—
Byrd (Jr.) (D – Va.)	—	—	—	—	—	—	—
Hansen (R – Wyo.)	—	—	—	—	—	—	—
Carlson (R – Kans.)	—	—	—	—	—	—	N/A
Jordan (D – N.C.)	—	N/A	—	—	—	—	—
Mundt (R – S.Dak.)	—	N/A	—	—	—	—	—
Smathers (D – Fla.)	—	—	—	—	—	N/A	N/A
Morton (R – Ky.)	—	—	—	—	—	N/A	N/A

91st Congress

	Civil rights	Social security	Poverty program	Housing and urban affairs	War powers	Civil liberties	Military expenditure
Ribicoff (D – Conn.)	L	L	L	L	L	L	L
Hughes (D – Iowa)	L	L	L	L	L	L	L
McCarthy (D – Minn.)	L	L	L	L	L	L	L
Mondale (D – Minn.)	L	L	L	L	L	L	L
Metcalf (D – Mont.)	L	L	L	L	L	L	L
Goodell (R – N.Y.)	L	L	L	L	L	L	L
Young (D – Ohio)	L	L	L	L	L	L	L
Harris (D – Okla.)	L	L	L	L	L	L	L
Nelson (D – Wis.)	L	L	L	L	L	L	L
McGovern (D – S.Dak.)	L	L	L	L	L	N/A	L
Hartke (D – Ind.)	L	L	L	L	L	N/A	L
Cranston (D – Calif.)	L	L	L	L	L	—	L
Williams (D – N.J.)	L	L	L	L	L	—	L
Muskie (D – Maine)	L	—	L	L	L	L	L
Hart (D – Mich.)	L	—	L	L	L	L	L
Javits (R – N.Y.)	L	L	L	L	L	L	—
Mansfield (D – Mont.)	L	L	L	—	L	—	L
Proxmire (D – Wis.)	L	L	L	—	L	—	L

91st Congress (*continued*)

	Civil rights	Social security	Poverty program	Housing and urban affairs	War powers	Civil liberties	Military expenditure
Bayh (D – Ind.)	L	L	L	N/A	L	—	L
Case (R – N.J.)	L	L	—	L	L	—	L
Hatfield (R – Oreg.)	L	L	—	L	L	—	L
Brooke (R – Mass.)	L	L	L	L	L	—	—
Gravel (D – Alaska)	L	—	L	L	L	N/A	L
Kennedy (D – Mass.)	N/A	L	L	L	L	L	—
Symington (D – Mo.)	L	L	L	—	L	—	—
Burdick (D – N.Dak.)	L	L	L	—	L	—	—
Schweiker (R – Pa.)	L	L	L	—	L	—	—
Pell (D – R.I.)	L	L	L	—	L	—	—
Moss (D – Utah)	L	L	L	—	L	—	—
Magnuson (D – Wash.)	L	L	L	—	L	—	—
Eagleton (D – Mo.)	L	—	L	—	L	—	L
Inouye (D – Hawaii)	L	—	L	—	L	L	—
Church (D – Idaho)	L	—	L	L	L	—	—
Tydings (D – Md.)	L	—	L	L	L	—	—
Mathias (R – Md.)	L	—	L	L	L	—	—
Fulbright (D – Ark.)	—	—	L	L	L	—	L
Montoya (D – N.Mex.)	L	—	L	N/A	L	—	—
Pastore (D – R.I.)	L	—	L	—	L	—	—
McIntyre (D – N.H.)	L	L	—	—	L	—	—
Jackson (D – Wash.)	L	L	L	—	—	—	—
McGee (D – Wyo.)	L	—	L	N/A	—	L	—
Yarborough (D – Tex.)	—	L	L	N/A	L	N/A	—
Percy (R – Ill.)	L	—	L	—	—	—	—
Saxbe (R – Ohio)	L	—	L	—	—	—	—
Scott (R – Pa.)	L	—	L	—	—	—	—
Dodd (D – Conn.)	L	N/A	L	—	—	—	—
Anderson (D – N.Mex.)	L	N/A	L	N/A	—	—	—
Gore (D – Tenn.)	L	N/A	L	N/A	—	—	—
Stevens (R – Alaska)	L	—	—	—	—	—	—
Allott (R – Colo.)	L	—	—	—	—	—	—
Boggs (R – Del.)	L	—	—	—	—	—	—
Fong (R – Hawaii)	L	—	—	—	—	—	—
Jordan (R – Idaho)	L	—	—	—	—	—	—
Pearson (R – Kans.)	L	—	—	—	—	—	—
Cook (R – Ky.)	L	—	—	—	—	—	—
Cooper (R – Ky.)	L	—	—	—	—	—	—
Smith (R – Maine)	L	—	—	—	—	—	—
Griffin (R – Mich.)	L	—	—	—	—	—	—

Bellmon (R – Okla.)	L	—	—	—	—	—	—
Baker (R – Tenn.)	L	—	—	—	—	—	—
Packwood (R – Oreg.)	L	—	—	N/A	—	—	—
Aiken (R – Vt.)	L	—	—	—	—	N/A	—
Prouty (R – Vt.)	L	—	—	—	—	N/A	—
Bible (D – Nev.)	—	—	L	—	—	—	—
Spong (D – Va.)	—	—	L	—	—	—	—
Randolph (D – W.Va.)	—	—	L	—	—	—	—
Sparkman (D – Ala.)	—	—	—	L	—	—	—
Stevenson (D – Ill.)	N/A	L	N/A	N/A	N/A	N/A	N/A
Allen (D – Ala.)	—	—	—	—	—	—	—
Fannin (R – Ariz.)	—	—	—	—	—	—	—
McClellan (D – Ark.)	—	—	—	—	—	—	—
Murphy (R – Calif.)	—	—	—	—	—	—	—
Dominick (R – Colo.)	—	—	—	—	—	—	—
Williams (R – Del.)	—	—	—	—	—	—	—
Holland (D – Fla.)	—	—	—	—	—	—	—
Gurney (R – Fla.)	—	—	—	—	—	—	—
Talmadge (D – Ga.)	—	—	—	—	—	—	—
Miller (R – Iowa)	—	—	—	—	—	—	—
Dole (R – Kans.)	—	—	—	—	—	—	—
Ellender (D – La.)	—	—	—	—	—	—	—
Long (D – La.)	—	—	—	—	—	—	—
Stennis (D – Miss.)	—	—	—	—	—	—	—
Curtis (R – Nebr.)	—	—	—	—	—	—	—
Hruska (R – Nebr.)	—	—	—	—	—	—	—
Cannon (D – Nev.)	—	—	—	—	—	—	—
Cotton (R – N.H.)	—	—	—	—	—	—	—
Ervin (D – N.C.)	—	—	—	—	—	—	—
Jordan (D – N.C.)	—	—	—	—	—	—	—
Young (R – N.Dak.)	—	—	—	—	—	—	—
Hollings (D – S.C.)	—	—	—	—	—	—	—
Thurmond (R – S.C.)	—	—	—	—	—	—	—
Mundt (R – S.Dak.)	—	—	—	—	—	—	—
Tower (R – Tex.)	—	—	—	—	—	—	—
Bennett (R – Utah)	—	—	—	—	—	—	—
Byrd (Jr.) (D – Va.)	—	—	—	—	—	—	—
Byrd (D – W.Va.)	—	—	—	—	—	—	—
Hansen (R – Wyo.)	—	—	—	—	—	—	—
Russell (D – Ga.)	—	N/A	—	N/A	—	—	—
Smith (R – Ill.)	—	N/A	—	N/A	—	—	—
Eastland (D – Miss.)	—	—	N/A	N/A	—	—	—
Goldwater (R – Ariz.)	—	N/A	—	N/A	—	N/A	—

92nd Congress

	Civil rights	Social security	Poverty program	Consumer and environmental protection	War powers	Military expenditure	Foreign aid
Cranston (D – Calif.)	L	L	L	L	L	L	L
Stevenson (D – Ill.)	L	L	L	L	L	L	L
Bayh (D – Ind.)	L	L	L	L	L	L	L
Hughes (D – Iowa)	L	L	L	L	L	L	L
Kennedy (D – Mass.)	L	L	L	L	L	L	L
Hart (D – Mich.)	L	L	L	L	L	L	L
Mondale (D – Minn.)	L	L	L	L	L	L	L
Williams (D – N.J.)	L	L	L	L	L	L	L
Moss (D – Utah)	L	L	L	L	L	L	L
Ribicoff (D – Conn.)	L	L	L	L	L	—	L
Brooke (R – Mass.)	L	L	L	L	L	—	L
Humphrey (D – Minn.)	L	L	L	L	L	—	L
Case (R – N.J.)	L	L	L	L	L	—	L
Tunney (D – Calif.)	L	L	L	L	—	L	L
Javits (R – N.Y.)	L	L	L	L	—	L	L
Gravel (D – Alaska)	L	L	L	L	L	L	—
Hartke (D – Ind.)	L	L	L	L	L	L	—
Church (D – Idaho)	L	—	L	L	L	L	—
Nelson (D – Wis.)	L	—	L	L	L	L	—
Metcalf (D – Mont.)	L	N/A	L	L	L	L	—
McGovern (D – S.Dak.)	L	N/A	L	L	L	L	—
Schweiker (R – Pa.)	L	L	L	L	—	—	L
Jackson (D – Wash.)	L	L	L	L	—	—	L
Inouye (D – Hawaii)	L	—	L	L	—	L	L
Hatfield (R – Oreg.)	L	L	L	—	—	L	L
Mathias (R – Md.)	L	L	L	—	L	—	L
Pell (D – R.I.)	L	L	N/A	L	L	—	L
Pastore (D – R.I.)	L	L	L	L	L	—	—
Montoya (D – N.Mex.)	L	—	L	L	L	—	—
Burdick (D – N.Dak.)	L	—	L	L	L	—	—
Symington (D – Mo.)	L	—	L	L	L	—	—
McIntyre (D – N.H.)	L	L	L	L	—	—	—
Stevens (R – Alaska)	L	L	L	L	—	—	—
Fulbright (D – Ark.)	—	—	L	L	L	L	—
Percy (R – Ill.)	L	L	L	—	—	—	L
Scott (R – Pa.)	L	L	L	—	—	—	L
Proxmire (D – Wis.)	—	—	L	L	L	L	—
Eagleton (D – Mo.)	L	N/A	L	L	—	L	—

McGee (D – Wyo.)	L	N/A	L	L	—	—	L
Cooper (R – Ky.)	L	L	N/A	—	L	—	L
Muskie (D – Maine)	L	L	N/A	N/A	N/A	L	N/A
Harris (D – Okla.)	L	N/A	L	N/A	L	N/A	N/A
Magnuson (D – Wash.)	L	—	L	L	—	—	—
Aiken (R – Vt.)	L	L	—	—	—	—	L
Weicker (R – Conn.)	L	L	L	—	—	—	—
Chiles (D – Fla.)	—	—	L	L	—	—	L
Boggs (R – Del.)	L	—	—	—	—	—	L
Pearson (R – Kans.)	L	—	—	—	—	—	L
Bellmon (R – Okla.)	L	—	N/A	—	—	—	L
Sparkman (D – Ala.)	—	—	L	—	—	—	L
Fong (R – Hawaii)	—	—	L	—	—	—	L
Stafford (R – Vt.)	L	L	N/A	—	—	—	—
Mansfield (D – Mont.)	L	—	N/A	—	L	—	—
Beall (R – Md.)	—	L	—	—	—	—	L
Randolph (D – W.Va.)	—	—	L	L	—	—	—
McClellan (D – Ark.)	—	—	L	—	—	—	—
Long (D – La.)	—	—	L	—	—	—	—
Cannon (D – Nev.)	—	—	L	—	—	—	—
Hollings (D – S.C.)	—	—	L	—	—	—	—
Bentsen (D – Tex.)	—	—	L	—	—	—	—
Spong (D – Va.)	—	—	L	—	—	—	—
Jordan (D – N.C.)	—	—	L	—	—	—	—
Miller (R – Iowa)	L	—	—	—	—	—	—
Anderson (D – N.Mex.)	L	—	N/A	—	—	—	—
Saxbe (R – Ohio)	L	—	—	—	—	—	—
Griffin (R – Mich.)	—	—	—	—	—	—	L
Taft (R – Ohio)	—	—	—	—	—	—	L
Bennett (R – Utah)	—	—	—	—	—	—	L
Smith (R – Maine)	—	L	—	—	—	—	—
Byrd (D – W.Va.)	—	—	—	L	—	—	—
Allen (D – Ala.)	—	—	—	—	—	—	—
Fannin (R – Ariz.)	—	—	—	—	—	—	—
Dominick (R – Colo.)	—	—	—	—	—	—	—
Prouty (R – Vt.)	—	—	—	—	—	—	—
Gurney (R – Fla.)	—	—	—	—	—	—	—
Gambrell (D – Ga.)	—	—	—	—	—	—	—
Talmadge (D – Ga.)	—	—	—	—	—	—	—
Jordan (R – Idaho)	—	—	—	—	—	—	—
Dole (R – Kans.)	—	—	—	—	—	—	—
Cook (R – Ky.)	—	—	—	—	—	—	—
Stennis (D – Miss.)	—	—	—	—	—	—	—
Curtis (R – Nebr.)	—	—	—	—	—	—	—
Hruska (R – Nebr.)	—	—	—	—	—	—	—
Buckley (C – N.Y.)	—	—	—	—	⊷	—	—

92nd Congress (*continued*)

	Civil rights	Social security	Poverty program	Consumer and environmental protection	War powers	Military expenditure	Foreign aid
Ervin (D – N.C.)	—	—	—	—	—	—	—
Packwood (R – Oreg.)	—	—	—	—	—	—	—
Thurmond (R – S.C.)	—	—	—	—	—	—	—
Brock (R – Tenn.)	—	—	—	—	—	—	—
Tower (R – Tex.)	—	—	—	—	—	—	—
Byrd (Jr.) (I – Va.)	—	—	—	—	—	—	—
Hansen (R – Wyo.)	—	—	—	—	—	—	—
Ellender (D – La.)	—	N/A	—	—	—	—	—
Eastland (D – Miss.)	—	N/A	—	—	—	—	—
Baker (R – Tenn.)	—	N/A	—	—	—	—	—
Bible (D – Nev.)	—	—	N/A	—	—	—	—
Cotton (R – N.H.)	—	—	N/A	—	—	—	—
Young (R – N.Dak.)	—	—	N/A	—	—	—	—
Allot (R – Colo.)	—	N/A	N/A	—	—	—	—
Goldwater (R – Ariz.)	—	N/A	—	N/A	—	—	N/A
Edwards (D – La.)	N/A	—	N/A	N/A	N/A	N/A	N/A
Mundt (R – S.Dak.)	N/A	N/A	N/A	N/A	N/A	N/A	N/A

Distribution of Senators' Scale Rankings, 1959–1972

Distribution of Senators' Scale Rankings, 1959–1972

		Number of scores	Proportion of scores ranked liberal (%)	Proportion of scores ranked moderate (%)	Proportion of scores ranked conservative (%)
Alabama					
Hill	(D)	27	25.9	22.2	51.8
Sparkman	(D)	40	25.0	35.0	40.0
Allen	(D)	14	0.0	35.7	64.3
Alaska					
Bartlett	(D)	27	74.1	22.2	3.7
Gruening	(D)	27	74.1	7.4	18.5
Gravel	(D)	13	84.6	15.4	0.0
Stevens	(R)	14	35.7	42.9	21.4
Arizona					
Hayden	(D)	23	56.5	21.7	21.7
Goldwater	(R)	20	0.0	20.0	80.0
Fannin	(R)	29	0.0	3.4	96.5
Arkansas					
Fulbright	(D)	38	47.4	26.3	26.3
McClellan	(D)	41	2.4	21.9	75.6
California					
Engle	(D)	12	100.0	0.0	0.0
Kuchel	(R)	27	51.8	29.6	18.5
Murphy	(R)	22	0.0	9.1	90.9
Cranston	(D)	14	92.9	7.1	0.0
Tunney	(D)	7	85.7	14.3	0.0
Colorado					
Carroll	(D)	7	85.7	14.3	0.0
Allott	(R)	39	12.8	20.5	66.7
Dominick	(R)	34	5.9	17.6	76.5
Connecticut					
Dodd	(D)	33	66.7	21.2	12.1
Bush	(R)	14	71.4	7.1	21.4

Distribution of Senators' Scale Rankings, 1959–1972 (*continued*)

		Number of scores	Proportion of scores ranked liberal (%)	Proportion of scores ranked moderate (%)	Proportion of scores ranked conservative (%)
Connecticut (cont.)					
Ribicoff	(D)	27	85.2	11.1	3.7
Weicker	(R)	7	42.9	42.9	14.3
Delaware					
Frear	(D)	3	0.0	100.0	0.0
Boggs	(R)	37	24.3	32.4	43.2
Williams	(R)	34	0.0	17.6	82.3
Roth	(R)	7	0.0	42.9	57.1
Florida					
Holland	(D)	34	5.9	26.5	67.6
Smathers	(D)	25	24.0	36.0	40.0
Gurney	(R)	14	0.0	0.0	100.0
Chiles	(D)	7	42.9	28.6	28.6
Georgia					
Russell	(D)	30	0.0	10.0	90.0
Talmadge	(D)	41	2.4	34.1	63.4
Gambrell	(D)	7	0.0	57.1	42.9
Hawaii					
Long	(D)	6	100.0	0.0	0.0
Fong	(R)	39	30.7	30.7	38.5
Inouye	(D)	34	73.5	20.6	5.9
Idaho					
Church	(D)	41	63.4	31.7	4.9
Dworshak	(R)	7	0.0	28.6	71.4
Jordan	(R)	34	2.9	20.6	76.5
Illinois					
Douglas	(D)	19	100.0	0.0	0.0
Dirksen	(R)	27	14.8	14.8	70.4
Percy	(R)	22	40.9	45.4	13.6
Smith	(R)	5	0.0	40.0	60.0
Stevenson	(D)	8	100.0	0.0	0.0
Indiana					
Hartke	(D)	40	95.0	2.5	2.5

Indiana (cont.)

Capehart	(R)	7	28.6	14.3	57.1
Bayh	(D)	33	84.8	12.1	3.0

Iowa

Hickenlooper	(R)	26	7.8	11.5	80.8
Miller	(R)	37	5.4	27.0	67.6
Hughes	(D)	14	100.0	0.0	0.0
Martin	(R)	4	50.0	50.0	0.0

Kansas

Carlson	(R)	26	11.5	26.9	61.5
Pearson	(R)	34	11.7	41.2	47.1
Dole	(R)	14	0.0	42.9	57.1
Schoeppel	(R)	6	0.0	16.7	83.3

Kentucky

Cooper	(R)	40	40.0	50.0	10.0
Morton	(R)	25	12.0	48.0	40.0
Cook	(R)	14	7.1	50.0	42.9

Louisiana

Ellender	(D)	40	10.0	25.0	65.0
Edwards	(D)	1	0.0	0.0	100.0
Long	(D)	41	19.5	31.7	48.9

Maine

Muskie	(D)	36	86.1	13.9	0.0
Smith	(R)	41	31.7	39.0	29.3

Maryland

Beall (Sr.)	(R)	12	33.3	16.7	50.0
Beall (Jr.)	(R)	7	28.6	28.6	42.9
Butler	(R)	6	0.0	16.7	83.3
Brewster	(D)	20	80.0	15.0	5.0
Tydings	(D)	22	77.3	18.2	4.5
Mathias	(R)	14	64.3	28.6	7.1

Massachusetts

Kennedy, J.	(D)	4	100.0	0.0	0.0
Saltonstall	(R)	19	26.3	26.3	47.4
Kennedy, E.	(D)	31	93.5	6.4	0.0
Brooke	(R)	22	81.8	9.1	9.1
Smith	(D)	3	100.0	0.0	0.0

Michigan

Hart	(D)	41	95.1	4.9	0.0

Distribution of Senators' Scale Rankings, 1959–1972 (*continued*)

		Number of scores	*Proportion of scores ranked liberal (%)*	*Proportion of scores ranked moderate (%)*	*Proportion of scores ranked conservative (%)*
Michigan (cont.)					
McNamara	(D)	17	82.3	17.6	0.0
Griffin	(R)	22	18.2	31.8	50.0
Minnesota					
Humphrey	(D)	19	89.5	10.5	0.0
McCarthy	(D)	34	91.2	5.9	2.9
Mondale	(D)	29	96.5	3.4	0.0
Mississippi					
Eastland	(D)	38	0.0	10.5	89.5
Stennis	(D)	41	2.4	17.1	80.5
Missouri					
Hennings	(D)	4	100.0	0.0	0.0
Long	(D)	20	75.0	25.0	0.0
Symington	(D)	41	68.3	17.1	14.6
Eagleton	(D)	13	61.5	23.1	15.4
Montana					
Mansfield	(D)	40	70.0	27.5	2.5
Murray	(D)	4	75.0	25.0	0.0
Metcalf	(D)	36	86.1	13.9	0.0
Nebraska					
Curtis	(R)	41	0.0	9.8	90.2
Hruska	(R)	41	0.0	7.3	92.7
Nevada					
Bible	(D)	40	17.5	57.5	25.0
Cannon	(D)	41	26.8	53.7	19.5
New Hampshire					
Cotton	(R)	40	2.5	22.5	75.0
McIntyre	(D)	33	60.6	24.2	15.1
Bridges	(R)	6	0.0	16.7	83.3
New Jersey					
Williams	(D)	41	90.2	9.8	0.0
Case	(R)	41	82.9	14.6	2.4

New Mexico

Anderson	(D)	38	52.6	34.2	13.2
Chavez	(D)	6	50.0	50.0	0.0
Mechem	(R)	5	0.0	0.0	100.0
Montoya	(D)	27	66.7	25.9	7.4

New York

Javits	(R)	41	87.8	12.2	0.0
Keating	(R)	12	50.0	41.7	8.3
Kennedy, R.	(D)	13	92.3	7.7	0.0
Goodell	(R)	7	100.0	0.0	0.0
Buckley	(C)	7	0.0	28.6	71.4

North Carolina

Ervin	(D)	41	0.0	31.7	68.3
Jordan	(D)	40	2.5	35.0	62.5

North Dakota

Langer	(R)	2	100.0	0.0	0.0
Brunsdale	(R)	1	0.0	100.0	0.0
Burdick	(D)	37	67.6	24.3	8.1
Young	(R)	36	2.8	25.0	72.2

Ohio

Lausche	(D)	27	7.4	37.0	55.5
Young	(D)	34	91.2	2.9	5.9
Saxbe	(R)	14	21.4	35.7	42.9
Taft	(R)	7	14.3	28.6	57.1

Oklahoma

Kerr	(D)	7	42.9	28.6	28.6
Monroney	(D)	27	63.0	18.5	18.5
Edmonson	(D)	5	40.0	60.0	0.0
Bellmon	(R)	13	23.1	7.7	69.2
Harris	(D)	24	79.2	16.7	4.2

Oregon

Morse	(D)	27	88.9	0.0	11.1
Lusk	(D)	1	0.0	100.0	0.0
Neuberger, R.	(D)	3	100.0	0.0	0.0
Neuberger, M.	(D)	15	100.0	0.0	0.0
Hatfield	(R)	21	66.7	28.6	4.8
Packwood	(R)	13	7.7	61.5	30.8

Pennsylvania

Clark	(D)	27	100.0	0.0	0.0

Distribution of Senators' Scale Rankings, 1959–1972 (*continued*)

		Number of scores	Proportion of scores ranked liberal (%)	Proportion of scores ranked moderate (%)	Proportion of scores ranked conservative (%)
Pennsylvania (cont.)					
Scott	(R)	41	39.0	39.0	21.9
Schweiker	(R)	14	64.3	14.3	21.4
Rhode Island					
Pastore	(D)	41	70.7	26.8	2.4
Pell	(D)	36	75.0	22.2	2.8
Green	(D)	4	50.0	50.0	0.0
South Carolina					
Johnston	(D)	12	25.0	16.7	58.3
Russell	(D)	5	0.0	0.0	100.0
Thurmond	(D/R)	41	0.0	2.4	97.6
Hollings	(D)	22	9.1	54.5	36.4
South Dakota					
Case	(R)	7	14.3	14.3	71.4
Mundt	(R)	33	6.1	12.1	81.8
McGovern	(D)	30	90.0	10.0	0.0
Tennessee					
Gore	(D)	29	58.6	34.5	6.9
Kefauver	(D)	7	71.4	14.3	14.3
Walters	(D)	4	0.0	75.0	25.0
Bass	(D)	6	83.3	16.7	0.0
Baker	(R)	21	9.5	19.0	71.4
Brock	(R)	7	0.0	0.0	100.0
Texas					
Yarborough	(D)	32	65.6	18.7	15.6
Tower	(R)	36	0.0	5.5	94.4
Johnson	(D)	4	75.0	25.0	0.0
Bentsen	(D)	7	14.3	71.4	14.3
Utah					
Moss	(D)	41	87.8	12.2	0.0
Bennett	(R)	41	4.9	9.8	85.4
Vermont					
Aiken	(R)	40	37.5	50.0	12.5

Vermont (cont.)

Prouty	(R)	33	18.2	60.6	21.2
Stafford	(R)	6	33.3	50.0	16.7

Virginia

Byrd (Sr.)	(D)	17	0.0	0.0	100.0
Robertson	(D)	19	0.0	10.5	89.5
Byrd (Jr.)	(D)	23	0.0	21.7	78.3
Spong	(D)	22	13.6	50.0	36.4

Washington

Jackson	(D)	41	65.8	21.9	12.2
Magnuson	(D)	41	61.0	24.4	14.6

West Virginia

Byrd	(D)	41	26.8	39.0	34.1
Randolph	(D)	41	53.7	36.6	9.8

Wisconsin

Proxmire	(D)	41	75.6	17.1	7.3
Wiley	(R)	7	42.9	42.9	14.3
Nelson	(D)	34	94.1	5.9	0.0

Wyoming

Hickey	(D)	3	66.7	0.0	33.3
O'Mahoney	(D)	4	75.0	25.0	0.0
McGee	(D)	38	73.7	13.2	13.2
Simpson	(R)	12	0.0	8.3	91.7
Hansen	(R)	22	0.0	9.1	90.9

Classification of Senators into Individual Attitude Types

Alabama

Hill	(D)	Conservative-to-liberal
Sparkman	(D)	Conservative-to-moderate
Allen	(D)	Conservative-to-moderate

Alaska

Bartlett	(D)	Liberal-to-moderate
Gruening	(D)	Liberal-to-conservative
Gravel	(D)	Liberal
Stevens	(R)	Moderate-to-liberal

Arizona

Hayden	(D)	Liberal-to-moderate/conservative
Goldwater	(R)	Conservative
Fannin	(R)	Conservative

Classification of Senators into Individual Attitude Types (*continued*)

Arkansas
| Fulbright | (D) | Liberal-to-moderate-conservative |
| McClellan | (D) | Conservative |

California
Engle	(D)	Liberal
Kuchel	(R)	Liberal-to-moderate
Murphy	(R)	Conservative
Cranston	(D)	Liberal
Tunney	(D)	Insufficient data for classification

Colorado
Carroll	(D)	Liberal
Allott	(R)	Conservative-to-moderate
Dominick	(R)	Conservative

Connecticut
Dodd	(D)	Liberal-to-moderate
Bush	(R)	Liberal-to-conservative
Ribicoff	(D)	Liberal
Weicker	(R)	Insufficient data for classification

Delaware
Frear	(D)	Insufficient data for classification
Boggs	(R)	Conservative-to-moderate
Williams	(R)	Conservative
Roth	(R)	Insufficient data for classification

Florida
Holland	(D)	Conservative-to-moderate
Smathers	(D)	Conservative-to-moderate
Gurney	(R)	Conservative
Chiles	(D)	Insufficient data for classification

Georgia
Russell	(D)	Conservative
Talmadge	(D)	Conservative-to-moderate
Gambrell	(D)	Insufficient data for classification

Hawaii
Long	(D)	Liberal
Fong	(R)	Conservative-to-moderate/liberal
Inouye	(D)	Liberal-to-moderate

Idaho
Church	(D)	Liberal-to-moderate
Dworshak	(R)	Conservative-to-moderate
Jordan	(R)	Conservative

Illinois
Douglas	(D)	Liberal
Dirksen	(R)	Conservative-to-moderate/liberal
Percy	(R)	Moderate-to-liberal
Smith	(R)	Insufficient data for classification
Stevenson	(D)	Liberal

Indiana
Hartke	(D)	Liberal
Capehart	(R)	Conservative-to-liberal
Bayh	(D)	Liberal

Iowa
Hickenlooper	(R)	Conservative
Miller	(R)	Conservative-to-moderate
Hughes	(D)	Liberal
Martin	(R)	Insufficient data for classification

Kansas
Carlson	(R)	Conservative-to-moderate
Pearson	(R)	Conservative-to-moderate
Dole	(R)	Conservative-to-moderate
Schoeppel	(R)	Conservative

Kentucky
Cooper	(R)	Moderate-to-liberal
Morton	(R)	Moderate-to-conservative
Cook	(R)	Moderate-to-conservative

Louisiana
Ellender	(D)	Conservative-to-moderate
Edwards	(D)	Insufficient data for classification
Long	(D)	Moderate-to-conservative

Maine
Muskie	(D)	Liberal
Smith	(R)	Moderate-to-liberal/conservative

Maryland
Beall (Sr.)	(R)	Conservative-to-liberal
Beall (Jr.)	(R)	Insufficient data for classification

Classification of Senators into Individual Attitude Types (*continued*)

Maryland (cont.)
Butler	(R)	Conservative
Brewster	(D)	Liberal
Tydings	(D)	Liberal
Mathias	(R)	Liberal-to-moderate

Massachusetts
Kennedy, J.	(D)	Insufficient data for classification
Saltonstall	(R)	Conservative-to-moderate/liberal
Kennedy, E.	(D)	Liberal
Brooke	(R)	Liberal
Smith	(D)	Insufficient data for classification

Michigan
Hart	(D)	Liberal
McNamara	(D)	Liberal
Griffin	(R)	Conservative-to-moderate

Minnesota
Humphrey	(D)	Liberal
McCarthy	(D)	Liberal
Mondale	(D)	Liberal

Mississippi
Eastland	(D)	Conservative
Stennis	(D)	Conservative

Missouri
Hennings	(D)	Insufficient data for classification
Long	(D)	Liberal
Symington	(D)	Liberal-to-moderate
Eagleton	(D)	Liberal-to-moderate

Montana
Mansfield	(D)	Liberal-to-moderate
Murray	(D)	Insufficient data for classification
Metcalf	(D)	Liberal

Nebraska
Curtis	(R)	Conservative
Hruska	(R)	Conservative

Nevada
Bible	(D)	Moderate-to-conservative
Cannon	(D)	Moderate-to-liberal

New Hampshire
Cotton   (R)   Conservative
McIntyre   (D)   Liberal-to-moderate
Bridges   (R)   Conservative

New Jersey
Williams   (D)   Liberal
Case   (R)   Liberal

New Mexico
Anderson   (D)   Liberal-to-moderate
Chavez   (D)   Liberal/moderate
Mechem   (R)   Insufficient data for classification
Montoya   (D)   Liberal-to-moderate

New York
Javits   (R)   Liberal
Keating   (R)   Liberal-to-moderate
Kennedy, R.   (D)   Liberal
Goodell   (R)   Insufficient data for classification
Buckley   (C)   Insufficient data for classification

North Carolina
Ervin   (D)   Conservative-to-moderate
Jordan   (D)   Conservative-to-moderate

North Dakota
Langer   (R)   Insufficient data for classification
Brunsdale   (R)   Insufficient data for classification
Burdick   (D)   Liberal-to-moderate
Young   (R)   Conservative-to-moderate

Ohio
Lausche   (D)   Conservative-to-moderate
Young   (D)   Liberal
Saxbe   (R)   Conservative-to-moderate
Taft   (R)   Insufficient data for classification

Oklahoma
Kerr   (D)   Liberal-to-moderate/conservative
Monroney   (D)   Liberal-to-moderate/conservative
Edmonson   (D)   Insufficient data for classification
Bellmon   (R)   Conservative-to-liberal
Harris   (D)   Liberal

Classification of Senators into Individual Attitude Types (*continued*)

Oregon

Morse	(D)	Liberal
Lusk	(D)	Insufficient data for classification
Neuberger, R.	(D)	Insufficient data for classification
Neuberger, M.	(D)	Liberal
Hatfield	(R)	Liberal-to-moderate
Packwood	(R)	Moderate-to-conservative

Pennsylvania

Clark	(D)	Liberal
Scott	(R)	Liberal/moderate
Schweiker	(R)	Liberal-to-conservative

Rhode Island

Pastore	(D)	Liberal-to-moderate
Pell	(D)	Liberal
Green	(D)	Insufficient data for classification

South Carolina

Johnston	(D)	Insufficient data for classification
Russell	(D)	Insufficient data for classification
Thurmond	(D/R)	Conservative
Hollings	(D)	Moderate-to-conservative

South Dakota

Case	(R)	Conservative-to-moderate/liberal
Mundt	(R)	Conservative
McGovern	(D)	Liberal

Tennessee

Gore	(D)	Liberal-to-moderate
Kefauver	(D)	Liberal-to-moderate/conservative
Walters	(D)	Insufficient data for classification
Bass	(D)	Insufficient data for classification
Baker	(R)	Conservative-to-moderate
Brock	(R)	Insufficient data for classification

Texas

Yarborough	(D)	Liberal-to-moderate
Tower	(R)	Conservative
Johnson	(D)	Insufficient data for classification
Bentsen	(D)	Insufficient data for classification

Utah
Moss	(D)	Liberal
Bennett	(R)	Conservative

Vermont
Aiken	(R)	Moderate-to-liberal
Prouty	(R)	Moderate-to-conservative
Stafford	(R)	Insufficient data for classification

Virginia
Byrd (Sr.)	(D)	Conservative
Robertson	(D)	Conservative
Byrd (Jr.)	(D)	Conservative
Spong	(D)	Moderate-to-conservative

Washington
Jackson	(D)	Liberal-to-moderate
Magnuson	(D)	Liberal-to-moderate

West Virginia
Byrd	(D)	Moderate-to-conservative/liberal
Randolph	(D)	Liberal-to-moderate

Wisconsin
Proxmire	(D)	Liberal
Wiley	(R)	Liberal/moderate
Nelson	(D)	Liberal

Wyoming
Hickey	(D)	Insufficient data for classification
O'Mahoney	(D)	Insufficient data for classification
McGee	(D)	Liberal-to-moderate/conservative
Simpson	(R)	Conservative
Hansen	(R)	Conservative

Notes

CHAPTER 1

1. James Madison, "Federalist Paper Number 10," in James Madison, Alexander Hamilton, and John Jay, *The Federalist Papers* (New York: Mentor Books, 1961), p. 384.

2. John C. Donovan, *The Policy Makers* (New York: Pegasus Books, 1970), p. 158.

3. U.S. Congress, *Congressional Record* (Washington, D.C.: GPO, 1963), 19 February 1963, p. 2559. Some empirical support is given to Clark's position by Wayne Swanson, "Committee Assignments and the Nonconformist Legislator: Democrats in the U.S. Senate," *Midwest Journal of Political Science* 13, no. 1 (February 1969): 84–94.

4. U.S. Congress, *Congressional Record* (Washington, D.C.: GPO, 1963), 19 February 1963, pp. 2562–66; 20 February 1963, pp. 2664–67.

5. Donald R. Matthews, *U.S. Senators and Their World* (New York: Vintage Books, 1960); William S. White, *Citadel: The Story of the U.S. Senate* (New York: Harper & Bros., 1956).

6. White, *Citadel: The Story of the U.S. Senate*, p. 113.

7. Ibid., p. 70.

8. Matthews, *U.S. Senators and Their World*, p. 95.

9. A. J. Beitzinger, *A History of American Political Thought* (New York: Dodd, Mead, 1972), pp. 377–87; Richard Hofstadter, *The American Political Tradition* (London: Jonathan Cape, 1967), pp. 67–91; Clinton Rossiter, *Conservatism in America: The Thankless Persuasion*, 2d ed. rev. (New York: Vintage Books, 1962), pp. 120–26.

10. Rossiter, *Conservatism in America: The Thankless Persuasion*, p. 123.

11. White, *Citadel: The Story of the U.S. Senate*, p. 111.

12. Ibid., p. 115.

13. Matthews, *U.S. Senators and Their World*, p. 101.

14. White, *Citadel: The Story of the U.S. Senate*, p. 94.

15. Ibid., p. 72.

16. Ibid., p. 11.

17. Ibid., p. 86.

18. James Sundquist, *Politics and Policy: The Eisenhower, Kennedy and Johnson Years* (Washington, D.C.: The Brookings Institution, 1968), p. 400; Roger H. Davidson, David M. Kovenock, and Michael K. O'Leary, *Congress in Crisis: Politics and Congressional Reform* (Belmont, Calif.: Wadsworth, 1966), ch. 5; Ralph K. Huitt, "The Outsider in the Senate: An Alternative Role," *American Political Science Review* 55, no. 3 (September 1961): 566–75; Rowland Evans and Robert Novak, *Lyndon B. Johnson: The Exercise of Power* (London: Allen & Unwin, 1967), ch. 10; Tom Wicker, "The Winds of Change in the Senate," *New York Times Magazine*, 12 September 1965; Randall B. Ripley, *Power in the Senate* (New York: St. Martin's Press, 1969), ch. 3; Joseph P. Harris, *Congress and the Legislative Process* (New York: McGraw-Hill, 1972), pp. 76–78; Harry McPherson, "The Senate Observed," *Atlantic Monthly*, May 1972; Charles M. Roberts, "Nine Men Who Control Congress," *Atlantic Monthly*, April 1964.

19. White, *Citadel: The Story of the U.S. Senate*, p. 225.

20. Ibid., pp. 8-9.

21. Matthews, *U.S. Senators and Their World*, p. 253.

22. Ibid., p. 113.

23. Ibid.

24. Huitt, "The Outsider in the Senate: An Alternative Role," p. 571.

25. Although Matthews selected the only two folkways (i.e., legislative work and specialization) which would lend themselves to some form of measurement, his attempts at assessing degrees of conformity demonstrates the inherent problems in measuring informal behavior.

His index of specialization was determined by the "proportion of all public bills and resolutions introduced by each Senator that were referred to the committee receiving the largest number of the bills and resolutions he sponsored" (p. 275). Apart from the fact that specialization could have been measured in many other ways (e.g., the number of speeches and articles on limited subject areas, the range of committee assignments, specialist reputations), the actual index used was not a reliable guide. For example, bills directed to the same committee need not necessarily be related in subject matter. The subjects of bills are often ambiguous in respect to the area of committee jurisdiction—bearing in mind the enthusiasm of sponsors in arranging for their bills to be sent to the most favorable committees. In addition, the introduction of bills and resolutions does not necessarily reflect the range of legislative activity on the part of senators; it ignores the possibility that the few bills introduced by a Senate "conformist" which were not sent to his two main committees may have been major proposals concerning diverse areas of policy.

The index of legislative work was assessed by the degree to which a senator limited his speeches from the floor. As he is expected to concentrate on detailed and specialized committee work, an orthodox Senate type will tend to avoid the public platform of the Senate floor. Matthews measures floor speaking simply by the number (not length) of speeches made from the floor. As with specialization, legislative work could have been measured in a variety of other ways (e.g., attendance record, research work, media exposure, committee diligence). There is no way of knowing that floor speaking is a more valid measurement of Matthews's concept of legislative work than are any of the others.

Since there is no proof of the reliability of these indices, there is no guarantee that the cross-tabulations derived from them are not inaccurate.

Legislative effectiveness was assessed by "the ability to get one's bills passed" (p. 115). Those who conformed to the two folkways mentioned above had greater success "in concrete legislative results" (p. 115). However, this unit of measurement can also be challenged. A sponsor of a bill may play a very small part in its passage, which ultimately may change the whole structure of the original draft. Introducing a bill may be no more than a form of advocacy or a means to publicize a personal platform. Alternatively, a member may sponsor legislation in the certain knowledge that it will not be passed. More important than all these qualifications is the fundamental objection against regarding the Senate solely as a means for passing legislation. It was Matthews's notion that legislative effectiveness could be equated with bill production that was objected to most strongly by Ralph K. Huitt in his seminal article "The Outsider in the Senate: An Alternative Role." In Huitt's words, "the enactment of legislation is but one and not the most important function of either house of Congress let alone of all members individually" (p. 574).

26. Nelson W. Polsby, "Goodbye to the Inner Club," in *Congressional Behavior*, ed. Nelson W. Polsby (New York: Random House, 1971), pp. 105–10. Polsby's position is that the notions of an "inner club" "vastly underplayed the extent to which *formal* position . . . conferred power and status on individual Senators almost regardless of their clubability. Second, it understated the extent to which power was spread by specialization and the need for co-operative effort" (p. 107). While the Senate has always been renowned for its relatively decentralized structure, it has never maintained an equitable distribution of power. During the 1950s and the early 1960s, formal positions of real leverage were not equitably distributed within the majority party. For one reason or another, it appeared that the provision of formal positions benefited a particular type of senator and discriminated against others in terms of region and ideology. Given the validity of the assertions that the limited number of formal positions bestowed great power and that this power was usually held by a particular group, it does not seem unreasonable to conclude that the institution was characterized by an identifiable elite—with substantial influence over policy and over internal leadership recruitment. This did not amount to a rigid conspiratorial oligarchy—it would be difficult to imagine anything so definite and so disciplined in the Senate. Nevertheless, neither an acknowledgment that individual senators could achieve infamous prominence through procedural objection and negative disruption, nor the appearance of an "unclubable" liberal with a minor subcommittee chairmanship, nor a clubable conservative without a chairmanship or party position are really sufficient to disprove the existence of a distinctive political elite during the period in question. In John F. Manley's words, "the attack of Clark and the liberals on the establishment cannot easily be turned aside by references to the capacious norms and the multiple vantage points of Senate power. . . . It appears, even by Polsby's account, that there was enough reality to the establishment notion under Lyndon Johnson to cause real concern among Senate liberals" (John F. Manley, *American Government and Public Policy* [New York: Macmillan, 1976], p. 215).

27. Ripley, *Power in the Senate*, ch. 3; Harris, *Congress and the Legislative Process*, pp. 76–78; Evans and Novak, *Lyndon B. Johnson: The Exercise of Power*, ch. 10; Davidson, Kovenock, and O'Leary, *Congress in Crisis: Politics and Congressional Reform*, ch. 5; John F. Bibby and Roger H. Davidson, *On Capitol Hill: Studies in the Legislative Process* (New York: Dryden Press, 1972), ch. 4; Wicker, "The Winds of Change in the Senate"; Huitt, "The Outsider in the Senate: An Alternative Role," 566–75.

28. Interview with Senator Gaylord Nelson, 27 March 1974.

29. Interview with Senator Frank Moss, 21 March 1974.

30. Interview with Senator Edmund Muskie, 28 March 1974.

31. U.S., Congress, *Congressional Record* (Washington, D.C.: GPO, 1963), 19 February 1963, pp. 2554–55.

32. John F. Manley, "The Conservative Coalition in Congress," in *Varieties of Political Conservatism*, ed. Matthew Holden, Jr. (Beverly Hills, Calif.: Sage, 1974), pp. 77–81.

33. Bibby and Davidson, *On Capitol Hill: Studies in the Legislative Process*, p. 145.

34. Donovan, *The Policy Makers*, p. 158.

35. For a representative selection of works asserting that the Senate *was* a predominantly conservative institution in the late 1950s and early 1960s and yet

had dramatically changed its policy positions and internal structure by the late 1960s, see Gary Orfield, *Congressional Power: Congress and Social Change* (New York: Harcourt Brace Jovanovich, 1975), ch. 1; John F. Manley, *American Government and Public Policy* (New York: Macmillan, 1976), pp. 206–40; Ripley, *Power in the Senate*, ch. 3; Davidson, Kovenock, and O'Leary, *Congress in Crisis: Politics and Congressional Reform*, pp. 144–54; Bibby and Davidson, *On Capitol Hill: Studies in the Legislative Process*, pp. 144–48; Wicker, "The Winds of Change in the Senate."

36. Marian D. Irish and James W. Prothro, *The Politics of American Democracy*, 4th ed. rev. (Englewood Cliffs, N.J.: Prentice-Hall, 1968), pp. 347–49; Emmette S. Redford, David B. Truman, Andrew Hacker, Alan F. Westin, and Robert C. Wood, *Politics and Government in the United States* (New York: Harcourt, Brace and World, 1965), p. 354; Ira Katznelson and Mark Kesselman, *The Politics of Power: A Critical Introduction to American Government* (New York: Harcourt Brace Jovanovich, 1975), pp. 305–06; Stephen Horn, *Unused Power: The Work of the Senate Committee on Appropriations* (Washington, D.C.: The Brookings Institution, 1970), pp. 88–101; William J. Keefe and Morris S. Ogul, *The American Legislative Process: Congress and the States* (Englewood Cliffs, N.J.: Prentice-Hall, 1964), pp. 242–44; Harris, *Congress and the Legislative Process*, pp. 75–79.

37. Dale Vinyard, *Congress* (New York: Scribner, 1968), pp. 85–87; David J. Olson and Philip Meyer, *To Keep the Republic* (New York: McGraw-Hill, 1975), p. 315; Leroy N. Rieselbach, *Congressional Politics* (New York: McGraw-Hill, 1973), ch. 6; Malcolm E. Jewell and Samuel C. Patterson, *The Legislative Process in the United States* (New York: Random House, 1966), ch. 15.

Matthews's piece on the folkways is reprinted in Lawrence K. Petit and Edward Keynes, eds., *The Legislative Process in the U.S. Senate* (Chicago: Rand McNally, 1969), pp. 41–71; Raymond E. Wolfinger, ed., *Readings on Congress* (Englewood Cliffs, N.J.: Prentice-Hall, 1971), pp. 90–108; George Goodwin, Jr., ed., *Congress: Anvil of Democracy* (Glenview, Ill.: Scott, Foresman, 1967), pp. 25–36; Joseph Palamountain and Martin M. Shapiro, eds., *Issues and Perspectives in American Government* (Glenview, Ill.: Scott, Foresman, 1971), pp. 304–14.

38. Donald R. Matthews, *U.S. Senators and Their World* (New York: W. W. Norton, 1973).

CHAPTER 2

1. For a closer analysis of this transitory period see Charles C. Alexander, *Holding the Line: The Eisenhower Era, 1952–1961* (Bloomington, Ind.: Indiana University Press, 1976), chs. 1, 2; Eric Goldman *The Crucial Decade—And After: America, 1945–1960* (New York: Vintage Books, 1960), chs. 8–11; Walter Goodman, *The Committee* (New York: Farrar, Straus and Giroux, 1968); Alan Harper, *The Politics of Loyalty: The White House and the Communist Issue 1946–1952* (Westport, Conn.: Greenwood Press, 1969); Herbert S. Parmet, *Eisenhower and the American Crusades* (New York: Macmillan, 1972); Cabell Phillips, *The Truman Presidency: The History of a Triumphant Succession* (New York: Macmillan, 1966).

2. See Robert J. Donovan, *Eisenhower: The Inside Story* (New York: Harper & Row, 1956), ch. 15; Dwight D. Eisenhower, *The White House Years: Mandate*

for a Change (London: Heinemann, 1963), ch. 9; Parmet, *Eisenhower and the American Crusades,* chs. 36, 37.

3. Eisenhower, *The White House Years: Mandate for a Change,* ch. 15; Aaron Wildavsky, *Dixon Yates: A Study in Power Politics* (New Haven, Conn.: Yale University Press, 1962).

4. Sherman Adams, *First-Hand Report: The Inside Story of the Eisenhower Administration* (London: Hutchinson, 1962), ch. 15; Parmet, *Eisenhower and the American Crusades,* chs. 21, 22.

5. Emmet J. Hughes, *The Ordeal of Power: A Political Memoir of the Eisenhower Years* (London: Macmillan, 1963), ch. 10.

6. Adams, *First-Hand Report: The Inside Story of the Eisenhower Administration,* ch. 11; Eisenhower, *The White House Years: Mandate for a Change,* ch. 23; Parmet, *Eisenhower and the American Crusades,* ch. 29.

7. Adams, *First-Hand Report: The Inside Story of the Eisenhower Administration,* ch. 16; Alexander, *Holding the Line: The Eisenhower Era 1952–1961,* ch. 6; Dwight D. Eisenhower, *The White House Years: Waging Peace* (London: Heinemann, 1965), ch. 4; Arthur Larson, *Eisenhower: The President Nobody Knew* (London: Leslie Frewin, 1969), ch. 7.

8. Donovan, *Eisenhower: The Inside Story,* ch. 11; Parmet, *Eisenhower and the American Crusades,* chs. 37, 38; Hughes, *The Ordeal of Power: A Political Memoir of the Eisenhower Years,* pp. 200–02, 241–45, 261.

9. Donovan, *Eisenhower: The Inside Story,* ch. 5; Eisenhower, *The White House Years: Mandate for a Change,* chs. 2, 11; Richard F. Fenno, Jr., *The President's Cabinet* (Cambridge, Mass.: Harvard University Press, 1959), chs. 3, 4; Hughes, *The Ordeal of Power: A Political Memoir of the Eisenhower Years,* ch. 4.

10. Hughes, *The Ordeal of Power: A Political Memoir of the Eisenhower Years,* p. 194.

11. Goldman, *The Crucial Decade—And After: America 1945–1960,* ch. 12.

12. Seymour Martin Lipset, *Political Man* (London: Heinemann, 1960), p. 406.

13. See Daniel J. Boorstin, *The Genius of American Politics* (Chicago: University of Chicago Press, 1953); Louis Hartz, *The Liberal Tradition in America: An Interpretation of American Political Thought since the Revolution* (New York: Harcourt, Brace and Co., 1955); Daniel Bell, ed., *The End of Ideology* (New York: Free Press, 1960).

14. William S. White, "Who Is Lyndon Johnson?," *Harpers,* March 1958, pp. 53–58; White, *The Professional: Lyndon B. Johnson* (New York: Fawcett, 1964), ch. 11; Doris B. Kearns, *Lyndon Johnson and the American Dream* (New York: Harper & Row, 1976), ch. 5.

15. Rowland Evans and Robert Novak, *Lyndon B. Johnson: The Exercise of Power* (London: Allen & Unwin, 1967), chs. 6, 7; Ralph K. Huitt, "Democratic Party Leadership in the Senate," *American Political Science Review* 55, no. 2 (June 1961): 333–44; Randall B. Ripley, *Majority Leadership in Congress* (Boston: Little, Brown, 1969), ch. 5; Alfred Steinberg, *Sam Johnson's Boy: A Close-up of the President from Texas* (London: Macmillan, 1968), chs. 43–54; John G. Stewart, "Two Strategies of Leadership: Johnson and Mansfield," in *Congressional Behavior,* ed. Nelson W. Polsby (New York: Random House, 1971).

16. Evans and Novak, *Lyndon B. Johnson: The Exercise of Power,* p. 143.

17. Ibid., ch. 8.

18. Steinberg, *Sam Johnson's Boy: A Close-up of the President from Texas,*

chs. 48, 50; Booth Mooney, *LBJ: An Irreverent Chronicle* (New York: T. Y. Crowell, 1976), ch. 6.

19. James L. Sundquist, *Politics and Policy: The Eisenhower, Kennedy and Johnson Years* (Washington, D.C.: The Brookings Institution, 1968), pp. 405–09; Evans and Novak, *Lyndon B. Johnson: The Exercise of Power*, pp. 144–47, 160–63.

20. Sundquist, *Politics and Policy: The Eisenhower, Kennedy and Johnson Years*, p. 395.

21. Ibid., pp. 441–66; Alexander, *Holding the Line: The Eisenhower Era, 1952–1961*, ch. 6; William G. Carleton, "A Grass-Roots Guide to '58 and '60," *Harper's Magazine*, July 1958; Parmet, *Eisenhower and the American Crusades*, ch. 37; William S. White, "The Changing Map of American Politics," *Harper's Magazine*, August 1959; Congressional Quarterly, *Congress and the Nation 1945–1964: A Review of Government and Politics in the Postwar Years* (Washington, D.C.: Congressional Quarterly, 1965), pp. 26–30.

22. Steinberg, *Sam Johnson's Boy: A Close-up of the President from Texas*, chs. 44–47.

23. Evans and Novak, *Lyndon B. Johnson: The Exercise of Power*, pp. 203–12.

24. John C. Donovan, *The Policy Makers* (New York: Pegasus Books, 1970), pp. 149–58; Mark F. Ferber, "The Formation of the Democratic Study Group," in *Congressional Behavior*, ed. Nelson W. Polsby (New York: Random House, 1971), pp. 249–69.

25. See Congressional Quarterly, *Congressional Quarterly Almanac 1959* (Washington, D.C.: Congressional Quarterly, 1960), Key Votes Appendix, Roll Call no. 5.

26. Malcom E. Jewell and Samuel C. Patterson, *The Legislative Process in the United States* (New York: Random House, 1966), pp. 196–98; Sundquist, *Politics and Policy: The Eisenhower, Kennedy and Johnson Years*, pp. 400–02; Randall B. Ripley, *Power in the Senate* (New York: St. Martin's Press, 1969), pp. 53–69; Thomas P. Murphy, *The New Politics Congress* (Lexington, Mass.: D. C. Heath, 1974), pp. 93–96; Robert G. Spivack, "Won't Do Democrats," *The Nation*, 29 August 1959; U.S., Congress, *Congressional Record* (Washington, D.C.: GPO, 1959), 23 February 1959, pp. 2814–20; 9 March 1959, pp. 3559–83; 15 April 1959, pp. 5956–58; William Proxmire, *Uncle Sam: The Last of the Bigtime Spenders* (New York: Simon & Schuster, 1972), pp. 241–44.

27. Daniel M. Berman, *A Bill Becomes a Law: The Civil Rights Act of 1960* (New York: Macmillan, 1962), pp. 117–23; Steinberg, *Sam Johnson's Boy: A Close-up of the President from Texas*, ch. 53; Wayne Morse, "Murder by the Moderates," *The Nation*, 7 November 1959.

28. Berman, *A Bill Becomes a Law: The Civil Rights Act of 1960*; Steinberg, *Sam Johnson's Boy: A Close-up of the President from Texas*, ch. 54.

29. Berman, *A Bill Becomes a Law: The Civil Rights Act of 1960*, pp. 57–70.

30. Evans and Novak, *Lyndon B. Johnson: The Exercise of Power*, p. 221.

31. Kearns, *Lyndon Johnson and the American Dream*, p. 162.

32. Carl M. Brauer, *John F. Kennedy and the Second Reconstruction* (New York: Columbia University Press, 1977); James T. Crown, *The Kennedy Literature: A Bibliographical Essay on John F. Kennedy* (New York: New York University Press, 1968); Henry Fairlie, *The Kennedy Promise: The Politics of Expectation* (New York: Dell, 1972); David Halberstam, *The Best and the Brightest* (New York: Fawcett, 1972); Allan Nevins, ed., *The Burden and the*

Glory (New York: Harper & Row, 1964); Edmund S. Ions, ed., *The Politics of John F. Kennedy* (London: Routledge & Kegan Paul, 1967); Kenneth O'Donnell, David F. Powers, and Joe McCarthy, *Johnny, We Hardly Knew Ye: Memories of John Fitzgerald Kennedy* (New York: Pocket Books, 1973); Randall B. Ripley, *Kennedy and Congress* (Morristown, N.J.: General Learning Press, 1972); Pierre Salinger, *With Kennedy* (London: Jonathan Cape, 1967); Arthur M. Schlesinger, Jr., *A Thousand Days: John F. Kennedy in the White House* (London: Mayflower-Dell, 1965); Theodore C. Sorensen, *Kennedy* (London: Pan Books, 1965); Tom Wicker, *JFK and LBJ: The Influence of Personality upon Politics* (Baltimore: Penguin Books, 1968); James M. Burns, *John Kennedy: A Political Profile* (New York: Harcourt, Brace and Co., 1960).

33. Ions, *The Politics of John F. Kennedy*, pp. 19–43.

34. *New York Times*, 15 January, 1960.

35. Ions, *The Politics of John F. Kennedy*, pp. 44–62; Fairlie, *The Kennedy Promise: The Politics of Expectation*, chs. 1, 2.

36. Wicker, *JFK and LBJ: The Influence of Personality upon Politics*, p. 86.

37. "President Kennedy Discusses the Presidency," in *The Politics of John F. Kennedy*, ed. Ions; Sorensen, *Kennedy*, ch. 15.

38. Philip E. Converse, Angus Campbell, Warren E. Miller, and Donald E. Stokes, "Stability and Change in 1960: A Reinstating Election," *American Political Science Review* 55, no. 2 (June 1961): 269–81; Theodore H. White, *The Making of the President 1960* (London: Jonathan Cape, 1961).

39. Sorensen, *Kennedy*, p. 382.

40. Evans and Novak, *Lyndon B. Johnson: The Exercise of Power*, pp. 222–24.

41. James A. Robinson, *The House Rules Committee*, (Indianapolis, Ind.: Bobbs-Merrill, 1963); Milton C. Cummings, Jr. and Robert L. Peabody, "The Decision to Enlarge the Committee on Rules: An Analysis of the 1961 Vote," in *New Perspectives on the House of Representatives*, ed. Robert L. Peabody and Nelson W. Polsby (Chicago: Rand McNally, 1963), pp. 167–94; Neil MacNeil, *The Forge of Democracy: The House of Representatives* (New York: David McKay, 1963).

42. Sundquist, *Politics and Policy: The Eisenhower, Kennedy and Johnson Years*, passim; Wicker, *JFK and LBJ: The Influence of Personality upon Politics*, ch. 3.

43. Wicker, *JFK and LBJ: The Influence of Personality upon Politics*, p. 54.

44. Sorensen, *Kennedy*, p. 377.

45. Sundquist, *Politics and Policy: The Eisenhower, Kennedy and Johnson Years*, p. 479.

46. Ted Lewis, "Kennedy's Legislative Strategy," *The Nation*, 25 March 1961; Ripley, *Kennedy and Congress*, passim.

47. Wicker, *JFK and LBJ: The Influence of Personality upon Politics*, ch. 6; Sorensen, *Kennedy*, pp. 385–90.

48. Sundquist, *Politics and Policy: The Eisenhower, Kennedy and Johnson Years*, pp. 254–59; Schlesinger, *A Thousand Days: John F. Kennedy in the White House*, ch. 35; Coretta S. King, *My Life with Martin Luther King* (London: Hodder and Stoughton, 1970), ch. 12; Brauer, *John F. Kennedy and the Second Reconstruction*, pp. 245–303; Benjamin Muse, *The American Negro Revolution: From Nonviolence to Black Power, 1963–1967* (Bloomington, Ind.: Indiana University Press, 1968), pp. 40–46.

49. Sundquist, *Politics and Policy: The Eisenhower, Kennedy and Johnson Years*, p. 474.

50. Gar Alperovitz and Kim Willenson, "The Leaderless Liberals," *The Nation*, 8 September 1962; Ted Lewis, "Congress versus Kennedy," *The Nation*, 14 July 1962; Helen Fuller, "Kennedy's Problem," *New Republic*, 9 March 1963; "Why Congress Doesn't Give Kennedy What He Wants," *U.S. News and World Report*, 18 March 1963; Carroll Kilpatrick, "The Kennedy Style in Congress," in *The Politics of John F. Kennedy*, ed. Ions.

51. For the most emphatic assertion of a conservative clique by two liberal Senators (Clark and Douglas), see Joseph S. Clark, *The Senate Establishment* (New York: Hill & Wang, 1963), pp. 21–41, 121–33.

52. Wicker, *JFK and LBJ: The Influence of Personality upon Politics*, p. 84.

53. Fairlie, *The Kennedy Promise: The Politics of Expectation*, ch. 12.

54. Sundquist, *Politics and Policy: The Eisenhower, Kennedy and Johnson Years*, p. 481.

55. Ibid., p. 482.

56. Wicker, *JFK and LBJ: The Influence of Personality upon Politics*, chs. 10, 11; Evans and Novak, *Lyndon B. Johnson: The Exercise of Power*, ch. 16.

57. Mooney, *LBJ: An Irreverent Chronicle*, chs. 2, 9; Kearns, *Lyndon Johnson and the American Dream*, chs. 1, 2.

58. Wicker, *JFK and LBJ: The Influence of Personality upon Politics*, p. 152.

59. Kearns, *Lyndon Johnson and the American Dream*, pp. 212–13.

60. White, *The Professional: Lyndon B. Johnson*, ch. 4; Kearns, *Lyndon Johnson and the American Dream*, pp. 152–57; Philip Geyelin, *Lyndon Johnson and the World* (London: Pall Mall, 1966), pp. 13–23, 28–35.

61. Kearns, *Lyndon Johnson and the American Dream*, p. 152.

62. Eric F. Goldman, *The Tragedy of Lyndon Johnson* (London: Macdonald, 1969), ch. 4; Kearns, *Lyndon Johnson and the American Dream*, pp. 210–17; Wicker, *JFK and LBJ: The Influence of Personality upon Politics*, pp. 209–16.

63. David S. Broder, "Consensus Politics: The End of an Experiment," *Atlantic Monthly*, October 1966.

64. Ibid.

65. For background analysis on the economic boom during the Kennedy-Johnson period, see Seymour E. Harris, *Economics of the Kennedy Years* (New York: Harper & Row, 1964), pp. 55–77, 176–95; Walter Heller, *New Dimensions of Political Economy* (Cambridge, Mass.: Harvard University Press, 1966), pp. 58–79; Arthur M. Okun, *The Political Economy of Prosperity* (Washington, D.C.: The Brookings Institution, 1970), pp. 37–62, 66–73; Leo Huberman and Paul Sweezy, "The Kennedy–Johnson Boom," in *The Great Society Reader: The Failure of American Liberalism*, ed. Marvin E. Gettleman and David Mermelstein (New York: Vintage Books, 1967).

66. U.S., Department of Commerce, Bureau of the Census, Industrial Production Indexes, by Industry: 1950 to 1970, *Statistical Abstract of the United States: 1970* (Washington, D.C.: GPO, 1970), p. 696.

67. U.S., Department of Commerce, Bureau of the Census, Employment Status of the Noninstitutional Population by Sex and Race: 1950 to 1970, *Statistical Abstract of the United States: 1970* (Washington, D.C.: GPO, 1970), p. 213.

68. Wicker, *JFK and LBJ: The Influence of Personality upon Politics*, p. 170.

69. Goldman, *The Tragedy of Lyndon Johnson*, pp. 67–72; Elizabeth Drew, "The Politics of Cloture," *The Reporter* 16 July 1964; Evans and Novak, *Lyndon*

B. Johnson: The Exercise of Power, pp. 376–80; Sundquist, Politics and Policy: The Eisenhower, Kennedy and Johnson Years, pp. 265–71; Wicker, JFK and LBJ: The Influence of Personality upon Politics, pp. 169–77; Hubert H. Humphrey, The Education of a Public Man: My Life and Politics (London: Weidenfeld and Nicholson, 1976), pp. 268–87; Daniel M. Berman, A Bill Becomes a Law, 2d ed. rev. (New York: Macmillan, 1060), Muse, The American Negro Revolution: From Nonviolence to Black Power, 1963–1967, ch. 6.

70. Philip E. Converse, Aage R. Clausen, and Warren E. Miller, "Electoral Myth and Reality: The 1964 Election," American Political Science Review 59, no. 2 (June 1965): 321–36; Theodore H. White, The Making of the President 1964 (London: Jonathan Cape, 1965).

71. Goldwater's contemporary philosophy is presented in Barry Goldwater, The Conscience of a Conservative (Shepardsville, Kentucky: Victor, 1960).

72. Broder, "Consensus Politics: End of an Experiment."

73. Wicker, JFK and LBJ: The Influence of Personality upon Politics, pp. 169–79.

74. Ibid., p. 178.

75. Quoted in Broder, "Consensus Politics: End of an Experiment."

76. Figures taken from Joseph Califano, A Presidential Nation (New York: W. W. Norton, 1975), p. 20.

77. Goldman, The Tragedy of Lyndon Johnson, ch. 12; Stephen K. Bailey, The New Congress (New York: St. Martin's Press, 1966); Lyndon B. Johnson, The Vantage Point: Perspectives of the Presidency, 1963–1969 (London: Weidenfeld and Nicholson, 1972), ch. 9.

78. Sundquist, Politics and Policy: The Eisenhower, Kennedy and Johnson Years, pp. 117–18; Daniel P. Moynihan, Maximum Feasible Misunderstanding: Community Action in the War on Poverty (New York: Free Press, 1969), pp. 65–66; John E. Moore, "Controlling Delinquency: Executive, Congressional and Juvenile, 1961–1964," in Congress and Urban Problems, ed. Frederic N. Cleaveland (Washington, D.C.: The Brookings Institution, 1969).

79. Moynihan, Maximum Feasible Misunderstanding: Community Action in the War on Poverty, pp. 61–81; John C. Donovan, The Politics of Poverty (New York: Pegasus Books, 1969), pp. 17–26, 39–41.

80. Bibby and Davidson, On Capitol Hill: Studies in the Legislative Process (New York: Dryden Press, 1972), p. 247.

81. Abraham Holtzman, Legislative Liaison: Executive Leadership in Congress (Chicago: Rand McNally, 1970); "From White House to Capitol Hill: How Things Get Done," U.S. News and World Report, 20 September 1965; Norman Thomas and Harold Wolman, "The Presidency and Policy Formulation: The Task Force Device," Public Administration Review 29, no. 5 (September–October 1969): 450–58; Adam Yarmolinsky, "Ideas into Programs," The Public Interest 2, no. 2 (Winter 1966): 70–79; Russell B. Pipe, "Congressional Liaison: The Executive Branch Consolidates Its Relations with Congress," Public Administration Review 26, no. 1 (March 1966): 14–24; Edward P. Morgan, "O'Brien Presses On With the Four P's," in Issues and Perspectives in American Government, ed. Joseph C. Palamountain and Martin M. Shapiro (Glenview, Ill.: Scott, Foresman, 1971); Carl Sapp, "Executive Assistance in the Legislative Process," in Public Administration and Policy, ed. Peter Woll (New York: Harper & Row, 1966); Bibby and Davidson, On Capitol Hill: Studies in the Legislative Process, pp. 225–50; Kearns, Lyndon Johnson and the American Dream, pp. 221–37;

Randall B. Ripley, *Majority Party Leadership in Congress* (Boston: Little, Brown, 1969), pp. 37–40; Berman, *A Bill Becomes a Law*, passim; Donovan, *The Politics of Poverty*, passim; Eugene Eidenburg and Roy D. Morey, *An Act of Congress* (New York: W. W. Norton, 1969), passim.

82. Kearns, *Lyndon Johnson and the American Dream*, p. 221.

83. Robert L. Allen, *A Guide to Black Power in America: An Historical Analysis* (London: Victor Gollanz, 1970), chs. 3, 4; Malcolm X and James Farmer, "Separation v. Integration," in *Black Protest in the Twentieth Century*, 2d ed., ed. August Meier, Elliott Rudwick, and Francis L. Broderick (Indianapolis, Ind.: Bobbs-Merrill, 1965); Muse, *The American Negro Revolution: From Nonviolence to Black Power, 1963–1967*, ch. 16; Eldridge Cleaver, *Soul on Ice* (New York: Dell, 1968); U.S., Commission on Civil Rights, *Federal Civil Rights Enforcement Effort: A Report of the U.S. Commission on Civil Rights* (Washington, D.C.: GPO, 1970); Joanne Grant, ed., *Black Protest* (New York: Fawcett, 1968); Jerry Cohen and William S. Murphy, *Burn, Baby, Burn* (New York: E. P. Dutton, 1966); Julius Lester, *Look Out, Whitey!* (London: Allison and Busby, 1970).

84. Anthony Downs, *An Economic Theory of Democracy* (New York: Harper & Row, 1957), pp. 55–60; John E. Mueller, *War, Presidents and Public Opinion* (New York: Wiley, 1973), pp. 205–08, 219–31.

85. Mueller, *War, Presidents and Public Opinion*, p. 205.

86. Richard Blumenthal, "The Bureaucracy: Anti-poverty and the Community Action Program," in *American Political Institutions and Public Policy: Five Contemporary Studies*, ed. Allan P. Sindler (Boston: Little, Brown, 1969); Ralph J. Kramer, *Participation of the Poor* (Englewood Cliffs, N.J.: Prentice-Hall, 1969); Donovan, *The Politics of Poverty*, chs. 3, 4; Moynihan, *Maximum Feasible Misunderstanding: Community Action in the War on Poverty*, chs. 3–5.

87. Kearns, *Lyndon Johnson and the American Dream*, pp. 218–20, 286-95; Califano, *A Presidential Nation*, pp. 19–34.

88. Califano, *A Presidential Nation*, p. 21.

89. Herbert S. Parmet, *The Democrats: The Years after FDR* (New York: Macmillan, 1976), pp. 248–84; Eugene J. McCarthy, *Year of the People* (New York: Doubleday, 1969); Jack Newfield, *Robert Kennedy: A Memoir* (London: Jonathan Cape, 1970), pp. 169–251; Norman Mailer, *Miami and the Siege of Chicago: An Informal History of the American Political Conventions of 1968* (Harmondsworth: Penguin Books, 1969), pp. 83–217.

90. Kearns, *Lyndon Johnson and the American Dream*, pp. 299–303, 310–14, 324–27.

91. Califano, *A Presidential Nation*, p. 63.

92. Two illustrative examples of the role played by liberal members of Congress in the defense and extension of Great Society programs in increasingly less favorable conditions are provided by Harold Wolman, *The Politics of Federal Housing* (New York: Dodd, Mead, 1971), pp. 72–81; and Robert A. Levine, *The Poor Ye Need Not Have with You: Lessons from the War on Poverty* (Cambridge, Mass.: Massachusetts Institute of Technology Press, 1970), pp. 72–82.

93. Arthur M. Schlesinger, Jr., *The Bitter Heritage: Vietnam and American Democracy, 1941–1966* (London: Andre Deutsch, 1967); Joseph Buttinger, *Vietnam: A Political History* (New York: Praeger, 1968), ch. 18; Frank Schurman, Peter D. Scott, and Reginald Zelnick, *The Politics of Escalation in Vietnam* (Greenwich, Conn., Fawcett Books, 1966); Frank N. Trager, *Why Vietnam?* (London: Pall Mall, 1966), ch. 8; Robert Shaplen, *The Road from War: Vietnam*

1965–1970 (London: Andre Deutsch, 1970), pp. 32–120; David Halberstam, *The Making of a Quagmire* (London: Bodley Head, 1964); Roger Hilsman, *To Move a Nation: The Politics of Foreign Policy in the Administration of John F. Kennedy* (Garden City, N.Y.: Doubleday, 1967), pp. 413–540.

94. John P. Roche, "The Impact of Dissent on Foreign Policy: Past and Future," in *The Vietnam Legacy: The War, American Society and the Future of American Foreign Policy,* ed. Anthony Lake (New York: New York University Press, 1976); Noam Chomsky, *At War with Asia* (New York: Vintage Books, 1969), ch. 1; *American Power and the New Mandarins* (London: Pelican Books, 1971), pp. 7–22, 291–305; J. William Fulbright, *The Crippled Giant: American Foreign Policy and Its Domestic Consequences* (New York: Random House, 1972), pp. 72–106, 150–76; Herbert Y. Schandler, *The Unmaking of a President: Lyndon Johnson and Vietnam* (Princeton, N.J.: Princeton University Press, 1977), pp. 194–217; Adam Yarmolinsky, *The Military Establishment: Its Impact on American Society* (New York: Harper & Row, 1971), pp. 355–63; I. F. Stone, *In a Time of Torment* (London: Jonathan Cape, 1968), pp. 178–327.

95. See Philip E. Converse, Warren E. Miller, Jerrold G. Rusk, and Arthur C. Wolfe, "Continuity and Change in American Politics: Parties and Issues in the 1968 Election," *American Political Science Review* 63, no. 4 (December 1969): 1083–1105; Johnson, *The Vantage Point: Perspectives of the Presidency, 1963–1969,* ch. 19.

96. Donovan, *The Policy Makers,* ch. 6; Schandler, *The Unmaking of a President: Lyndon Johnson and Vietnam,* pp. 218–28; Fulbright, *The Crippled Giant: American Foreign Policy and Its Domestic Consequences,* pp. 243–64; Okun, *The Political Economy of Prosperity,* pp. 62–66, 73–99; Heller, *The New Dimensions of Political Economy,* pp. 83–99; Murray L. Weidenbaum, *The Economic Impact of the Vietnam War* (Washington, D.C.: Georgetown University Center for Strategic Studies, 1967).

97. *United States* v. *Curtiss-Wright Export Corporation,* 299 U.S. 304 (1936).

98. Ibid.

99. Arthur M. Schlesinger, Jr., *The Imperial Presidency* (London: Andre Deutsch, 1974), chs. 5, 6.

100. Quoted in "Members Seek Veto over Executive Agreements," Congressional Quarterly, *Congressional Quarterly Guide to Current American Government,* Spring 1976 (Washington, D.C.: Congressional Quarterly, 1976), p. 47.

101. Ibid., p. 49.

102. Donald L. Robinson, "The President as Commander-in-Chief," in *Perspectives on the Presidency,* ed. Stanley Bach and George T. Sulzner (Lexington Mass.: D. C. Heath, 1974); Louis Fisher, *President and Congress: Power and Policy* (New York: Free Press, 1972), ch. 6.

103. Schlesinger, *The Imperial Presidency,* p. 176.

104. Aaron Wildavsky, "The Two Presidencies," in *The Revolt against the Masses,* ed. Aaron Wildavsky (New York: Basic Books, 1971), p. 327.

105. The initial disaffection toward, and first complaints against, the excessive presidential power perceived at this time are reflected in Henry S. Commager, "Presidential Power," *New Republic,* 6 April 1968; George Reedy, *The Twilight of the Presidency* (New York: New American Library, 1970), chs. 1, 3, 13; Arthur M. Schlesinger, Jr., *The Crisis of Confidence: Ideas, Power and Violence in America* (London: Andre Deutsch, 1969), pp. 286–300; Fulbright, *The Crippled Giant: American Foreign Policy and Its Domestic Consequences,* pp. 204–42;

Hans J. Morgenthau, "A Dangerous Concentration of Power," *New York Review of Books,* 31 March 1966.

106. Richard M. Scammon and Ben J. Wattenberg, *The Real Majority* (New York: Berkley Medallion Books, 1972), p. 107.

107. Haynes Johnson and Bernard M. Gwertzman, *Fulbright the Dissenter* (London: Hutchinson, 1968), p. 304.

108. Kearns, *Lyndon Johnson and the American Dream,* p. 220.

109. *Public Papers of the President of the United States, Richard Nixon, 1969* (Washington, D.C.: GPO, 1971), p. 2.

110. Hartz, *The Liberal Tradition in America: An Interpretation of American Political Thought since the Revolution,* p. 57.

111. Ibid., p. 58.

112. Gary Wills, *Nixon Agonistes: The Crisis of the Self-made Man* (New York: Signet Books, 1971), p. 43.

113. Paul Jacobs and Saul Landau, eds., *The New Radicals* (New York: Random House, 1966); Mitchell Cohen and Denis Hale, eds., *The New Student Left* (Boston: Beacon Press, 1966); Students for a Democratic Society, *The Port Huron Statement* (Chicago: S.D.S., 1966); Abbie Hoffman, *Revolution for the Hell of It* (New York: Dial Press, 1968); Jerry Rubin, *Do It!* (London: Jonathan Cape, 1970); James Glass, " 'Yippies': The Critique of Possessive Individualism," *The Political Quarterly* 43, no. 1 (January–March 1972): 60–78; Stokeley Carmichael and Charles V. Hamilton, *Black Power: The Politics of Liberation in America* (New York: Vintage Books, 1967); Huey P. Newton, *The Genius of Huey P. Newton* (Berkeley, Calif.: Black Panther Party, 1970); Bobby Seale, *Seize the Time* (New York: Random House, 1970); Schlesinger, *The Crisis of Confidence,* chs. 1, 2, 5; Priscilla Long, ed., *The New Left: A Collection of Essays* (Boston: Porter Sargent, 1969); Seymour M. Lipset and Gerald M. Schaflander, *Passion and Politics: Student Activism in America* (Boston: Little, Brown, 1971); Irving Louis Horowitz, *The Struggle Is the Message: The Organization and Ideology of the Anti-war Movement* (Berkeley, Calif.: The Glendassary Press, 1970).

114. Converse et al., "Continuity and Change in American Politics: Parties and Issues in the 1968 Election," p. 1088.

115. Bernard Crick, "The Strange Death of the American Theory of Consensus," *The Political Quarterly* 43, no. 1 (January–March 1972): 46–59.

116. Rubin, *Do It!,* p. 161.

117. Scammon and Wattenberg, *The Real Majority,* p. 171. See also John P. Robinson, "Public Reaction to Political Protest: Chicago 1968," *Public Opinion Quarterly* 34, no. 1 (Spring 1970): 1–10.

118. Scammon and Wattenberg, *The Real Majority,* p. 76.

119. Converse et al., "Continuity and Change in American Politics: Parties and Issues in the 1968 Election," p. 1088.

120. Theodore H. White, *The Making of the President 1968* (London: Jonathan Cape, 1969); Lewis Chester, Godfrey Hodgson, and Bruce Page, *An American Melodrama: The Presidential Campaign of 1968* (London: Andre Deutsch, 1969).

121. This famous remark has generally been attributed to Anthony Howard of the *New Statesman.*

122. Wills, *Nixon Agonistes: The Crisis of the Self-made Man,* pp. 135–44; Chester, Hodgson, and Page, *An American Melodrama: The Presidential Campaign of 1968,* pp. 495–99.

123. See Mueller, *War, Presidents and Public Opinion,* pp. 196–204.

124. Scammon and Wattenberg, *The Real Majority*, p. 76.

125. Ibid., pp. 76–78. For a deeper analysis of public's distinction between "ideological" liberalism and "operational" liberalism, see Lloyd A. Free and Hadley Cantril, *The Political Beliefs of Americans* (New Brunswick, N.J.: Rutgers University Press, 1968), pp. 1–40, 207–10.

126. Rowland Evans and Robert D. Novak, *Nixon in the White House: The Frustration of Power* (New York: Vintage Books, 1971), pp. 9–19; Theodore H. White, *The Making of the President 1972* (New York: Bantam Books, 1973), ch. 10; Richard P. Nathan, *The Plot That Failed: Nixon and the Administrative Presidency* (New York: Wiley, 1975), chs. 1, 3.

127. James D. Barber, *Presidential Character: Predicting Performance in the White House* (Englewood Cliffs, N.J.: Prentice-Hall, 1972), pp. 347–417; Bruce Mazlish, *In Search of Nixon* (New York: Basic Books, 1972).

128. Congressional Quarterly, *Congress and the Nation, Vol. III, 1969–1972* (Washington, D.C.: Congressional Quarterly, 1973), pp. 605–34; Daniel P. Moynihan *The Politics of a Guaranteed Income: The Nixon Administration and the Family Assistance Plan* (New York: Random House, 1973), ch. 1; U.S., Department of Commerce, Bureau of the Census, Social Welfare Expenditures under Public Programs: 1935 to 1972, *The American Almanac 1974* (New York: Grosset & Dunlap, 1974), p. 286.

129. *Public Papers of the President of the United States, Richard Nixon, 1971* (Washington, D.C.: GPO, 1973), p. 51.

130. Gary Orfield, *Congressional Power: Congress and Social Change* (New York: Harcourt Brace Jovanovich, 1975), pp. 302–06; Congressional Quarterly, *The Future of Social Programs* (Washington, D.C.: Congressional Quarterly, 1973), pp. 75–98.

131. Moynihan, *The Politics of a Guaranteed Income: The Nixon Administration and the Family Assistance Plan*, passim; Congressional Quarterly, *The Future of Social Programs*, pp. 15–19; Vincent J. Burke and Vee Burke, *Nixon's Good Deed: Welfare Reform* (New York: Columbia University Press, 1974), passim.

132. Congressional Quarterly, *The Future of Social Programs*, p. 76.

133. For a general review of President Nixon's treatment of this issue, see Evans and Novak, *Nixon in the White House: The Frustration of Power*, ch. 6; Eleanor H. Norton, "Civil Rights: Working Backward," in *What Is Nixon Doing to Us?*, ed. Alan Gartner, Colin Greer, and Frank Riessman (New York: Harper & Row, 1973); Leon E. Panetta and Peter Gall, *Bring Us Together: The Nixon Team and the Civil Rights Retreat* (Philadelphia: J. B. Lippincott, 1971).

134. Louis W. Koenig, *The Chief Executive*, 3d ed. rev. (New York: Harcourt Brace Jovanovich, 1975), p. 319.

135. Evans and Novak, *Nixon in the White House: The Frustration of Power*, pp. 146–47.

136. Barber, *Presidential Character: Predicting Performance in the White House*, pp. 425–29; Evans and Novak, *Nixon in the White House: The Frustration of Power*, pp. 159–72; Richard Harris, *Decision* (New York: E. P. Dutton, 1971); Orfield, *Congressional Power: Congress and Social Change*, pp. 103–16.

137. Evans and Novak, *Nixon in the White House: The Frustration of Power*, pp. 134–35.

138. Robert Sherrill, *Why They Call It Politics: A Guide to America's Government*, 2d ed. rev. (New York: Harcourt Brace Jovanovich, 1974), p. 264.

139. Figures taken from U.S., Department of Commerce, Bureau of the Census,

Consumer Price Indexes, by Commodity Groups: 1920 to 1973; and Employment Status of the Noninstitutional Population by Sex and Race: 1950 to 1973, *The American Almanac 1974*, pp. 354, 219.

140. Schlesinger, *The Imperial Presidency*, pp. 187–200; Frances Fitzgerald, *Fire in the Lake: The Vietnamese and the Americans in Vietnam* (London: Macmillan, 1972), pp. 403–24; John G. Stoessinger, *Henry Kissinger: The Anguish of Power* (New York: W. W. Norton, 1976), pp. 49–78.

141. Poll results given in Mueller, *War, Presidents and Public Opinion*, p. 97.

142. For a general review of the Senate's activism at this time, see Francis Wilcox, *Congress, the Executive and Foreign Policy* (New York: Harper & Row, 1971); John Lehman, *The Executive, Congress and Foreign Policy: Studies of the Nixon Administration* (New York: Praeger, 1974); Schlesinger, *The Imperial Presidency*, chs. 8, 9; Fisher, *President and Congress: Power and Policy*, ch. 7; Thomas F. Eagleton, *War and Presidential Power: A Chronicle of Congressional Surrender* (New York: Liveright, 1974), pp. 107–225; Jacob K. Javits with Don Kellerman, *Who Makes War: The President versus Congress* (New York: Morrow, 1973), pp. 262–74; Alan Frye and Jack Sullivan, "Congress and Vietnam: The Fruits of Anguish," in *The Vietnam Legacy: The War, American Society and the Future of American Foreign Policy*, ed. Anthony Lake (New York: New York University Press, 1976).

143. Congressional Quarterly, *Congress and the Nation, Vol. III, 1969–1972* (Washington, D.C.: Congressional Quarterly, 1973), pp. 899–931.

144. Ibid., pp. 917–19; Schlesinger, *The Imperial Presidency*, p. 194.

145. Lehman, *The Executive, Congress and Foreign Policy Studies of the Nixon Administration*, pp. 37–77; John Rothchild, "Cooing Down the War: The Senate's Lame Doves," *Washington Monthly*, August 1971.

146. Interview with Senator Mark Hatfield, 16 September 1975.

147. Evans and Novak, *Nixon in the White House: The Frustration of Power*, p. 331.

148. Louis Heren, "Agnew Hits Out at 'Eunuchs'," *The Times*, 1 November 1970.

CHAPTER 3

1. Thomas Jefferson, quoted in Richard Hofstadter, *The American Political Tradition* (London: Jonathan Cape, 1967), p. 37.

2. Kenneth M. Dolbeare and Patricia Dolbeare, *American Ideologies: The Competing Political Beliefs of the 1970s* (Chicago: Markham, 1971), ch. 3; David Spitz, "A Liberal Perspective on Liberalism and Conservatism," in *Left, Right and Center: Essays on Liberalism and Conservatism in the United States*, ed. Robert A. Goldwin (Chicago: Rand McNally, 1967).

3. Arthur M. Schlesinger, Jr., *The Politics of Hope* (London: Eyre and Spottiswoode, 1964), p. 63.

4. Louis Hartz, *The Liberal Tradition in America* (New York: Harcourt Brace and World, 1955).

5. Eugene J. McCarthy, *Frontiers in American Democracy* (Cleveland: World Publishers, 1960), ch. 5; William A. Kerr, "Untangling the Liberal–Conservative Continuum," *Journal of Social Psychology* 35 (1952), pp. 111–25.

6. C. Wright Mills, *The Power Elite* (Oxford: Oxford University Press, 1959), p. 336.

7. See Philip Converse, "The Nature of Belief Systems in Mass Publics," in *Ideology and Discontent*, ed. David Apter (New York: Free Press, 1964); David Minar, "Ideology and Political Behavior," *Midwest Journal of Political Science* 5, no. 4 (November 1961): 317–31; Aage R. Clausen, *How Congressmen Decide: A Policy Focus* (New York: St. Martin's Press, 1973), pp. 100–06; Donald J. Devine, *The Political Culture of the United States: The Influence of Member Values on Regime Maintenance* (Boston: Little, Brown, 1972), pp. 255–60; Willmoore Kendall and George W. Carey, *Liberalism versus Conservatism: The Continuing Debate in American Government* (Princeton, N.J.: D. Van Nostrand, 1966); Angus Campbell, Philip E. Converse, Warren E. Miller, and Donald E. Stokes, *The American Voter* (New York: Wiley, 1964), pp. 109–23, 129–35.

8. John P. Roche, *Shadow and Substance: Essays on the Theory and Structure of Politics* (London: Collier Macmillan, 1964); Hubert H. Humphrey *The Cause Is Mankind* (London: Methuen, 1964); Americans for Democractic Action, *Americans for Democratic Action: Where It's Been and Where It's At* (Washington, D.C.: Americans for Democratic Action); Richard Hofstadter, *The Age of Reform: From Bryan to F.D.R.* (London: Jonathan Cape, 1962); John K. Galbraith, "An Agenda for American Liberals," in *American Government: Behavior and Controversy*, ed. Leonard Lipsitz (Boston: Allyn and Bacon, 1967); Eugene J. McCarthy, *A Liberal Answer to the Conservative Challenge* (New York: MacFadden, 1964).

9. Barry Goldwater, *The Conscience of a Conservative* (Shepardsville, Kentucky: Victor, 1960); Goldwater, *The Conscience of a Majority* (New York: Pocket Books, 1971); Frank S. Meyer, "The Recrudescent American Conservatism," in *American Conservative Thought in the Twentieth Century*, ed. William F. Buckley (Indianapolis, Ind.: Bobbs-Merrill, 1970); Milton Friedman, *Capitalism and Freedom* (Chicago: University of Chicago Press, 1962); Stephen C. Shadegg, "Conservatism and Political Action," in *Left, Right and Center: Essays on Liberalism and Conservatism in the United States*, ed. Robert A. Goldwin (Chicago: Rand McNally, 1967); Russell Kirk, *The Conservative Mind* (Chicago: Henry Regnery, 1953).

10. Randall B. Ripley, *Power in the Senate* (New York: St. Martin's Press, 1969); see also Lewis A. Froman, *Congressmen and Their Constituencies* (Chicago: Rand McNally, 1963), ch. 6.

11. John F. Manley, "The House Committee on Ways and Means: Conflict Management in a Congressional Committee," *American Political Science Review* 59, no. 4 (December 1965): 927–40; see also Samuel C. Patterson, "Legislative Leadership and Political Ideology," *Public Opinion Quarterly* 27, no. 3 (Fall 1963): 339–410; Richard F. Fenno, Jr., "The House of Representatives and Federal Aid to Education," in *New Perspectives on the House of Representatives*, ed. Robert L. Peabody and Nelson W. Polsby (Chicago: Rand McNally, 1963).

12. The simple index is employed to "rank" senators by such interest groups as the Americans for Democratic Action, the AFL-CIO's Committee on Political Education, the League of Women Voters, the National Association of Businessmen, and the Americans for Constitutional Action.

13. See Herman C. Beyle, *Identification and Analysis of Attribute-Cluster-Blocs* (Chicago: University of Chicago Press, 1931); David B. Truman, "The State Delegations and the Structure of Party Voting in the United States House of Representatives," *American Political Science Review* 50, no. 4 (December 1956): 1020–40; *The Congressional Party* (New York: Wiley, 1959), chs. 3, 5; Duncan

MacRae, Jr., "A Method for Identifying Issues and Factions from Legislative Votes," *American Political Science Review* 59, no. 4 (December 1965): 909–26; MacRae, *Issues and Parties in Legislative Voting: Methods of Statistical Analysis* (New York: Harper & Row, 1970), ch. 3; Aage R. Clausen and Richard B. Cheney, "A Comparative Analysis of Senate House Voting on Economic and Welfare Policy: 1953–1964," *American Political Science Review* 64, no. 1 (March 1970): 138–52.

14. Clausen and Cheney, "A Comparative Analysis of Senate House Voting on Economic and Welfare Policy: 1953–64," p. 139.

15. C. A. Moser and Graham Kalton, *Survey Methods in Social Investigation,* 2d ed. rev. (London: Heinemann, 1971), p. 367; for additional analysis of Guttman scaling, see George Belknap, "Scaling Legislative Behavior," in *Legislative Behavior: A Reader in Theory and Research,* ed. John C. Wahlke and Heinz Eulau (New York: Free Press, 1959); MacRae, *Issues and Parties in Legislative Voting: Methods of Statistical Analysis,* ch. 2; Lee Anderson, Meredith W. Watts, and Allen R. Wilcox, *Legislative Roll Call Analysis* (Evanston, Ill.: Northwestern University Press, 1966), ch. 6.

16. See H. Douglas Price, "Are Southern Democrats Different? An Application of Scale Analysis to Senate Voting Patterns," in *Politics and Social Life,* ed. Nelson W. Polsby, Robert A. Dentler, and Paul A. Smith (Boston: Houghton Mifflin, 1963); Samuel C. Patterson, "Dimensions of Voting Behavior in a One-Party State Legislature," *Public Opinion Quarterly* 26, no. 2 (Summer 1962): 185–200; "Legislative Leadership and Political Ideology," *Public Opinion Quarterly* 27, no. 3 (Fall 1963): 399–410; Charles F. Andrain, "Senators' Attitudes toward Civil Rights," *The Western Political Quarterly* 17, no. 3 (September 1964): 488–503; Charles Gray, "A Scale Analysis of the Voting Records of Senators Kennedy, Johnson and Goldwater, 1957–60," *American Political Science Review* 59, no. 3 (September 1965): 615–22; Robert A. Bernstein and William W. Anthony, "The ABM Issue in the Senate, 1968–1970: The Importance of Ideology," *American Political Science Review* 68, no. 3 (September 1974): 1198–1206; Bruce M. Russett, *What Price Vigilance? The Burdens of National Defense* (New Haven, Conn.: Yale University Press, 1970), ch. 2; Edward Keynes, "The Senate Rules and the Dirksen Amendment: A Study in Legislative Strategy and Tactics," in *The Legislative Process in the U.S. Senate,* ed. Lawrence K. Petit and Edward Keynes (Chicago: Rand McNally, 1969); Lawrence K. Petit, "Constitutional Ambiguity and Legislative Decision Making: The Establishment Clause and Aid to Higher Education," in *The Legislative Process in the U.S. Senate,* ed. Petit and Keynes; John C. Wahlke, Heinz Eulau, William Buchanan, and LeRoy C. Ferguson, *The Legislative System: Explorations in Legislative Behavior* (New York: Wiley, 1962), p. 475; Leroy N. Rieselbach, "The Demography of the Congressional Vote on Foreign Aid, 1939–1958," *American Political Science Review* 58, no. 3 (September 1964): 577–88.

17. On the liberal side, attention was given to such well-known outlets of liberal opinion as the Americans for Democratic Action, the AFL-CIO's Committee on Political Education, Common Cause, the *Nation,* and the *New Republic.* The equivalent for the conservative side was provided by the Americans for Constitutional Action, the American Security Council, the National Association of Businessmen, and the *National Review.*

18. See appendix II.

19. See appendix II.

20. See the unusually high number of liberal scores recorded by southern Democrats in the union regulation scale for Eighty-sixth Congress in appendix II.

21. In the Ninety-first Congress, for example, Hatfield returned 5 liberal scores in 7 scales, Mathias recorded 4 liberal scores, and Schweiker recorded 4 liberal scores.

22. See Rowland Evans and Robert Novak, *Nixon in the White House: The Frustration of Power* (New York: Vintage Books, 1971) ch. 5; Louis Fisher, *President and Congress: Power and Policy* (New York: Free Press, 1972), pp. 228–31; "The Senate's Five Runaway Freshmen," *The Progressive*, August 1969.

23. A particular problem with the typology concerns the always difficult question of marginal cases. A member with 75 percent of his scores ranked liberal and 25 percent of his scores ranked conservative would be given an overall ranking of liberal. On the other hand, a member with 74 percent of his scores ranked liberal and 26 percent of his scores ranked moderate would be given an overall ranking of liberal-to-moderate. The only rationale that can be offered for this apparent injustice is that the scales have been employed primarily to assess consistency. Therefore, whereas the latter member may appear to be more liberal than the former, the former is the slightly more consistent supporter of liberal positions.

24. For those readers who wish to consult the full list of senatorial rankings, appendix IV provides a complete breakdown of senators into attitudinal scale types.

CHAPTER 4

1. William S. White, *Citadel: The Story of the U.S. Senate* (New York: Harper & Bros., 1956), p. 2.

2. Ibid., p. 7.

3. Ibid., p. 11.

4. Ibid., p. 5.

5. Ibid., p. 113.

6. Donald R. Matthews, *U.S. Senators and Their World* (New York: Vintage Books, 1960), ch. 5.

7. Ibid., pp. 110–14.

8. James L. Sundquist, *Politics and Policy: The Eisenhower, Kennedy and Johnson Years* (Washington, D.C.: The Brookings Institution, 1968), ch. 9; Ralph K. Huitt, "The Outsider in the Senate: An Alternative Role," *American Political Science Review* 55, no. 3 (September 1961): 566–75; Roger H. Davidson, David M. Kovenock, and Michael K. O'Leary, *Congress in Crisis: Politics and Congressional Reform* (Belmont, Calif.: Wadsworth, 1966), ch. 5; Rowland Evans and Robert Novak, *Lyndon B. Johnson: The Exercise of Power* (London: Allen & Unwin, 1966), ch. 10; Tom Wicker, "Winds of Change in the Senate," *New York Times Magazine*, 12 September 1965; Randall B. Ripley, *Power in the Senate* (New York: St. Martin's Press, 1969), ch. 3; Joseph P. Harris, *Congress and the Legislative Process* (New York: McGraw-Hill, 1972), pp. 76–78; Harry McPherson, "The Senate Observed," *Atlantic Monthly*, May 1972; Charles M. Roberts, "Nine Men Who Control Congress," *Atlantic Monthly*, April 1964; Clayton Fritchey, "Who Belongs to the Inner Club," *Harper's Magazine*, May 1967; Alfred Steinberg, *Sam Johnson's Boy: A Close-up of the President from Texas* (New York: Macmillan, 1968), chs. 44, 53.

9. White and Matthews are not the only analysts to stress the significance of

norms and customs in the Congress. Among those who have made the study of norms an integral part of their analyses of Congress or of organizational units within Congress are: Charles L. Clapp, *The Congressman: His Work as He Sees It* (Washington, D.C.: The Brookings Institution, 1963) chs. 1, 3; Richard F. Fenno, Jr., "The House Appropriations Committee as a Political System," in *New Perspectives on the House of Representatives*, ed. Robert L. Peabody and Nelson W. Polsby (Chicago: Rand McNally, 1963); Fenno, "The Internal Distribution of Influence: The House," in *The Congress and America's Future*, ed. David B. Truman (Englewood Cliffs, N.J.: Prentice-Hall, 1965); Fenno, *Congressmen in Committees* (Boston: Little Brown, 1973), ch. 2; John F. Manley, "The House Committee on Ways and Means: Conflict Management in a Congressional Committee," *American Political Science Review* 59, no. 4 (December 1965): 927–39; David B. Truman, *The Congressional Party* (New York: Wiley, 1959); Ralph K. Huitt, "The Morse Committee Assignment Controversy: A Study in Senate Norms," *American Political Science Review* 51, no. 2 (June 1957): 313–29; Huitt, "The Outsider in the Senate: An Alternative Role," *American Political Science Review* 55, no. 3 (September 1961): 566–75; Malcolm E. Jewell and Samuel C. Patterson, *The Legislative Process in the United States* (New York: Random House, 1966), ch. 15; Herbert B. Asher, "The Learning of Legislative Norms," *American Political Science Review* 67, no. 2 (June 1973): 499–513.

10. White, *Citadel: The Story of the U.S. Senate*, p. 82.

11. Ibid.

12. Matthews, *U.S. Senators and Their World*, p. 93.

13. Joseph S. Clark, *Congress: The Sapless Branch* (Westport, Conn.: Greenwood Press, 1976), pp. 1–2.

14. Evans and Novak, *Lyndon B. Johnson: The Exercise of Power*, pp. 165–67, 196–202; Doris B. Kearns, *Lyndon Johnson and the American Dream* (New York: Harper & Row, 1976), chs. 4, 5; Steinberg, *Sam Johnson's Boy: A Close-up of the President from Texas*, pp. 493–97.

15. Interview with Senator Edmund Muskie, 28 March 1974.

16. Matthews, *U.S. Senators and Their World*, pp. 110–14, 235–39.

17. It was not so much the Democrats who were winning their elections with small majorities in 1958 so much as the Republicans. Fourteen percent of all the Democrats elected in that year had majorities of 52.5 percent or under, yet the proportion of the Republicans who were returned with equally low majorities was 44 percent.

18. David Nevin, *Muskie of Maine* (New York: Random House, 1972), ch. 3.

19. Interview with Senator Edmund Muskie, 28 March 1974.

20. Sundquist, *Politics and Policy: The Eisenhower, Kennedy and Johnson Years*, ch. 9; Kearns, *Lyndon Johnson and the American Dream*, ch. 5; Also based on interview material from Senators Edmund Muskie (28 March 1974) and Frank Moss (21 March 1974).

21. White, *Citadel: The Story of the U.S. Senate*, p. 3.

22. Nevin, *Muskie of Maine*, ch. 3; William Proxmire, *Uncle Sam: The Last of the Bigtime Spenders* (New York: Simon and Schuster, 1972), pp. 243–44; Abigail McCarthy, *Private Faces Public Places* (New York: Curtis Books, 1972), pp. 261–63; Evans and Novak, *Lyndon B. Johnson: The Exercise of Power*, pp. 200–02. Also based on interview material from Howard E. Shuman (administra-

tive assistant to Senator William Proxmire, 3 September 1975) and from Senator William Proxmire (29 March 1974).

23. Nevin, *Muskie of Maine*, p. 105.

24. Steinberg: *Sam Johnson's Boy: A Close-up of the President from Texas*, chs. 52–4; Evans and Novak, *Lyndon B. Johnson: The Exercise of Power*, pp. 166–67, 216–17, 220–23; Theodore Sorensen, *Kennedy* (London: Pan Books, 1965), pp. 63–68.

25. In addition to all the other diversions, there was the simple problem of available manpower. The 1958 election had not only increased the number of pupils by 23, but had decreased the number of available teachers by 17—all of whom were members of the Republican party, which tends to have a very high regard for continuity, loyalty, and hierarchy.

26. Matthews, *U.S. Senators and Their World*, p. 94.

27. Study of Senator Harrison Williams is based on Congressional Quarterly, *Congress and the Nation 1945–1964: A Review of Government and Politics in the Postwar Years* (Washington, D.C.: Congressional Quarterly, 1965), pp. 648, 760; Royce Hanson, "Congress Copes with Mass Transit, 1960–64," in *Congress and Urban Problems*, ed. Frederic N. Cleaveland (Washington, D.C.: The Brookings Institution, 1969); interview material from an interview with Senator Harrison Williams (25 September 1975).

28. Study of Senator Eugene McCarthy is based on Sundquist, *Politics and Policy: The Eisenhower, Kennedy and Johnson Years*, pp. 77–83; U.S., Congress, Senate, Special Committee on Unemployment Problems, *Hearings, Unemployment Problems*, 86th Cong., 1st sess., 1959, passim.

29. Sundquist, *Politics and Policy: The Eisenhower, Kennedy and Johnson Years*, pp. 396–400.

30. Huitt, "The Outsider in the Senate: An Alternative Role," pp. 569–70.

31. Ibid., p. 569.

32. Ibid., p. 575.

33. This was reflected in the discomfort suffered by fellow liberals and freshmen by Proxmire's tactics. Proxmire was generally supported by Clark, Morse, and Douglas but not by his immediate contemporaries. See Steinberg, *Sam Johnson's Boy: A Close-up of the President from Texas*, pp. 495–97; Proxmire, *Uncle Sam: The Last of the Bigtime Spenders*, pp. 241–44; William Proxmire and Richard Neuberger, "The Struggle for a Liberal Senate: A Debate between Senators Proxmire and Neuberger," *The Progressive*, June 1959. This observation was also based on interview evidence—in particular an interview with Roy Cook (administrative assistant to Senator Gale McGee, 25 August 1975).

34. Interview with Senator Edmund Muskie, 28 March 1974.

35. Randall B. Ripley, *Power in the Senate* (New York: St. Martin's Press, 1969), pp. 55–69; Thomas P. Murphy, *The New Politics Congress* (Lexington, Mass.: D. C. Heath, 1974), pp. 96–105; Gary Orfield, *Congressional Power: Congress and Social Change* (New York: Harcourt Brace Jovanovich, 1975), pp. 3–12; John F. Bibby and Roger H. Davidson, *On Capitol Hill: Studies in the Legislative Process* (New York: Dryden Press, 1972), pp. 144–48; John F. Manley, *American Government and Public Policy* (New York: Macmillan, 1976), pp. 206–40; John C. Donovan, *The Policy Makers* (New York: Pegasus Books, 1970), ch. 7.

36. Dan Cordtz, "The Senate Revolution," *Wall Street Journal*, 6 August 1965.

37. For Mansfield's effect on the Senate, see Ripley, *Power in the Senate*,

pp. 91–96; Manley, *American Government and Public Policy*, pp. 258–79; Bibby and Davidson, *On Capitol Hill: Studies in the Legislative Process*, pp. 144–48; "A Critical Look at Congress," *U.S. News and World Report*, 1 December 1969; "Why Kennedy's Program Is in Trouble with Congress," *U.S. News and World Report*, 17 September 1962; "The Senate: A Crisis in Leadership," *Newsweek*, 18 November 1963; John G. Stewart, "Two Strategies of Leadership: Johnson and Mansfield," in *Congressional Behavior*, ed. Nelson W. Polsby (New York: Random House, 1971).

38. Interview with John Nolan (assistant to Senator Edward Kennedy), 5 March 1974.

39. Observation based on an interview with Howard Shuman (administrative assistant to Senator William Proxmire), September 3 1975, and on Rowland Evans and Robert Novak, "Mondale and Harris: Humphrey's Establishment Radicals," *Harper's Magazine*, October 1968.

40. Interview with Senator John Tower, 13 March 1974.

41. Ibid.

42. See works already listed under note 9.

43. Quoted in William Weaver, *Both Your Houses* (New York: Praeger, 1972), p. 49; Mark J. Green, James M. Fallows, and David E. Zwick, *Who Runs Congress?* (New York: Bantam Books, 1972), p. 168.

44. Weaver, *Both Your Houses*, pp. 21–22; Congressional Quarterly, *Congressional Quarterly Guide to Current American Government*, Fall 1975 (Washington, D.C.: Congressional Quarterly, 1975), pp. 47–49.

45. Robert S. Anson, *McGovern: A Biography* (New York: Holt, Rinehart and Winston, 1972), p. 138.

46. Interview with Gerry Frank (administrative assistant to Senator Mark Hatfield), 11 March 1974.

47. Interview with Leon Shull (national director, Americans for Democratic Action), 20 March 1974.

48. Information on the Dodd case was derived from Congressional Quarterly, *Congress and the Nation, Vol. II, 1965–68* (Washington, D.C.: Congressional Quarterly, 1969), pp. 900–02; Drew Pearson and Jack Anderson, *The Case against Congress* (New York: Pocket Books, 1969), pp. 17–93; Green, Fallows, and Zwick, *Who Runs Congress?*, pp. 148–50, 162.

49. See Congressional Quarterly, *Congressional Quarterly Almanac 1964* (Washington, D.C.: Congressional Quarterly, 1965), Key Votes Appendix, Roll Call no. 229.

50. Congressional Quarterly, *Congress and the Nation, Vol. III, 1969–72* (Washington, D.C.: Congressional Quarterly, 1973), pp. 425–33.

51. Quoted in *Time*, 8 May 1972; 17 February 1972.

52. Quoted in *The Guardian*, 1 June 1972.

53. Quoted in *The Observer*, 4 June 1972.

54. Quoted in *The Times*, 21 April 1972.

55. Quoted in *Time*, 10 July 1972.

56. Ibid., 3 July 1972.

57. White, *Citadel: The Story of the U.S. Senate*, p. 111.

58. Ibid., p. 115.

59. Ibid., p. 23.

60. U.S., Congress, *Congressional Record* (Washington, D.C.: GPO, 1959), 23 February 1959, pp. 2814–20; 9 March 1959, pp. 3559–83; 15 April 1959, pp.

5956–58. U.S., Congress, *Congressional Record* (Washington, D.C.: GPO, 1962), 1 August 1962, pp. 14182–83. U.S., Congress, *Congressional Record* (Washington, D.C.: GPO, 1963), 19 February 1963, pp. 2413–26; 20 February 1963, pp. 2524–31; 21 February 1963, pp. 2703–13; U.S., Congress, Joint Committee on the Organization of Congress, *Hearings, The Organization of Congress*, 89th Cong., 2d. sess., 1966, pp. 17–34, 631–49, 1499–1534.

61. Interview with William S. White, 29 March 1974.

62. The study of the Manpower Development and Training Act is based on Sundquist, *Politics and Policy: The Eisenhower, Kennedy and Johnson Years*, pp. 83–91; Congressional Quarterly, *Congressional Quarterly Almanac 1962* (Washington, D.C.: Congressional Quarterly, 1963), pp. 512–18.

63. Joseph S. Clark, *The Senate Establishment* (New York: Hill & Wang, 1963).

64. Interview with James McKenna (legislative assistant to Senator John Pastore), 21 March 1974.

65. Interview with Senator Frank Moss, 21 March 1974.

66. Congressional Quarterly, *Congress and the Nation, Vol. II, 1965–1968* (Washington, D.C.: Congressional Quarterly, 1969), pp. 151–63, 183–226, 240–51, 709–33, 779–824; Sundquist, *Politics and Policy: The Eisenhower, Kennedy and Johnson Years*, passim.

67. Figures derived from U.S., Department of Commerce, Bureau of the Census, Federal Food Stamp Program: 1961 to 1972; Federal Budget–Receipts, by Source, and Outlays, by Function: 1960 to 1973, *The American Almanac: The Statistical Abstract of the United States* (New York: Grosset & Dunlap, 1974), pp. 90, 390.

68. Figures derived from U.S., Department of Commerce, Bureau of the Census, Public Assistance—Payments and Recipients: 1950 to 1972, *The American Almanac: The Statistical Abstract of the United States*, p. 308; also Kenneth M. Dolbeare and Murray J. Edelman, *American Politics: Policies, Power and Change*, 2d ed. (Lexington, Mass.: D. C. Heath, 1974), pp. 104–05.

69. Dolbeare and Edelman, *American Politics: Policies, Power and Change*, p. 103.

70. Arthur H. Miller, "Political Issues and Trust in Government," *American Political Science Review*, 68, no. 3 (September 1974): 951–72.

71. Richard M. Scammon and Ben J. Wattenberg, *The Real Majority* (New York: Berkley Medallion Books, 1972), p. 73.

72. Lloyd A. Free and Hadley Cantril, *The Political Beliefs of Americans: A Study of Public Opinion* (New Brunswick, N.J.: Rutgers University Press, 1967), ch. 1.

73. See Scammon and Wattenberg, *The Real Majority*, pp. 93–105; Philip E. Converse, Warren E. Miller, Jerrold G. Rusk, and Arthur C. Wolfe, "Continuity and Change in American Politics: Parties and Issues in the 1968 Election," *American Political Science Review* 63, no. 4 (December 1969): 1084–90.

74. For an interesting case study on the ways in which the changed political environment of the late 1960s affected one liberal (Joseph Tydings), see Bibby and Davidson, *On Capitol Hill: Studies in the Legislative Process*, pp. 25–51.

75. See table 3.8.

76. Interview with Senator Gale McGee, 18 March 1974.

77. Interview with Gene Godley (legislative assistant to Senator Thomas Eagleton), 9 September 1975.

78. Figures derived from the Eighty-ninth and Ninetieth Congress sections of the 1959–72 voting study referred to in chapter 3.

79. The Long amendment lost by 12 votes to 68 votes. See Congressional Quarterly, *Congressional Quarterly Almanac 1968* (Washington, D.C.: Congressional Quarterly, 1969), Key Votes Appendix, Roll Call no. 117.

80. The Hart amendment lost by 11 votes to 62 votes. See Congressional Quarterly, *Congressional Quarterly Almanac 1970* (Washington, D.C.: Congressional Quarterly, 1971), Key Votes Appendix, Roll Call no. 5.

81. Comment based on material from interviews with William Drower (congressional liaison officer, British Embassy, Washington, D.C.), 21 February 1974; Knox Pitts (research officer, Democratic National Committee), 1 March 1974; Eugene Peters (chief of staff, Joint Committee on the Organization of Congress), 25 March 1974; Michael Pertshuk (chief counsel, Senate Commerce Committee), 3 March 1974; Senator Gale McGee, 18 March 1974; Senator Thomas Eagleton, 24 September 1975.

82. Interview with Senator Thomas McIntyre, 28 March 1974.

83. Interview with Senator Quentin Burdick, 22 March 1974.

84. Interview with Senator Edmund Muskie, 28 March 1974.

85. Interview with Senator Gaylord Nelson, 27 March 1974.

86. Interview with Merill Englund (legislative assistant to Senator Lee Metcalf), 26 August 1975.

87. Interview with Harold Wolman (legislative assistant to Senator Adlai Stevenson, III), 24 September 1975.

88. Interview with Senator Harrison Williams, 25 September 1975.

89. See Congressional Quarterly, *Congress and the Nation, Vol. III, 1969–1972*, pp. 196–98, 205–06, 512–17; Congressional Quarterly, *Guide to Current American Government*, Fall 1969 (Washington, D.C.: Congressional Quarterly, 1969), pp. 98–104; Nathan Miller, "The Making of a Majority: The Senate and the ABM," *Washington Monthly*, October 1969; Orfield, *Congressional Power: Congress and Social Change*, pp. 38–44, 176–82; Rowland Evans and Robert Novak, *Nixon in the White House: The Frustration of Power*, (New York: Vintage Books, 1971), pp. 110–14.

90. Interview with William S. White, 29 March 1974.

91. See White, *Citadel: The Story of the U.S. Senate*, ch. 9; Matthews, *U.S. Senators and Their World*, ch. 5.

92. Matthews, *U.S. Senators and Their World*, p. 95.

93. Interview with Ron Greenaway (legislative assistant to Senator Alan Cranston), 25 September 1975.

94. Interview with Howard Shuman (legislative assistant to Senator William Proxmire), 3 September 1975.

95. Over the 1960s liberal senators developed specialist expertise and legislative prominence in such areas as health (Edward Kennedy), labor (Harrison Williams), alcoholism/narcotics (Harold Hughes), air pollution (Abraham Ribicoff), hunger/poverty (George McGovern), intergovernmental relations (Edmund Muskie), drug industry (Gaylord Nelson), education (Wayne Morse), housing (Edward Brooke), consumer interests (Philip Hart), environmental protection (Frank Moss), and family assistance (Fred Harris).

96. U.S., Congress, Joint Committee on the Organization of Congress, *Hearings, The Organization of Congress*, 89th Cong., 2d sess., 1966, pp. 30–31.

97. Interview with William Hoffman (legislative assistant to Senator Mike Gravel), 24 September 1975.

98. Murphy, *The New Politics Congress*, p. 295; Green, Fallows, and Zwick, *Who Runs Congress?*, p. 174.

99. Interview with Roy Cook (legislative assistant to Senator Gale McGee), 25 August 1975.

100. Interview with Michael Baroody (legislative assistant to Senator Robert Dole), 20 August 1975.

101. Interview with Jerry Udell (executive assistant to Senator Mike Gravel), 26 August 1975.

102. Matthews, *U.S. Senators and Their World*, p. 168; Richard F. Fenno, Jr., "The Appropriations Committee as a Political System," in *New Perspectives on the House of Representatives*, ed. Robert L. Peabody and Nelson W. Polsby (Chicago: Rand McNally, 1963), p. 84.

103. Fenno, "The Appropriations Committee as a Political System," p. 84.

104. Although liberal members had secured 4 seats on the Finance Committee by 1972, they had still only made a marginal impression on the Armed Services Committee (1 seat) and on the larger Appropriations Committee (3 seats).

105. Interview with Maynard Toll (legislative assistant to Senator Edmund Muskie), 22 August 1975.

106. (1) Environmental and Consumer Protection Subcommittee of the Appropriations Committee; (2) Air and Water Pollution Subcommittee of the Public Work Committee; (3) Environment Subcommittee of the Commerce Committee; (4) Oceans and Atmosphere Subcommittee of the Commerce Committee; (5) Oceans and the International Environmental Protection Subcommittee of the Foreign Relations Committee.

107. Charles McCarry, *Citizen Nader* (New York: Saturday Review Press, 1972), pp. 3–29, 65–79; Michael Davie, "Citizen Nader," *Observer Review*, 17 October 1971; "The U.S.'s Toughest Customer," *Time*, 12 December 1969.

108. U.S., Congress, Joint Economic Committee, Subcommittee on Economy, *Hearings, The Economics of Military Procurement*, 91st Cong., 1st sess., 1969.

109. Peter H. Schuck, Mark J. Green, Martha T. Kumar, Irene Till, and Michael E. Ward, *The Judiciary Committees* (New York: Grossman, 1975), p. 208.

110. Ibid., pp. 207–21.

111. See Members of Congress for Peace through Law: Military Spending Committee, *The Economics of Defense: A Bipartisan Review of Military Spending* (New York: Praeger, 1971); Congressional Quarterly, *The Power of the Pentagon* (Washington, D.C.: Congressional Quarterly, 1972), pp. 39–92; Louis Fisher, *President and Congress: Power and Policy* (New York: Free Press, 1972), pp. 212–31; Jacob Javits with Don Kellerman, *Who Makes War: The President versus Congress* (New York: Morrow, 1973), pp. 262–75; John C. Donovan, *The Policy Makers* (New York: Pegasus Books, 1970), ch. 7; William Proxmire, *Report from Wasteland: America's Military-Industrial Complex* (New York: Praeger, 1970), pp. 76–122; Proxmire, *Uncle Sam: The Last of the Bigtime Spenders*, pp. 65–89; Berkeley Rice, *The C5A Scandal: An Inside of the Military-Industrial Complex* (Boston: Houghton Mifflin, 1971), pp. 111–27; Anson, *McGovern: A Biography*, ch. 8; and the national security and foreign policy sections from successive *Congressional Quarterly Yearly Almanacs 1969, 1970, 1971, 1972* (Washington, D.C.: Congressional Quarterly, 1969–73).

112. Interview with Senator Gale McGee, 18 March 1974.

113. Fenno, *Congressmen in Committees*, p. 182.

114. Matthews, *U.S. Senators and Their World*, p. 94.

115. White, *Citadel: The Story of the U.S. Senate,* pp. 107–20; Matthews, U.S. *Senators and Their World,* pp. 94–95.

116. Matthews, *U.S. Senators and Their World,* p. 95.

117. White, *Citadel: The Story of the U.S. Senate,* p. 84.

118. Ibid., p. 9.

119. Congressional Quarterly, *Congressional Quarterly Almanac 1972* (Washington, D.C.: Congressional Quarterly, 1973), p. 54.

120. Interview with Senator Alan Cranston, 23 September 1975.

121. Interview with William S. White, 29 March 1974.

122. Interview with Senator Claiborne Pell, 21 March 1974.

123. Interview with Michael Baroody (administrative assistant to Senator Robert Dole), 20 August 1975.

124. Interview with Senator Gaylord Nelson, 27 March 1974.

125. White, *Citadel: The Story of the U.S. Senate,* p. 218.

126. Ibid., p. 85.

127. Interview with William S. White, 29 March 1974.

128. Congressional Quarterly, *Congressional Quarterly Almanac 1960* (Washington, D.C.: Congressional Quarterly, 1961), p. 103; Congressional Quarterly, *Congressional Quarterly Almanac 1972* (Washington, D.C.: Congressional Quarterly, 1973), p. 54.

129. Interview with Senator Abraham Ribicoff, 18 September 1975.

130. "The Tortoise and the Hare," *Time,* 1 February 1971; Bibby and Davidson, *On Capitol Hill: Studies in the Legislative Process,* p. 180; Murphy, *The New Politics Congress,* p. 309; Stanford Ungar, "The Man Who Runs the Senate," *Atlantic Monthly,* September 1975; Robert L. Peabody, *Leadership in Congress: Stability, Succession and Change* (Boston: Little, Brown, 1976), pp. 391–421.

131. Peabody, *Leadership in Congress: Stability, Succession and Change,* p. 415.

132. Figures based on the yearly voting participation records presented in the *Congressional Quarterly Almanacs 1965, 1966, 1967, 1968, 1969, 1970, 1971, 1972* (Washington, D.C.: Congressional Quarterly, 1966–73).

CHAPTER 5

1. These attributes have been established as the crucial elements in informal legislative groups by a number of major studies on the subject. See Alan Fiellin, "The Functions of Informal Groups in Legislative Institutions," *Journal of Politics* 24, no. 1. (February 1962): 72–91; Mark F. Ferber, "The Formation of the Democratic Study Group," in *Congressional Behavior,* ed. Nelson W. Polsby (New York: Random House, 1971); Charles Clapp, *The Congressman: His Work As He Sees It* (Washington, D.C.: The Brookings Institution, 1964), pp. 36–45; Kenneth Kofmehl, "The Institutionalization of a Voting Bloc," *Western Political Quarterly* 17, no. 2. (June 1964): 256–72; Sven Groennings, "The Clubs in Congress: The House Wednesday Group," in *To Be a Congressman: The Promise and the Power,* ed. Sven Groennings and Jonathan P. Hawley (Washington, D.C.: Acropolis Books, 1973), pp. 73–98; Arthur G. Stevens, Arthur H. Miller, and Thomas E. Mann, "Mobilization of Liberal Strength in the House, 1955–70: The Democratic Study Group," *American Political Science Review* 68, no. 2. (June 1974): 667–81.

2. Ferber, "The Formation of the Democratic Study Group," pp. 242–52;

Stevens, Miller, and Mann, "Mobilization of Liberal Strength in the House, 1955–70: The Democratic Study Group," pp. 667–68.

3. Stevens, Miller, and Mann, "Mobilization of Liberal Strength in the House, 1955–70: The Democratic Study Group," p. 667.

4. Leroy N. Rieselbach, *Congressional Politics* (New York: McGraw-Hill, 1973), p. 163.

5. Observation based on interviews with Senators Edmund Muskie, 28 March 1974; Philip Hart, 28 March 1974; and Lee Metcalf, 8 March 1974.

6. Observation based on an interview with Merill Englund (administrative assistant to Senator Lee Metcalf), 26 August 1975.

7. Quoted in *Time*, 24 July 1972, and confirmed in an interview with Senator Thomas Eagleton, 24 September 1975.

8. Gary Wills, "Cato's Gang," *New York Review of Books*, 4 March 1976.

9. U.S., Congress, *Congressional Record* (Washington, D.C.: GPO, 1959), 23 February 1959, pp. 2816–17.

10. Interview with Sidney Woolner (administrative assistant to Senator Philip Hart), 12 March 1974.

11. See chapter 2, pp. 28–31.

12. Congressional Quarterly, *Congressional Quarterly Almanac 1959* (Washington, D.C.: Congressional Quarterly, 1959), p. 398.

13. Ibid.

14. Robert S. Anson, *McGovern: A Biography* (New York: Holt, Rinehart and Winston, 1972), p. 135.

15. Congressional Quarterly, *Congress and the Nation 1945–64: A Review of Government and Politics in the Postwar Years* (Washington, D.C.: Congressional Quarterly, 1965), p. 736.

16. Congressional Quarterly, *Congress and the Nation, Vol. II, 1965–68* (Washington, D.C.: Congressional Quarterly, 1969), pp. 323–28.

17. Interview with Senator Philip Hart, 28 March 1974.

18. In 1972 the following Senate liberals were regarded as Presidential "possibles"—Hartke, Bayh, Hughes, Muskie, Kennedy, Humphrey, Harris, McGovern, and Proxmire.

19. Interview with Senator Lee Metcalf, 8 March 1974.

20. Interview with Sidney Woolner (administrative assistant to Senator Philip Hart), 12 March 1974.

21. The drive for subcommittee chairmanships on the part of junior liberal members is particularly well presented in Randall B. Ripley, *Power in the Senate* (New York: St. Martin's Press, 1969), pp. 66–69.

22. Interview with Senator Gale McGee, 18 March 1974.

23. Interview with Sidney Woolner (administrative assistant to Senator Philip Hart), 12 March 1974.

24. Ibid.

25. Members of Congress for Peace through Law: Military Spending Committee, *The Economics of Defense: A Bipartisan Review of Military Spending* (New York: Praeger, 1971).

26. Ibid. See also Congressional Quarterly, *Congressional Quarterly Almanac 1970* (Washington, D.C.: Congressional Quarterly 1971), pp. 303, 313.

27. See Congressional Quarterly, "Armed Services Committees: Advocates or Overseers?," *Congressional Quarterly Weekly Report*, 25 March 1972, pp. 673–77. Observation also based on an interview with Maynard Toll (administrative assistant to Senator Edmund Muskie), 22 August 1975.

28. Observations on the Wednesday Group based on interviews with the following group members—Senators Mark Hatfield, 13 September 1975; Richard Schweiker, 19 September 1975; and Charles Mathias, 24 September 1975.

29. Interview with Senator Richard Schweiker, 19 September 1975.

30. Interview with Senator Mark Hatfield, 16 September 1975.

31. See table 4.2.

32. See Joseph S. Clark, *The Senate Establishment* (New York: Hill & Wang, 1963); Clark, *Congress: The Sapless Branch* (Westport; Conn.: Greenwood Press, 1976), pp. 166–76; Roger H. Davidson, David M. Kovenock, and Michael K. O'Leary, *Congress in Crisis: Politics and Congressional Reform* (Belmont, Calif.: Wadsworth, 1966), pp. 144–62; Edward A. Kolodziej, "Joe Clark (Reformer, Pa.): Profile of a New Senatorial Style," in *The Legislative Process in the U.S. Senate*, ed. Lawrence Petit and Edward Keynes (Chicago: Rand McNally, 1969), pp. 27–40.

33. U.S., Congress, *Congressional Record* (Washington, D.C.: GPO, 1959), 23 February 1959, p. 2816.

34. See Andrew J. Glass, "Mansfield Reforms Spark 'Quiet Revolution' in Senate," *National Journal*, 6 March 1971, p. 500; and U.S., Congress, *Congressional Record* (Washington, D.C.: GPO, 1970), 3 December 1970, pp. 39706–08.

35. Malcom E. Jewell and Samuel C. Patterson, *The Legislative Process in the United States* (New York: Random House, 1966), p. 197.

36. Glass, "Mansfield's Reforms Spark 'Quiet Revolution' in Senate," pp. 500, 504–06; John F. Bibby and Roger H. Davidson, *On Capitol Hill: Studies in the Legislative Process* (New York: Dryden Press, 1972), pp. 144–48.

37. Interview with Harold Wolman (legislative assistant to Senator Adlai Stevenson, III), 24 September 1975.

38. Observation based on an interview with Louis Hansen (legislative assistant to Senator Gaylord Nelson), 22 August 1975. Also see Walter Shapiro, "Gaylord Nelson and the Myth of the White Knight," *Washington Monthly*, July/August 1975.

39. Interview with Senator Alan Cranston, 23 September 1975.

40. Observations based on interviews with the legislative assistants of three of the senators involved in various moves against the military budget—Gene Godley (Senator Thomas Eagleton), 9 September 1975; George Cunningham (Senator George McGovern), 17 September 1975; and Sidney Woolner (Senator Philip Hart), 12 March 1974.

41. For further discussion of the staff's role, see David E. Price, *Who Makes the Laws?: Creativity and Power in Senate Committees* (Cambridge, Mass.: Schenkman, 1972); John S. Saloma, III, *Congress and the New Politics* (Boston: Little, Brown, 1969), pp. 149–68; Jewell and Patterson, *The Legislative Process in the United States*, ch. 10; Harrison W. Fox, Jr., and Susan W. Hammond, "Congressional Staffs and Congressional Change," paper presented to the American Political Science Association, New Orleans, September 1973; Fox and Hammond, *Congressional Staffs: The Invisible Force in American Lawmaking* (New York: Free Press, 1977).

42. Interview with Harold Wolman (legislative assistant to Senator Adlai Stevenson, III), 24 September 1975.

43. Interview with Roy Cook (administrative assistant to Senator Gale McGee), 25 August 1975.

44. Interview with Maynard Toll (legislative assistant to Senator Edmund Muskie), 22 August 1975.

45. Interview with Merill Englund (administrative assistant to Senator Lee Metcalf), 26 August 1975.

46. Interview with Louis Hansen (legislative assistant to Senator Gaylord Nelson), 22 August 1975.

47. Interview with Senator Joseph Tydings, 12 September 1975.

48. Senator Hart's campaign against the anti-ballistic missile project from outside the Armed Services Committee and Senator McGovern's critique of the Vietnam war from outside the Foreign Relations Committee provide two noteworthy examples of extra-committee liberal campaigns.

49. Interview with Senator Thomas Eagleton, 24 September 1975.

50. Interview with Senator Abraham Ribicoff, 18 September 1975.

51. This study is based on information obtained from Anson, *McGovern: A Biography,* pp. 218–42; Bertram G. Waters, III, "The Politics of Hunger; Forming a Senate Select Committee," in *To Be a Congressman: The Promise and the Power,* ed. Groennings and Hawley, pp. 151–67; U.S., Congress, Senate, Select Committee on Nutrition and Human Needs, *Hearings, Nutrition and Human Needs,* 91st Cong., 1st sess., 1969; Duane J. Lockard, *The Perverted Priorities of American Politics* (New York: Macmillan, 1971), pp. 160–65.

52. See Congressional Quarterly, *Congressional Quarterly Almanac 1968* (Washington, D.C.: Congressional Quarterly, 1969), pp. 152–69; Congressional Quarterly, *Congressional Quarterly Guide to Current American Government, Fall 1968* (Washington, D.C.: Congressional Quarterly, 1968), pp. 66–70.

53. Congressional Quarterly, *Congress and the Nation, Vol. II, 1965–68* (Washington, D.C.: Congressional Quarterly, 1969), p. 387.

54. Interview with William Hoffman (legislative assistant to Senator Mike Gravel), 24 September 1975.

55. See James L. Sundquist, *Politics and Policy: The Eisenhower, Kennedy and Johnson Years* (Washington, D.C.: The Brookings Institution, 1968), pp. 397–400; Ted Siff and Alan Weil, *Ruling Congress: A Study of How the House and Senate Rules Govern the Legislative Process* (New York: Grossman, 1975), pp. 70–71.

56. Interview with Roy Cook (administrative assistant to Senator Gale McGee), 25 August 1975.

57. Information on the mass transit example derived from Royce Hanson, "Congress Copes with Mass Transit, 1960–64," in *Congress and Urban Problems,* ed. Frederick N. Cleaveland (Washington, D.C.: The Brookings Institution, 1969), pp. 311–49; and on an interview with Senator Harrison Williams, 25 September 1975.

58. Interview with Louis Hansen (administrative assistant to Senator Gaylord Nelson), 22 August 1975.

59. Anson, *McGovern: A Biography,* p. 175.

60. Ibid., p. 176.

61. See Congressional Quarterly, *Congressional Quarterly Almanac 1970* (Washington, D.C.: Congressional Quarterly, 1971), Key Votes Appendix, Roll Call no. 258.

62. David Nevin, *Muskie of Maine* (New York: Random House, 1972), pp. 115–18.

63. Hanson, "Congress Copes with Mass Transit," 1960–64," pp. 315–17.

64. Congressional Quarterly, *Congressional Quarterly Guide to Current American Government, Fall 1969* (Washington, D.C.: Congressional Quarterly, 1969), pp. 98–104.

65. Theodore Jacqueney, "Common Cause Lobbyists Focus on the Structure and Process of Government," *National Journal*, 9 January 1973, p. 1299.

66. Elizabeth Drew, "The Quiet Victory of the Cigarette Lobby," *Atlantic Monthly*, September 1965.

67. Sundquist, *Politics and Policy: The Eisenhower, Kennedy and Johnson Years*, pp. 349–53; Randall B. Ripley, "Congress and Clean Air: The Issue of Enforcement 1963," in *Congress and Urban Problems*, ed. Cleaveland, pp. 237–51, 259–61, 274–78; James Ridgeway, *The Politics of Ecology* (New York: E. P. Dutton, 1971), pp. 62–64.

68. Charles McCarry, *Citizen Nader* (New York: Saturday Review Press, 1972), chs. 1, 4.

69. Observation based on interview evidence and on Price, *Who Makes the Laws?: Creativity and Power in Senate Committees*, passim.

70. See David E. Price, "Professionals and 'Entrepreneurs': Staff Orientations and Policy Making on Three Senate Committees," *Journal of Politics* 33, no. 2 (May 1971): 332; Hanson, "Congress Copes with Mass Transit, 1960–64," pp. 316–17.

71. Unpublished memorandum by Michael Pertshuk (chief counsel to the Senate Commerce Committee), "Some Observations on Commerce Committee Staffing and Strategy," 17 September 1974.

72. "From White House to Capitol . . . How Things Get Done," *U.S. News and World Report*, 20 September 1965; Russell B. Pipe, "Congressional Liaison: The Executive Consolidates Its Relations with Congress," *Public Administration Review* 26, no. 1 (March 1966): 14–24; Carl Sapp, "Executive Assistance in the Legislative Process," in *Public Administration and Policy*, ed. Norton E. Long (New York: Harper & Row, 1966); Doris B. Kearns, *Lyndon Johnson and the American Dream* (New York: Harper & Row, 1976), pp. 221–37; Eric F. Goldman, *The Tragedy of Lyndon Johnson* (London: Macdonald, 1969), ch. 12; Ralph K. Huitt, "White House Channels to the Hill," in *Congress against the President*, ed. Harvey C. Mansfield (Montpelier, Vt.: Capital City Press, 1975).

73. Interview with Senator Edmund Muskie, 28 March 1974.

74. Interview with Senator Harrison Williams, 25 September 1975.

75. Ibid. See also Hanson, "Congress Copes with Mass Transit, 1960–64," pp. 321–28.

76. See Price, *Who Makes the Laws?: Creativity and Power in Senate Committees*, pp. 25–37; Congressional Quarterly, *Congressional Quarterly Almanac 1966* (Washington, D.C.: Congressional Quarterly, 1967), pp. 355–62, 1296–1301.

77. See Congressional Quarterly, *Congressional Quarterly Almanac 1966*, pp. 1260–62; *Congressional Quarterly Almanac 1967* (Washington, D.C.: Congressional Quarterly, 1968), pp. 717–26.

78. For an excellent presentation of the diverse and complex roots of presidential policies, see Sundquist, *Politics and Policy: The Eisenhower, Kennedy and Johnson Years*, passim.

79. See Gary Orfield, *Congressional Power: Congress and Social Change* (New York: Harcourt Brace Jovanovich, 1975), chs. 4, 5, 9, 13.

80. The Haynsworth case is based on Orfield, *Congressional Power: Congress and Social Change*, pp. 103–09; Rowland Evans and Robert Novak, *Nixon in the White House: The Frustration of Power* (New York: Vintage Books, 1971), pp. 159–64; Congressional Quarterly, *Congress and the Nation, Vol. III, 1969–72* (Washington, D.C.: Congressional Quarterly, 1973), pp. 292–95; "Haynsworth at Home," *Time*, 24 October 1969; Prentice Bowsher, "Senate Rejects Hayns-

worth under Crossfire of Pressure," *National Journal*, 22 November 1969; Bowsher, "Nixon Administration Measures Impact of Haynsworth Defeat," *National Journal*, 29 November 1969.

81. The Carswell case is based on Orfield, *Congressional Power: Congress and Social Change*, pp. 109–16; Evans and Novak, *Nixon in the White House: The Frustration of Power*, pp. 164–72; Congressional Quarterly, *Congress and the Nation, Vol. III, 1969–72*, pp. 295–97, "The Seventh Crisis of Richard Nixon," *Time*, 20 April 1970; Douglass Lea, "Nomination of Carswell Shows Nixon Effort to Change Court," *National Journal*, 31 January 1970; Andrew J. Glass, "Late Campaign against Carswell Ruins Nixon's Hopes for Easy Confirmation," *National Journal*, 4 April 1970; Richard Harris, *Decision* (New York: E. P. Dutton, 1971).

82. Evans and Novak, *Nixon in the White House: The Frustration of Power*, p. 164.

83. Harris, *Decision*, pp. 60–7.

84. Orfield, *Congressional Power: Congress and Social Change*, pp. 112–13.

85. Congressional Quarterly, *Congress and the Nation, Vol. III, 1969–72*, p. 296.

86. *Time*, 20 April 1970.

87. Ibid.

88. Interview with Joseph Lipman (director of Congress Watch), 28 February 1974.

89. Anson, *McGovern: A Biography*, p. 140.

90. Interview with David Cohen (director of operations, Common Cause), 25 March 1974.

91. For the background on the oil depletion case, see Drew Pearson and Jack Anderson, *The Case against Congress* (New York: Pocket Books, 1969), ch. 5; Lockard, *The Perverted Priorities of American Government*, pp. 153–54.

92. In the roll calls included in the voting study, the liberal position on votes in the congressional reform field was supported on average by 33 members. The equivalent figures for liberal support in the military expenditure and civil liberties issue areas were 25 and 26, respectively.

93. Anson, *McGovern: A Biography*, pp. 174–78; James Rothschild, "Cooing Down the War: The Senate's Lame Doves," *Washington Monthly*, August 1971; John Lehman, *The Executive, Congress and Foreign Policy: Studies of the Nixon Administration* (New York: Praeger, 1974), pp. 45–61; N. Gordon Levin, Jr., "Nixon, the Senate and the War," *Commentary*, November 1970.

94. McCarry, *Citizen Nader*, ch. 8.

95. Drew, "The Quiet Victory of the Cigarette Lobby"; Price, *Who Makes the Laws?: Creativity and Power in Senate Committees*, pp. 37–49.

96. See Congressional Quarterly, *Congressional Quarterly Almanac 1961* (Washington, D.C.: Congressional Quarterly 1962), Key Votes Appendix, Roll Call no. 114.

97. Interview with Senator Frank Moss, 21 March 1974.

98. Interview with William Cochrane (senior staff counsel to the Senate Rules Committee), 4 September 1975.

99. Interview with Louis Hansen (administrative assistant to Senator Gaylord Nelson), 22 August 1975.

100. Interview with Merill Englund (administrative assistant to Senator Lee Metcalf), 26 August 1975.

101. Interview with Senator Gaylord Nelson, 27 March 1974.

102. Interview with Murray Zwebin (assistant senate parliamentarian), 18 March 1974.

103. Orfield, *Congressional Power: Congress and Social Change,* pp. 38–44.

104. Interview with Senator Alan Cranston, 23 September 1975.

105. Congressional Quarterly, *Congress and the Nation, Vol. III, 1969–72,* pp. 512–17.

106. Interview with Roy Greenaway (administrative assistant to Senator Alan Cranston), 23 September 1975.

107. Interview with Murray Zwebin (assistant senate parliamentarian), 18 March 1974.

108. Interview with Floyd Riddick (senate parliamentarian), 4 September 1975.

109. Frank V. Fowlkes, "Foes of Lockheed Loan Guarantee Challenge Basic Premises behind Proposal," *National Journal,* 29 May 1971; Congressional Quarterly, *The Power of the Pentagon* (Washington, D.C.: Congressional Quarterly, 1972), pp. 87–92; U.S., Congress, *Congressional Record* (Washington, D.C.: GPO, 1971), 22 July 1971, pp. 26779–80, 26813–14; 23 July 1971, pp. 26987–88, 26993; 27 July 1971, pp. 27472–74; 28 July 1971, pp. 27581, 27583, 27596, 27599, 27606, 27612.

110. Interview with Senator Alan Cranston, 23 September 1975.

111. Taken from interviews with Paul Wieck (political columnist for the *New Republic*), 15 March 1974 and with Senator Gale McGee, 18 March 1974.

112. Interview with Senator Gale McGee, 18 March 1974.

113. Congressional Quarterly, *Congressional Quarterly Almanac 1968* (Washington, D.C.: Congressional Quarterly, 1969), Key Votes Appendix, Roll Call no. 160.

114. Congressional Quarterly, *Congressional Quarterly Almanac 1964* (Washington, D.C.: Congressional Quarterly, 1965), Key Votes Appendix, Roll Call no. 218.

115. Interview with William Hoffman (administrative assistant to Senator Mike Gravel), 24 September 1975.

116. Hubert H. Humphrey, *The Education of a Public Man: My Life and Politics* (London: Weidenfeld and Nicholson, 1976), p. 274.

117. See Sundquist, *Politics and Policy: The Eisenhower, Kennedy and Johnson Years,* chs. 9, 11.

118. Sar A. Levitan and Robert Taggart, "The Great Society Did Succeed," *Political Science Quarterly* 91, no. 4 (Winter 1976–77): 601.

119. Interview with David Cohen (director of operations, Common Cause), 25 March 1974.

120. Interview with Gerry Udell (executive officer to Senator Mike Gravel), 26 August 1975.

121. Interview with George Cunningham (legislative assistant to Senator George McGovern), 17 September 1975.

122. Interview with Louis Hansen (administrative assistant to Senator Gaylord Nelson), 22 August 1975.

CHAPTER 6

1. These epithets are quoted in Doris B. Kearns, *Lyndon Johnson and the American Dream* (New York: Harper & Row, 1976), pp. 137, 147; and Hubert H. Humphrey, *The Education of a Public Man: My Life and Politics* (London: Weidenfeld and Nicholson, 1976), p. 274, respectively.

2. Randall B. Ripley, *Power in the Senate* (New York: St. Martin's Press, 1969), p. 69.

3. David S. Broder, "Consensus Politics: The End of an Experiment," *Atlantic Monthly*, October 1966.

1. Interview with Senator Frank Moss, 21 March 1074.

5. See Sam Kernell, "Is the Senate More Liberal Than the House?" *Journal of Politics* 35, no. 2 (May 1973): 332–66.

6. Talcott Parsons, *The Social System* (New York: Free Press, 1951); Robert K. Merton, *Social Theory and Social Structure* (New York: Free Press, 1957); Neal Gross, Ward S. Mason, and Alexander W. McEachern, *Explorations in Role Analysis* (New York: Wiley, 1958); David Easton, "An Approach to the Analysis of Political Systems," *World Politics* 9, no. 2 (April 1957): 383–400; John C. Wahlke, Heinz Eulau, William Buchanan, and LeRoy C. Ferguson, *The Legislative System: Explorations in Legislative Behavior* (New York: Wiley, 1962); Richard F. Fenno, Jr., "The Appropriations Committee as a Political System," *American Political Science Review* 56, no. 2 (June 1962): 310–24; Brian M. Barry, *Sociologists, Economists and Democracy* (London: Collier Macmillan, 1970).

7. Nelson W. Polsby, "Legislatures," in *Handbook of Political Science: Governmental Institutions and Processes*, ed., Fred I. Greenstein and Nelson W. Polsby (Reading, Mass.: Addison-Wesley, 1975), p. 286.

8. See Joseph S. Clark, *The Senate Establishment* (New York: Hill & Wang, 1963); Clark, *Congress: The Sapless Branch* (Westport; Conn.: Greenwood Press, 1976). It is interesting and revealing that, while the majority leader in the early 1960s (Mansfield) always denied unfair treatment of the new liberal group at that time, he did disclose in an interview (5 September 1975) that the Senate probably had not responded adequately to its new liberal members in the early 1960s.

9. Lewis A. Froman, Jr., *The Congressional Process: Strategies, Rules and Procedures* (Boston: Little, Brown, 1967), p. 185.

10. Ripley, *Power in the Senate*, pp. 62–69; Kearns, *Lyndon Johnson and the American Dream*, pp. 110–17.

11. Ripley, *Power in the Senate*, p. 7.

12. The five committees in question were the Labor and Public Welfare Committee, the Banking and Currency Committee, the District of Columbia Committee, the Government Operations Committee, and the Public Works Committee.

13. See chapter 2, note 15.

14. See John G. Stewart, "Two Strategies of Leadership: Johnson and Mansfield," in *Congressional Behavior*, ed. Nelson W. Polsby (New York: Random House, 1971).

15. Randall B. Ripley, *Congress: Process and Policy* (New York: W. W. Norton, 1975), p. 61.

16. See p. 130.

17. Richard F. Fenno, Jr., *Congressmen in Committees* (Boston: Little, Brown, 1973), ch. 5.

18. See Nelson W. Polsby, "Strengthening Congress in National Policymaking," in *Congressional Behavior*, ed. Polsby.

19. See Nelson W. Polsby, *Congress and the Presidency*, 2d ed. rev. (Englewood Cliffs, N.J.; Prentice-Hall, 1971), pp. 67–70; "Goodbye to the Inner Club," in *Congressional Behavior*, ed. Nelson W. Polsby; Donald R. Matthews, "Presidential Nominations: Process and Outcomes," in *Choosing the President*, ed. James D. Barber (Englewood Cliffs, N.J.: Prentice-Hall, 1974); Robert L. Peabody, Norman J. Ornstein, David W. Rohde, "The United States Senate as a Presidential Incubator: Many Are Called but Few Are Chosen," *Political Science Quarterly* 91, no. 2 (Summer 1976): 237–58.

20. See John Lehman, *The Executive, Congress, and Foreign Policy: Studies of the Nixon Administration* (New York: Praeger, 1974); Louis Fisher, *President and Congress: Power and Policy* (New York: Free Press, 1972).

21. Ripley, *Power in the Senate,* pp. 67–77.

22. Donald R. Matthews, *U.S. Senators and Their World* (New York: Vintage Books, 1960), ch. 5.

23. John F. Manley, "The Conservative Coalition in Congress," in *Varieties of Political Conservatism,* ed. Matthew Holden, Jr., (Beverly Hills, Calif.: Sage, 1974).

24. Interview with Senator Clifford Case, 26 March 1974.

25. See Eugene J. McCarthy, *The Hard Years: A Look at Contemporary America and American Institutions* (New York: Viking, 1975), ch. 3.

26. Clark, *The Senate Establishment,* pp. 21–36.

27. Quoted in Tom Wicker, "The Winds of Change in the Senate," *New York Times Magazine,* 12 September 1965.

28. Aage R. Clausen, *How Congressmen Decide: A Policy Focus* (New York: St. Martin's Press, 1973), p. 2.

29. For the classic statement on this view, see Samuel P. Huntington, "Congressional Responses to the Twentieth Century," in *The Congress and America's Future,* ed. David B. Truman (Englewood Cliffs, N.J.: Prentice-Hall, 1965), pp. 5–32.

30. Huntington, "Congressional Responses to the Twentieth Century," p. 29.

31. See Gary Orfield, *Congressional Power: Congress and Social Change* (New York: Harcourt Brace Jovanovich, 1975); Lehman, *The Executive, Congress, and Foreign Policy: Studies of the Nixon Administration;* Nelson W. Polsby, "Policy Analysis and Congress," *Public Policy* 18 (September 1969): 61–74.

32. James L. Sundquist, *Politics and Policy: The Eisenhower, Kennedy and Johnson Years* (Washington, D.C.: The Brookings Institution, 1968), chs. 4, 7.

33. David E. Price, *Who Makes the Laws? Creativity and Power in Senate Committees* (Cambridge, Mass.: Schenkman, 1972); Jack L. Walker, "Setting the Agenda in the U.S. Senate: A Theory of Problem Selection," *British Journal of Political Science,* 7, no. 4 (October 1977): 423–45.

34. Nelson W. Polsby, "Strengthening Congress in National Policymaking," in *Congressional Behavior,* ed. Nelson W. Polsby (New York: Random House, 1971), p. 8.

35. See Arthur M. Schlesinger, *The Imperial Presidency* (London: Andre Deutsch, 1974), pp. 235–66, 298–328; Fisher, *President and Congress: Power and Policy,* chs. 6, 7.

36. See Congressional Quarterly, "Cameras in Committees: A Senate Tradition," *Congressional Quarterly Guide to Current American Government,* Spring 1976, (Washington, D.C.: Congressional Quarterly, 1976), p. 38; Michael J. Robinson, "A Twentieth-Century Medium in a Nineteenth-Century Legislature: The Effects of Television on the American Congress," in *Congress in Change,* ed. Norman J. Ornstein (New York: Praeger, 1975).

37. Peabody, Ornstein, and Rohde, "The United States Senate as a Presidential Incubator: Many Are Called but Few Are Chosen," pp. 252–58; Robert L. Peabody and Eve Lubalin, "The Making of Presidential Candidates," in *The Future of the American Presidency,* ed. Charles W. Dunn (Morristown, N.J.: Learning Press, 1975).

38. Interview with William S. White, 29 March 1974.

39. William S. White, "The Decline of Congress," *Washington Post,* 2 February 1974.

40. Interview with William S. White, 29 March 1974.

41. *Newsweek*, 25 January 1971.

42. Interview with Charles D. Ferris (staff director, Democratic Policy Committee), 12 March 1974.

43. Interview with Senator Philip Hart, 28 March 1974.

APPENDIX II

1. Lee F. Anderson, Meredith W. Watts, Jr., and Allen R. Wilcox, *Legislative Roll Call Analysis* (Evanston, Ill.: Northwestern University Press, 1966), pp. 100–06.

2. Andrew F. Henry, "A Method of Classifying Non-scale Response Patterns in a Guttman Scale," *Public Opinion Quarterly* 16 (Summer 1952): 105.

3. Charles F. Andrain, "Senators' Attitudes toward Civil Rights," in *American Legislative Behavior: A Reader,* ed. Samuel C. Patterson (Princeton, N.J.: D. Van Nostrand, 1968), p. 349.

4. C. A. Moser and Graham Kalton, *Survey Methods in Social Investigation,* 2d ed. rev. (London: Heinemann, 1971), p. 369.

5. Louis Guttman, "The Basis for Scalogram Analysis," in *Measurement and Prediction,* ed. Samuel A. Stouffer et al. (Princeton, N.J.: Princeton University Press, 1950), p. 77.

Index

Adams, Sherman, 25, 305n
Administrative Practice and Procedure
 Subcommittee, Senate Judiciary
 Committee, 158
Aeronautical and Space Sciences
 Committee, Senate, 146, 155
Agriculture and Forestry Committee,
 Senate, 146, 155
Aid to Families with Dependent
 Children (AFDC), 42, 143
Aiken, George, 199
Air and Water Pollution Subcommittee,
 Senate Public Works Committee, 241
Alexander, Charles C., 304n, 305n, 306n
Allen, Robert L., 310n
Alliance for Progress, 43
Alperovitz, Gar, 308n
American Federation of Labor-Con-
 gress of Industrial Organizations
 (AFL–CIO), 184, 192, 201, 210
American Municipal Association, 202
Americans for Democratic Action
 (ADA), 133, 202, 203
Ames, Ardee, 204
Anderson, Clinton, 27, 30, 95
Anderson, Jack, 320n, 329n
Anderson, Lee, 264n, 316n, 333n
Andrain, Charles F., 266, 316n, 333n
Anson, Robert S., 320n, 323n, 325n,
 327n, 329n
Anthony, William W., 316n
Antiballistic Missile System (ABM),
 157, 190, 202, 222, 327n
Apprenticeship folkway, 4, 120–32
Appropriations Committee, Senate,
 146, 155, 156
Area Redevelopment, 31, 39, 42, 127
Armed Services Committee, Senate,
 146, 155, 157, 189
Arms Control and Disarmament
 Agency, 43
Armstrong, Louis, 118

Asher, Herbert B., 318n

Bailey, Stephen K., 309n
Baker, Howard, 131
Banking and Currency Committee,
 Senate, 145–46, 155–56, 186, 193
Barber, James D., 313n
Baroody, Michael, 323n, 324n
Barry, Brian M., 331n
Bartlett, E. L., 130
Bayh, Birch, 94, 107–08, 129, 177,
 185, 199–200, 209–11, 241
Beitzinger, A. J., 301n
Belknap, George, 316n
Bell, Daniel, 305n
Bennett, Wallace, 2, 135
Berman, Daniel M., 306n, 309n
Bernstein, Robert A., 316n
Beyle, Herman C., 315n
Bibby, John, 11–12, 303n–04n, 309n,
 319n–21n, 324n, 326n
Bible, Alan, 27
Biemiller, Andrew, 192
Black Caucus, 174
Blumenthal, Richard, 310n
Boll Weevil Group, 174
Boorstin, Daniel J., 305n
Bowsher, Prentice, 328n–29n
Brauer, Carl M., 306n–07n
Brewster, Daniel B., 66, 94–95, 107–
 08, 129, 144, 199–200, 209–11, 241
Bricker, John W., 122
Bridges, Styles, 2
Broder, David, 235, 308n–09n, 331n
Brooke, Edward, 107–09, 197, 200,
 209–10
Buchanan, William, 316n, 331n
Buckley, James L., 131
Burdick, Quentin, 147, 322n
Burke, Vee, 313n
Burke, Vincent J., 313n
Burns, James M., 307n
Busing, 149, 222

Butler, John, 2
Butler, Paul, 23–25, 30, 56
Buttinger, Joseph, 310n
Byrd, Harry F., 2, 7, 37
Byrd, Robert, 151, 167, 188

Calhoun, John C., 5
Califano, Joseph, 309n–10n
Cambodia, 73–75, 216–17
Campbell, Angus, 307n, 315n
Cantril, Hadley, 143, 313n, 321n
Carleton, William G., 306n
Carlson, Frank, 2
Carmichael, Stokeley, 312n
Carroll, John, 27–28, 107–08, 121, 137
Carswell, Harold G., 200, 208–12
Case, Clifford, 107–09, 116, 134, 137,
    196, 199, 332n
Center for Study of Responsive Law,
    159
Chavez, Dennis, 27
Cheney, Richard B., 316n
Chester, Lewis, 312n
Chomsky, Noam, 311n
Chowder and Marching Society, 174
Church, Frank, 95, 106, 216
Civil liberties issue, 88, 95, 97, 99,
    105, 144, 155
Civil Rights Act (1957), 20, 32
Civil Rights Act (1960), 32
Civil Rights Act (1964), 49–50, 54, 71,
    95, 141, 198, 213
Civil rights issue, 20, 22–23, 26, 31–
    33, 39–44, 49–50, 54–55, 69, 71–72,
    80, 87–88, 91, 94–95, 98–100, 105,
    127, 138, 141, 145, 150, 155, 198,
    205, 208, 213, 219–20, 234, 236
Clapp, Charles L., 318n, 324n
Clark, Joseph S., 2–3, 11–13, 27–28,
    66, 95, 106–08, 121, 125, 134, 137–
    40, 144, 161, 181, 186, 188, 195,
    204, 224, 239, 253, 308n, 318n, 321n,
    326n, 331n–32n
Class of 1958, 27, 30–31, 51, 58, 94,
    96, 106, 109, 121, 123
Clausen, Aage R., 84–85, 309n, 315n–
    16n, 332n
Cochrane, William, 320n
Cohen, David, 203, 214, 329n–30n
Cohen, Jerry, 310n

Cohen, Mitchell, 312n
Colmer, William, 39
Commager, Henry S., 311n
Commerce Committee, Senate, 132,
    146, 155, 193, 204
Common Cause, 159, 185, 201, 203,
    214
Concurrent majority doctrine, 5, 137,
    141–42, 179
Congressional Quarterly, 82, 87–88, 90,
    306n, 311n, 313n, 319n–25n, 327n–
    30n, 332n
Congressional Record, 132–33, 301n,
    306n, 320n–21n, 325n–26n, 330n
Congressional reform issue, 22, 29–30,
    32, 88, 95, 97–98, 100, 105, 138
Constitutional Amendments Subcom-
    mittee, Senate Judiciary Commit-
    tee, 241
Consumer and environmental protec-
    tion issue, 97, 99, 150, 158, 203,
    206–07, 217–19
Consumer Federation of America, 185,
    201
Converse, Philip E., 307n, 309n, 311n–
    12n, 315n, 321n
Cook, Marlow, 211
Cook, Roy, 319n, 323n, 326n–27n
Cooper, John Sherman, 96, 190, 202,
    216
Cooper-Church Amendment (1970), 75
Cordz, Dan, 319n
Cotton, Norris, 133
Council for a Livable World, 202
Courtesy folkway, 132–37
Cranston, Alan, 106–08, 116, 150, 162,
    165, 189, 191, 196, 198, 201, 221–
    22, 326n, 330n
Crick, Bernard, 312n
Crown, James T., 306n
Cuban missile crisis, 41, 44, 60
Cummings, Milton C., 307n
Cunningham, George, 326n, 330n
Curtis, Carl, 2

Daley, Richard, 65
Davidson, Roger H., 11–12, 14, 301n,
    303n–04n, 309n, 317n, 319n–21n,
    324n, 326n
Davie, Michael, 323n

Democratic Advisory Council (DAC), 24–25, 30–31
Democratic National Committee, 23–24
Democratic Party Caucus, Senate, 31, 187, 239
Democratic Party Convention, *1968,* 64–65
Democratic Policy Committee, Senate, 31, 187–88, 210, 239
Democratic Steering Committee, Senate, 31, 187–88
Democratic Study Group (DSG), 29, 171–75, 178–79, 182
Development Loan Fund, 43
Devine, Donald J., 315n
Dirksen, Everett, 28, 135, 176, 197–98, 257
District of Columbia Committee, Senate, 146, 155
Dodd, Thomas, 130, 133–34, 211
Dolbeare, Kenneth M., 314n, 321n
Dolbeare, Patricia, 314n
Dole, Robert, 131, 135, 154, 195
Donovan, John C., 13–14, 301n, 303n, 306n, 309n–11n, 319n, 323n
Donovan, Robert J., 304n–05n
Douglas, Paul, 12–13, 27–28, 30, 95, 106–08, 116, 119, 130, 137–38, 140, 144, 155, 161, 176, 199–201, 207, 215, 239
Downs, Anthony, 55, 310n
Drew, Elizabeth, 308n, 328n–29n
Drower, William, 322n

Eagleton, Thomas F., 106, 173, 314n, 322n, 325n, 327n
Eastland, James O., 2, 7, 130, 135, 151, 241
Easton, David, 331n
Economic issue (Scammon and Wattenberg), 68
Economy in Government Subcommittee, Joint Economic Committee, 158
Edelman, Murray J., 321n
Education issue, 23, 26, 31, 39, 41, 43–44, 49, 69, 87–88, 99–100, 105, 127, 138, 140, 143, 145, 205, 213, 232, 234
Eidenburg, Eugene, 310n

Eisenhower, Dwight D., 17–36, 49, 93, 175, 232, 237, 304n–05n
Election *1956,* 24–25
Election *1958,* 25–27, 37
Election *1960,* 30, 36–38
Election *1962,* 94
Election *1964,* 50–51, 94
Election *1966,* 55, 62, 95
Election *1968,* 62–67, 95–96
Election *1970,* 96
Elementary and Secondary Education Act (*1965*), 213
Ellender, Allen, 195
Employment, Manpower and Poverty Subcommittee, Senate Labor and Public Welfare Committee, 195
Engle, Clair, 27, 107–08, 116, 122
Englund, Merill, 322n, 325n, 327n, 329n
Environment Subcommittee, Senate Commerce Committee, 241
Ervin, Sam, 135, 159
Eulau, Heinz, 316n, 331n
Evans, Rowland, 11, 32, 209, 301n, 303n, 305n–08n, 313n–20n, 322n, 328n–29n
Executive Reorganization Subcommittee, Senate Government Operations Committee, 158, 203

Fair Housing Act (*1968*), 196–98
Fairlie, Henry, 44, 306n–08n
Fallows, James, 320n
Family Assistance Plan (FAP), 70–71
Farmer, James, 310n
Federal Housing Administration, 40
Federal Trade Commission, 218–19
Federation of American Scientists, 202
Fenno, Richard F., 156, 160, 305n, 315n, 318n, 323n, 331n
Ferber, Mark F., 306n, 324n
Ferguson, LeRoy C., 316n, 331n
Ferris, Charles, 333n
Fiellin, Alan, 324n
Filibuster. *See* Rule XXII
Finance Committee, Senate, 127, 146, 155, 157, 215
Financial disclosure, senators', 134–35
Fisher, Louis, 311n, 314n, 317n, 332n
Fitzgerald, Frances, 314n

Folkways, 4–9, 118–20, 165–69, 233–34, 243–51, 302n
Fong, Hiram, 211
Food stamp program, 142–43, 195–96
Foreign aid issue, 88, 99–100, 105
Foreign Relations Committee, Senate, 146, 155, 157
Fowlkes, Frank V., 330n
Fox, Harrison W., 326n
Frank, Gerry, 320n
Frear, Allen, 27
Free, Lloyd, 143, 313n, 321n
Friedman, Milton, 315n
Friends of the Earth, 185
Fritchey, Clayton, 317n
Froman, Lewis A., 240, 315n, 331n
Frye, Alan, 314n
Fulbright, J. William, 107, 151, 177, 216, 311n
Fuller, Helen, 308n

Galbraith, John K., 315n
Gall, Peter, 313n
Geyelin, Philip, 308n
Glass, Andrew J., 326n, 329n
Glass, James M., 312n
Godley, Gene, 321n, 326n
Goldman, Eric F., 304n–05n, 308n–09n, 328n
Goldwater, Barry, 2, 50, 95, 164, 248, 309n, 315n
Goodell, Charles, 135, 152, 181, 201
Goodman, Walter, 304n
Goodwin, George, 304n
Gore, Albert, 177
Government Operations Committee, Senate, 145–46, 155, 158, 203
Grant, Joanne, 310n
Gravel, Mike, 107–08, 110, 135, 152–53, 177, 181, 194, 198, 229
Gray, Charles, 316n
Green, Mark J., 320n, 323n
Green, Theodore, 119
Greenaway, Roy, 322n, 330n
Groennings, Sven, 324n
Gross, Neal, 331n
Gruening, Ernest, 95, 106
Gun control, 177
Guttman, Louis, 266, 333n

Guttman scaling technique, 85–92, 264–67
Gwertzman, Bernard M., 312n

Hacker, Andrew, 304n
Halberstam, David, 306n, 311n
Hale, Denis, 312n
Halleck, Charles, 28
Hamilton, Charles V., 312n
Hammond, Susan W., 326n
Hansen, Louis, 326n–27n, 329n–30n
Hanson, Royce, 319n, 327n–28n
Harper, Alan, 304n
Harris, Fred, 51, 94, 107–08, 116, 130, 151–52, 164, 177, 187, 201
Harris, Joseph P., 11, 301n, 303n–04n, 317n
Harris, Richard, 313n, 329n
Harris, Seymour E., 308n
Hart, Philip A., 27, 95, 106–08, 122, 125, 127, 145, 165, 169, 175, 177–78, 180, 185, 190, 193, 196–99, 202, 206–08, 210–11, 325n, 333n
Hartke, Vance, 27, 107–08, 122–23, 127, 130, 176, 181
Hartz, Louis, 63, 305n, 312n, 314n
Hatfield, Mark, 79–80, 96, 106, 182, 201, 314n, 326n
Hawley, Jonathan P., 324n
Hayden, Carl, 27, 216
Haynsworth, Clement, 200, 208–09
Heller, Walter, 308n, 311n
Henry, Andrew F., 333n
Heren, Louis, 314n
Hill, Lister, 151, 241
Hilsman, Roger, 311n
Hodgson, Godfrey, 312n
Hoffman, Abbie, 312n
Hoffman, William, 327n, 330n
Hofstadter, Richard, 301n, 314n–15n
Holtzman, Abraham, 309n
Hoover, Herbert, 66
Horn, Stephen, 304n
Horowitz, Irving L., 312n
House of Representatives, 1, 6, 75, 171–74, 206, 245, 254, 256
Housing and urban affairs issue, 23, 38–39, 42, 54, 57, 150, 155, 205, 232, 234, 255

Housing Subcommittee, Senate Labor and Public Welfare Committee, 127
Huberman, Leo, 308n
Hughes, Emmet J., 305n
Hughes, Harold, 107–08, 110, 155, 181, 185, 201
Huitt, Ralph K., 10–11, 128, 153, 237–38, 302n, 305n, 317n–19n, 328n
Humphrey, Hubert H., 27, 30, 80, 87–88, 100, 106–09, 119, 121, 125, 130, 136–37, 164, 169, 185, 197, 199–200, 215, 225, 308n, 315n, 330n
Huntington, Samuel P., 254, 256, 332n

Inner Club, 7–12
Inouye, Daniel, 95, 106
Institutional loyalty folkway, 6, 160–65
Interior and Insular Affairs Committee, Senate, 146, 155
Ions, Edmund S., 307n
Irish, Marian D., 304n

Jackson, Henry, 136, 151, 164, 178, 248
Jacobs, Paul, 312n
Jacqueney, Theodore, 328n
Javits, Jacob, 96, 106–08, 115, 137, 151–52, 186, 196, 199–200, 219–20, 221, 314n, 323n
Jenner, William, 122
Jewell, Malcolm E., 304n–05n, 318n, 326n
Johnson, Haynes, 312n
Johnson, Lyndon B., 7, 22–25, 27–32, 37, 45–65, 67–69, 73–74, 77, 82, 93, 121, 125, 127, 129, 138, 140, 146, 161, 164, 175–76, 192, 196–97, 205–08, 213–14, 224–27, 232, 234, 242, 309n, 311n
Johnson, Olin, 107
Judiciary Committee, Senate, 145–46, 151, 155–56, 158, 186, 193, 196–98, 200, 210–11, 241

Kalton, Graham, 316n, 333n
Katznelson, Ira, 304n
Kearns, Doris B., 46, 53, 305n–06n, 308n–10n, 312n, 318n, 328n, 330n–31n
Keefe, William J., 304n
Kefauver, Estes, 24, 28, 106–07, 177

Kellerman, Don, 314n, 323n
Kendall, Willmoore, 315n
Kennedy, Edward M., 79, 94, 106–08, 116, 129–30, 151, 153, 158–59, 165, 178, 186, 193–94, 197, 200, 210–11
Kennedy, John F., 33–45, 48–53, 56, 60, 67, 79, 82, 93–94, 125, 129–30, 138–40, 206–07, 214, 226, 248
Kennedy, Robert F., 51, 62, 79, 94–95, 106–08, 116, 130, 135, 177, 194–96, 203
Kernell, Sam, 331n
Kerr, Robert, 257
Kerr, William, 314n
Kesselman, Mark, 304n
Keynes, Edward, 304n, 316n
Kilpatrick, Carroll, 308n
King, Coretta S., 307n
Kirk, Russell, 315n
Knowland, William, 7, 122
Koenig, Louis, 313n
Kofmehl, Kenneth, 324n
Kolodziej, Edward A., 326n
Kovenock, David M., 11, 14, 301n, 303n–04n, 317n, 326n
Kramer, Ralph J., 310n
Kumar, Martha T., 323n

Labor and Public Welfare Committee, Senate, 127, 139, 145–46, 151, 155–56, 186, 193, 195, 241–42
LaFollette, Robert, 152
Landau, Saul, 312n
Landrum-Griffin Labor Reform Act (1959), 31
Langer, William, 135
Laos, 73–74
Larson, Arthur, 305n
Lausche, Frank, 27
Lea, Douglass, 329n
Leadership Conference on Civil Rights, 210
League of Women Voters, 201
Lee, Charles, 204
Legislative reorganization, 240–41, 259, 302n
Legislative work folkway, 4–5, 160–65
Lehman, Herbert, 12, 27, 119
Lehman, John, 314n, 329n, 332n
Lester, Julius, 310n
Levin, N. Gordon, 329n

Levine, Robert A., 310n
Levitan, Sar A., 330n
Lewis, Ted, 307n–08n
Liberalism, 79–85
Lipman, Joseph, 329n
Lipset, Seymour M., 21, 305n, 312n
Little Rock, 26
Lockard, Duane, 327n, 329n
Lockheed Loan (1971), 222
Long, Edward, 66, 107–08, 110, 129, 144–45
Long, Oren, 27, 107–08, 110, 122–23
Long, Priscilla, 312n
Lubalin, Eve, 332n
Lubell, Sam, 52

McCarry, Charles, 323n, 328n–29n
McCarthy, Abigail, 318n
McCarthy, Eugene J., 27, 62, 95, 106–08, 110, 122, 125, 127, 136, 191, 310n, 314n–15n, 332n
McCarthy, Joe, 307n
McClellan, John, 130, 151
McEachern, Alexander W., 331n
McGee, Gale, 95, 144, 153, 179, 223, 321n–23n, 325n, 330n
McGovern, George, 94–95, 106–09, 116, 129, 132, 136, 153, 164–65, 169, 173, 177, 181, 190, 194–96, 201, 212
McGovern-Hatfield Amendment (1970), 201, 216–17
McIntyre, Thomas, 95, 147, 322n
McKenna, James, 321n
McNamara, Patrick, 12, 27–28, 43, 107–08, 121, 125, 137
MacNeil, Neil, 307n
McPherson, Harry, 301n, 317n
MacRae, Duncan, 316n
Madison, James, 1, 8
Magnuson, Warren, 202, 216
Mailer, Norman, 310n
Malcolm X, 310n
Manley, John F., 14, 82, 303n–04n, 315n, 318n–20n, 332n
Mann, Thomas E., 324n–25n
Manpower development and training, 42, 70, 139
Mansfield, Mike, 75, 95, 129, 187–88, 197, 216, 235, 242–44, 252
Mason, Ward S., 331n
Mathias, Charles, 96, 106, 181, 326n

Matthews, Donald R., 3–7, 9–14, 16, 118–22, 126, 138, 150, 156, 160–61, 166, 160 70, 231 32, 235, 247, 249, 301n–02n, 304n, 317n–19n, 322n–24n, 331n–32n
Mazlish, B., 313n
Medicare, 26, 31, 39, 41, 43–44, 49, 127, 138, 143, 145, 205, 213
Members of Congress for Peace through Law (MCPL), 180–81, 189
Merton, Robert K., 331n
Metcalf, Lee, 29, 106–08, 116, 129, 148, 165, 177–78, 185, 191, 221, 325n
Meyer, Frank S., 315n
Mields, Hugh, 203
Migratory Labor Subcommittee, Senate Labor and Public Welfare Committee, 127
Military expenditures issue, 88, 95, 97, 99, 105, 149, 158–59, 180–81, 189–90, 224
Miller, Arthur H., 321n, 324n–25n
Miller, Nathan, 322n
Miller, Warren E., 307n, 309n, 311n–12n, 315n, 321n
Millikin, Eugene, 7
Mills, C. Wright, 314n
Minar, David W., 315n
Minimum wage, 22, 38–39, 41–42
Model Cities Act (1966), 201, 206
Mondale, Walter F., 94–95, 107–09, 130, 165, 169, 178, 181, 189, 196–97, 199–200, 203, 208–09, 217
Monday Morning Meeting (MMM), 180
Monroney, Michael, 216
Montoya, Joseph, 106, 217
Mooney, Booth, 306n, 308n
Moore, John E., 309n
Morey, Roy D., 310n
Morgan, Edward P., 309n
Morgenthau, Hans J., 312n
Morse, Wayne, 12–13, 27–28, 44, 66, 95, 106–08, 110, 137–38, 140, 144, 161, 177, 204, 207, 306n
Moser, C. A., 316n, 333n
Moss, Frank, 11, 27, 106–08, 116, 122–23, 125, 127, 169, 177, 185, 236, 303n, 310n, 321n, 329n, 331n
Moynihan, Daniel P., 309n–10n, 313n
Mueller, John E., 55, 310n, 312n, 314n

Mundt, Karl, 135
Murphy, Thomas P., 306n, 319n, 323n–24n
Murphy, William S., 310n
Murray, James, 27
Muse, Benjamin, 307n, 309n–10n
Muskie, Edmund, 11, 27, 107–08, 110, 116, 121–23, 125, 127–28, 147, 153, 157, 164, 178, 185, 191, 201, 203, 206, 241, 303n, 318n–19n, 322n, 325n, 328n

Nader, Ralph, 158–59, 185, 203
Nathan, Richard P., 313n
National Association for the Advancement of Colored People (NAACP), 210
National Committee for a Sane Nuclear Policy, 202
National Education Association, 210
National Governors' Conference, 201
National Nutrition Survey, 195
National Traffic and Motor Vehicle Safety Act (1966), 203
Naval Ration Act (1902), 177
Nelson, Gaylord, 11, 94–95, 107–08, 129, 147, 163, 177, 181, 185, 189, 191, 200–01, 221, 303n, 322n, 324n, 329n
Neuberger, Maurine, 107–08, 110, 129, 203
Nevin, David, 318n–19n, 327n
Nevins, Allan, 306n–07n
Newfield, Jack, 310n
Newton, Huey P., 312n
Nixon, Richard M., 36, 63–78, 80, 82, 93, 95–96, 125, 151, 195, 208–09, 214, 216, 222, 227, 255
Nolan, John, 320n
Norton, Eleanor H., 313n
Novak, Robert D., 11, 32, 209, 301n, 303n, 305n–08n, 313n–14n, 317n–20n, 322n, 328n–29n

O'Brien, Larry, 207
O'Donnell, Kenneth, 307n
Ogul, Morris S., 304n
Oil depletion allowance, 177, 215
Okun, Arthur M., 308n, 311n
O'Leary, Michael K., 11, 14, 301n, 303n–04n, 317n, 326n

Olson, David J., 304n
Orfield, Gary, 13, 304n, 313n, 319n, 322n, 328n–30n, 332n
Ornstein, Norman J., 331n–32n

Packwood, Robert, 211
Page, Bruce, 312n
Palamountain, Joseph, 304n, 309n
Panetta, Leon E., 313n
Parmet, Herbert S., 304n–06n, 310n
Parsons, Talcott, 331n
Patterson, Samuel C., 304n–05n, 315n–16n, 318n, 326n
Peabody, Robert L., 307n, 324n, 331n–32n
Peace Corps, 43
Pearson, Drew, 320n, 329n
Pell, Claiborne, 95, 106–08, 110, 129, 163, 324n
Percy, Charles, 211
Pertschuk, Michael, 204, 322n, 328n
Peters, Eugene, 322n
Petit, Lawrence K., 304n, 316n
Phillips, Cabell, 304n
Pipe, Russell B., 309n, 328n
Pitts, Knox, 322n
Polsby, Nelson W., 10, 237–38, 255, 303n, 307n, 331n–32n
Post Office and Civil Service Committee, Senate, 146, 155–56
Poverty issue, 53–54, 57, 70, 88, 100, 138, 143, 150, 205, 224, 234, 236
Powers, David F., 307n
Price, David E., 326n, 328n, 332n
Price, H. Douglas, 316n
Prothro, James W., 304n
Prouty, Winston, 100, 211
Proxmire, William, 12–13, 28, 106–08, 127–28, 130, 133, 135, 137, 151–53, 155, 158, 165, 174, 177–78, 181, 187, 194, 200, 207, 215, 239, 306n, 318n–19n, 323n
Public Buildings and Grounds Subcommittee, Senate Public Works Committee, 153
Public Works Committee, Senate, 144, 146, 153, 155–56

Randolph, Jennings, 130
Rayburn, Sam, 22–24, 29, 38–40
Reciprocity folkway, 5, 137–49

Redford, Emmette S., 304n
Reedy, George, 311n
Ribicoff, Abraham, 94–95, 106–08, 110, 129, 151, 158, 164–65, 185, 194, 203, 324n, 327n
Rice, Berkeley, 323n
Riddick, Floyd, 330n
Ridgeway, James, 328n
Rieselbach, Leroy N., 304n, 316n, 325n
Ripley, Randall B., 11, 13, 235, 240–41, 301n, 303n–07n, 310n, 315n, 317n, 319n, 325n, 328n, 330n–32n
Roberts, Charles M., 301n, 317n
Robertson, A. Willis, 2
Robinson, Donald L., 311n
Robinson, James A., 307n
Robinson, John P., 312n
Robinson, Michael J., 332n
Roche, John P., 311n, 315n
Rohde, David W., 331n–32n
Roosevelt, Franklin D., 20, 34, 48, 51
Rossiter, Clinton, 301n
Rothchild, John, 314n, 329n
Rubin, Jerry, 312n
Rule XXII, 29, 30, 32, 138, 141–42, 176, 221–23, 247
Rules Committee, House of Representatives, 38–40, 42
Rules Committee, Senate, 146, 155
Rusk, Jerrold G., 311n–12n, 321n
Russell, Richard, 2, 7, 161, 164
Russett, Bruce M., 316n

Salinger, Pierre, 307n
Saloma, John S., 326n
Sapp, Carl, 309n, 328n
Scammon, Richard M., 61–62, 312n–13n, 321n
Schaflander, Gerald M., 312n
Schandler, Herbert Y., 311n
Schlesinger, Arthur M., 60, 307n, 310n–12n, 314n, 332n
Schoeppel, Andrew, 2
Schuck, Peter H., 323n
Schurman, Frank, 310n
Schweiker, Richard, 96, 106, 181, 326n
Scott, Peter D., 310n
Seale, Bobby, 312n
Select Committee on Nutrition and Human Needs, Senate, 195
Select Committee on Standards and

Conduct (Ethics Committee), Senate, 134–35
Senate liberals (1959–72), identity of, 106–08
Shadegg, Stephen C., 315n
Shapiro, Martin, 304n, 309n
Shapiro, Walter, 326n
Shaplen, Robert, 310n–11n
Sherrill, Robert, 313n
Shull, Leon, 133, 320n
Shuman, Howard E., 318n–20n, 322n
Siff, Ted, 327n
Smith, Howard, 39
Smith, Margaret C., 199, 210
Social issue (Scammon and Wattenberg), 64, 67–68
Social security issue, 22, 23, 26, 80, 99–100, 234, 236
Social welfare issue, 22, 69, 98, 100, 105, 127, 155
Sorensen, Theodore C., 307n, 319n
Southern Christian Leadership Conference, 202
Special Committee on Unemployment, Senate, 127
Specialization folkway, 5, 150–60, 302n
Spitz, David, 314n
Spivack, Robert G., 306n
Staff, Senatorial and Committee, 190–91, 203–05
Steinberg, Alfred, 305n–06n, 317n–19n
Stennis, John, 130, 135
Stevens, Arthur G., 324n–25n
Stevenson, Adlai (governor), 17, 24
Stevenson, Adlai (senator), 107–08, 148
Stewart, John G., 305n, 320n, 331n
Stoessinger, John G., 314n
Stokes, Donald E., 307n, 315n
Stone, I. F., 311n
Subcommittees, 151–52, 242
Sullivan, Jack, 314n
Sundquist, James L., 44, 204, 301n, 306n–09n, 317n–19n, 327n–28n, 330n, 332n
Supersonic transport plane (SST), 222
Supreme Court, 26, 57, 68, 72
Swanson, Wayne, 301n
Symington, Stuart, 125, 216

Taft, Robert A., 7, 161, 164, 257

Taft-Hartley Labor Relations Act
(*1947*), 26, 31, 55, 94
Taggart, Robert, 330*n*
Tax cut (*1964*), 43–44, 48–49
Thomas, Norman, 309*n*
Thurmond, Strom, 132
Thye, Edward, 122
Till, Irene, 323*n*
Toll, Maynard, 323*n*, 325*n*–26*n*
Tower, John, 131, 320*n*
Trager, Frank N., 310*n*
Truman, David B., 304*n*, 315*n*, 317*n*
Truman, Harry S., 17, 20, 24, 35–36
Truth in Lending Act (*1966*), 207
Truth in Packaging Act (*1968*), 206–07
Twenty-fifth Amendment, 241
Twenty-second Amendment, 26
Tydings, Joseph D., 51, 94–95, 107–08,
144, 193, 197, 210–11, 327*n*

Udell, Gerry, 323, 330
Ungar, Stanford, 324
Union regulation issue, 23, 26, 31, 55,
94, 98, 100, 105
United Auto Workers, 201–02, 210
U.S. Conference of Mayors, 201–03
U.S. v. *Curtiss-Wright Export Corporation* (*1936*), 59

Vietnam, 33, 57–62, 65, 73–76, 80, 143,
146, 196, 208, 216–17, 224, 226, 255
Vinyard, Dale, 304*n*
Voting Rights Act (*1965*), 95, 198

Wahlke, John C., 316*n*, 331*n*
Walker, Jack L., 332*n*
Wallace, George, 62, 65–66
Ward, Michael, 323*n*
War powers issue, 74–76, 97, 100, 201,
216–17
Waters, Bertram G., 327*n*
Watkins, Arthur, 122
Wattenberg, Ben J., 61–62, 312*n*–13*n*,
321*n*

Watts, Meredith W., 264, 316*n*, 333*n*
Weaver, William, 320*n*
Wednesday Club, 180–82, 189, 210
Weidenbaum, Murray L., 311*n*
Weil, Alan, 327*n*
Westin, Allan F., 304*n*
White, Theodore H., 307*n*, 309*n*, 312*n*–13*n*
White, William S., 3–14, 16, 27, 118–
21, 135, 137–38, 149–50, 156, 160–
64, 166, 169–70, 231–32, 235, 247,
249, 257, 301*n*–02*n*, 308*n*, 317*n*–18*n*,
320*n*–22*n*, 324*n*, 332*n*–33*n*
Wholesome Meat Act (*1967*), 217
Wicker, Tom, 11, 13, 35, 39, 43, 301*n*,
303*n*–09*n*, 317*n*, 332*n*
Wieck, Paul, 330*n*
Wilcox, Allen R., 264*n*, 316*n*, 333*n*
Wilcox, Francis, 314*n*
Wildavsky, Aaron, 61, 305*n*, 311*n*
Willenson, Kim, 308*n*
Williams, Harrison, 27, 106–08, 116,
122–23, 127, 148, 169, 185, 193, 200,
202, 204, 206, 319*n*, 322*n*, 327*n*–28*n*
Williams, John, 2
Wills, Garry, 174, 312*n*, 325*n*
Wilson, Woodrow, 36, 187
Wolfe, Arthur C., 311*n*–12*n*, 321*n*
Wolfinger, Raymond E., 304*n*
Wolman, Harold, 309*n*–10*n*, 322*n*, 326*n*
Wood, Robert C., 304*n*
Woolner, Sidney, 325*n*–26*n*

Yarborough, Ralph, 100, 106–07, 132,
177
Yarmolinsky, Adam, 309*n*, 311*n*
Young, Stephen, 27, 95, 107–08, 122,
127, 176, 199
Youth Conservation Corps, 127

Zelnick, Reginald, 310*n*
Zwebin, Murray, 330*n*
Zwick, David E., 320*n*

Date Due

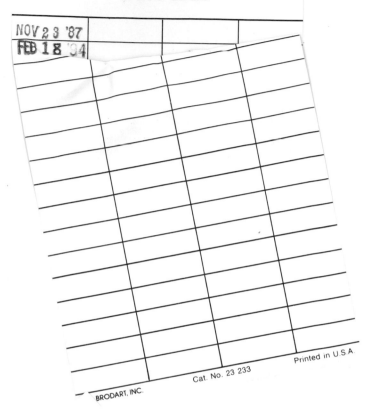